SUPPLY-SIDE TAX POLICY

Its Relevance to Developing Countries

Ved P. Gandhi

Liam P. Ebrill
George A. Mackenzie
Luis A. Mañas-Antón
Jitendra R. Modi
Somchai Richupan
Fernando Sanchez-Ugarte
Parthasarathi Shome

International Monetary Fund
Washington, D.C. • 1987

Cover design by the IMF Graphics Section

Library of Congress Cataloging-in-Publication Data

Supply-side tax policy.

Bibliography: p.
1. Taxation—Developing countries. 2. Supply-side economics—Developing countries. I. Gandhi, Ved P. (Ved Parkash)
HJ2351.7.S86 1987 336.2'009172'4 87-29890
ISBN 0-939934-91-4

Price: $20.00

Contents

Part III. Tax Policy for Efficiency and Growth: Aspects of Basic Supply-Side Tax Policy

Appendices

Foreword

The decade of the 1980s is likely to be remembered as the time when tax reform became fashionable around the world. Not only many industrial countries but also many developing and centrally planned countries have felt the need to reform, sometimes drastically, their tax systems. While in earlier periods reforms often had the objective of raising revenue and of making the tax system more progressive, during the 1980s most tax reforms have been revenue neutral in intention, if not always in actual results, in spite of the large fiscal deficits that have characterized many of these countries. The main objective of the recent reforms has been the removal of obstacles to growth. In the industrial countries, the concern about the relationship between the tax system and the rate of economic growth has been heightened by the high and increasing unemployment rates that have accompanied the slowdown of their rate of economic growth in recent years. In the developing countries, there has been the realization that heavy debt burdens could only be reduced by accelerating the rate of growth of these economies. Furthermore, in view of the low levels of income in these countries, growth had always been a major objective for their policymakers.

In this period, both economists and policymakers have rediscovered the importance of supply-side aspects of economic policy. While up to recently economic policy had been driven by the Keynesian assumption that regulating aggregate demand would go a long way toward achieving whatever economic objectives the policymakers wanted to achieve, during the 1980s the focus of policymakers' attention shifted from the demand to the supply side of the economy. They came to believe that it would be possible to squeeze a larger growth rate out of the existing resources if certain changes were made in economic policies. For the tax system, these changes were often thought to require reductions in tax rates accompanied by broadening of bases. They also required reductions in the differential treatments of economic sectors and economic activities.

In spite of the fact that many observers think of the Fund as an institution concerned mainly with stabilization, it has, in fact, always paid attention to the objective of economic development. As a consequence, it was natural that it would be influenced, like everybody else, by the current thinking about the role of incentives in general and tax incentives in particular. The Fund has paid increasing attention to the structural components of adjustment policies. It has accepted the conclusion that without major structural adjustments developing countries might achieve stability, but only at the cost of a slower rate of growth. Stability with growth requires that many changes in the structure of their economies must take place in these countries. There must be changes in the external sector through the liberalization of imports and the removal of impediments to exports, in addition to the more traditional adjustments in the exchange rate. There must be changes in the financial markets, through the removal of obstacles to the flow of financial resources within the economy, through the raising of real interest rates to realistic levels, and through the reduction of the proportion of total credit that is administratively allocated. There must be realignments in relative prices in order to eliminate disincentives to producers, when the prices that they receive are too low to keep them producing the cash crops for which the countries have comparative advantages. There must also be changes in the relative prices of consumer goods to reduce the consumption of products that must be imported or that could be exported in larger quantities.

The restructuring of economies will inevitably involve also the reform of the tax system. This is the aspect addressed in this book. Under the direction of Ved Gandhi, Chief of the Tax Policy Division, the Fiscal Affairs Department has made a systematic attempt at surveying what is known about the disincentive effects of taxes. This research has relied on hard evidence in order not to be swayed by claims that may be fashionable but that are often not fully substantiated. This reliance on hard evidence has obvious scientific merits, but it has also some shortcomings. The merits are that the conclusions reached are based on firm evidence. The shortcomings are that those conclusions are based on work which has already been done; that work may itself have been biased by earlier preconceptions about the effect of taxes. In any case, I hope that enough interesting conclusions are provided by this book to make it a valuable addition to the literature on taxation in developing countries. I also hope that policymakers will find some of its conclusions useful for the conduct of their economic policy. I should perhaps conclude by adding that the views presented reflect the thinking of the authors and do not necessarily reflect official Fund positions.

VITO TANZI
Director
Fiscal Affairs Department

Preface

A striking feature of the 1980s has been the sharp decline in the rates of growth witnessed by countries in the developing world. According to the World Bank's *World Development Report, 1986,* the average annual rate of growth of these countries declined from 6.6 percent during 1965–73 and 5.4 percent in 1973–80 to 2 percent in 1982 and 1983 (Statistical Appendix Table A.3, page 115). Countries all over Africa as well as Latin America and the Caribbean have experienced a significant erosion of the standard of living of their populations in recent years, as their economic growth rates have fallen far short of their population growth rates, and there is little hope for early reversal of these trends. Given the uncertain prospects for growth, many economists have expressed the belief that exclusive reliance on traditional demand management policies, which can certainly achieve successful stabilization around a trend growth path, may not be enough to improve economic welfare and that these policies may have to be combined with policies aimed at raising the trend growth path itself. This belief has renewed the interest of economists and policymakers alike in the determinants of growth and supply-side economics with its fundamental claim to enhancing the country's potential for growth.

Although supply-side economics addresses all aspects of aggregate supply, it focuses particularly on the appropriate role of government in encouraging growth through its expenditure and taxation policies. This book examines the relevance to developing countries of the tax policy recommendations of supply-side economists and attempts to delineate policy guidelines to ensure that fiscal management enhances rather than inhibits growth and efficiency in the wider economy.

The book is the product of a research project initiated in 1984 in the Fiscal Affairs Department of the International Monetary Fund to assess the relevance to the special circumstances of developing countries of tax policy aspects of the popular supply-side revolution in the United States. The main emphasis of the popular version of this revolution has been to stress the negative effects of high income tax rates on incentives to produce, save, and invest and, through these, on the growth of the economy.

Assessing the relevance of supply-side tax policy for developing countries is no easy task. First, there are many forms of taxes and the effects of each tax on incentives have many aspects. Effects of tax rates, the primary focus of the popular supply-siders, on the behavior of the economic agents are interwoven with the type and scope of the tax base, tax reliefs, and tax incentives, and many other special provisions of the tax system. Second, tax policy frequently interacts with other economic policies of the government in very many complicated ways so that the economic effects of a tax cut become a function of the institutional and economic policy environment within which it operates. Furthermore, statistical and other information relevant to estimating the disincentive effects of various tax policies or the incentive effects of the reform of such policies are not readily available.

The book does not purport to be comprehensive; it covers only selected aspects of supply-side tax policy. In particular, it attempts to deal with the following eleven questions:

- What are the most important price elasticities that determine the effects of income tax reductions on aggregate supply?
- How price-sensitive are labor supply, savings, and investment in developing countries?
- To what extent do income tax policies, given certain other economic policies, reduce financial savings in developing countries?
- To what extent do income and corpopate tax policies, given generous tax incentives and other tax provisions, reduce corporate investment in developing countries?
- Do high and progressive income tax rates significantly increase income tax evasion in developing countries?
- Are there certain examples from the developing world where a reduction of top marginal income tax rates has increased government revenue significantly in the short run as predicted by the "Laffer curve?"
- What is the econometric evidence on the negative relationship between reliance of developing countries on income taxes and their growth rates?
- What will the tax systems of developing countries look like in theory if incentives and efficient allocation of resources were the major concern of policymakers?
- How efficient are the generous tax incentives that are frequently given to investors in developing countries in order to induce economic growth?
- Under what circumstances are export duties justified on grounds of efficiency and growth?
- What is the precise role of tax policy in removing the various structural bottlenecks to economic development and helping the growth of developing countries?

Chapters 2 through 12 deal with each of these questions, while Chapter 1 brings together the findings and conclusions of the analyses and suggests ideas for supply-side tax reform relevant for developing countries.

The research project was carried out by a staff team headed by Ved P. Gandhi of the Tax Policy Division of the Fiscal Affairs Department. In addition, the team consisted of Liam P. Ebrill, Jitendra R. Modi, Somchai Richupan, Fernando Sanchez-Ugarte, and Parthasarathi Shome. The papers included in this book were prepared by the staff members as and when they found time in the course of their regular operational work for the Fund. The papers by George A. Mackenzie and Luis A. Mañas-Antón were not prepared as a part of the project; the former was completed before the research project was initiated, while the latter was prepared when the author served as a summer intern in the Tax Policy Division.

The research project was a cooperative effort, and the author of each paper has benefited from the comments of the other members of the staff team. In addition, many friends and colleagues in the Fiscal Affairs Department, as well as in other departments of the Fund, took pains to read the draft papers and provide guidance, and their advice is gratefully acknowledged. The team is particularly indebted to Vito Tanzi, Director of the Fiscal Affairs Department, who took interest in the research project from its inception, provided an exciting environment, and guided the work of the team; the book owes a great deal to him. The team also wishes to thank Alan Tait, Leif Mutén, Robert Schneider, Richard Hemming, Sheetal Chand, David Nellor, and Charles Sisson, who gave constructive criticisms on one or more draft papers. Extensive comments on the entire manuscript and valuable suggestions were received from Professor Roy Bahl of Syracuse University and Professor Charles McLure, Jr., of Stanford University and the authors wish to express their gratitude to them. However, none of the foregoing can be held responsible for any errors or omissions that may remain. The authors also wish to express appreciation for the painstaking and skillful editing of the manuscript by Esha Ray. Finally, thanks are due to Lyndsey Livingstone and Ahwerah Vichailak for their patience and superb job of typing and retyping successive drafts of each paper until the final manuscript stage.

VED P. GANDHI

PART I
Overview and Summary

1

Relevance of Supply-Side Tax Policy to Developing Countries

A Summary

Ved P. Gandhi

Within the short span of a few years, "supply-side economics" has come to be considered in some quarters to be the "new" economics that is most relevant to policymaking for solving the economic problems of the 1980s. However, the basic propositions of supply-side economics, including the belief that taxes affect economic behavior and the substitution effects of taxes are important for the efficient allocation of resources, are as old as neoclassical economics itself. What is *new* is the conviction of some supply-side economists that a substantial reduction of tax burdens, in general, and the rates of income tax, in particular, will have significant effects on the level of output and growth rates. In 1984, the Fiscal Affairs Department of the International Monetary Fund undertook a research project to analyze the relevance to developing countries of the tax policy recommendations of supply-side economics made in the context of developed countries. This volume contains the studies that were prepared as part of this research project.

As explained in greater detail in Section I of this chapter, there are at least two interpretations of supply-side economics, and, consequently, of supply-side tax policy—the traditional or the "basic" view and the new or the "popular" view. Most of the studies included in this book assess the validity of the arguments of popular supply-side economics, while others deal with the validity of selected propositions of basic supply-side economics.

The volume is in three parts. Part I provides an overview and summary of findings and conclusions. Part II presents seven papers reviewing the evidence on the validity of popular supply-side tax policy. Part III contains four papers dealing with selected aspects of basic supply-side tax policy or tax policy for efficiency and growth. The book also has two appendices. Appendix I contains statistical information that is readily available on the revenue structures of developing and developed countries relevant to the various studies. Appendix II presents a selected bibliography of publications on popular supply-side economics of interest to the general reader.

The term supply-side economics originated in the United States in the mid-1970s primarily as a reaction to government economic policies based on Keynesian macroeconomic theory and represents a new way of looking at government economic policies.[1] The term, however, has evolved over time and has come to mean different things to different people. It is, therefore, important at the outset to clarify in broad terms what supply-side economics stands for and then to define with greater precision those aspects of supply-side tax policy that have received the most attention in the United States and whose relevance is analyzed in the context of developing countries in the papers included in this volume.

These concepts are explained in Section I of this chapter. Section II describes the scope of the project and the broad conclusions reached under it. Sections III and IV contain the main findings and conclusions of individual papers on the validity and relevance of popular supply-side tax policy and tax policy for efficiency and growth. Finally, Section V summarizes several supply-side-oriented proposals for tax reform that have emerged from the various studies.

I. Scope of Supply-Side Economics

Supply-side writers have founded their work on the strong conviction that free markets, with few exceptions, allocate resources most efficiently.[2] This belief drives both their economic tenets and the way they view politics and the social order.

On the political side, supply-side economists see governments, which are usually monopolists and not subject to the requirement of profit maximization, as inherently inefficient because of their lack of market discipline and as subject to a tendency to grow without bound. Because the agents of government have personal objectives which, by definition, differ from the

[1]Bartlett (1985, p. 18) points out that the term was coined by Professor Herbert Stein of the University of Virginia in April 1976, as described in Stein (1984, p. 241).

[2]Supply-siders accept that the existence of pure public goods, such as defense and internal security, and some merit goods, such as protecting the welfare of the extremely needy, provides a rationale for social action. However, they believe that policymakers would not necessarily provide even these goods in the optimum quantity or at the lowest possible cost.

goals of the society at large, neither politicians nor bureaucrats in policy-making positions can be trusted to act effectively in the social interest.[3]

On the economic side, the belief that any policy that distorts free-market-determined relative prices distorts resource allocation has led supply-siders to espouse at least three important propositions that have major consequences for government policy. (1) Most government regulations aimed at protecting consumers and workers are generally costly and indefensible in terms of their cost-benefit ratios; eliminating them would, therefore, improve resource allocation in the economy; (2) most welfare and entitlement programs discourage work effort (including retraining); limiting access to such programs to the really needy would, therefore, restore work incentives; and (3) personal income tax is inherently biased against work effort (on the ground that work is taxed but leisure is not), as well as against savings (since income saved is taxed twice, while income consumed is taxed only once) and investment (since productive investment is taxed but unproductive investment is not) and that high marginal income tax rates exacerbate these biases significantly; reducing marginal income tax rates would, therefore, increase labor supply, savings, and investment. As will be shown below, many of the propositions of supply-side economists are implicit in the behavioral and market structure assumptions made by most neoclassical economists.

In general, thus, supply-side economists emphasize minimizing the distortions in market-determined relative prices that result from regulations, subsidies, and high income taxes and believe that the reduction of such distortions would encourage savings and production by allowing the economic incentives of a free market to work. They also believe that the private sector is generally capable of bringing about sustained economic growth, so that there is no need to tolerate the inefficiencies of large government in the economy. At least two interpretations of supply-side economics, and, consequently, of supply-side tax policy have evolved within this general framework over time. These interpretations have been referred to in this volume as basic supply-side economics and popular supply-side economics.

Basic Supply-Side Economics: Return to Classical and Neoclassical Economics

The first interpretation, basic supply-side economics, is simply an application of classical and neoclassical economic theory to government policy-

[3]The political philosophy underlying supply-side economics derives from the writings of Downs (1957), Buchanan and Tullock (1969), Niskanen (1971), and Breton (1974).

making. According to this view of supply-side economics, government economic policies should focus on aggregate supply rather than on aggregate demand. As aggregate supply is the result of the economic behavior of producers, they, rather than consumers, should be considered the driving force in the economy and their economic behavior should be considered the most important determinant of real and nominal economic activity. As government economic policies can, and frequently do, have significant negative substitution effects (drive economic agents away from rational —welfare maximizing—economic decisions), they should be structured in such a way so as to minimize the substitution effect.

If one follows this interpretation, supply-side economics is essentially no different from mainstream classical and neoclassical economics. It emphasizes the objective of efficient allocation of resources more than any other objective of economic policy and recognizes the importance of negative substitution effects of government economic policies and, particularly, of tax policies. These beliefs were also held by Smith, Say, Mill, Marshall, Pigou, and Ramsey and others who obviously were supply-siders long before the term was coined.

A basic supply-side economist believes that government tax policy can, and does, create a "wedge" between pretax and posttax producer prices as well as rates of return to factors of production and, given the negative substitution effect, is likely to distort the economic behavior of producers as well as the suppliers of factor inputs. Given the importance of efficient resource allocation to aggregate output, a basic supply-side economist seeks to reduce distortions in resource allocation that individual taxes and tax structures can cause. Distortions can arise because of a number of factors such as (1) the economic aggregate or the base on which taxes are levied; (2) tax rules and provisions that affect the taxable base for individual producers and factor suppliers; (3) the height of nominal tax rates and the degree of progression in the tax rate schedule; and (4) the interaction between inflation, the taxable base, and tax liabilities. A basic supply-side economist is one who seeks to reform all of these aspects of a tax structure.

The recommendation that tax policy be reformed along these lines is also not new; it is well known in public finance literature. Most books on traditional public finance, for example, contain detailed analyses of the effects of various forms of taxation on the efficiency of resource allocation.[4] The relative merits of income and consumption as alternative tax bases

[4]Recent literature on "optimal taxation" also deals extensively with this subject. The optimal taxation literature takes this objective and the neoclassical framework as starting points but reaches very different conclusions on tax reform. For a discussion of the difference between a supply-side tax economist and an optimal tax economist, see Gandhi (Chapter 9).

and their possible effects on savings are frequently discussed at length. Similarly, the effects of alternative tax rules and provisions—relating to depreciation allowances and inventory valuation, loss-offset and carry-forward privileges, debt versus equity, etc.—on capital formation, risk-taking, and financial policies are discussed in considerable detail in the literature. The argument that the "excess burden" of a tax depends on the nominal rate of the tax is also well known to students of public finance.[5] The resource allocation costs of the lack of inflation-adjustment of the income tax system, which have been dealt with extensively as the rates of inflation have accelerated in the 1970s, are also well known.

Thus, basic supply-side tax policy would seem to be no different from the views of fiscal economists who, on efficiency grounds, recommend the reform of (1) the economic base on which taxes are levied; (2) various tax breaks and loopholes that signify distortionary economic signals; (3) the levels and progressivity of nominal tax rates; and (4) tax rules and provisions that raise the effective tax rates in inflationary times. If these are the aims of supply-side tax policy, then fiscal economists such as Pigou, Simon, Haig, Kaldor, Harberger, Feldstein, Boskin, and McLure obviously were supply-siders long before the term "supply-side tax policy" was conceived.[6]

In a sense, supply-side economics is as old as economics itself, if all that it stands for is that efficiency of resource allocation is an important objective of economic policy *and* that market-determined resource allocation is basically optimal. Most economists would find it hard to disagree with its contents in theory and under normal circumstances. As a clone of classical and neoclassical economics, basic supply-side economics contains policy prescriptions based on the latter's specific assumptions relating to, first, what the proper role of the government should be and, second, how developed the commodity and factor markets are or how well they function. But

[5]The argument that "excess burden" rises monotonically with the nominal tax rate belongs to the partial equilibrium tax theory. According to this argument, an income tax by its very nature causes an excess burden vis-à-vis a lump sum tax (i.e., it causes a reduction of utility in excess of that which would have occurred had the tax been collected as a lump sum) and that partial equilibrium analysis suggests that, in an economy completely free of distortions, including distortions caused by other taxes, the higher the rate of tax, the higher the excess burden. In fact, under highly simplified assumptions regarding the shapes of demand and supply curves, the excess burden of a tax (which is not lump sum) is given by the square of the rate of the tax. Theoretically, thus, the rate of the tax does have a very significant effect on the economic behavior of the taxpayers. See Rosen (1985, Chapter 12).

[6]Ture (1982b), Hall and Rabushka (1983), and the authors of the report by the U.S. Treasury Department (1984) also belong to the basic supply-side school since they seek tax reform in a wider sense, as described above.

one can still question whether both of these assumptions are strictly valid in the special circumstances of developing countries. To what extent, for example, should one whole-heartedly accept the "appropriate" role of the government implicit in supply-side economics (as well as in classical and neoclassical economics) which states that the main aim of the government should be ensure an efficient allocation of the economy's resources through private initiative and enterprise and that all other roles of state, such as its role as an active agent of income redistribution or of economic stabilization or of the growth of the economy, whenever in conflict with the former, should receive lesser priority? Similarly, to what extent should one accept the fundamental faith of supply-side economists (as well as of classical and neoclassical economists) that private markets are capable of delivering "appropriate" levels of goods and services and that, in the interest of achieving maximum welfare of the society, governments should ensure a smooth working of free markets and provide few goods and services other than essential public goods, such as defense and internal security?

Popular Supply-Side Economics: Elasticity Optimism

It is not the views of the basic supply-siders, however, that have caught the public attention since the mid-1970s. Rather, it is the views of what can be called popular supply-side economics and the extravagant claims made by its proponents for efficiency-enhancing government economic policies, in general, and income tax policies, in particular, that have become the subject of major debate in the United States and other developed countries.[7] The major proponents of popular supply-side economics have written a number of articles and books during the last few years.[8]

Of the many policy recommendations of popular supply-side economics, the lowering of marginal income tax rates is the most important and also the best known. As one leading popular supply-side economist has stated, "The term supply-side economics has in recent years become closely associated with . . . a set of policy prescriptions, the most prominent of which has been a recommendation that tax rates be lowered both in the United States and in many other countries."[9]

Never before have economists given so much importance to the marginal

[7]Cf., Feldstein (1986).

[8]For the views of popular supply-siders, see Laffer and Seymour (1979); Meyer (1981); U.S. Congress (1981); Bartlett (1982); Fink (1982); Raboy (1982); Hailstones (1982a, 1982b); Roberts (1982, 1984); Gilder (1981); and Canto, Joines, and Laffer (1983). Also see Appendix II for additional references.

[9]Canto, Joines, and Laffer (1983, p. ix).

rates of income taxation, and particularly to the top marginal income tax rates, and made reduction of the progressivity of income taxation the centerpiece of reform of government economic policies. This elevation by popular supply-siders of nominal marginal income tax rates to such a height is a reaction to two major trends of recent years.

First, it is a reaction to the perceived overwhelming equity bias of traditional literature on taxation. With its preoccupation with the ability-to-pay basis of taxation and the principles of sacrifice, traditional literature generally justifies the progressivity of nominal rates of income taxation.

Second, it is a reaction to the progressive income tax systems found in all countries. The progressivity has been accentuated in recent years because of the interaction between rates of inflation and tax brackets based on nominal incomes, as a result of which taxpayers have been constantly pushed into higher income brackets during inflationary times and have been subjected to even higher tax rates under unindexed income tax systems.[10] Such steep progressivity, in the opinion of popular supply-siders, intensifies the relative price effects and biases of taxation and creates "crushing" effects on all incentives to produce.[11]

Therefore, the first characteristic of popular supply-siders that sets them apart from basic supply-side economists is their preoccupation with tax policy and, within tax policy, a focus on the nominal progressivity of income taxation and the top marginal income tax rates rather than on the reform of the tax system in all its aspects.

Another characteristic that distinguishes the popular supply-siders from the basic supply-siders is the extravagance of their claims with regard to the effects of a reduction of marginal income tax rates on the economy. It is their conviction that because the negative substitution effects of income taxes are extremely high, reductions in marginal income tax rates will result in "rapid growth, dramatic increases in tax revenue, a sharp rise in saving, and a relatively painless reduction in inflation."[12] The popular supply-siders believe that a reduction in marginal income tax rates, especially the top rates, would increase the supply of labor significantly by inducing marked shifts from leisure to work and from nonmarket to market activity as after-tax wages increase, thereby raising marketed output and slowing down the rate of inflation. It would also increase the supply of savings and capital significantly by encouraging large shifts from con-

[10]"Under current law, everyone will face the top rate sooner or later," Kemp (1981, p. 94).

[11]Wanniski (1981, p. 38).

[12]This is how Feldstein (1986, p. 27) has summed up the position of popular supply-siders; he, however, does not believe in it.

sumption to savings, thereby lowering interest rates. Finally, it would redirect resources from unproductive investment and nonmarket activity to more productive uses of capital and market activity, thereby lowering unit costs, raising productivity, and removing supply bottlenecks. In short, a reduction of marginal rates of income taxes will significantly change the economic behavior of households and businesses in favor of work, savings, and productive investments and against leisure, consumption, and unproductive investments. Lower top marginal income tax rates and less progressive income taxation would also greatly discourage tax avoidance and reduce tax evasion. In a word, the popular supply-siders believe that the short-run price elasticity in the behavior of various economic agents is extremely large. Feldstein, therefore, rightly points out, "what distinguished the new [popular] supply siders from the traditional [basic] supply sider . . . was not the policies they advocated, but the claims that they made for those policies."[13]

It is this elasticity optimism that also underlies the "Laffer curve," supported by all popular supply-siders. According to its author, Arthur Laffer, government revenues first rise with tax rates (as long as tax rates are in the "normal range"), reaching a peak (the "Laffer hill"), and then falling (as tax rates rise to a "prohibitive range").[14] A reduction of income tax rates from the prohibitive range is believed by Laffer and all leading popular supply-siders to result in a very large expansion of economic activity and tax compliance, and hence income tax revenues.[15]

Thus, the popular supply-side economist aims to reduce the "exciseness" (relative price effects) of income tax rates.[16] As high marginal income tax rates have large negative substitution effects, the popular supply-siders would like particularly to see the marginal rates of personal income tax reduced and expect significant increases in output and real incomes

[13]Feldstein (1986, p. 27).

[14]For an elaboration of the Laffer curve, see Canto, Joines, and Laffer (1983, pp. 2–24) and Wanniski (1983, pp. 97–115). The Laffer curve is not essential to the basic premise of supply-side economics that leaner governments are better.

[15]Comments on the Laffer curve can be found in Hemming and Kay (1980), Blinder (1981), Moszer (1982), Henderson (1982), Buchanan and Lee (1982), Fullerton (1982), Mirowski (1982), and Malcolmson (1986). For a test of the validity of the Laffer curve in one developed country and two developing countries, see Feige and McGee (1983) and Ebrill (Chapter 7), respectively. Also see Wanniski (1983, Chapter 11).

[16]See Kemp (1981, p. 68). Comments on supply-side economics can be found in Tobin (1982).

even in the short run.[17] They believe that an income tax cut would actually increase tax revenue (by moving the economy back from the "prohibitive range" of the Laffer curve) rather than raise the budget deficit, because it would unleash an enormously depressed supply of labor and work effort and reduce tax evasion. And even if a tax cut did lead to an increased budget deficit, that would not "crowd out" resources available for private investment and capital formation, because a tax cut would significantly raise the private savings rate by increasing the after-tax rewards to savers. Nor would the increased budget deficit result in inflation, because increased nominal demand resulting from a budget deficit would be matched by an increased supply of goods and services, resulting from increased incentive to work and save, due to the tax cut.[18]

To conclude Section I, the tax systems as well as economic and other conditions of developing countries are quite different from those of developed countries. Therefore, the views of popular supply-side economists on tax policy, espoused primarily in the context of developed countries, as well as the validity of market and other assumptions made by basic supply-side economists, need to be scrutinized closely before appropriate conclusions can be drawn regarding the nature of tax reforms that would be of relevance to developing countries.

II. The Scope of the Studies and Overall Conclusions

Sections II and III highlight the findings and conclusions of individual studies included in this book. However, it is important to define the scope of the studies as well as clarify what the studies do and do not cover. Most developing countries depend on import duties and domestic commodity

[17]Wanniski (1981, p. 43) and Ture (1982a, p. 26). The nominal marginal tax rates are important for incentives, while the average effective tax rates are important for their implications about the size of government and income distribution. Both Wanniski and Kemp would like to see the marginal income tax rates ultimately range between 5 percent and 35 percent. See Wanniski (1981, pp. 45–46 and p. 49) and Kemp (1981, p. 52). Both of them favor the top rate of 35 percent, which is merely expression of an opinion and is not derived from any theoretical or economic arguments. The popular supply-siders do not want, as one might think, to do away with progressivity in the marginal rates of income taxation in the short run, although they would probably prefer a flat but low rate income tax in the long run. In their opinion, excessive progressivity of tax rates is often evaded and avoided, and never achieves the intended reduction in income inequalities.

[18]Keynes also believed in tax cuts, but only if they were not accompanied by expenditure cuts, so as to make fiscal deficits stimulative during recessions. Popular supply-siders, on the other hand, do not consider the size of the budget deficit to be of any macroeconomic relevance. See also Bechter (1982).

taxes to a significant extent (see Tables A2 and A3 in the Statistical Appendix) and some countries depend heavily on mineral taxation. These taxes have not been analyzed from a supply-side perspective in this book in view of existing research on the subject.[19] The supply-side effects of excessive effective protection, implicit in the high and complicated structures of import duties prevalent in most developing countries, are well known in the literature on international trade and development economics. Also well known are their negative effects on the efficiency of resource allocation, export prospects, and growth rates, especially when they are combined with quotas and other trade restrictions, as is also usually the case in developing countries.[20] Various studies carried out by the World Bank and the Fund have also convincingly alluded to the distortionary effects and anti-export biases of high import duties. Papers produced in the Fund's Fiscal Affairs Department have reviewed natural resource taxation and excise taxation in developing countries, respectively, from the viewpoint of efficiency.[21] The studies prepared under this research project, therefore, concentrated primarily on the economic effects of direct taxes, viz., income tax, corporation tax, and export duties, and attempted to review their optimality in the real (second-best) world prevalent in developing countries.[22]

[19]Nontax revenue policies of the government, including prices charged for various government services as well as outputs of autonomous public enterprises, can also have taxes or subsidies implicit in them. The supply-side effects of such implicit taxes, if any, were not analyzed under the research project either.

[20]For a theoretical exposition of and empirical evidence on this see Corden (1974, 1975). Empirical work on the effect of foreign trade regimes on the economic development of ten developing countries has been carried out under the auspices of the National Bureau of Economic Research. The results of this work are summarized in Bhagwati (1978) and Krueger (1978). Sce also Balassa (1971).

[21]See Palmer (1980), Nellor (1984), and Ferron (1986).

[22]Given the importance of foreign investment to the growth of most developing countries, the effects of tax policies on foreign investment should have been covered. However, this was omitted because experience shows that foreign investment decisions are usually affected by a number of economic (e.g., market size, availability of raw materials and skilled manpower), financial (e.g., development of capital market, registration and financial disclosure requirements for mobilizing domestic equity), institutional (e.g., entry and ownership regulations), and political factors, and tax policy is frequently of lesser importance in these decisions. To the extent tax policy is important, however, it seems from the survey of the literature that each developing country's tax policy will have to be tailor-made to suit its special circumstances. In this process, all tax rules and tax incentives (not tax rates alone) affecting the net return on retentions in, and remittances from, the "host" developing country will have to be reformed. The tax policies of neighboring countries and of countries in similar situations will have to be taken into account. Full account will also have to be taken of the tax systems of the "home" country of potential investors, including the availability of tax deferral, tax sparing, and foreign tax credit provisions. The scope of the double taxation treaty agreements between the

Although the research project focused primarily on the tax policy recommendations of the popular supply-side economists and their relevance to developing countries, some comments on the objective of efficient resource allocation emphasized by all supply-side economists seem necessary. Developing countries have some very special circumstances which make the neoclassical model (achievement of efficient allocation of resources through primary reliance on private initiative and enterprise) underlying supply-side economics less than fully valid. Many of these countries, especially the low-income ones, suffer from a number of disadvantages, such as (1) highly skewed income distribution; (2) "population trap," that is, large and rapidly growing population with high levels of absolute poverty; (3) large structural unemployment, both rural and urban, with little hope of a solution for want of appropriate labor-intensive technology; (4) dominance of agriculture, particularly less-productive peasant agriculture, sometimes resulting from existing land tenure systems; (5) unstable prices of export commodities; and (6) lack of adequate economic infrastructure, education, and human resources.[23] Thus, to the extent that the governments of such countries have to concern themselves with objectives other than the efficient allocation of given resources, for example, income redistribution,[24] economic stabilization,[25] or the creation of social and economic infrastructure for economic growth,[26] the supply-side approach generally has tended to be seen as being of limited relevance to these countries. Similarly, to the extent that most factor, product, and financial markets are inadequately developed in these countries, their development by the government has been considered an important objective in itself. As a result, the role of the state has been seen as far larger than that "implicit" in the supply-side approach.[27] Finally, as Shome (Chapter 12) stresses, savings

---

"host" country and the "home" country will also need to be considered. Finally, the nature of foreign investment (whether it is "footloose" or "country-specific") and its volatility as well as the existence of tax havens will also be relevant. For the importance of some of these factors see International Monetary Fund (1985b). Also see Ebrill (Chapter 3).

[23]Cf., Todaro (1985, especially Part II).

[24]There is ample evidence that the distribution of income is far more skewed in developing countries than in developed countries. See Lecaillon and others (1984, especially Table 9 and p. 41).

[25]See Killick and others (1984, especially Part I).

[26]Cf., World Bank (1980, especially pp. 36-39 and Chapters 5 and 6).

[27]As Todaro (1985) has pointed out, "whether one likes it or not, Third World governments must inevitably assume a more active responsibility for the future well-being of their countries than the governments of the more developed nations. . . . Central to this new role will be institutional and structural reform in the fields of land tenure, taxation [to mobilize resources for investment, lacking private financial markets], asset ownership and distribution, educa-

alone are not enough for growth, they require "complementary factors" if they are to become investment in reality, especially the removal of external constraints (such as foreign exchange availability) and domestic constraints (such as expanding the size of the market, facilitating the transfer of technology, and establishing adequate financial intermediary institutions).[28] Also, growth by itself would not mean development unless it is accompanied by certain institutional reforms involving human capital formation and the creation of essential social and economic structure, agricultural reforms, population control, etc. Growth and development of developing countries are, thus, objectives that are much more complex than ensuring the efficient allocation of *given* resources only, and they call for a much bigger role of the state than supply-side economists are perhaps willing to concede.

The broad conclusion of the research project is that the supply-side tax policy which focuses on marginal income tax rates alone (the popular version) is too narrow and is of limited relevance to many developing countries, especially the low-income countries. The view of supply-side tax policy which stresses broadening the tax base and rationalizing the rates of not only income tax but also of other taxes so as to remove all tax-related distortions (the basic version) is of greater relevance to such countries.[29] In addition, the research project has established that the impact of the tax system of a developing country on the potential for its development depends on a variety of factors such as (1) the reliance of the tax system on income-related taxes; (2) the interaction between tax rates, the tax base, specific tax incentives for savings and capital formation, and the tax administrative capacity, as they each affect savers and income earners; (3) the rate of inflation and the degree of inflation-indexation of depreciation and other provisions of the tax system, which determine the effective tax burdens of producers and income earners and their after-tax rewards; (4) the interaction between tax policy and other macroeconomic policies of the government, which affects the prices of foreign exchange, capital, and labor; and (5) the degree of imperfection in or the level of development of the labor market, the capital market, the foreign exchange market, financial

tional and health delivery systems, credit rationing, labor market relations, pricing policies, the organization and orientation of technological research and experimentation . . . and the very machinery of government and planning itself" (pp. 526–27).

[28]Cf., Streeten (1979, pp. 21–52).

[29]Recent income tax reform efforts in Indonesia, India, the Philippines, and Jamaica and a few other developing countries reflect this strategy. See Gillis (1985), India, Ministry of Finance (1985), Yoingco (1986), and Bahl and others (1987) for descriptions of these efforts.

institutions, credit markets, etc. As is shown by the papers that follow, these factors are of fundamental importance and developing countries have some very special circumstances with respect to all of these, so that the advice of lowering the marginal income tax rates must be examined in this wider context. Once this approach is taken, the high degree of elasticity and growth optimism, which the popular supply-siders frequently take for granted subsequent to a reduction of high marginal income tax rates, must be moderated in the special circumstances of the developing countries.

More specifically, the research project has established that while the popular view of supply-side tax policy (that the height of nominal tax rates matters for incentives) has to be valid for developing countries, other tax and nontax factors are equally important, if not more important for growth and development. While tax policy undeniably affects the behavior of taxpayers, factors such as inflation and rigid nontax policies of developing countries are frequently more severe disincentives to economic agents. Similarly, though labor supply, financial savings, and investment in developing countries do respond to economic incentives and tax policy, they are frequently affected by market imperfections and institutional factors as well and their price elasticities tend to be low in the short run. In relation to income taxation in particular, the finding is that the overall reliance of developing countries, particularly the low-income ones, on this tax is extremely low. Hence, any policy reform in the area of income taxation can, at best, be expected to have a limited impact on the growth of the economy. Furthermore, while the present nominal levels of personal income taxation are high in many developing countries, their negative economic effects on capital incomes are frequently neutralized, partially if not fully, by the very generous tax incentives granted to savers and investors. Indeed, lowering marginal personal income tax rates, while at the same time broadening the tax base and removing the liberal tax incentives in order to contain the short-run revenue loss, in the context of many developing countries could well lead to an increase in the tax burden on savings and investments. There is also some evidence that in developing countries, given their inflationary situations, the disincentive effects of high rates of taxes other than individual income tax, such as of export duties, and certain provisions of corporation tax, such as historic cost depreciation, first-in-first-out basis of inventory valuation, and other provisions, are far greater than those of high marginal income tax rates on individuals. In light of all this, several efficiency and growth-oriented tax reform ideas have emerged from the research project, which are consistent with the views of basic supply-side tax policy. These are highlighted in Section V, below.

III. Validity and Relevance of Popular Supply-Side Tax Policy

This section summarizes the findings and conclusions of the papers contained in Part II of the book which assess the validity and relevance of the policy prescriptions of popular supply-side economics in the context of the special circumstances of developing countries.

Validity of Popular Supply-Side Tax Policy

The validity of the popular supply-side tax policy prescription for developing countries requires positive answers to the following five questions.

- Are labor supply, savings, and investment highly price-sensitive?
- Do income tax policies (tax rates combined with liberal tax incentives for savings) significantly reduce savings, especially the availability of financial savings?
- Do income tax policies (tax rates combined with generous tax incentives and other tax provisions affecting investors) significantly reduce investment?
- Do high and progressive income tax rates significantly increase income tax evasion?
- Have government revenues increased significantly in the short run, in line with the Laffer curve, when top marginal income tax rates have been reduced?

A positive answer to all these questions in the institutional and economic circumstances of the developing world would imply that the tax policy prescriptions of the popular supply-side school are valid and require careful consideration by the policymakers of developing countries. Six papers included in Part II of this book attempt to answer the above-mentioned five questions, while the seventh paper reviews some econometric evidence on the interrelationship between reliance of developing countries on income taxes and their growth rates.

Price Responsiveness of Labor Supply, Savings, and Investment

Using some simple macroeconomic models, Mackenzie (Chapter 2) establishes that, theoretically, a reduction of income tax rates can have aggregate supply effects as well as effects on aggregate demand and liquidity. However, he also shows that the supply effects are far less significant than the demand and liquidity effects unless the income tax reductions are drastic and the price elasticities of labor supply and savings are very high. To illustrate his point, he takes the readily available empirical estimates of elasticities for a well-integrated and well-functioning competitive market economy as that of the United States. (Economies of some middle-income developing countries may well have similar features.) Even for such an economy, he establishes that for the income tax cut to be self-financing, labor supply elasticity will have to be 15, when savings elasticity is assumed to be within the limits of reported empirical research. He shows that if the labor supply and savings elasticities are low (as they, in fact, are for the United States where savings elasticity has been estimated by some studies to be between 0.2 and 0.4 and labor supply elasticity has been estimated to be around 0.2), the increases in the rate of growth of real output would not be particularly great in the first ten years following a significant reduction of income tax rates. He estimates that a 20 percent across-the-board reduction of income tax rates for both capital and labor, given a savings elasticity of 0.4 and a labor supply elasticity of 0.2, and other economic parameters similar to those of the U.S. economy, will raise the average annual growth rate of 3 percent over a ten-year period to at most 3.14 percent. In the extreme case, when both elasticities equal 1.0 and the tax rate on labor incomes is reduced by 20 percent and that on capital incomes by 50 percent, the average annual growth rate of 3 percent over a ten-year period increases to 3.77 percent. Mackenzie, thus, concludes from his theoretical analysis that some positive supply-side effects are certain from an across-the-board reduction of income tax rates but how large the effect will be will depend upon the price elasticities of labor supply, savings, and investment. The size of these elasticities is an empirical question and must depend on the structural features of the economy or economies in question. However, on balance, the potential impact of sweeping income tax rate cuts on the growth rates of a representative economy of the type some middle-income developing countries may have does not seem to be very high.

Ebrill (Chapter 3) surveys the empirical evidence on the price responsiveness of labor supply, savings, and investment in developing countries. He finds a dearth of solid empirical work and the direct evidence on price responsiveness to be rather limited. He, therefore, looks for indirect evidence.

On labor supply, he reviews studies on subjects such as rural-urban migration, the effects of minimum wage laws, and the determinants of earning functions and concludes that "some indirect support" does exist for the proposition "that supply-side considerations have a role in the determination of the equilibrium wage" (p. 67). He also concludes that "although the empirical work supports the existence of a well-defined aggregate labor supply function, it appears not to be very elastic" (p. 67). In rural areas, in particular, the evidence is that labor supply decisions are determined by a variety of factors other than the wage rate (labor markets are frequently interlocked with other factor markets and widespread land-lease contracts and sharecropping arrangements make for imperfect labor markets). As a result, the labor supply function is price inelastic.

On savings, he finds that savings data in developing countries are very inadequate and that the development economics literature has dealt little with the question of interest elasticity of savings. Ebrill, therefore, seeks out indirect evidence again. Most available estimates of consumption functions in developing countries, for example, reveal that aggregate savings are affected more by income as well as by noneconomic factors, such as demographic factors, income distribution, life span, occupational patterns, and urban-rural distinction, than by interest rates. However, the empirical literature evaluating the effects of financial repression (artificially low interest rate ceilings) widely prevalent in developing countries demonstrates that financial savings may be sensitive to changes in interest rates. He, therefore, concludes that "even though aggregate savings may not be very interest-sensitive, the allocation of that aggregate between conventional financial assets and alternatives such as curb market funds and works of art is indeed responsive to economic incentives" (p. 74). Of course, changes in income tax rates may be powerless in influencing even the allocation of aggregate savings if financial policy is "wrong."

On investment, Ebrill finds much of the empirical evidence from developing countries to be against the neoclassical framework which explains investment simply in terms of the cost of capital. Foreign investment is said to be influenced by factors such as the presence of natural resources, proven record of economic performance of a country, threat of expropriation, degree of urbanization, and the availability of advanced infrastructure rather than by the availability of fiscal incentives. Domestic investment, on the other hand, is shown to be influenced by factors such as the availability of domestic savings, retained earnings of businesses, public investment outlays in support of private productive activity, trade policy, and the degree of protection, and, in the specific case of agricultural investment, by distortions associated with price support systems and marketing boards. Ebrill, therefore, concludes that while investors do react to economic incentives, "investment [in developing countries] is influenced by a number of factors" (p. 81).

Ebrill sums up his findings on the subject of price responsiveness in developing countries as follows: "Although the empirical literature examining the impact of tax policy on labor supply, savings, and investment leaves much to be desired, it nonetheless appears that changes in tax policy will have some effects. The behavior of these aggregates appears, however, to be determined as much by other elements. . . . Given the existence of widespread market failure in many developing countries, the impact of changes in tax policies may be quite difficult to predict . . . [and] it may be the case that a more promising supply-side approach might be one that also aims at alleviating the most obvious sources of market failure" (p. 82).

Tax Policies and Financial Savings

What is the optimal tax policy toward financial savings in developing countries and is the sharp reduction of marginal income tax rates its most important element? In Chapter 4, Ebrill reviews the existing literature in search of a theoretical answer to these questions and finds that the literature is inconclusive; in addition, the literature does not adequately accommodate the special circumstances of developing countries. He identifies at least four characteristics of developing country situations (they exist in all developing countries although their magnitudes may vary): (1) artificially low interest rate ceilings which, given the rates of inflation, frequently result in financial repression; (2) relatively underdeveloped financial institutions and capital markets; (3) the existence of unorganized capital markets; and (4) the use of compulsory savings schemes by the governments.

Ebrill then develops a modified illustrative optimal tax framework to take into account some of the characteristics of the financial structures of developing countries, in particular the existence of financial repression and curb markets. To start with, his model shows that, under normal circumstances, the optimal tax on financial savings depends on its own-price elasticity. While the evidence indicates that financial savings are interest-elastic to some degree, he admits that no useful point estimates can be made of the relevant price elasticity and, therefore, of the optimal tax rates. Once, however, the special circumstances of developing countries are taken into account, the model suggests that the optimal taxation of financial savings changes. If the degree of financial repression in a developing country is large, and if for some reason this distortion cannot be removed, his modified optimal tax framework indicates that "a subsidy rather than a tax is appropriate" (p. 106). In turn, if the use of subsidies is precluded for fiscal or other reasons, then "consumption . . . is more appropriate than income as a tax base" (p. 106).

Ebrill argues that the optimal tax treatment of financial savings depends critically on the degree of financial repression, which varies widely both across countries and over time. "Accordingly, there is no single recommended policy such as reducing marginal tax rates. Each country has to be considered individually" (p. 108). Depending on the particular country that is under consideration, "the optimal tax treatment of financial savings runs the gamut from subsidies to substantial taxation" (p. 92).

Tax Policies and Investment

The rate of tax affects the cost of capital and, therefore, affects the level of investment—this much is built into the neoclassical framework of investment behavior. In many developing countries, the nominal rate of corporation income tax is high but, as Table A15 in the Statistical Appendix shows, tax incentives and deductions for investment are relatively liberal and it is the combination of both of these, along with the rate of inflation as it interacts with capital allowances, capital gains, and interest deductibility provisions, that determines the cost of capital. In Chapter 5 Ebrill reviews the income and corporate tax structures of 31 developing countries and makes cost-of-capital estimates. His results show that "Indeed . . . the tax system in many countries subsidizes the cost of investment at low inflation rates."At high rates of inflation, on the other hand, their tax systems (especially those featuring depreciation allowances and inventory valuations based on historic costs) are such as to be a "source of investment disincentives." For several countries with very high inflation rates, he finds the disincentive effects to be pronounced (p. 126).

Relating the share of gross domestic investment in gross domestic product (GDP) to his cost-of-capital estimates for 31 developing countries, Ebrill shows that while after-tax cost of capital has a significant impact on investment levels, other variables, especially the rate of inflation and the growth of exports, are equally important which, at least, "raises the question of which is the most promising path for policy to take" (p. 132).

He concludes, therefore, that strong policy recommendations concerning the effectiveness of income and corporate tax rate reductions alone for encouraging investment in developing countries should be resisted and attention should be paid to controlling inflation and alleviating distortions to exports. All this suggests "that supply-side based tax reform proposals [advocated by popular supply-siders] are only of limited use" (pp. 133–34) and additional tax reforms, such as indexation of depreciation allowances or taxing corporations on a cash flow basis (i.e., full expensing of all investment and disallowing the deductibility of interest payments on debt), are equally important.

Progressivity and Income Tax Evasion

The effect of high and progressive taxation on income tax evasion is commonly taken for granted and with ample justification. Richupan (Chapter 6) surveys the theoretical and empirical literature on income tax evasion to locate the basis of this perceived relationship. He concludes that "the theoretical literature does not support the claim that an increase in the tax rate will lead to an increase in tax evasion" (p. 148) or "that a progressive tax rate schedule stimulates tax evasion" (p. 151). The empirical studies on the subject are, however, sketchy and indirect and do not yield a definitive conclusion on the subject.

Richupan, however, finds that the theoretical literature contains stronger conclusions regarding the role of other tax and nontax factors in encouraging income tax evasion. In particular, high penalty rates and high probability of detection are shown to have a negative effect on tax evasion. Income tax evasion is also shown to be strongly influenced by nontax factors such as the type of income and perception of fiscal equity. In the special circumstances of developing countries, nontax factors such as price controls, government regulations, and civil service salaries, are all shown to contribute positively to income tax evasion.

Thus, Richupan ends up doubting the effect that a reduction of income tax rates alone or even income tax reforms generally will have on the degree of income tax evasion which is far higher in developing countries than in developed countries.

Evidence on the Laffer Curve

One important assumption of popular supply-side economics is that if tax rates are sufficiently high (the "prohibitive range") then a reduction in tax rates would lead to an increase in tax revenues. The implicit assumption in this relationship is that the substitution effect of a tax cut is positive and the factor elasticities are very large.

Ebrill (Chapter 7) tests the validity of this assumption and the Laffer curve with data from Jamaica and India, two developing countries that had very high marginal income tax rates and where in the 1970s the top marginal income tax rates were significantly reduced. He points out that an ideal test of the Laffer curve would involve relating income tax yield among the highest income groups with proxies for tax rate reductions and other explanatory variables. Using the data for PAYE taxpayers in Jamaica between 1979 and 1981 only, and adjusting it for changes in income distribution, real growth rates, and inflation over time, Ebrill concludes that "data are consistent with the existence of a Laffer curve in Jamaica" (p. 188); however, he mentions many reservations about this conclusion. Data availability is better for India and Ebrill's analysis of the effects of a marginal income tax reduction introduced in that country in 1975 leads him to conclude that "the data on India, at least for the years selected . . . do not support the Laffer curve hypothesis" (p. 192).

Ebrill recognizes the limitations of his methodology, which had to be tailored to use the available (rather poor quality and inadequate) data, and admits that existence of market imperfections, improvements in income tax administration, and other variables may account for his results. Nevertheless, he concludes that "assertions to the effect that developing countries are operating in regions of the Laffer curve, where tax rate reductions would lead to revenue increases, should be treated with caution" (p. 175) and that "the results [obtained for Jamaica and India] could easily be rationalized using non-Laffer curve explanations" (p. 193). He, therefore, cautions that none of his results can be seen as a complete endorsement of the narrow (popular) supply-side approach (marginal income tax rate reductions) and that the broader (basic) supply-side approach (removal of tax distortions irrespective of the source) may still induce significant supply-side response.

The answers to the five questions set out at the beginning of this subsection can be summed up as follows. Although there is some indirect evidence that the assumptions underlying the popular supply-side tax policy may be valid for developing countries, the research has highlighted many other factors, special to the circumstances of developing countries, which may be of equal or greater importance to the expansion of labor supply, savings, and investment as well as the reduction of income tax evasion, considered desirable by supply-side economists. In particular, the research shows that developing countries need to pay attention to the development of labor and capital markets and to removing other economic policy distortions such as high minimum wages, overvalued exchange rates, interest rate ceilings, and inflationary financing of the budget. Even in the area of income tax policy, the alternatives of inflation-adjustment of depreciation allowances and inventory valuations, conversion of income tax to some form of consumption tax (i.e., the exemption of savings or, at least, a moderation of the tax burden on capital incomes), and the replacement of a corporation tax based on profits by a tax based on cash flow may affect savings and investment more significantly than a simple reduction of marginal income tax rates. Similarly, raising income tax penalties and increasing the probability of detection of income tax evaders, through legislative and administrative improvements, may also be more effective in reducing income tax evasion in developing countries than just lowering marginal tax rates and reducing the progressivity of income taxation.

Thus, the conclusion of the research is that it is not that the popular supply-side tax policy prescription of reducing the excessively high marginal income tax rates, in the interest of improving growth prospects, is invalid but that there are other important tax and nontax determinants of the behavior of economic agents and economic growth in developing countries. The fact that developing countries are quite heterogeneous and that their governments must, at this stage of development, pursue a variety of objectives (including redistribution, economic stabilization, and mobilizing revenue for providing essential social and economic infrastructure and its maintenance) further complicates the task of arriving at a unique conclusion about the levels and structure of taxation that will be valid for all developing countries. Advice on tax policies must, therefore, struggle with this multiplicity of objectives; in doing so it must also take into account the uses to which government revenues are put and assess their economic and social necessity.[30]

Relevance of Popular Supply-Side Tax Policy

In assessing the relevance to developing countries of the popular view of supply-side tax policy, one needs to assess the reliance of developing countries on income taxes, in particular (1) the relative importance of income tax revenues in such countries; (2) the height of their income tax rates; and (3) the scope and generosity of various tax reliefs to savings and investments and the impact of these on the effective tax rates on capital incomes. These topics are treated below. Furthermore, one also needs to consider the empirical evidence on the growth rates of the developing countries that rely heavily on income taxes, which is explored by Mañas-Antón in Chapter 8.

Relative Insignificance of Individual Income Taxation

The data given in Tables A2–A4 in the Statistical Appendix confirm that the individual income tax is a relatively unimportant source of revenue in many developing countries, particularly in those that do not have large and significant mining sectors. While there are important differences among countries of the developing world, on average, the individual income tax accounts for only 2 percent of GDP and 11 percent of all tax revenue, compared with 8 percent and 29 percent, respectively, in developed countries. From a limited number of developing countries for which it has been possible to collect information (see Tables A5 and A6 in the Statistical Appen-

[30]As Rosen (1985) points out, "The fact that a tax generates an excess burden is not necessarily 'bad.' One hopes, after all, that the tax will be used to obtain something beneficial for society either in terms of purchase of public goods or income redistribution" (p. 296). The uses to which government revenues are put are, therefore, not entirely irrelevant. Available data suggest that central governments of developing countries devote an average of over 40 percent of their total expenditure (including net lending) to the provision of economic services (viz., agriculture, electricity, roads, and transport and communications) and for capital formation as against an average of about 15 percent by those of developed countries. See International Monetary Fund (1985a, pp. 46–63). Unfortunately, expenditure data are not readily available to make a similar comparison for all levels of government.

dix), it is clear that individual income tax, on average, is paid by less than 5 percent of the population (mostly wage and salary earners) and the income assessed to tax is less than 14 percent of GDP (mostly through withholding taxes). Richupan (1985) has listed a variety of factors that may be responsible for the relative insignificance of personal income taxation in developing countries.[31]

Even though income tax is an unimportant source of tax revenue and affects a relatively small proportion of high income earners, the progressivity of its nominal rate structure may still be such as to have serious disincentive effects on income earners who matter. Data given in Table A9 of the Statistical Appendix throw light on the rate structures of personal income taxation in selected developing countries.

Levels of Individual Income Taxation

The income tax rate schedules of 32 developing countries, summarized in Table A9 of the Statistical Appendix, show that the top marginal income tax rate exceeds 55 percent in nearly one half of the 32 selected countries. In 4 developing countries, the top marginal rates exceed 65 percent (Table 1). The threshold levels of income at which income tax starts applying in most developing countries are the equivalent of about one time the per capita GDP before personal allowances are taken into account and less than twice the per capita GDP after personal allowances are taken into account (see Table A12 in the Statistical Appendix). The availability of personal allowances, deductions, and preferences (see Statistical Appendix Table A10) does neutralize some of the burden of high marginal tax rates, and in most developing countries the top marginal income tax rates apply only to very high income levels, as high as 50 times the per capita income. However, in 3 developing countries, top marginal tax rates are payable by income earners earning less than 10 times the per capita GDP (Table 2), which is relatively low.

Tax Reliefs for Personal Savings and Investments

Individual income taxpayers in many developing countries enjoy a number of incentives for personal savings and investments which reduce the

[31]In addition to fundamental factors such as the underdeveloped structure of the economy (e.g., the prevalence of subsistence agriculture and small and poorly equipped production and business units in the manufacturing and service sectors) and the consequent lack of adequate tax handles, Richupan stresses the roles of government economic policies and the low efficiency of tax administration.

Table 1. Thirty-Two Selected Developing Countries: Frequency Distribution of Top Marginal Income Tax Rates, Around 1981 and 1985

Maximum or Top Marginal Tax Rates	Number of Countries		Applies to Income Less Than 25 Times PCGDP[1]		Applies to Income over 25 Times PCGDP[1]	
	1981	1985[2]	1981	1985[2]	1981	1985[2]
Up to 35	0	3	0	1	0	2
36–45	4	7	1	2	3	3
46–55	6	7	3	0	3	7
56–60	11	9	6	4	5	3
61–65	4	2	0	0	4	4
66–70	6	2	2	2	4	0
Over 70	1	2	1	0	0	2
Total[3]	32	32	13	9[3]	19	21[3]

Source: Jitendra R. Modi, "Levels of Personal Income Taxation in Selected Developing Countries" (unpublished, International Monetary Fund, February 1985) and the sources cited therein.

[1]PCGDP = per capita gross domestic product at current market prices.

[2]The shift in the distribution of countries is due to the major revisions in the tax rate schedules implemented by some countries.

[3]Frequency distribution of income levels (in terms of PCGDP) for 1985 does not add to total number of countries in the sample because the relevant information is not available for two countries.

effective tax rates on capital incomes, and these have important supply-side implications. The former include deductions for life insurance premiums and pension contributions and exemptions from income taxation of interest and dividend incomes (see Table A10 in the Statistical Appendix), while the latter include, among other things, the levy of a final withholding tax on selected investment incomes at rates substantially lower than the top marginal income tax rates (Statistical Appendix Table A11). Furthermore, income tax holidays for periods between five to ten years are widespread in developing countries for those taxpayers whose incomes are derived from the establishment of new businesses or the expansion of existing businesses (see Statistical Appendix Table A15).

All these features of the income tax systems take away much of the "bite" of high nominal income tax rates, especially with respect to savings and investment incomes, and selected forms of capital incomes enjoy substantial "subsidies" under the income tax systems of developing countries. As Ebrill (Chapter 5) shows, under zero rates of inflation, the cost of capital in most developing countries is extremely small (some countries even "subsidize" capital) and it is only the lack of indexation or inadequate indexation of the income tax systems that raises the cost of capital in high-

Table 2. Selected Developing Countries: Estimates of Total Income Levels at Which Top Marginal Tax Rates Must Apply

	Top Nominal Marginal Tax Rate	Estimated Total Income (As multiple of PCGDP)[1]
Brazil	45	18.3
Cyprus	60	10.9
Egypt	50	199.8
Ghana	60	3.5
Guyana	70	17.4
India	66	71.3
Indonesia	50	54.9
Jamaica	58	8.1
Kenya	65	84.7
Korea	60	53.9
Malaysia	55	30.1
Morocco	45	287.1
Nigeria	70	77.6
Pakistan	66	40.5
Papua New Guinea	50	56.9
Peru	65	102.6
Philippines	60	84.3
Singapore	45	68.6
Thailand	65	128.7
Trinidad and Tobago	70	7.9
Tunisia	80	16.2
Venezuela	45	423.7
Zaïre	60	95.3

Source: Jitendra R. Modi, "Levels of Personal Income Taxation in Selected Developing Countries" (unpublished, International Monetary Fund, February 1985) and the sources cited therein.

[1]Estimated total incomes take into account the personal exemptions, the personal allowances, and an estimate of the various deductions and tax preferences available to the taxpayer at that income level in each country. PCGDP = per capita gross domestic product at market prices.

inflation developing countries. However, as only "selected" forms of capital incomes are preferentially treated, tax-caused distortions in the use of savings continue to prevail in many developing countries, and investments not enjoying preferential tax treatment (usually speculative and unproductive investments) obviously are the ones that are taxed at the high marginal income tax rates noted earlier. In addition, as various studies included in this book show, savings and investment decisions in developing countries are also distorted by other governmental policies such as administered interest rates (Chapter 4) and overvalued exchange rates, quantitative trade restrictions, and producer price ceilings (Chapter 11).

Relationship Between Income Tax Ratios and Growth Rates

If the levels of income taxation have the significantly detrimental effects on growth rates that popular supply-siders claim, countries whose governments rely less heavily on income taxation should enjoy relatively higher growth rates than those whose governments rely more heavily on such taxation. Taking this as his starting point, Mañas-Antón (Chapter 8) presents some empirical evidence on the interrelationship in selected developing countries between output growth and the reliance on income taxes. He uses readily available cross-country and pooled cross-country time-series data and estimates of multiple regression equations with a variety of specifications, all containing important determinants of growth derived from the Dennison growth accounting tradition.

His regressions show that the ratio of income taxes to total tax revenue (as well as to GDP) and the growth rate of output are negatively related and that the regression coefficients are significant, but this result does not hold in all specifications. When the ratios of individual and corporate income taxes to total tax revenue are related to growth rates, the regression coefficients are still negative but statistically insignificant in both cases.

Mañas-Antón, therefore, concludes that "while there is some evidence supporting a negative relationship between output growth rates and the reliance of a country on income taxes, this relationship cannot be asserted with much confidence" (p. 218). He calls this conclusion "tentative" and recognizes the many limitations of his analysis: cross-section regression analysis, for example, can be easily criticized as an improper test of a time-series proposition; the model specification itself was limited by the available data and, therefore, may be inadequate.

Evidence thus far suggests that, given the limited scope of income taxation in most low-income developing countries, and the very few taxpayers who are subject to top marginal income tax rates in many developing countries, lowering the top marginal income tax rates alone (the popular supply-side tax policy) may well be of lesser consequence from an efficiency point of view than reforming the scope of the tax base, various tax rules and provisions, and other aspects of the income tax structure. For supply-side tax policy to be relevant to developing countries, it must also encompass reforms in the rates and bases of taxes other than income tax, which are more important in developing countries and which may have more significant supply-side effects than the level and structure of income tax rates. A review of the other characteristics of the tax systems of developing countries is, therefore, essential and a supply-side look at other aspects of their tax policies is called for. The papers included in Part III of the book review selected aspects of the tax systems of developing countries that are significant from the point of view of efficiency and growth.

IV. Tax Policy for Efficiency and Growth

The overall level of taxation is claimed by all supply-side economists to have significant effects on the growth rates in developing countries, and the structure of taxation is believed to have significant effects on the incentives of economic agents and the efficiency of resource allocation in the economy. One must, therefore, ask the following questions.

- What will the tax systems of developing countries look like in theory if incentives and the efficient allocation of resources were the major concern of the policymakers?
- How efficient are the very generous tax incentives that are frequently given to agricultural, manufacturing, and other enterprises by the policymakers of developing countries in order to induce economic growth?
- When are export duties, which are so dominant in the revenue structures of many low-income developing countries, justified on grounds of efficiency and growth?
- What is the precise role of tax policy in removing the various structural bottlenecks to economic development and helping the growth of developing countries?

The answers to these questions are explored in the four papers included in Part III.

Tax Structure for Incentives and Efficient Resource Allocation

Gandhi (Chapter 9) points out that taxation has always been an instrument with multiple objectives. It is not that the traditional literature on taxation has ignored the efficiency objective of taxation, or the distortionary economic effects of various taxes, but that a tax system based solely on efficiency criteria would not be viable on political and other grounds. It would ignore entirely the equity objective and is unlikely to generate adequate revenue to run a modern government or to allow for the provision and maintenance of basic social and economic infrastructure that is necessary for economic development. Furthermore, it would contain certain taxes that would not be easy to administer.

He establishes what the tax systems of developing countries would look like if efficient allocation of resources were the sole concern of the policymakers. They would consist of a poll tax, a tax on land area, a tax on windfall profits, a tax on potential income, taxes on items with inelastic demand or supply, and taxes for internalizing the negative production and consumption externalities; they would not consist of any other taxes such as income tax, corporation tax, capital gains tax, payroll tax, wealth tax, gift tax, and inheritance tax. Export duties and import duties would also not be included in such tax systems except under very exceptional circumstances. The rates of taxation under an "efficient" tax system would be strictly dictated by optimizing formulas based on price elasticities and would contain little or no progression—in any case, they could not be raised simply for revenue reasons. Also, there would be no place for special tax incentives and preferences in such a tax system. The efficiency-oriented tax structure is, thus, shown by Gandhi to be no more than a theoretical ideal which could not be realistically adopted by any developing country.

Role of Tax Incentives

Tables A13 to A15 in the Statistical Appendix examine the structure of corporation tax and corporate tax incentives in 32 developing countries.[32] They show that only a few developing countries have high corporate tax rates (55 percent or over) but most do have very liberal tax deductions and incentives. Most developing countries offer tax depreciation allowances on a replacement basis or accelerated basis and investment tax credits or investment allowances ranging between 5 percent and 30 percent of the cost of capital assets. Many developing countries give special deductions for intangible expenditures, such as manpower training and research and development expenditures, as well as for expenditure related to export production. Carry forward of unutilized holiday period depreciation and losses for almost indefinite periods is also permitted in most developing countries. Many developing countries also offer favorable tax treatment of capital gains and partial indexation provisions, and almost one third of the selected developing countries permit liberal inventory valuations for tax purposes. Shareholders frequently enjoy relief from double taxation of dividends through partial imputation of the corporation tax. However, the most significant of all tax incentives to corporate investment is the complete income tax holidays, for varying durations (often extendable) and for a variety of purposes, which are offered in most developing countries; dividends and capital gains earned by individual and corporate stockholders during the tax holiday period are also frequently tax exempt.

Thus, in developing countries investment incentives are generous enough to reduce the cost of capital considerably and to lower the average tax burden on capital incomes as compared to what is incorporated in the

[32]For a fuller description of the features of corporate tax structures in developing countries, see Modi (1987).

nominal tax rate schedules. In fact, as Ebrill (Chapter 7) shows, the governments of many developing countries "subsidize" productive investments in priority sectors of their economies.

Given the widespread use of liberal tax incentives in developing countries to achieve a variety of developmental goals, Sanchez-Ugarte (Chapter 10) looks at tax incentives from the supply-side point of view and concludes that "even though the granting of tax incentives under certain circumstances might be economically rational, this policy presents severe limitations and drawbacks. . . . The attempt by some developing countries to use a vast array of liberal tax incentives to counteract the negative economic effects of high marginal tax rates of narrowly based taxes and/or wrong economic policies with regard to wage rates, interest rates, exchange rates, and so on is likely to be ineffective and even counterproductive" (p. 273). Sanchez-Ugarte divides the efficiency case for tax incentives into a "pure" case and an "impure" case. A pure case for tax incentives exists whenever externalities exist and tax incentives for regional development, encouragement of risk-taking and savings, dampening the short-run output disturbances, and promoting research and development are all justified on this basis. The impure case for tax incentives exists only as an offset to distortions created by other economic policies whose reform is considered infeasible by policymakers for one reason or another. Sanchez-Ugarte then describes the distortions created by inappropriate trade, tax, and wage policies and shows how tax incentives can be designed to counteract their distortionary effects. He concludes that tax incentives "are never the most appropriate policy to follow" (p. 258) because they are prone to induce diverse and often unpredictable distortions in the economy and illustrates this by examining specific tax incentives in terms of the criterion of efficiency.

As stated earlier, Sanchez-Ugarte points out that tax incentives as applied in most developing countries are often ineffective. For tax incentives to be effective, he lists five conditions: (1) they should be directed to limited objectives which should be economic and not political; (2) there should be little red tape and discretion in granting them; (3) they should be predictable, though not necessarily permanent; (4) the specific tax incentive should closely match the objective which is being pursued; and (5) the design of the tax incentive should attempt to take into account its general equilibrium effects on the economy. It is, thus, no simple task to design effective tax incentives and Sanchez-Ugarte concludes that "tax incentives are no substitute for an efficient tax system" (p. 274).

Optimality of Export Duties

Many low-income developing countries rely as much on export duties as on income tax. Sanchez-Ugarte and Modi (Chapter 11) examine a sample of 71 developing countries that levy export duties and find that 29 countries derive more than 10 percent of their tax revenue and more than 1 percent of GDP from such duties. Almost all of the 71 developing countries rely heavily on one or more export items, generally coffee, cocoa, tea, bananas, rubber, groundnuts, tin, bauxite, and phosphates, and the average rates of these duties are frequently high, thus affecting incentives for production and exports.

Sanchez-Ugarte and Modi review the levels and structures of existing imposts, both explicit and implicit, on exports in selected developing countries and reach three important conclusions. First, they find the actual level of export taxation in the majority of developing countries to be higher than the level that can be considered even country optimal, let alone world optimal. This result arises primarily due to the high implicit export taxes, in the form of overvalued or multiple exchange rates, producer price ceilings, or quantitative restrictions on exports, prevalent in many developing countries. Given the small but significant values of the supply elasticities of agricultural products estimated in the literature, they show that the detrimental effects of the high export taxation existing in many developing countries on the level of their exports are significant. Second, they find that the taxation of "windfall" profits through export taxes will be nondistortionary only when the tax is unexpected and temporary—which is difficult to attain in practice. Finally, they show that the operation of producer income stabilization schemes reduces significantly the present value of revenue to producers, without significantly reducing riskiness. Hence, such schemes are distortionary and discourage production and exports.

Thus, Sanchez-Ugarte and Modi show that in the majority of developing countries analyzed in the chapter, the reduction of export taxes can be expected not only to increase exports but also to enhance the economic well-being of the specific country and the world as a whole. However, the authors conclude that over the short and medium runs the existence of market imperfections in commodity markets could well preclude many developing countries from benefiting from the supply-side effects of lowering export taxes, while the government revenues would be lowered. With respect to revenues, they argue, however, that many developing countries can reduce effective levels of export taxation without losing revenue (in a few cases even gaining revenue) if the nonrevenue-yielding implicit export taxes (exchange rate overvaluation, quantitative restrictions on exports, etc.) are removed, so that the base of explicit export taxes expands.

Limits of Tax Policy for Economic Development

Shome (Chapter 12) forcefully argues that in a developing country, "tax policy can theoretically be a powerful instrument in targeting all . . . factors of development" (p. 327) but only under appropriate conditions. He shows how tax policies can and have in practice operated in certain developing countries to influence the conditions of development such as raising the investment rate, closing the foreign exchange gap, encouraging financial intermediation, assisting in human resource development, and controlling population, where necessary. But, then, taxation has its limitations and difficulties: it simply cannot be effective in the attainment of too many objectives; frequently, not all individuals in a developing country are covered by the tax regime; the capacity to administer even moderately sophisticated taxes is limited in many of these countries; and the taxpayer's economic behavior is not always affected solely by prices. In addition, tax policy must be supported by complementary changes in other policies of developing countries, especially those relating to the monetary and financial sector, as well as the removal of structural bottlenecks to development. Shome, therefore, rightly states, "Thus, while economists have to, and indeed, do assign a major role to tax policy in tackling development and growth, and sometimes successfully, it must be done with perspicacity" (p. 330). Similar sentiment is expressed in other chapters, viz., in Ebrill (Chapter 4), where a strong case is made from the supply-side point of view for removing financial repression and other distortions to the development of the capital markets; in Ebrill (Chapter 5), where a strong case is made for the control of inflation; and in Sanchez-Ugarte and Modi (Chapter 11), where a strong case is made for the removal of distortions to exports, including overvalued exchange rates.

To sum up Section IV, the research has established that tax structures of most developing countries depend a lot more on commodity taxes, such as import and export duties, sales taxes, and excise duties, than on income taxes. Even income taxes in these countries take on the characteristics of consumption taxes because of the very generous tax incentives and tax reliefs granted to savings and investments. In addition, many facets of a given tax, other than tax rate, such as the tax base, exemptions, and allowances, can significantly distort taxpayer behavior. If developing countries are to reach their full growth potential, they may need efficiency-oriented reforms of the entire tax systems, corporate tax incentives, export duties, and other important elements of their tax structures, and not only of the marginal rates of income tax, considered sufficient by popular supply-siders.

V. Supply-Side Tax Reforms for Developing Countries

Various supply-side tax proposals relevant to developing countries, as well as the limitations of tax policy in developing country circumstances, emerge from the papers included in the book. This section summarizes what should or should not be expected from strictly supply-side tax reforms.

Acknowledging the limited influence of tax policy in the current developing country environment, as stressed by Shome (Chapter 12), is the first step toward adopting feasible supply-side tax reforms. Then there are other limitations that have to be acknowledged. For tax policy to have a strict efficiency orientation, it should not be used as an instrument of major redistribution. However, income and wealth distribution is highly skewed in developing countries, and few policy instruments, other than land reforms and social welfare expenditures, are readily available to governments to affect major redistribution. Consequently, the policymakers of developing countries will have to take bold political decisions on this issue viz., the extent to which they want the tax system to be *the* main instrument of redistribution and are willing to control tax avoidance and evasion and make the nominal tax structure truly effective. Finally, as Gandhi (Chapter 9) argues, a tax system dictated by efficiency considerations would certainly be desirable except that the benefits of such a tax structure would be large only when many assumptions, which may not be readily descriptive of the special circumstances of developing countries, are satisfied. As a result, he shows that such a tax system is not going to be easily accepted by policymakers. Indeed, very radical reforms in tax bases as well as tax rates will be needed strictly in the interest of efficiency objectives and may involve the substitution of existing taxes with entirely new and even administratively difficult taxes, such as replacing the income tax by the levy of a tax on ability and potential income.

In practice, tax systems in most countries attempt to fulfill multiple objectives, including many politically motivated ones, and end up having distortionary economic effects, and the tax systems of developing countries are no exception. From a supply-side perspective, it would be desirable if taxation were used only for the attainment of as few objectives as possible, for example, correcting "market failures" and providing adequate government revenues with minimal distortions to resource allocation and disincentives to factor supplies. Achieving a limited degree of redistribution can easily be accommodated in the framework of supply-side tax policy, if that were to be politically acceptable. The papers presented in this book contain a number of proposals for reform relevant to the longer-term tax systems of developing countries that are, at once, practical and in the supply-side spirit.[33]

First, the tax systems should over time attempt to reduce their reliance on narrowly based taxes unless such taxes fall on real windfall profits and scarcity rents or correct some negative externality. The views of Gandhi (Chapter 9) on the efficient tax system and Sanchez-Ugarte and Modi (Chapter 11) on export duties more than amply bear this out.

Second, on income taxation, there is a case for lowering the excessively high marginal tax rates presently existing in many developing countries while (1) expanding the tax base through the removal of most allowances, deductions, exclusions, and tax credits; (2) indexing the tax base for inflation; and (3) improving income tax laws and administration, particularly raising the penalty rates and probability of detection. There is no case for a separate capital gains tax; real capital gains can be treated as ordinary incomes and taxed under income tax without any preferential tax treatment. Similarly there is no case for a separate payroll tax or social security taxes on labor incomes. The arguments in support of these positions are amplified in Ebrill (Chapter 5), Richupan (Chapter 6), and Gandhi (Chapter 9).

Third, in relation to income taxation again, a strong case is made by Ebrill (Chapter 4) for the removal of savings from the base of income taxation (i.e., for increased reliance on broad-based consumption taxation), especially in circumstances where, for a variety of noneconomic reasons, interest rates must remain at artificially low levels and adequate pretax rates of return to savings are precluded.

Fourth, on corporate taxation, the case is made on efficiency grounds to (1) reduce the scope of tailor-made tax incentives and (2) index depreciation allowances and inventory valuation for inflation. Sanchez-Ugarte (Chapter 10) suggests that tax incentives be restricted only to the efficiency-oriented ones, such as those that encourage risk-taking and savings, research and development, and, under certain circumstances, regional distribution of economic activity. Ebrill (Chapter 5) proposes indexation of the corporate tax base and even taxation of corporations, on a cash-flow basis, which will allow all capital outlays to be immediately expensed and disallow the deductibility of interest payments, thereby eliminating many of the distortions of existing corporation taxes. Gandhi

[33]In the short run, the needs of economic stabilization and demand management could well preclude the immediate adoption of some of the reform proposals dictated by supply-side objectives. Under such circumstances, government revenue, needed to manage fiscal deficits in the short run, should preferably be raised through consumption taxes and not through an increase in the rates of income taxes if the negative supply-side effects are to be minimized.

(Chapter 9) restates various arguments made in the literature against the levy of any separate corporation tax and for the removal of double taxation of dividends.

Fifth, on export taxation, the recommendation is made by Sanchez-Ugarte and Modi (Chapter 11), on efficiency grounds, that tax levels be reduced in most of the developing countries in the medium term; it is only under circumstances of temporary high world prices that temporarily the levy of high export duties to mop up excess demand generated by "windfall profits" is justified. However, given the developing countries' present reliance on export tax revenue and the limitations of tax handles and tax administration capacity in these countries, the reforms in this area may have to be gradual. Furthermore, the effectiveness of such a course of action will depend on the removal of many obstacles to free world trade that still exist. Nevertheless, the unwanted supply-side effects of export duties can be reduced by avoiding export duties on agricultural products with relatively high supply elasticity and imposing them on others on a sliding scale of tax rates to approximate them as much as possible to a tax on "windfall" incomes. In the long run, the rates of export duties should be such as to allow the exporters to earn an "adequate" after-tax rate of return on labor and capital; under no circumstance should this be less than what is achievable in other sectors of the economy. In relation to commodity stabilization schemes, the suggestion is made in Sanchez-Ugarte and Modi (Chapter 11) to streamline the administration of marketing boards in order to reduce the costs of their operations and to return to producers, over time, all profits generated in the process of commodity price stabilization.

Sixth, on wealth taxes, Gandhi (Chapter 9) shows that, in the interest of neutrality and removing distortions in the use of savings, the tax systems of developing countries should not rely on the highly differentiated and narrowly based wealth taxes (such as taxes on income-generating agricultural land). Nor should they rely on taxes that are levied on productive wealth (financial assets, capital equipment, and the like) if the wealth creation process is not to be damaged. Wealth taxes should primarily be directed toward those elements of wealth that have inelastic supply, such as land, or are for personal use, such as homes, automobiles, and yachts. Taxation of transfers of wealth, through gifts and bequests, is also justified, on grounds of intergenerational equity, as are taxes on unproductive wealth, especially holdings of jewelry, precious metals, and land and real estate for speculative purposes, on grounds of controlling negative externalities.[34]

[34]Taxation of unproductive wealth can present certain administrative and compliance problems.

Finally, on commodity taxes, though these have not been explicitly analyzed in the papers contained in this volume, a few reform proposals suggest themselves in the interest of promoting efficiency and positive supply-side effects and growth.[35] Among others, the following need to be particularly mentioned: (1) Only final consumption goods, and not raw materials, intermediate goods, or capital goods, should be taxed to avoid cascading.[36] (2) Commodity taxes should not discriminate between alternative sources of supply for consumption, viz., domestic output and imports, through the levy of differential rates of taxation. (Separate taxes can be imposed on imports if protection for "infant industry" is desired; however, the policymakers must ensure that import taxes are not too high or too diverse to begin with and that a timetable has been set for their gradual removal.) (3) Both consumer goods and consumer services should be taxed to avoid distortions in consumption patterns.[37] (4) Commodity taxes should be levied as close as possible to the retail stage of the production/distribution process to avoid pyramiding. All these can be achieved through the adoption of a broad-based retail sales tax or, better still, a value-added tax of the consumption type preferably at rates which are not unreasonably high or excessively differentiated. (5) Excise duties can justifiably be levied on items that have relatively inelastic demand (such as selected necessities), or have negative externalities (such as alcohol, tobacco, and gasoline), or are complementary to leisure (such as recreational vehicles, ski equipment, and other "luxury" goods).[38] Levy of excise duties as substitutes for "user fees," whenever the latter are administratively difficult, is also justified.[39] (6) Exports, which are subject to domestic commodity taxes, deserve to receive complete drawback of such taxes. The arguments in support of some, though not all, of these reform proposals are discussed in Gandhi (Chapter 9).

All the above-mentioned tax reform proposals are consistent with the

[35]Theoretically, from an efficiency point of view, there should be no commodity taxation if the income tax rate schedule has been chosen optimally. This is so because, under fairly reasonable assumptions, the levy of differential commodity taxes is not likely to improve social welfare. However, if for some reason, income tax is not optimal, differential commodity taxes can be designed to improve welfare.

[36]Consumption of leisure being nontaxable, allocative efficiency requires that consumption of goods and services should not be taxed too highly.

[37]Gandhi (1977).

[38]The basic argument underlying the latter is the nontaxability of leisure itself. An efficient tax system here is an equity-oriented tax system as well.

[39]For example, if the use of roads by motorists causes wear and tear and road fees cannot be easily collected, taxation of gasoline can be a good substitute for appropriate road user charges.

efficiency objective, if not the equity objective; they are also consistent with the view of basic supply-side tax policy as described at the beginning of this chapter. Quite a few of them could well imply a significant revenue loss in the short run.[40] Gandhi (Chapter 9), therefore, stresses that in the short run, supply-side and efficiency-oriented tax reforms must go hand-in-hand with expenditure reforms and reforms of public enterprise pricing if high and unsustainable fiscal deficits and their inflationary consequences are to be avoided by developing countries. He also points out that the positive results of supply-side tax reforms on growth rates should more realistically be expected in the longer run and then only if such tax reforms are (1) significant and permanent and (2) coupled with very substantial reforms in other macroeconomic policies (such as exchange rates, interest rates, wage rates, and agricultural and other prices). Mackenzie (Chapter 2) establishes the importance of the former, while Ebrill (Chapters 3, 4, and 5), Sanchez-Ugarte (Chapter 10), and Sanchez-Ugarte and Modi (Chapter 11) stress the importance of the latter. Finally, given the heterogeneity of individual country situations with respect to market conditions and existing tax systems, it is clear from the research that supply-side and efficiency-oriented tax reform packages would need to be tailored to the specific needs and circumstances of individual developing countries, including the distributional and stabilization objectives of their governments, if any.

REFERENCES

Bahl, Roy, and others, *Tax Reform and Private Sector Growth: Proceedings of a Conference Held July 10, 1986*, Monograph No. 18 (Syracuse, New York: Metropolitan Studies Program, Maxwell School of Citizenship and Public Affairs, Syracuse University, February 1987).

Balassa, Bela, and associates, *The Structure of Protection in Developing Countries* (Baltimore: Johns Hopkins University Press, 1971).

Bartlett, Bruce R., *Reaganomics: Supply Side Economics in Action* (New York: Quill, updated ed., 1982).

———, "Supply-Side Economics: Theory and Evidence," *Quarterly Review*, National Westminster Bank (London), February 1985, pp. 18–29.

Bechter, Dan M., "Budget Deficits and Supply-Side Economics: A Theoretical Discussion," *Economic Review*, Federal Reserve Bank of Kansas City, Vol. 67 (June 1982), pp. 14–27.

[40]This is likely to be so as existing tax systems of developing countries frequently have (1) double or multiple taxation of the same base; (2) nonindexation of tax bases with respect to inflation; and (3) inefficient taxes such as export duties.

Bhagwati, Jagdish N., *Foreign Trade Regimes and Economic Development: Anatomy and Consequences of Exchange Control Regimes* (Cambridge, Massachusetts: Ballinger Publishing Co., 1978).

Blinder, Alan S., "Thoughts on the Laffer Curve," in *The Supply-Side Effects of Economic Policy*, ed. by Laurence H. Meyer (Boston, Massachusetts: Kluwer-Nijhoff, 1981).

Breton, Albert, *The Economic Theory of Representative Government* (Chicago: Aldine Publishing Co., 1974).

Buchanan, James M., and Dwight R. Lee, "Politics, Time, and the Laffer Curve," *Journal of Political Economy* (Chicago), Vol. 90 (August 1982), pp. 816–19.

Buchanan, James M., and Gordon Tullock, *The Calculus of Consent: Logical Foundations of Constitutional Democracy* (Ann Arbor, Michigan: University of Michigan Press, 1969).

Canto, Victor A., Douglas H. Joines, and Arthur B. Laffer, *Foundations of Supply-Side Economics: Theory and Evidence* (New York: Academic Press, 1983).

Corden, W.M., *Trade Policy and Economic Welfare* (Oxford: Clarendon Press, 1974).

———, "The Costs and Consequences of Protection: A Survey of Empirical Work," in *International Trade and Finance: Frontiers for Research*, ed. by Peter B.Kenen (Cambridge, England: Cambridge University Press, 1975).

Downs, Anthony, *An Economic Theory of Democracy* (New York: Harper & Row, 1957).

Federal Reserve Bank of Atlanta and Emory University Law and Economics Center, *Supply-Side Economics in the 1980s: Conference Proceedings* (Westport, Connecticut: Quorum Books, 1982).

Feldstein, Martin, "Supply-Side Economics: Old Truths and New Claims," *American Economic Review, Papers and Proceedings of the Ninety-Eighth Annual Meeting of the American Economic Association* (Nashville, Tennessee), Vol. 76 (May 1986), pp. 26–30.

Ferron, Mark J., "Issues in Excise Taxation," in *Fiscal Issues in South-East Asia: Comparative Studies of Selected Economies*, ed. by Parthasarathi Shome (Singapore: Oxford University Press, 1986).

Feige, Edgar L., and Robert T. McGee, "Sweden's Laffer Curve: Taxation and the Unobserved Economy," *Scandinavian Journal of Economics* (Stockholm), Vol. 85, No. 4 (1983), pp. 499–519.

Fink, Richard H., ed., *Supply-Side Economics: A Critical Appraisal* (Frederick, Maryland: University Publications of America, 1982).

Fullerton, Don, "On the Possibility of an Inverse Relationship Between Tax Rates and Government Revenues," *Journal of Public Economics* (Amsterdam), Vol. 19 (October 1982), pp. 3–22.

Gandhi, Ved P., "Sales Taxation of Services in Developing Countries" (unpublished, International Monetary Fund, December 1, 1977).

Gilder, George, *Wealth and Poverty* (New York: Basic Books Inc., 1981).

Gillis, Malcolm, "Micro and Macroeconomics of Tax Reform: Indonesia," *Journal of Development Economics* (Amsterdam), Vol. 19 (December 1985), pp. 221-54.

Hailstones, Thomas J. (1982a), *A Guide to Supply-Side Economics* (Richmond, Virginia: Robert F. Dame, Inc., 1982).

——— (1982b), ed., *Viewpoints on Supply-Side Economics* (Richmond, Virginia: Robert F. Dame, Inc., 1982).

Hall, Robert E., and Alvin Rabushka, *Low Tax, Simple Tax, Flat Tax* (New York: McGraw-Hill, 1983).

Hemming, R., and J. A. Kay, "The Laffer Curve," *Fiscal Studies* (London), Vol. 1 (March 1980), pp. 83-90.

Henderson, David, "Limitations of the Laffer Curve as a Justification for Tax Cuts," in *Supply-Side Economics: A Critical Appraisal*, ed. by Richard H. Fink (Frederick, Maryland: University Publications of America, 1982).

India, Ministry of Finance, Department of Economic Affairs, *Long Term Fiscal Policy* (New Delhi, December 1985).

International Monetary Fund (1985a), *Government Finance Statistics Yearbook, 1985*, Vol. 9 (Washington, 1985).

——— (1985b), *Foreign Private Investment in Developing Countries: A Study by the Research Department of the International Monetary Fund,* Occasional Paper No. 33 (Washington, January 1985).

Kemp, Jack, "The Classical Economic Case for Cutting Marginal Income Tax Rates," in *Supply-Side Economics, Hearing Before the Task Force on Tax Policy of the Committee on the Budget, House of Representatives*, 97th Congress, 1st Session, March 10, 1981 (Washington: Government Printing Office, 1981).

Killick, Tony, ed., *The Quest for Economic Stabilisation: The IMF and the Third World* (New York: St. Martin's Press, 1984).

Krueger, Anne O., *Foreign Trade Regimes and Economic Development: Liberalization Attempts and Consequences* (Cambridge, Massachusetts: Ballinger Press, 1978).

Laffer, Arthur B., and Jan P. Seymour, eds., *The Economics of the Tax Revolt: A Reader* (New York: Harcourt Brace Jovanovich, 1979).

Lecaillon, Jacques, and others, *Income Distribution and Economic Development: An Analytical Survey* (Geneva: International Labor Office, 1984).

Malcomson, James M., "Some Analytics of the Laffer Curve," *Journal of Public Economics* (Amsterdam), Vol. 29 (April 1986), pp. 263-79.

Marsden, Keith, "Links Between Taxes and Economic Growth: Some Empirical Evidence," World Bank Staff Working Paper No. 605 (Washington, 1983).

Meyer, Laurence H., ed., *The Supply-Side Effects of Economic Policy* (Boston, Massachusetts: Kluwer-Nijhoff, 1981).

Mirowski, Philip, "What's Wrong With the Laffer Curve?" *Journal of Economic Issues* (Sacramento, California), Vol. 16 (September 1982), pp. 815-28.

Modi, Jitendra R., "Levels of Personal Income Taxation in Selected Developing Countries" (unpublished, International Monetary Fund, February 1985).

———, "Major Features of Corporate Profit Taxes in Selected Developing Countries," *Bulletin*, International Bureau of Fiscal Documentation (Amsterdam), Vol. 41 (February 1987), pp. 65–74.

Moszer, Max, "A Comment on the Laffer Model," in *Supply-Side Economics: A Critical Appraisal*, ed. by Richard H. Fink (Frederick, Maryland: University Publications of America, 1982).

Nellor, David C.L., "Natural Resource Tax Policy in Developing Countries" (unpublished, International Monetary Fund, March 2, 1984).

Niskanen, William A., Jr., *Bureaucracy and Representative Government* (Chicago: Aldine-Atherton, 1971).

Palmer, Keith F., "Mineral Taxation Policies in Developing Countries: An Application of Resource Rent Tax," *Staff Papers*, International Monetary Fund (Washington), Vol. 27 (September 1980), pp. 517–42.

Raboy, David G., ed., *Essays in Supply Side Economics* (Washington: Institute for Research on the Economics of Taxation, 1982).

Richupan, Somchai, "Revenue Significance of the Individual Income Tax in Developing Countries" (unpublished, International Monetary Fund, April 22, 1985).

Roberts, Paul C., "The Breakdown of the Keynesian Model," in *Supply-Side Economics: A Critical Appraisal*, ed. by Richard H. Fink (Frederick, Maryland: University Publications of America, 1982).

———, *The Supply-Side Revolution: An Insider's Account of Policymaking in Washington* (Cambridge, Massachusetts: Harvard University Press, 1984).

Rosen, Harvey S., *Public Finance* (Homewood, Illinois: Richard D. Irwin, 1985).

Stein, Herbert, *Presidential Economics: The Making of Economic Policy from Roosevelt to Reagan and Beyond* (New York: Simon and Schuster, 1984).

Streeten, Paul, "Development Ideas in Historical Perspective," in Albert O. Hirschman and others, *Toward a New Strategy for Development: A Rothko Chapel Colloquium* (New York: Pergamon Press, 1979).

Tobin, James, "Supply-Side Economics: What Is It? Will It Work?" in *Viewpoints on Supply-Side Economics*, ed. by Thomas J. Hailstones (Richmond, Virginia: Robert F. Dame, Inc., 1982).

Todaro, Michael P., *Economic Development in the Third World* (New York: Longman, 3rd ed., 1985).

Ture, Norman B. (1982a), "Supply Side Analysis and Public Policy," in *Essays in Supply Side Economics*, ed. by David G. Raboy (Washington: Institute for Research on the Economics of Taxation, 1982).

——— (1982b), "The Economic Effects of Tax Changes: A Neoclassical Analysis," in *Supply-Side Economics: A Critical Appraisal*, ed. by Richard H. Fink (Frederick, Maryland: University Publications of America, 1982).

United States, Department of the Treasury, *Tax Reform for Fairness, Simplicity, and Economic Growth: The Treasury Department Report to the President*, Vols. I–III (Washington: Office of the Secretary, Department of the Treasury, November 1984).

U.S. Congress, House Committee on the Budget, *Supply-Side Economics, Hearing Before the Task Force on Tax Policy of the Committee on the Budget, House of Representatives*, 97th Congress, 1st Session, March 10, 1981 (Washington: Government Printing Office, 1981).

Wanniski, Jude, "Taxes, Revenues, and the 'Laffer Curve,'" *The Public Interest*, National Affairs, Inc. (New York), Winter 1978, pp. 3-16.

———, Statement Before the Task Force on Tax Policy, in *Supply-Side Economics, Hearing Before the Task Force on Tax Policy of the Committee on the Budget, House of Representatives*, 97th Congress, 1st Session, March 10, 1981 (Washington: Government Printing Office, 1981).

———, *The Way the World Works* (New York: Simon and Schuster, rev. and updated ed., 1983).

World Bank, *World Development Report, 1980* (New York: Oxford University Press, 1980).

———, *World Development Report, 1981* (New York: Oxford University Press, 1981).

Yoingco, Angel Q., "Tax Reform in the Philippines," in *Tax Reform in the Asian-Pacific Countries: Papers Presented at the 4th Asian-Pacific Tax Conference*, November 17-18, 1986 (Singapore: Asian-Pacific Tax and Investment Research Center, 1986).

PART II

Income Taxes and Growth: Evidence on Popular Supply-Side Tax Policy

2

A Simple Model of the Effects of Income Tax Rate Reductions on Economic Growth and Aggregate Supply

George A. Mackenzie

Both mainstream neoclassical economists and popular supply-side writers have in recent years espoused the view that labor supply, investment, and savings may be a good deal more sensitive to their after-tax rate of remuneration or return than had previously been supposed. If this is the case, then a tax reform that reduces appreciably marginal rates of income taxation may have a substantial impact on the rate of growth of the supply of labor and the capital stock and hence on the rate of growth of potential output.

The principal aim of this chapter is to illustrate the possible range of this impact with the aid of the basic one-sector neoclassical growth model. The version of the model presented here includes a tax on income from both labor and capital, and can be used to simulate the effect of a reduction in marginal income tax rates once values are assumed for its parameters.

The limitations inherent in the use of such a rudimentary model need to be stated at the outset. First, it should be stressed that the neoclassical model of growth presupposes well-functioning markets and flexibility of production techniques. Thus, it cannot be the model of choice for dealing with such problems as the constraints on growth in developing countries that may be created because of a shortage of foreign exchange when production techniques allow little substitution between domestic labor and capital and imported capital. Nor would it be appropriate for the analysis of financial repression, because it assumes in effect that the capital stock is directly owned by savers. A further consequence of this is that the decision to save is also a decision to invest, so that the two cannot be analyzed separately.

Second, the model incorporates only income taxes. However, revenues from personal income taxes in industrial countries are generally much higher than in developing countries both in relation to gross domestic product and as a share of total tax revenue. Presumably, this explains why the great bulk of the literature on the incentive effects of tax regimes and of changes in marginal tax rates on labor, savings, and investment decisions pertains to the developed world. Third, a one-sector model cannot be used to analyze allocational questions such as the effect of different tax regimes on the composition of investment.

Finally, the model cannot be used to analyze the question of how the size of the supply response generated by income tax reductions might compare with the increase in aggregate demand that income tax reductions might generate. This question is examined in the Annex to this chapter.

Despite these limitations, the simple neoclassical model can shed some light on the possible magnitude of the impact on growth of reductions in marginal income tax rates and on the conditions under which marginal tax rate reductions could have an appreciable impact. Unless prices and wages are of no consequence at all in the allocation of resources in developing countries, changes in income tax rates that alter relative prices should have some impact on decisions in the labor and capital markets. Moreover, the personal income tax is, or may become, an important source of revenue in some middle-income developing countries, and the marginal income tax rate faced by the average taxpayer might conceivably create disincentives against working or saving.

The various experiments with the model illustrate the conditions under which reductions in marginal income tax rates are likely to have a substantial impact. One basic conclusion is that when other things, and in particular the elasticities of savings and labor supply are held constant, the response to given proportional reductions in marginal tax rates is greater the higher the marginal rates of income tax. Another important but more surprising conclusion is that when labor and capital are substitutable and the marginal product of labor is high relative to its average, that is, when labor's share of output is high, the response of output to a reduction in marginal tax rates is more sensitive to changes in the assumed labor supply elasticity than to changes in the savings elasticity. In other words, the elasticity of savings is by no means the only relevant parameter.

The experiments also underscore the limitations of a policy aimed at accelerating the rate of growth of aggregate output in developing countries by reducing marginal income tax rates alone. The conditions under which marginal income tax reductions would spark a significant increase in growth are more likely to be present in industrial countries rather than in developing countries. Marginal rates of income tax are typically high in industrial countries, and these countries probably approximate more closely the neoclassical model in terms of the flexibility of their labor and savings markets. Finally, the scope for revenue-neutral income tax reforms, which reduce marginal rates without reducing tax revenue excessively, is probably greater in industrial countries, given the importance in so many of these countries of allowable deductions from taxable income that erode the tax base.

I. Incorporating Marginal Income Tax Rates in the One-Sector Neoclassical Model

The basic assumptions incorporated in the model are as follows. First, the supply of labor grows at a constant rate, other things being equal, but is also made a function of the marginal real wage after tax. Second, saving in one period adds to the stock of capital in the following period, and is also a function of the after-tax rate of return to capital at the margin. Third, the neoclassical production function chosen is the Cobb-Douglas. This choice implies a substantial degree of substitutability between capital and labor, and has an important bearing on the simulation results. Fourth, the before-tax wage rate equals the marginal product of labor, and the before-tax return to capital equals the marginal product of capital. Both the wage rate and the return to capital are expressed in units of final product. Finally, technical progress is assumed to be labor-augmenting and exogenous: that is, it is independent of the rate of investment. The assumption of labor-augmenting technical progress permits the measurement of labor in terms of efficiency units. Endogenous technical progress is subsequently introduced into the model by making the rate of technical progress partly a function of the share of output saved.

With these assumptions, the variables of the model are determined by the following relationships:

$$Y(t) = AK(t)^{a} L(t)^{1-a} \quad (1)$$
$$L(t) = (w(t)(1 - t_w))^{els} LA(1 + g)^{t} \quad (2)$$
$$w(t) = (1 - a)AK(t)^{a}L(t)^{-a} \quad (3)$$
$$K(t) = K(t - 1) + SY(t - 1)(r(t - 1)(1 - t_r))^{ess} \quad (4)$$
$$r(t) = aAK(t)^{a-1}L(t)^{1-a}, \quad (5)$$

where

$Y(t)$ = output at time t;
$K(t)$ = capital stock at time t;
$L(t)$ = labor supply at time t;
$w(t)$ = before-tax wage rate at time t;
$r(t)$ = before-tax rate of return to capital at time t;
els = elasticity of labor supply with respect to after-tax wage;
ess = elasticity of savings with respect to after-tax rate of return;
g = rate of increase in "efficiency units" of labor supply;
t_w = tax on labor income;
t_r = tax on capital income; and
A = constant term.

Equation (1) represents the production function; equation (2) is the supply curve of labor; equation (3) is an inverted demand for labor curve; equation (4) is the savings function; and equation (5) determines the rate of return to capital.

One very important characteristic of the one-sector neoclassical growth model when technical progress is exogenous is the constancy of the steady-state rate of growth, which is given by g, the rate of growth of labor measured in efficiency units. This characteristic does not depend on the specific parameters of the production function. It has the well-known implication that increases in the savings rate cannot permanently raise the rate of growth, although they can raise it above its steady-state rate for a substantial period of time.

Once initial values for the variables Y, L, and K and for the parameters a, g, t_w, and t_r are chosen, it is possible to simulate the impact of changes in the two income tax rates.[1] The value of a, the share of capital income, is set initially at 0.2, and the value of g, the steady-state rate of growth of output, at 3 percent. The estimates are not derived from an empirical study of any one economy, but they would nonetheless approximate the characteristics of a number of industrial economies. It is not necessary to worry over the choice of the steady-state capital output and savings ratios, because, as may be shown, the choice does not affect the simulation.

The scale parameters in equations (2) and (4), LA and S, are made functions of *els* and *ess* in such a way that the economy remains on its steady-state growth path when the two taxes are held at their initial values regardless of the assumed values for the two elasticities. This assumption

[1]The choice of initial values for Y, K, and L determines the value of A, the scale parameter in equation (1).

permits a comparison of the effect of changing the income tax rates under a variety of assumptions regarding the elasticity of savings and labor.

II. Assumed Elasticities and Simulation Results

The elasticities of labor and savings were each allowed to range from 0 to 1.0. The upper bound of 1.0 substantially exceeds most estimates for the elasticity of aggregate savings and labor supply made for the United States, where most of the empirical work has been done. Nonetheless, it needs to be emphasized that there is no firm consensus as to the most likely value for either parameter, and in particular for the elasticity of savings.[2]

Rosen (1980) summarizes some earlier research on labor supply elasticity in two "stylized facts": (1) for prime-age males, the substitution effect of changes in the net wage on hours worked is small and often statistically insignificant and the hours of work are unresponsive to changes in net wages; and (2) the hours of work and the decisions of married women as to labor force participation are quite sensitive to changes in the net wage, with some elasticity estimates exceeding 1.0. Fullerton (1982) calculated a measure of aggregate labor supply elasticity of 0.15 based on the estimates of elasticities for male and female workers in various econometric studies. The study by Hausman (1981) estimated uncompensated supply elasticities for secondary female earners of close to 1.

An often-cited study by Boskin (1978) estimated the elasticity of savings with respect to the expected after-tax interest rate at between 0.2 and 0.4. While this is not the highest estimate ever reported, it is higher than most previous studies.[3] Boskin's estimate may even understate the elasticity of financial savings with respect to changes in after-tax rates of interest, because even if an increased rate of return has little effect on total saving, it may increase the desired rate of accumulation of financial assets at the expense of real assets (i.e., consumer durables and housing).

The first set of simulations of the model were performed with t_w set at 40 percent and t_r set at 50 percent. The elasticities of labor supply and savings ranged from 0 to 1. A 30 percent reduction in both tax rates—that is, a reduction of t_w to 28 percent and t_r to 35 percent—can generate substantial increases in growth in the initial years following the reduction, if the

[2] A discussion of the problems involved in the econometric estimation of savings elasticities may be found in McLure (1980).

[3] Evans (1982, pp. 251–52), having surveyed some studies of the interest elasticity of savings, notes that the more circumspect and careful studies favor a small positive interest elasticity of aggregate saving—in the United States—but that the issue is far from closed.

labor supply elasticity is sufficiently high, even if the savings elasticity is zero. For example, with a labor supply elasticity of 0.4, the model generates an increase in the average annual rate of growth in the first ten years following the tax reductions from its steady-state value of 3 percent to 3.59 percent.

However, the initial increase in growth is not greatly affected by the increase in the elasticity of saving: for example, when this is 0.4 instead of zero, the average annual rate of growth in the first ten years following the tax reductions is raised to 3.69.

The initial spurt in growth is not much influenced by the assumed savings elasticity because even if savings—and thus investment—is boosted substantially by the income tax reductions, the impact on the total stock of capital cannot be very great. This point can be illustrated by a simple numerical example. With a savings rate of 9 percent and a capital output ratio of 3, savings and investment are 3 percent of the capital stock. An increase in savings of as much as 33 percent adds only 1 percent to the growth of the capital stock, and given the assumption that capital's share is 0.2, this increase in the stock of capital adds just 0.2 percent to output. However, with a labor supply elasticity of 0.4, an increase in the after-tax real wage at the margin of 10 percent generates an increase in labor supply of 4 percent—and the increase in labor supply produces an increase in output of 3.2 percent.

The initial spurt in growth quickly tapers off, because the response of labor to its after-tax real wage is immediate and not lagged. Thus, with both the elasticity of savings and the elasticity of labor equal to 0.4, the average annual rate of growth in years 11–20 is 3.09 percent, which is not much different from its steady-state value (Table 1).

After the initial spurt in growth is over, growth is fostered by two processes. First, the initial increase in the supply of labor raises the ratio of labor to capital, and hence output to capital. With a given savings rate, the rate of accumulation of capital is raised and remains above its steady-state rate for some time. Second, if savings are responsive to their after-tax rate of remuneration, the savings rate increases, and this in turn increases the rate at which capital accumulates.

Although in the initial impact on growth, the labor supply elasticity is the more important parameter, in later years the savings elasticity's effect becomes relatively more important as a result of the processes described above. For example, with a labor supply elasticity of 0.4 and a zero elasticity of savings, the average annual rate of growth tapers off to 3.03 percent by years 11–20. With a savings elasticity also equal to 0.4, growth is 3.09 percent (Table 1).

What the simulations do make clear is that, given the assumptions of

Table 1. Average Annual Growth Rate of Output for Indicated Periods When Tax Rates Are Reduced by 30 Percent in Period 1 from Initial Values of 40 Percent for Labor Income Tax and 50 Percent for Capital Income Tax, for Various Combinations of Elasticities

(In percent)

		Labor Supply Elasticity				
Savings Elasticity	Period	0	0.2	0.4	0.8	1.0
	0–10	3.00	3.31	3.59	4.12	4.37
0	11–20	3.00	3.01	3.03	3.07	3.10
	21–30	3.00	3.01	3.03	3.06	3.08
	0–10	3.03	3.34	3.64	4.19	4.44
0.2	11–20	3.02	3.04	3.06	3.12	3.15
	21–30	3.02	3.03	3.05	3.09	3.11
	0–10	3.06	3.38	3.69	4.25	4.52
0.4	11–20	3.04	3.06	3.09	3.16	3.20
	21–30	3.03	3.05	3.07	3.12	3.14
	0–10	3.11	3.45	3.78	4.39	4.67
0.8	11–20	3.07	3.10	3.14	3.22	3.27
	21–30	3.04	3.06	3.09	3.14	3.18
	0–10	3.14	3.49	3.82	4.45	4.75
1.0	11–20	3.08	3.12	3.16	3.25	3.30
	21–30	3.05	3.07	3.09	3.15	3.18

capital-labor substitutability, the impact on the growth of aggregate output is greatly affected by the elasticity of labor supply. Growth is not simply a function of the volume of savings and the elasticity of savings.

The importance of the magnitude of the elasticity of labor supply is further illustrated by reducing only the tax on capital income and not the tax on labor income, because the impact on growth that results is much diminished (Table 2). For example, even with a savings elasticity of 0.4, the average annual rate of growth over the first ten periods increases to just 3.06 percent when a zero elasticity of labor supply is assumed. Nonetheless, even though only the tax on capital income and not the tax on labor income has been lowered, the impact on growth does depend on the assumed labor supply elasticity. With a labor supply elasticity of 0.8, the average annual rate of growth increases to 3.09 percent (Table 2).

The impact on growth of the tax rate reductions simulated above is substantially increased if it is assumed that technical progress is partly a function of the share of output saved. This assumption of endogenous technical progress also increases the significance of the elasticity of savings.

To illustrate this, the model was resimulated with the assumption that

Table 2. Average Annual Growth Rate of Output for Indicated Periods When the Tax Rate on Capital Is Reduced by 30 Percent in Period 1, with Initial Values of 40 Percent for Labor Income Tax and 50 Percent for Capital Income Tax, for Various Combinations of Elasticities

(In percent)

Savings Elasticity	Period	Labor Supply Elasticity 0	0.2	0.4	0.8	1.0
0.2	0–10	3.03	3.03	3.04	3.04	3.05
	11–20	3.02	3.02	3.03	3.03	3.04
	21–30	3.02	3.02	3.02	3.03	3.03
0.4	0–10	3.06	3.07	3.07	3.09	3.10
	11–20	3.04	3.05	3.05	3.07	3.07
	21–30	3.03	3.03	3.04	3.05	3.05
0.8	0–10	3.11	3.13	3.15	3.18	3.19
	11–20	3.07	3.08	3.09	3.12	3.13
	21–30	3.04	3.05	3.06	3.08	3.09
1.0	0–10	3.14	3.16	3.18	3.22	3.24
	11–20	3.08	3.09	3.11	3.14	3.15
	21–30	3.05	3.06	3.07	3.09	3.10

the rate of labor-augmenting technical progress increased by 0.4 percent for every 1 percentage point increase in the savings rate above its initial value. With savings and labor supply elasticities each set equal to 0.4, this results in an increase in the average annual rate of growth to 4.06 percent during the first ten years after the reductions (Table 3). Moreover, the steady-state rate of growth can be higher than 3 percent, so that the growth rate does not fall sharply in latter years as it does with the original version of the model.

It is interesting to note that when both taxes are reduced in this second version of the model, the growth rate is still considerably influenced by the assumed elasticity of labor supply. For example, with a zero elasticity of labor supply and an elasticity of savings of 0.4, the average growth rate in the first ten years is 3.39 percent.

The increases in growth generated by both versions of the model in response to reductions in the marginal income tax rates when both elasticities are greater than zero depend to a considerable degree on the initial marginal income tax rates and not just the proportional size of the reduction. When the marginal rates of tax assumed above of 40 percent for labor income and 50 percent for capital income are reduced by 30 percent to 28 percent and 35 percent, respectively, after-tax labor income increases at

Table 3. Average Annual Growth Rate of Output for Indicated Periods When Tax Rates Are Reduced by 30 Percent in Period 1 from Initial Values of 40 Percent for Labor Income Tax and 50 Percent for Capital Income Tax, for Various Combinations of Elasticities: Case of Endogenous Technical Progress

(In percent)

Savings Elasticity	Period	Labor Supply Elasticity 0	0.2	0.4	0.8	1.0
0	0–10	3.00	3.31	3.59	4.12	4.37
	11–20	3.00	3.01	3.03	3.07	3.10
	21–30	3.00	3.01	3.03	3.06	3.08
0.2	0–10	3.19	3.34	3.82	4.38	4.64
	11–20	3.19	3.04	3.25	3.31	3.34
	21–30	3.20	3.03	3.23	3.28	3.30
0.4	0–10	3.39	3.74	4.06	4.66	4.93
	11–20	3.41	3.44	3.48	3.56	3.61
	21–30	3.42	3.44	3.46	3.51	3.54
0.8	0–10	3.85	4.23	4.60	5.28	5.60
	11–20	3.93	3.97	4.02	4.13	4.19
	21–30	4.02	4.00	3.99	4.02	4.04
1.0	0–10	4.10	4.52	4.91	5.64	5.98
	11–20	4.26	4.30	4.34	4.45	4.51
	21–30	4.51	4.39	4.32	4.27	4.27

the margin by 20 percent and after-tax capital income by 30 percent.[4] Thus, it is perhaps not surprising that a substantial response of output can take place when the elasticity of savings and labor supply are positive.

Marginal rates this high may be representative of rates facing the *average* taxpayer in many industrial countries, but they are clearly well above the rates that would characterize even most middle-income developing countries.

When the initial value of the marginal rate of tax on labor income is 20 percent instead of 40 percent and the initial value of the tax on capital income is 25 percent instead of 50 percent, a proportional reduction of 30 percent in each tax has far less impact on output. When labor supply is completely inelastic, the response is practically negligible (Table 4). Nonetheless, even with these lower tax rates the average rate of growth in the

[4]For a given gross wage rate W, the after-tax wage increases from $((100 - 40)/100)*W$ to $((100 - 28)/100)*W$ or from $0.6*W$ to $0.72*W$. The increase for after-tax income from capital at the margin for gross income YK is from $0.5*YK$ to $0.65*YK$.

Table 4. Average Annual Growth Rate of Output for Indicated Periods When Tax Rates Are Reduced by 30 Percent in Period 1 from Initial Values of 20 Percent for Labor Income Tax and 25 Percent for Capital Income Tax, for Various Combinations of Elasticities

(In percent)

		Labor Supply Elasticity				
Savings Elasticity	Period	0	0.2	0.4	0.8	1.0
	0–10	3.00	3.12	3.23	3.44	3.54
0	11–20	3.00	3.01	3.01	3.03	3.04
	21–30	3.00	3.00	3.01	3.02	3.03
	0–10	3.01	3.13	3.25	3.47	3.56
0.2	11–20	3.01	3.02	3.02	3.05	3.06
	21–30	3.01	3.01	3.02	3.04	3.04
	0–10	3.02	3.15	3.27	3.49	3.59
0.4	11–20	3.01	3.02	3.03	3.06	3.07
	21–30	3.01	3.02	3.03	3.04	3.05
	0–10	3.04	3.17	3.30	3.53	3.64
0.8	11–20	3.02	3.04	3.05	3.08	3.10
	21–30	3.02	3.02	3.03	3.06	3.07
	0–10	3.05	3.18	3.31	3.55	3.66
1.0	11–20	3.03	3.04	3.06	3.09	3.11
	21–30	3.02	3.03	3.04	3.06	3.07

first ten-year period does increase to 3.27 percent when elasticities of 0.4 are assumed for both savings and labor supply.

III. Conclusions

These few experiments give some idea of the variety of characteristics of an economy that would have to be taken into account to determine the conditions under which reductions in marginal income tax rates would have an impact on the rate of growth. In particular, they illustrate the basic importance of the nature of the process of growth itself. The assumption of endogenous technical progress makes a good deal of difference to the results.

The experiments show that the impact of marginal income tax rate reductions depends on the values of many parameters and that the elasticity of savings, somewhat surprisingly, may be relatively unimportant. The experiments also show the importance of the level of marginal income tax rates. If these are low to begin with, and the elasticities of savings and labor supply only moderate, then the impact of income tax rate reductions on growth is very limited. Finally, they illustrate indirectly how little impact marginal income tax rate reductions would have in an economy where marginal rates were low to begin with and capital labor substitutability was limited.

ANNEX

A Simple Model of the Impact of Income Tax Reductions on the Aggregate Demand-Supply Balance

The effect of an income tax reduction on aggregate supply and demand is examined in this Annex with the aid of a version of the elementary Keynesian model, where aggregate supply, instead of being fixed, is a function of a fixed capital stock and a supply of labor that varies directly with the after-tax real wage. Prices are fixed in this model, so that financial effects cannot be examined.

The model is specified as follows:

$$Y_D = E + C \tag{6}$$
$$Y_S = AK^a L^{1-a} \tag{7}$$
$$C = C[(1 - a)Y_D(1 - gt_w),\ aY_D(1 - gt_r),\ r(1 - t_r)] \tag{8}$$
$$L_S = F(w(1 - t_w))^b \tag{9}$$
$$L_D = [(1 - a)AK^a]^{1/a} w^{-1/a} \tag{10}$$
$$L_S = L_D = L \tag{11}$$
$$at_r = cat_w \tag{12}$$
$$t_w = gat_w \tag{13}$$
$$t_r = gat_r, \tag{14}$$

where

Y_D = aggregate demand;
Y_S = aggregate supply;
E = autonomous expenditure;
C = aggregate consumption;
K = capital stock;
L_S = labor supply;
L_D = labor demand;
L = actual employment;
Y = actual aggregate output;
at_w = average tax on labor income;
t_w = marginal tax on labor income;
at_r = average tax on capital income;
t_r = marginal tax on capital income;
w = real wage rate (in units of output);

r = real rate of return to capital (assumed equal to before-tax return to saving); and

A, F, c, g = constant terms.

Average tax rates must be incorporated in the model if it is to be used to analyze the effects of a tax reduction on aggregate demand. Marginal rates are related to average rates by equations (13) and (14). For simplicity, the tax on capital income is assumed to be proportional to the tax on labor income (equation (12)).

Because it is desired to investigate the conditions under which the increase in aggregate demand caused by an income tax reduction would be offset by an increase in aggregate supply, an equilibrium condition for the product market has not been included. In the specification of the model, it has been assumed that the labor market always clears (the real wage playing the equilibrating role). Equations (9), (10), and (11) determine labor market equilibrium. Labor supply (equation (9)) is a function of the after-tax real wage. The demand for labor (equation (10)) is a function of the fixed capital stock and the real wage.

Employment and, hence, aggregate supply are a function of t_w, the marginal tax on labor income, as may be seen by solving equation (10) for w, substituting this expression for w in equation (9), making use of the labor market equilibrium condition, and solving for L as a function of t_w. The standard production relationship of equation (7) makes aggregate supply a simple function of employment, as the capital stock is assumed to be fixed. The production relationship of equation (7) implies that the shares of labor (LS) and capital (KS) in national income are fixed and are equal to $(1 - a)$ and a, respectively. The consumption function (equation (8)) makes consumption a function of labor income, profits, and the after-tax rate of interest. Given the assumptions of this model, the only strictly supply-side effect of a tax reduction is its effect on the supply of labor. However, the model allows for the possibility that changes in the tax rate on capital income may affect the savings propensity.

It is assumed that aggregate demand (Y_D) and aggregate supply (Y_S) are initially equal. To determine the effect of a change in income tax rates, the responsiveness of both Y_D and Y_S to such a change must be calculated.

By appropriate substitutions, aggregate supply can be expressed as a function of $(1 - t_w)$, as follows:

$$\log Y_S = D + [(1 - a)\, b/(ba + 1)] \log (1 - t_w), \tag{15}$$

with D being a constant term.

This in turn implies the following expression for the elasticity of aggregate supply with respect to at_w, the average tax rate on labor income:

$$dY_S/Y_S\, dat_w/at_w = [(1 - a)b/ba + 1]\,(-gat_w)/(1 - gat_w). \tag{16}$$

The elasticity of aggregate demand with respect to at_w can be expressed as follows (superscripts denoting partial derivatives):

$$dY_D/Y_D\ dat_w/at_w = \frac{[C^1LS + C^2cKS + C^3rcg/Y_D]\,(-at_w)}{1 - C^1LS(1 - at_w) - C^2KS(1 - cat_w)}. \tag{17}$$

C^1 and C^2 are, respectively, the marginal propensities to consume from labor and capital income and are both positive in sign. C^3 is the partial derivative of consumption with respect to the after-tax rate of return on capital, whose sign is uncertain.

Because the elasticity of savings is related to C^3 by the formula

$$ess = -C^3r(1 - t_r)/SAVING,$$

equation (17) can be re-expressed as follows, with S representing the savings rate:

$$dY_D/Y_D\ dat_w/at_w = \frac{[C^1LS + C^2cKS - Scgess/(1 - t_r)]\,(-at_w)}{1 - C^1LS(1 - at_w) - C^2KS(1 - at_r)}. \tag{17a}$$

Thus, given initial values for the marginal propensities to consume from capital and labor income, the share of capital and labor, the marginal and average tax rates, the savings rate and the elasticity of savings, equations (16) and (17a) can be solved for that value of b, the elasticity of labor supply with respect to the after-tax marginal wage, for which the responses of supply and demand to a change in the two tax rates will equal one another. It should be noted that the supply response is determined uniquely by b, given a and t_w.

The savings rate was set initially at 9 percent, the average tax rate of labor income at 20 percent, and the average tax rate on capital income at 25 percent. In the first set of simulations, the parameter g in equations (13) and (14) was set at 1, so that average and marginal rates of tax are equal.

When the marginal propensity to consume from labor income is set at 0.8, the marginal propensity to consume from capital income at 0.5, and when savings are completely unresponsive to changes in their rate of remuneration, a labor supply elasticity of 2.9 is required to maintain the equilibrium of aggregate demand and aggregate supply (Table 5). Even when the savings elasticity is set at higher levels,

Table 5. Labor Supply Elasticity Required for Maintenance of Aggregate Supply-Demand Equilibrium Following an Income Tax Reduction: Marginal Tax Rates Equal Average Tax Rates

Elasticity of Savings with Respect to After-Tax Rate of Return	0	0.2	0.4	0.6	0.8	1.0	1.5	2.0
	2.9	2.8	2.6	2.4	2.3	2.1	1.8	1.5

the required labor supply elasticity remains at a value well above reported empirical estimates of aggregate labor supply elasticity (Table 5). Similarly, when the labor supply elasticity is less than 1.5, the required savings elasticity must exceed 2.

However, it should be noted that any positive response of either savings or labor supply to an increase in the real after-tax rate of return and in the real wage rate, respectively, means that the conventional multiplier analysis overstates the extent to which an income tax cut creates an inflationary gap or reduces a deflationary one. Table 6 presents illustrative calculations of the relative magnitude of the supply and demand effects in the simple Keynesian model resulting from a reduction in t_w under a range of assumed values for the elasticities of savings and labor supply. The ratio displayed in the main body of the table represents the ratio of the elasticities with respect to t_w of aggregate supply and aggregate demand, given, respectively, by equations (16) and (17a) and expressed in percentage form. The relative size of the supply effect is not insignificant in all cases, even in cases of modest values for labor supply and savings elasticities.

These results are very sensitive to the parameters of the tax functions. If the value of g is set at 2 instead of 1, so that marginal tax rates are twice average tax rates, a given proportionate reduction in average tax rates results in a much greater increase in marginal after-tax rates of remuneration to savings and labor. For example, with the average tax rate on labor of 20 percent and on capital of 25 percent and marginal tax rates on labor of 40 percent and on capital of 50 percent, a 10 percent reduction in taxes increases after-tax labor income by 6.7 percent and capital income by 10 percent.

If, instead, the marginal rate of tax on labor is 20 percent and that on capital is 25 percent, a 10 percent reduction increases after-tax labor income by just 2.5 percent and capital income by 3.3 percent.

Table 6. Comparison of Demand and Supply Effects of an Income Tax Reduction

		Labor Supply Elasticity				
		0.2	0.4	0.6	0.8	1.0
	Supply Effect	0.038	0.074	0.107	0.138	0.167
Savings Elasticity	Demand Effect	Supply Effect as Percentage of Demand Effect				
0	0.370	10.4	20.0	28.9	37.2	45.0
0.2	0.358	10.8	20.8	30.1	38.8	46.8
0.4	0.345	11.3	21.7	31.4	40.4	48.8
0.6	0.332	11.8	22.7	32.8	42.2	51.0
0.8	0.319	12.3	23.7	34.3	44.2	53.4
1.0	0.307	12.9	24.9	36.0	46.3	56.0

Note: The demand effect is the arithmetic inverse of the elasticity of aggregate demand of the simple Keynesian model with respect to t_w. The supply effect is the arithmetic inverse of the elasticity of aggregate supply with respect to t_w.

Table 7. Labor Supply Elasticity Required for Maintenance of Aggregate Supply-Demand Equilibrium Following an Income Tax Reduction: Marginal Tax Rates Double Average Tax Rates

Elasticity of Savings with Respect to After-Tax Rate of Return	0	0.2	0.4	0.6	0.8	1.0	1.5	2.0
	0.8	0.7	0.6	0.5	0.4	0.3	0.1	−0.1

With g set at 2, the labor supply elasticity required to maintain the balance of aggregate demand and supply when the savings elasticity is zero is much less: 0.8 instead of 2.9 (Table 7).

REFERENCES

Boskin, Michael J., "Taxation, Saving, and the Rate of Interest," *Journal of Political Economy* (Chicago), Vol. 86, No. 2, Part 2 (April 1978), pp. S3–S27.

Evans, Owen J., *The Life Cycle Inheritance: Theoretical and Empirical Essays on the Life Cycle Hypothesis of Saving* (unpublished doctoral dissertation, Philadelphia: University of Pennsylvania, 1982).

Fullerton, Don, "On the Possibility of an Inverse Relationship Between Tax Rates and Government Revenues," *Journal of Public Economics* (Amsterdam), Vol. 19 (October 1982), pp. 3–22.

Hausman, Jerry A., "Labor Supply," in *How Taxes Affect Economic Behavior*, ed. by Henry J. Aaron and Joseph A. Pechman (Washington: Brookings Institution, 1981).

McLure, Charles E., Jr., "Taxes, Saving and Welfare: Theory and Evidence," *National Tax Journal* (Columbus, Ohio), Vol. 33 (September 1980), pp. 311–20.

Rosen, Harvey S., "What Is Labor Supply and Do Taxes Affect It? " *American Economic Review, Papers and Proceedings of the Ninety-Second Annual Meeting of the American Economic Association* (Nashville, Tennessee), Vol. 70 (May 1980), pp. 171–76.

3

Are Labor Supply, Savings, and Investment Price-Sensitive in Developing Countries?

A Survey of the Empirical Literature

Liam P. Ebrill

This chapter aims to summarize the available empirical estimates of the impact of a number of direct tax instruments on labor supply, investment, and savings in developing countries with a view to determining whether supply-side policies are relevant for such countries. Theoretical contributions are also discussed to the extent that they elucidate the empirical results.

Given that the concern is over the applicability of supply-side tax policies to developing countries, some discussion of what is meant by the concept "supply-side policy" is appropriate. As the term has come to be used in the context of developed economies and, in particular, in the context of the United States, it has, in general, referred to certain changes in tax policy—particularly those pertaining to corporate and personal income taxes—that are viewed as likely to stimulate domestic savings, investment, and labor supply. It has also come to refer more specifically to the views of those who believe that the responses of the various relevant agents to relative price changes are so elastic that tax rates can be reduced without any loss in tax revenue (see Gandhi (Chapter 1)). It should be noted, however, that the views of these elasticity optimists are not unanimously accepted (Blinder (1981), Hausman (1981)).

Supply-side policies, as they apply to developing countries, must be defined more broadly. First, the role of government as an agent for savings and capital formation is more important in developing countries. How should the government perform this role? Second, there is some concern over the implications of changes in tax rates for tax revenue but this concern is overshadowed by the belief that the judicious use of tax policies (for example, tax incentives) will lead to an acceleration in growth rates. This emphasis on rates of economic growth immediately suggests that the applicability of supply-side concepts depends on income effects in addition to relative price effects. In particular, the availability of adequate savings in a developing country will depend not only on the interest elasticity of savings behavior but also on the marginal propensity to save.

Third, as noted above, supply-side analysis of developed countries concentrates on the role of direct taxes, both corporate and personal, on income. In developing countries, although these taxes can be of importance, it would be unwise to ignore other commonly used tax instruments. Many developing countries rely heavily on trade taxes both as a source of revenue and as an instrument of protection. Presumably, these taxes also have implications for the workings of the labor and capital markets in these countries. Further, even though the broad range of existing taxes offers considerable scope for the implementation of tax based supply-side policies, the efficacy of such policies may nonetheless be quite limited. Thus, many economists believe that developing countries suffer from structural problems that cannot be greatly alleviated by tinkering with tax rates.

This survey attempts to accommodate such a broader definition of the supply-side approach, although it cannot claim, in the space available, to provide a comprehensive evaluation of the empirical significance of supply-side effects in developing country contexts. It will conclude, however, that while reform of direct tax structures in developing countries in some cases would be useful, it may well be the case that alternative nontax reform strategies would yield greater efficiency gains.

Before considering specific contributions, a comment on the quality of much of the empirical work is appropriate. The time-series data available for developing countries is well known to be deficient. As a result, much of the empirical work uses data that typically consist of aggregate macroeconomic quantities. Such studies are of limited value, particularly for evaluating microeconomic tax reform proposals. Further, the cross-section analyses abstract from the great heterogeneity of the countries selected. It is a suspect strategy to proceed as if the data sources are observations on a typical country, ignoring the possibility of income-type effects associated with the level of development. Taking tax systems as an example, it has been shown that cross-country differences can be large and, what is more important for regression analysis, systematic (Martin and Lewis

(1956), Williamson (1961), Hinrichs (1965), Tanzi (1982, 1987), and Abizadeh and Wyckoff (1982)).[1]

The implications of tax policy for labor supply, saving, and investment are discussed in Sections I, II, and III below.

I. Labor Supply

Theoretical Background

When evaluating the implications of tax policy for the labor market, the traditional approach has been to estimate the elasticity of labor supply with respect to real wage changes. The view has been that, given the assumption that factor taxes are borne where they are levied,[2] such an elasticity estimate will indicate labor supply responses to tax changes. The major problem, as perceived by this traditional approach, is that economic theory provides little guidance on the magnitude of the elasticity since the Slutsky equation permits an ambiguous result.[3]

This view, that all the implications of the taxation of labor supply can be evaluated by considering the elasticity of labor supply with respect to real wage changes, can be challenged on a number of accounts. First, and most obviously, in most frameworks the incidence of a tax on labor income and the elasticity of labor supply are directly related. The more elastic the supply of labor, the less the net wage received by labor will change and the greater will be the effect of the introduction of the tax on other factor and

[1]It should be noted that, in the case of consumer analysis within a country, the discrepancies between cross-section and time-series results are frequently resolved by arguing that cross-section observations include those who are experiencing transitory income blips (Friedman (1957), Ando and Modigliani (1963)). Such a device, which permits the assumption of a typical consumer, does not carry over to countries with structural differences.

[2]As is traditional, unless otherwise stated, it is assumed that whatever revenue is raised is spent in a neutral fashion. There is, therefore, no need to take account of whether there are changes in net wages, and hence, labor supply effects, because of government expenditures.

[3]In the absence of taxation, the relevant Slutsky equation is

$$\frac{\partial L}{\partial w} = \left(\frac{\partial L}{\partial w}\right)_{\bar{u}} + L\frac{\partial L}{\partial M},$$

where L refers to labor supply, w to the wage rate, and M to income; $\bar{u}$ refers to the fact that the first term on the right-hand side is compensated. This is the substitution effect and is known to be positive. The second term is the income effect. Given that leisure is conventionally assumed to be normal ($\partial L/\partial M < 0$), the net effect of an increase in the wage rate on a consumer's labor supply is ambiguous (cf., Atkinson and Stiglitz (1980)). Note that the compensated elasticity of labor supply is the relevant quantity to consider when evaluating efficiency losses, while the uncompensated elasticity is relevant when evaluating the revenue implication of tax changes.

goods markets. Second, as pointed out by Hausman (1983), the simple Slutsky equation may not apply because of the presence of nonlabor income and nonlinear (i.e., nonproportional) tax structures. This has a number of implications. The existence of nonlabor income makes the nature of the tax instruments important. Is it a wage tax or an income tax? Further, the nature of the income effect associated with tax changes becomes more complicated—indeed, Hausman (1983) suggests that the interaction between typical nonproportional tax systems and earnings functions produces an income effect over and above the conventional Slutsky term where this effect may well be the source of the backward-bending labor supply curve found in so many empirical studies.

The widespread use of nonproportional tax systems has a further serious implication. There is a possibility, particularly if there are positive transfer receipts at low-income levels, that the individual budget set is nonconvex, with the concomitant potential outcome of multiple equilibria. In graphical terms, this means that there is the possibility of a budget line with multiple kinks being tangent to the consumer's indifference curve at more than one point. Accordingly, in order to predict accurately the impact of taxation on labor supply in those circumstances, one would have to know the typical individual's entire preference structure (Hausman (1983)).

The above observations refer to all labor supply analyses, irrespective of whether they pertain to developed or developing countries. A third challenge to the view that tax policy analysis of the labor market can be reduced to a simple aggregate elasticity estimate of labor supply is most relevant in the case of developing countries. It is contained implicitly in the component of development literature that characterizes rural labor markets as frequently being noncompetitive. Wages are assumed to be institutionally set with the resultant outcome of persistent underemployment and unemployment of labor (e.g., Lewis (1954), Ranis and Fei (1961), Sen (1966)). If this framework is accurate, then the incidence of a general tax on labor income may be dramatically altered. Instead of facing an inelastic supply of labor in the aggregate, where this implies that labor will bear a general factor tax levied on its earnings, labor supply to the economy is now infinitely elastic. The incidence of a wage/income tax then depends on the institutional mechanisms in place and, in particular, on what happens to the net wage. More important, this nonneoclassical framework suggests that the net effect of tax policy will be determined on the demand side. If there remains an excess supply of labor after the tax has been absorbed, then any change that occurs in employment will be because of changes in demand.

Finally, it should be noted that, as far as developing countries are concerned, the focus is on the labor supply behavior of urban households, as rural household incomes are taxed little if at all by means of direct taxes such as the income tax.

As pointed out at the beginning of this section, it is often assumed that the incidence of an income/wage tax is such that it is borne by labor. In the short run, this may well be an accurate assumption. It is worth noting, however, that, in the very long run, circumstances may be quite different. Indeed, following Feldstein (1974a, 1974b), if one uses a traditional neoclassical growth model to gauge long-run incidence effects, then the critical factor in determining the impact of a tax is whether it affects aggregate savings by changing the propensity to save. Feldstein shows that, within the context of his model for the case of wage tax, the steady-state equilibrium is completely independent of the extent to which the supply of labor responds to the net wage. The intuition is clear. In the long run in that type of model, labor affects output growth through the rate of population growth rather than through the labor participation rate. Accordingly, when assessing the impact of a wage/income tax, account must be taken of how the revenue raised is spent—in particular, is aggregate savings, and therefore the rate of capital formation, unaltered? (Note that the Feldstein approach relaxes the assumption that tax revenue is neutrally spent.) This implies that, if the full range of supply-side effects associated with wage taxes are to be appreciated, it is not enough to consider only the elasticity of labor supply. We will return to this point in Section II where the behavior of savings is examined.

The above discussion has also implicitly assumed that the only taxes on labor income are broad-based wage or income taxes. More specific taxes such as taxes (subsidies) on the use of a factor in an industry or on the price of the given output are also possible. In a neoclassical context, these taxes have general equilibrium effects that occur as a result of differing capital labor ratios and elasticities of substitution across industries and demand effects precipitated by alterations in the distribution of income. Such effects make it difficult to analyze the incidence of these taxes, as evidenced by Harberger (1962), Mieszkowski (1969), McLure (1975), and Vandendorpe and Friedlaender (1976). In the case of developing countries, the authors typically have some modified two-sector model in the background. Notable examples of contributions in this area are afforded by Ahluwalia (1973) and Bird (1982). For example, Ahluwalia analyzes the implications of tax incentives for employment within the framework of a two-sector surplus labor economy. In this context, mention should also be made of Gandhi (1981), who discusses the efficacy of investment incentives for increasing employment. It should be noted that these papers focus on the creation of a demand for labor rather than on the definition of circumstances in which supply would be forthcoming.

Empirical Evidence: Urban Workers

Unfortunately, even for the case of the aggregate labor supply elasticity of urban workers, the available empirical literature has little to offer. What direct evidence there is suggests that, at least for Africa, the aggregate supply curve for labor for the monetized economy as a whole is positively sloped (Berg (1961)). This view is in marked contrast to the earlier presumption that African labor supply functions were backward sloping. The two views are not contradictory. To elaborate, using data drawn from the copper belt of Africa and from Kenya, respectively, Miracle and Fetter (1970) and Miracle (1976) argue that the earlier observations of backward-sloping supply curves are consistent with conventional microeconomic theory when account is taken of the costs associated with working at that time. In particular, these two papers document that, in the early part of the twentieth century, the risk of dying from a disease while at work in an urban area was considerable. It was not surprising, therefore, that the income effect associated with an increase in the wage rate tended to outweigh the substitution effect. The more recent findings of a positive labor supply response to increases in wages may then be ascribed at least in part to a reduction in the costs associated with urban employment and, in particular, to an improvement in health conditions.

Although the remainder of the empirical literature does not directly provide estimates on the labor supply behavior of urban workers, by documenting other aspects of the labor markets of developing countries, it does provide some useful indirect evidence.

One component of that literature considers the economics of urbanization. This component can be further subdivided into studies that examine the determinants of migration and studies that document the migrant experience in urban locations. Both streams are surveyed by Yap (1977). The consensus of this literature is that migration flows do respond to economic incentives in selecting employment locations. To take two recent examples, Schultz (1982), working with Venezuelan data, concluded that the elasticity of the migration rate with respect to destination wages ranges from 1.4 to 2.9. This result is analogous to that discovered by Fields (1982) for the case of Colombia.

Migrants appear not only to gain by moving to cities but to do so more rapidly than had been assumed hitherto. For example, in a paper on the experience of migrants in Brazil, Yap (1976) argues that the evidence indicates that migrants are, within a short period of time, indistinguishable from the urban born as far as income and employment patterns are concerned.

The contributions on the experiences of migrants are closely related to studies estimating the earnings functions of urban workers in general. The picture that emerges is one of earnings being a function of objective measures such as a skill level (years of schooling) (e.g., House and Rempel (1976)). Further, turning to the earnings functions that have been estimated for urban workers in the informal sectors of developing countries' economies, there is growing evidence that these sectors also respond to market forces and that, in particular, they offer to the workers they employ a higher real income than had generally been believed to be the case (Teilhet-Waldorf and Waldorf (1983)). This observation is of interest in its own right in that proponents of the Harris-Todaro framework view this sector as affording low living standards, given its presumed role of permitting migrants to queue up for employment in the modern sector (Fields (1975)).

The literature on statutory minimum wages also provides some indirect evidence on the behavior of labor supply. Irrespective of the motivation for introducing a floor to wages (Starr (1981)), the effects of such a floor are of interest. In a study of the introduction of a minimum wage in Tanganyika in 1963, Chesworth (1967) noted that employment among the categories of workers covered by labor enumeration fell by 14.3 percent between 1962 and 1963. Unfortunately, given the potential for disequilibrium in developing country labor markets, it is impossible to discern whether this observation is recording a movement along the demand curve or the supply curve of labor. There is, however, some additional evidence. As pointed out by Watanabe (1976), minimum wage floors in developing countries are frequently set at a relatively high level, which leads to widespread cheating. This suggests that, in these countries, there are well-defined demand and supply schedules for labor.

Empirical Evidence: Rural Workers

Literature examining the behavior of rural labor markets is of interest not only because of the further insight it provides into the labor supply behavior of urban workers but also because rural labor may itself be affected by taxes such as those on international trade. The relevant literature is large and varied. For example, in a paper estimating labor supply functions in peasant agriculture on the basis of a data set collected from some 4,900 rural households, Bardhan (1979a) finds evidence against the existence of the horizontal supply curve of labor predicted by the Lewis framework. In particular, he finds, "The wage response of labor supply seems to be significantly positive for the set of agricultural laborers and small cultivators, and also for that of women in the *usual* labor force. The wage response is not significant for *total* labor supply for the set of cultivators of all size groups taken together" (p. 81). The author concludes that labor supply decisions are determined by factors other than the wage rate, that is, the labor supply function is wage inelastic. Hansen (1969), working with data drawn from rural Egypt, concludes that the evidence is consistent with a competitive framework and that, in particular, there is a strong positive correlation between rural wages and hours worked per day during the year for males, females, and children. Rosenzweig (1980) also tested the assumption of competitive labor markets using household survey data collected in India. He concludes that, "Empirical results based on micro data from rural India stratified by sex and landholding status were generally supportive of the neoclassical framework suggesting that the annual number of [wage days] of employment observed for individuals in rural India is *mainly* supply rather than demand determined, as implied by competitive models" (p. 53). Finally, in a related demonstration of the thesis that rural wage levels in developing countries are not exogenously determined, Rosenzweig (1978) observed the existence of a negative correlation between rural wage levels and a measure of landholding inequality. His data consisted of a survey of more than 5,000 households in India.[4]

Assessment

The above contributions afford some indirect support to those who argue that supply-side considerations have a role in the determination of the equilibrium wage. However, although the empirical work supports the existence of a well-defined aggregate labor supply function, it appears not to be very elastic. Against this, the evidence does indicate that more elastic responses can be observed at the disaggregated level. Nonetheless, in view of the other reservations mentioned above, until some assumptions are made concerning the aggregate structure of all the taxes on labor income, little can be said about the supply-side implications of tax changes.

It should be further noted that this research does not demonstrate the superiority of simple tax-based policies over alternative measures. A distinguishing feature of developing countries is the degree to which their markets appear to be distorted. There is a growing body of literature that explicitly addresses these imperfections and accordingly raises alternative policy prescriptions. This literature begins with the observation that interlocking factor markets are observed in many rural communities where these may be, at least in part, an economic response to market imperfections. To be more specific, the cost of hiring and supervising labor leads

[4]Further evidence on the endogeneity of wages can be found in Bardhan (1979b) and Sumner (1981).

landowners to seek land-lease contracts. In addition, given that the intensity and quality of labor input is difficult to monitor, landowners tend to prefer sharecropping (i.e., risk-sharing) arrangements. Finally, capital markets are not complete in the sense that, because of information costs, many farmers do not have ready access to them. Landlords tend to fill this gap by providing loans, using the tenancy contract itself as collateral. This framework suggests that there are a series of nontax measures whereby the government by its intervention could induce output increases. Examples are the creation of futures markets and/or commodity price stabilization programs.[5] This literature is extensively discussed in Bardhan (1980, 1983), Newbery and Stiglitz (1981), and Braverman and Stiglitz (1982).

Although nontax policies of this type afford some possibility for output increases, they should be viewed as being primarily one-shot efforts. That is, they ensure that the existing stock of factors is more efficiently employed but do not affect the long-run rate of growth.[6]

Even though the gains that would result from removing labor market distortions may be primarily static rather than dynamic, this is not to say that they are necessarily negligible. Some empirical work exists in which estimates of the welfare gains associated with the removal of distortions are presented. For example, Harberger (1959) concluded that, for Chile, the total cost of both product and factor market distortions was between 9 percent and 15 percent of gross national product. Not all studies, however, are as optimistic about the potential welfare gains. In a more recent study in which they examine the effect of wage differentials between different industrial sectors in Colombia, Dougherty and Selowsky (1973) conclude that the output effects associated with those differentials are relatively insignificant. The methodology of that paper was to ascribe unexplained wage variations to distortions where the latter are presumably due to many factors. However, as pointed out by de Melo (1977), their approach was a partial equilibrium one in that they held product and factor prices fixed. For his part, reconsidering the case of removing labor market distortions in Colombia in a general equilibrium context, de Melo (1977) finds the potential gains to be significant.

We turn now to consider how tax policies affect savings and investment.

[5]It should be emphasized that the value of these measures lies solely in their increasing the efficiency of the market system. No account is taken of the equity implications either of the sharecropping arrangements or of the government policy measures. As pointed out by Braverman and Stiglitz (1982), interlinking markets can, but need not, increase the utility of both landlords and tenants since such arrangements unambiguously shift the utility possibilities schedule outward.

[6]This assertion has to be modified to the extent that devices such as price stabilization systems alter savings behavior. For a discussion of these possibilities, see Newbery and Stiglitz (1981).

II. Savings Behavior

Theoretical Background

The theoretical microeconomic literature on how savings behavior is affected by tax policy has tended to concentrate on the issue of how various tax instruments affect the net rate of interest. The presumption of much of that literature is that, once the incidence of a tax has been determined, all that remains is to calculate the interest elasticity of savings. In this, the relevant literature parallels that in which the effects of taxes on labor supply are discussed. It is easy to show, within the context of a two-period life-cycle framework, that the impact of a change in interest rates is ambiguous, since it depends on a balancing of substitution and wealth effects (Atkinson and Stiglitz (1980)). Some of the ambiguity is removed when it is recognized that the balanced-budget incidence analysis used in the optimal tax framework allows one to concentrate on the compensated rather than on the total price elasticity. Ambiguity remains, however, in that, within the two-period life-cycle framework, the elasticities are defined in terms of consumption, whereas the compensated elasticity of savings to interest rate changes is of greater concern to the analysis here. The conclusion is that that interest elasticity can take on any sign.[7]

Some writers question the relevance of the life-cycle framework, either because it is too limited, or because it represents an inappropriate specification of consumer preferences. Under the former critique is the work of Kotlikoff and Summers (1981), who argue for the inclusion of a bequest motive, while, under the latter critique, should be included the work of those who favor a myopic consumption function (e.g., Ball and Drake (1964), Clower and Johnson (1968)). Indeed, in the Clower and Johnson formulation of the myopic consumption function, interest rates do not even play a direct role in the savings process.

The results of the literature on the myopic consumption function may be particularly relevant for developing countries. Thus, it is quite possible that, in these countries, the precautionary motive for savings is more im-

[7]Following Feldstein (1978), savings are defined as $S = PC$, where S designates savings, C retirement consumption, and $P = 1/(1 + r)$ the "price" of consumption in retirement (r is the interest rate). In compensated terms this yields

$$\left(\frac{\partial S}{\partial P}\right)_{\bar{u}} = C + P\left(\frac{\partial C}{\partial P}\right)_{\bar{u}},$$

where $\partial C/\partial P < 0$ by assumption. The compensated effect of a change in the rate of interest is, therefore, ambiguous. A compensated increase in r (a decrease in the "price" of future consumption) is guaranteed to result in an increase in the demand for retirement consumption (C). However, savings might not increase since one does not have to save as much as before to ensure a given consumption level.

portant than the life-cycle motive. For example, account must be taken of the role of children in providing for the retirement of their parents.[8]

As pointed out in the introduction, the supply-side perspective as it applies to developing countries should also be concerned with the question of savings behavior in countries experiencing growth, that is, how does aggregate savings respond to increases in income? A substantial theoretical literature exists on this subject. This literature was the outcome of an attempt to reconcile early empirical work undertaken in developed countries in which it emerged that cross-section data indicated the existence of a nonproportional relationship between consumption and income, while time-series data suggested that the relationship is proportional. The best known reconciliation (the permanent-income hypothesis) of these two observations can be reduced to the argument that the cross-section regressions tend to estimate short-run consumption functions, while the time-series regressions estimate the analogous long-run function (Modigliani and Brumberg (1954), Friedman (1957), and Ando and Modigliani (1963)). From a development perspective, the long-run function is most relevant. Should the proportional relation hold for developing countries, it implies that the income elasticity of savings would be unity—with economic growth, the share of output devoted to savings would remain constant, everything else being held equal.

The above macroeconomic debate took place in the absence of tax considerations. When taxes are accommodated in this framework, as they are, for example, in Feldstein (1974a, 1974b), the crucial link is viewed as being how the redistribution of income from the private sector to the government affects aggregate savings. If the government's marginal propensity to save exceeds that of the private sector, the net effect of an increase in taxation with a concomitant increase in government expenditures is an increase in capital formation.

Just as in the case of labor-market behavior, there are difficulties in uncritically applying the results of the above literature to developing countries. Indeed, the situation in many developing countries is such that the efficacy of tax-based savings incentives programs may be questioned. Issues associated with the mobilization and deployment of domestic savings are often viewed as being central. Financial institutions may not be well developed (e.g., Miracle, Miracle, and Cohen (1980)). Further, the ex-

[8]Indeed, Kotlikoff and Spivak (1981) suggest that the current instability of family arrangements in the United States may in part be due to the improvement in the completeness of U.S. capital markets where this reduces the need for risk-sharing behavior on the part of the family!

change rate and domestic climate may be such as to encourage capital flight.

Finally, it has often been pointed out (e.g., Galbis (1979b)) that, in many developing countries, interest rates are often set at artificially low rates. This has resulted in a large literature in which it is argued that such an institutional constraint will result in financial repression. Thus, with the incentive for financial savings being greatly weakened (Galbis (1979a), World Bank (1983)), it is argued that the reduced supply of such savings requires the introduction of rationing mechanisms as far as investment is concerned. The work of Shaw (1973) and McKinnon (1973) is perhaps the best known. More recent contributions have refined their original work. Spellman (1976) attempts to introduce the role of financial intermediation into a one-sector growth model; Vogel and Buser (1976) argue that the degree of financial repression is sensitive to changes in risk as well as to changes in the mean return to financial investments; van Wijnbergen (1983) examines the implications of relaxing McKinnon's assumption that the alternative investment opportunity to financial assets consists of "unproductive assets" by allowing for curb market funds, where these have been documented to be of considerable empirical importance (e.g., Tun Wai (1977)). Finally, Galbis (1981) raises the question that, in a second-best world, it may not be optimal for interest rates to be market determined.[9]

Empirical Evidence

Much of the empirical development economics literature on savings behavior has not addressed the issue of the interest elasticity of savings. Data availability is a major reason for this. As Mikesell and Zinser (1973) point out in their survey, data on savings are inaccurate by the very nature of their method of calculation, that is, savings figures are frequently obtained residually. As a result, it is quite conceivable, for example, that the result obtained by Krishna and Raychaudhuri (1982) for India of a marginal propensity to save out of permanent income exceeding that out of transitory income—an unexpected outcome—is the product of inaccurate data. Further, given the widespread use of interest rate ceilings, it is not clear what should be the appropriate choice of a rate of return variable. As a result of all of these difficulties, many of the empirical results should be approached with great caution. So as to emphasize that the difficulties are genuine, it should be noted that Williamson (1968) found interest rates to have an

[9]Special conditions of financial markets in developing countries and their impact on optimal taxation of financial savings are highlighted in Ebrill (Chapter 4).

insignificant impact on savings in India, while Gupta (1970), using a different data set, found that, for some specifications, they had a significant positive effect. (Some of the statistical and conceptual difficulties associated with measuring saving (and investment) in India are discussed in Gothoskar and Venkatachalam (1979).)

Instead, a large proportion of the available empirical research has been concerned more with the macroeconomic issues raised above. Thus, a major effort has been made to estimate consumption functions for developing countries. Various hypotheses are tested. In particular, the life-cycle model is frequently tested, as is the hypothesis that savings rates increase with income levels. Many of the early contributions have been exhaustively surveyed elsewhere (Mikesell and Zinser (1973), Snyder (1974)). A good example of this literature is Landau (1971). Also notable is Leff and Sato (1975), in which a simultaneous equations model of aggregate savings is developed. Other examples of recent additions to this literature are Song (1981) and McDonald (1983). The consensus of this literature is that some relationship between savings and income does exist and, further, that some versions of the life cycle/permanent income hypotheses are appropriate. More specifically, McDonald (1983), in his study of savings behavior in Latin America, found that the income elasticities of consumption were, with a few exceptions, in the range of 0.7 to 1.1. This lends some support to the hypothesis that the proportionality result of the permanent-income framework applies to developing countries. Of course, it also implies that, as countries develop, there is no particular tendency for the savings rate to increase.

The empirical work also shows that there are other important determinants of savings, where these include demographic factors (e.g., dependency rates and age distribution (Bilsborrow (1979)), occupation, income distribution, life span (Ram and Schultz (1979)), and the urban-rural distinction). Note that to the extent that growth affects these variables, savings rates will change. Further, insofar as income distributions can be altered by tax policy (Goode (1961)), that provides a potential lever for government intervention. The policy might prove to be unpalatable, however, to the extent that the government tries to increase aggregate savings by distributing income from the poor (low propensity to save) to the rich (high propensity to save).

A large number of papers examine the impact of the growth in the government sector on aggregate savings. These papers constitute the empirical analogue of Feldstein's (1974a, 1974b) theoretical contributions, although it must be emphasized that the concept of government savings is particularly difficult to pin down. The relevant papers have concentrated on evaluating the "Please effect," where this can take either a strong or a weak form (Please (1967, 1970)). The strong form maintains that aggregate savings will decline with the growth of the share of tax revenues in gross domestic product (GDP), whereas the weak form contends that under such circumstances aggregate savings may increase but not by much. Papers in which this and related hypotheses are tested include those by Bhatia (1967), Morss (1968), Thimmaiah (1977), and Tahari (1979). The consensus of this literature seems to be that the Please effect is not valid. Bhatia concludes that aggregate savings increase quite sharply on the basis of a cross-sectional study of 20 African countries—for every 1 percent increase in the tax-GDP ratio, private consumption declined by 0.21 percent of GDP, while public consumption increased by 0.05 percent of GDP. Morss, using data drawn from a cross-section of 46 developing countries, felt confident in rejecting the Please effect. Tahari reached a similar conclusion. Thimmaiah, using time-series data from India, could not reject the weak form of the Please effect. On the other hand, Landau (1971) did find evidence to support the Please effect in the case of Latin American countries.

There is also an important body of literature that attempts to evaluate the empirical significance of the financial repression which is presumed to be an inevitable outcome of institutionally setting interest rates at artificially low rates. The consensus is that financial repression does exist and can be a severe drag on economic development. For example, in a paper by the Research Department of the Fund (International Monetary Fund (1983)), the authors concluded that there is good prima facie evidence to support the assertion that countries with positive real rates of interest experience a higher rate of growth than that enjoyed by countries in which the real rate of interest is negative. Fry (1980a) finds that savings are affected positively by the real deposit rate of interest. He argues that his estimates of savings and growth functions are such as to allow him to conclude that the cost of financial repression is around one half of a percentage point in growth forgone for every percentage point by which the real rate falls below the equilibrium rate. In another paper, Fry (1978) finds further evidence of the importance of financial repression. He concludes that the specific transmission mechanism proposed by Shaw (1973) appears to fit the facts better than that proposed by McKinnon (1973). In particular, McKinnon's twin assumptions to the effect that investments are lumpy and entirely self-financed which, taken together, imply that potential investors must accumulate money balances prior to investing, leads to the testable hypothesis that money and physical capital are complements. This hypothesis is not sustained by the data. Shaw's alternative approach, which assumes that investors are not constrained to self-finance because of the emergence of noninstitutional markets in response to financial repression, does receive support. Other papers, in which it is argued that financial repression can be important, are Chandavarkar (1971) and Vogel and Buser (1976). Also noteworthy are two papers by Fry (1980b) and Leff and Sato (1980), in which it is pointed out that artificially low interest rates affect not only long-term growth rates but also short-term macroeconomic adjustment processes.

All of the above suggests that, even though aggregate savings may not be very interest-sensitive, the allocation of that aggregate between conventional financial assets and alternatives such as curb market funds and works of art is indeed responsive to economic incentives.[10] Presumably, this responsiveness extends to the behavior of asset holders as they determine their portfolio allocations within the category of conventional financial assets. There is, unfortunately, little empirical work addressing this issue. An exception is a paper by Bürkner (1982), in which he concludes on the basis of financial data collected for the Philippines, that investors in the Philippines react to relative changes in rates of return just as their counterparts do in developed countries.

Assessment

To the extent that the empirical literature on savings behavior addresses the concerns of supply-side economists, it does it best in its evaluation of the financial repression hypotheses of Shaw and McKinnon. While the empirical work in this area demonstrates that savings may be sensitive to changes in interest rates and, therefore, are also sensitive to changes in tax policy, it also raises the issue of whether savings-based tax incentives represent the most effective reform route for countries to pursue. Specifically, the distortion to savings decisions implied by the existence of financial repression may be far larger than that associated with the fact that interest income is subject to income tax.[11] To place the relative magnitudes of these distortions in some context, consider that, for Ghana during the late 1970s, official market interest rates on savings deposits rarely exceeded 10 percent, while the rate of inflation was frequently in the neighborhood of 100 percent.

As for the remainder of the empirical literature, most of it is concerned with macroeconomic aggregates rather than supply-side issues. In particu-

[10]In this context, note that the alternatives include placing savings overseas. This alternative emphasizes the important role of confidence in the determination of savings allocation decisions.

[11]This issue is treated in greater depth in the next chapter. That chapter also discusses some of the factors that should be taken into account when trying to determine how to use taxes so as to enhance the return to financial savings.

lar, inadequate attention has been devoted to the question of whether aggregate savings, as opposed to its components, is affected by the type of tax structure. Is a consumption-based tax preferable to an income-based tax, for example, as argued by Due (1976)? This is an important issue since it raises the possibility that the substantial reliance of developing countries on broad-based consumption taxes may have been conducive to savings. As an aside on this, it is interesting to note that Tahari (1979) has found on the basis of his cross-section work that (private) savings behavior appears to be stimulated more by direct than indirect taxation! While theoretically possible, too much store should not be placed on this somewhat surprising conclusion given the heterogeneous nature of the countries in his sample and the aggregative nature of his regression results. Besides, the net effect of government's actions on aggregate savings depends on the manner of disposition of the tax revenues.

As is well known, aggregate savings do not necessarily equal gross investment for any single country. Thus, for a given country, investments can be made by domestic or foreign investors. Further, since this survey is concerned with results that have implications for supply-side policies, the term "investment" is interpreted here in a restricted sense as referring to those increments in the stock of a nation's capital which result in increases in market output. Investment in works of art and so on are accordingly excluded. Given this potential difference between savings and investment and given that there exists a wide range of specifically targeted tax instruments, for example, those aimed at manufacturing and tourism investment, we turn now to consider investment behavior as a separate topic.

III. Investment Behavior

Theoretical Background

The theory of how investment behavior responds to changes in tax policy has been heavily influenced by the neoclassical framework established by Jorgenson (1963). The most important conclusions of the literature can be found in Hall and Jorgenson (1971), Stiglitz (1973), King (1975), Flemming (1976), Atkinson and Stiglitz (1980), and King and Fullerton (1984). For our purposes, it is important to note the observation that attempting to gauge the impact of tax policy on the cost of capital (and, therefore, on the rate of investment) by concentrating on the corporate tax rate is misleading. In many countries, the corporate tax structure interacts with the personal tax system (for example, through the tax treatment of dividends and capital gains) and, further, the specific provisions of the corporate tax are of critical importance.[12] On the latter point, the corporate tax will not affect the cost of capital if companies are allowed to make deductions against their tax liabilities that accurately reflect the contribution of capital to the production process. For example, in the context of the U.S. tax system, there are two approaches to ensuring that the tax system would be neutral with respect to the cost of capital. First, if the corporation uses debt finance on the margin and if debt interest is deductible and depreciation allowances accurately measure the value of the capital used up (a difficult quantity to measure in an inflationary environment), then increases in the corporate tax rate will leave the cost of capital unaffected. The alternative approach, easier to implement administratively, would disallow interest deductions and replace depreciation allowances with expensing.[13] The two approaches are equivalent in present value terms.[14]

The above literature refers to the effects of taxes in a world without risk. There is, however, an additional body of work that relaxes this constraint and allows for the existence of risk. The emphasis has been on the role of the government as a risk-sharer through its tax instruments. The question of interest has been whether taxation encourages more or less risk taking. The answer depends on factors such as the degree of investor risk aversion and the extent of loss-offset provisions (cf., Atkinson and Stiglitz (1980)). It should be noted, with respect to the latter, that the present value of loss-offset provisions are of greatest relevance—the fact that many countries permit full loss-offset for an indefinite period in nominal terms does not take account of the cost associated with the postponement of the tax benefits.

When one turns to consider that part of the theoretical literature concerned with developing country issues, one finds that it differs from the papers cited above in a number of important respects. First, given the variety of developing country experiences, it is more concerned with the multitude of direct tax structures in existence (cf., Lent (1967), Usher (1977)). Many of these tax structures employ devices not commonly used in devel-

[12]Moreover, as emphasized by King and Fullerton (1984), within a country, capital income taxes can be quite variable in their treatment of different transactions.

[13]It might be worth noting that this alternative approach is also automatically inflation-proof.

[14]It must be recognized that, in practice, the two systems may not be equivalent. Thus, for example, start-up companies will not in general have the profits against which they can deduct their investment expenditures. While it is true that these companies can be compensated by allowing them to carry their expensing allowances forward, for equivalence to be maintained, these carry-forward provisions would have to be indexed for inflation and the real rate of return.

oped countries. For example, Agell (1983) shows how tax holidays can be accommodated with the neoclassical cost of capital model.

Second, there is a belief that the neoclassical model may not apply readily to developing countries. Capital markets are imperfect. Therefore, financial policy and, in particular, policies concerning dividend/retained earnings behavior, are no longer irrelevant to aggregate investment behavior. More important, the structure of a country's system of financial intermediation can be significant. Thus, as pointed out in the previous section, the fact that interest rates are maintained at an artificially low level in some countries could well lead to financial disintermediation with the result that the demand for investment funds must be met by rationing. This manifestation of financial repression raises the possibility that investment may increase with interest rates as a result of an increase in available savings.

Third, and related to the possibility that financial repression may imply that investment behavior is quantity-constrained rather than price-constrained, is the argument that the growth performance of some countries (where this is influenced by their investment efforts) may be limited by the availability of foreign exchange. This possibility, commonly referred to as the two-gap hypothesis, is discussed by McKinnon (1964) among others.

Fourth, recognition of the fact that aggregate investment consists of a number of components in addition to private domestic investment has stimulated research. Attention has been devoted to the determinants of foreign direct investment and foreign aid. To what do these capital flows respond? It is clear, for example, that if a complete explanation of how taxes affect private foreign investment flows is to be determined, the interactions of differing national tax systems must be taken into account. For example, Hartman (1981a) considers how U.S. foreign direct investment might be influenced by U.S. tax policies. An important element of the current U.S. tax structure is that income from foreign sources is liable to taxation only on repatriation, which implies that firms should finance foreign investment out of foreign earnings to the greatest extent possible. Work in this area is still at an early stage.[15]

Fifth, at this macroeconomic level, there has been concern over the degree of complementarity or substitutability between the components of aggregate investment. In particular, are capital inflows a substitute for domestic saving and investment? Thus, Chenery and Strout (1966) viewed all capital inflows as net addition to a developing country's capital stock,

[15]In particular, the interaction between national tax systems can be expected to have interesting side effects. For example, foreign capital may not be attracted by reductions in a developing country's marginal tax rates due to tax treaties, tax sparing, etc.

whereas Weisskopf (1972b) viewed such inflows as being a substitute for domestic savings. Papanek (1972) argued for an intermediate position. There has also been concern over the impact of public investment on private investment.

Finally, as mentioned in the introduction, investment behavior can be influenced by taxes and distortions other than direct income-based taxes. Notable among these other instruments are trade taxes or marketing boards and agricultural price support systems. While these devices may be introduced for a number of reasons (e.g., with a view to levying an optimum export tax whereby a country exploits its market power in world markets (Corden (1974), Sanchez-Ugarte and Modi (Chapter 11)), they can frequently have unintended effects, particularly at the level of individual industries.

Empirical Evidence

The available empirical work reflects the bias mentioned above against the neoclassical framework. For example, Bilsborrow (1977) tests an eclectic theory of investment behavior that allows for variables representing the internal financial structure of the firm. He finds, using data drawn from Colombia, that accelerator effects, cash flow effects, balance sheet risk variables, and, most notably, the availability of foreign exchange were important determinants of investment flows. However, the rate of return to investors can still be an important determinant of investment behavior. In her study of the inflationary process in India, Ahluwalia (1979) found that the interest elasticity of private investment exceeded 2, which would suggest that a tax policy aimed at altering the rate of return could be stimulative. In contrast to this result, the papers cited earlier, in which the financial repression hypotheses are evaluated, find—almost as a corollary to the existence of artificially low interest rates—that investment is quantity-constrained by rationing. For example, Fry (1978) finds for his sample of countries that an increase in the real rate of interest has a positive effect on growth. Related to this is the work of Thirlwall (1974), who discovered, for his global sample of countries, that inflation exercises a positive influence on investment, but on further examination found that, if the sample is limited to developing countries, this influence is negative. If the role of the inflation variable for the case of developing countries is interpreted as its being a proxy for the degree of financial repression, then the sign of the effect is understandable. (This result is similar to one reported in Ebrill (Chapter 5).) It should be noted that, to the extent that these effects are important, they reduce the effectiveness of tax incentive programs for investment.

More neoclassical in nature is the example of Lim (1983). He concentrates on the specifics of the investment incentive programs in peninsula Malaysia, calling attention, in particular, to the role of generous tax holidays that tend to be awarded on an indiscriminate basis. He finds that there is some evidence of investor reactions to these incentives—there is some tendency for both capital intensity and utilization rates to increase.

The empirical literature evaluating the two-gap hypothesis, that is, the argument that growth prospects are often constrained by the availability of foreign exchange, is inconclusive. Weisskopf (1972a) and Blomqvist (1976) cast some doubt on this argument. On the other hand, for the case of Sudan, Wynn (1980) finds some evidence to support it. All authors agree, however, that testing the hypothesis is particularly difficult since, given the accounting identity between the excess of imports over exports and the corresponding excess of savings over investment, it is not easy to identify ex post the true constraint on a country's development.

There is little empirical work on the determinants of foreign investment flows. Hartman (1981b) finds that U.S. aggregate foreign direct investment does, in fact, respond to changes in tax policy. In particular, it is influenced negatively and quite strongly by the after-tax rate of return to domestic investment. As further evidence of the sensitivity of foreign investment flows to economic variables, Hartman (1982) shows that foreign investment flows into the United States respond to changes in U.S. tax policy. However, when one considers the experience of developing countries, there are fewer grounds for optimism over the ability of tax policies to attract investment flows. Lim (1983) finds in his work on a cross-section of 27 developing countries that the presence of natural resources and a proven record of economic performance were far more important than fiscal incentives in attracting such flows. Although they do not consider the impact of tax incentives per se, Root and Ahmed (1979) corroborate Lim's results for nonextractive industries in that they find that those countries that have attracted the most foreign investment have substantial urbanization, relatively advanced infrastructures, and so on.[16]

The issue of whether capital inflows are a substitute for domestic savings and investment has been examined empirically by Papanek (1973), Stoneman (1975), and Gupta and Islam (1983), among others. Given their careful empirical methodology, Gupta and Islam's (1983) work would appear to be the most interesting. They find, after decomposing aggregate capital inflows, that foreign aid had a more negative impact on savings than for-

[16]As an aside, it is worth noting that the other component of foreign capital flows, mentioned above, namely, foreign aid, to the extent that is increasingly being associated with structural adjustment, is responsive to changes in tax policy.

eign investment, although these effects never appeared to be very large. In a related paper looking at the other side of this issue, Feldstein and Horioka (1980) show that, for the developed countries, international differences in savings rates correspond to almost equal differences in domestic investment rates, again suggesting, as do Gupta and Islam (1983) in the context of developing countries, that domestic savings are the most important determinant of domestic investment.

Sundararajan and Thakur (1980), using data collected on India and Korea, test a modified neoclassical framework to see the impact of public investment on private investment. Simulations show that, in India, increases in public investment initially lead to substantial crowding out of private investment with a weak reversal of this tendency occurring in subsequent periods. In Korea, in marked contrast, there is evidence of a strong complementarity between public and private investment. Tun Wai and Wong (1982), using data drawn from a number of countries, found evidence of financial crowding out in some countries (Malaysia and Mexico). Further, on the subject of financial structure, they find that, in the case of Korea, retained earnings play a less important role than credit availability in determining investment flows, that is, again the financial structure is important.

The allocation effects of various trade taxes, notably export taxes, and price support systems have been extensively evaluated in the literature. The thrust of the work has been to estimate the relevant supply elasticities for the commodities whose prices are affected, thereby providing additional insight into the degree to which investment changes in response to changes in incentives.

Most of the papers are concerned with agricultural commodities. Booth (1980), in her consideration of the role of export taxes in member countries of the Association of South East Asian Nations, points out that Thailand's export tax on rice, levied at a fairly high rate in the 1970s, has led many producers to shift out of rice production. While the resultant production distortion is a cost to the economy, it does indicate that Thai farmers respond to economic circumstances.[17] Further evidence of the sensitivity of agricultural interests to government intervention can be found in Tolley, Thomas, and Wong (1982). They cite, for example, the fact that Korea

[17]As an aside, it should be noted that, even though the export tax distorts Thailand's production, there could be a net benefit to the economy. Thailand has market power in the world rice market and the net effect of the export tax with its concomitant reduction in the supply of rice is for Thailand to get a higher price for its rice exports than previously (cf., Tolley, Thomas, and Wong (1982)).

attained self-sufficiency in rice production during the 1970s, a period in which the Government's farm purchase price increased by more than 70 percent in real terms. (They argue that a supply elasticity of 0.3 is appropriate for this case.) Finally, mention should be made of Tanzi (1976), who shows that the export tax levied by Haiti on its coffee exports has had a major negative impact on production.

Intervention in agricultural markets need not take as explicit a form as a price support. Marketing boards, which sell a country's product at a different (usually higher) price than that which it pays to domestic suppliers, are indirectly performing the role of an export tax. In his discussion of the case of the Cocoa Marketing Board in Ghana, Leith (1974) cites evidence which suggests that the short-run supply elasticities for cocoa are of the order of 0.15 to 0.20, while the corresponding long-run elasticities range from 0.71 to 1.0.

The above results draw on a large body of research in which agricultural supply response to price changes in general is evaluated. Much of this literature, a good example of which is Dowling and Jessadachatr (1979), is surveyed in Askari and Cummings (1977). The short-run and long-run supply elasticities (the latter are particularly important for perennials) of previous researchers are tabulated. The authors comment that there is an enormous range of elasticity estimates where, disturbingly, this range occurs not only across commodities but also within commodities. It is also notable that the majority of the long-run elasticity estimates cited are less than unity. This implies that substantial price incentives are needed to stimulate increases in output.

Assessment

All of the above implies that investors do react to economic incentives and that, therefore, a tax-based policy of incentives could have some role to play. However, the empirical results above also suggest that investment is influenced by a number of factors. These run the range from the existence of capital market imperfections due to financial repression as evidenced by the role of liquidity effects to the existence of other distortions such as those associated with price support systems and marketing boards. The fact that Askari and Cummings (1977) reported such a broad range of supply elasticities may be due not to the vagaries of the econometric techniques employed but rather to the differing circumstances that farmers in different countries experience. For example, is the market for inputs free or regulated? If regulated, the observed supply elasticity might be lower.

IV. Conclusions

Although the empirical literature examining the impact of tax policy on labor supply, savings, and investment leaves much to be desired, it nonetheless appears that changes in tax policies will have some effects. The behavior of these aggregates appears, however, to be determined as much by other elements such as the sophistication of financial intermediaries and the completeness of capital markets as by these tax policies. Given the existence of widespread market failure in many developing countries, the impact of changes in tax policies may be quite difficult to predict as the costs associated with such changes are potentially large. This is not to deny that there may be circumstances in which most would agree on what would constitute useful tax reforms. The reduction of large export taxes comes to mind in this respect (see Sanchez-Ugarte and Modi (Chapter 11)). However, it may be the case that a more promising supply-side approach might be one that also aims at alleviating the most obvious sources of market failure. This fact seems to have been appreciated by researchers who examine the economics of sharecropping structures and interlinked factor markets.

REFERENCES

Abizadeh, Sohrab, and J.P. Wyckoff, "Tax System Components and Economic Development: An International Perspective," *Bulletin*, International Bureau of Fiscal Documentation (Amsterdam), Vol. 36 (November 1982), pp. 483–91.

Agell, Jonas, "Subsidy to Capital Through Tax Incentives in the ASEAN Countries: An Application of the Cost of Capital Approach Under Inflationary Situations," *Singapore Economic Review* (Singapore), Vol. 28 (October 1983), pp. 98–128.

Ahluwalia, I.J., *Behaviour of Prices and Outputs in India: A Macro-Econometric Approach* (New Delhi: Macmillan, 1979).

Ahluwalia, Montek S., "Taxes, Subsidies, and Employment," *Quarterly Journal of Economics* (Cambridge, Massachusetts), Vol. 87 (August 1973), pp. 393–409.

Ando, Albert, and Franco Modigliani, "The 'Life-Cycle' Hypothesis of Saving: Aggregate Implications and Tests," *American Economic Review* (Nashville, Tennessee), Vol. 53 (March 1963), pp. 55–84.

Askari, Hossein, and John Thomas Cummings, "Estimating Agricultural Supply Response with the Nerlove Model: A Survey," *International Economic Review* (Osaka, Japan), Vol. 18 (June 1977), pp. 257–92.

Atkinson, Anthony B., and Joseph E. Stiglitz, *Lectures on Public Economics* (New York: McGraw-Hill, 1980).

Ball, R.J., and Pamela S. Drake, "The Relationship Between Aggregate Consumption and Wealth," *International Economic Review* (Osaka, Japan), Vol. 5 (January 1964), pp. 63-81.

Bardhan, Pranab K. (1979a), "Labor Supply Functions in a Poor Agrarian Economy," *American Economic Review* (Nashville, Tennessee), Vol. 69 (March 1979), pp. 73-83.

——— (1979b), "Wages and Unemployment in a Poor Agrarian Economy: A Theoretical and Empirical Analysis," *Journal of Political Economy* (Chicago), Vol. 87 (June 1979), pp. 479-500.

———, "Interlocking Factor Markets and Agrarian Development: A Review of Issues," *Oxford Economic Papers* (New Series), Vol. 32 (March 1980), pp. 82-98.

———, "Labor-Tying in a Poor Agrarian Economy: A Theoretical and Empirical Analysis," *Quarterly Journal of Economics* (Cambridge, Massachusetts), Vol. 98 (August 1983), pp. 501-14.

Berg, Elliot J., "Backward-Sloping Labor Supply Functions in Dual Economies—The Africa Case," *Quarterly Journal of Economics* (Cambridge, Massachusetts), Vol. 75 (August 1961), pp. 468-92.

Bhatia, Rattan J., "A Note on Consumption, Income, and Taxes" (unpublished, International Monetary Fund, November 2, 1967).

Bilsborrow, Richard E., "The Determinants of Fixed Investment by Manufacturing Firms in a Developing Country," *International Economic Review* (Osaka, Japan), Vol. 18 (October 1977), pp. 697-717.

———, "Age Distribution and Savings Rates in Less Developed Countries," *Economic Development and Cultural Change* (Chicago), Vol. 28 (October 1979), pp. 23-45.

Bird, Richard M., "Taxation and Employment in Developing Countries," *Finanzarchiv* (Tübingen), Vol. 40, No. 2 (1982), pp. 211-39.

Blinder, Alan S., "Thoughts on the Laffer Curve," in *The Supply-Side Effects of Economic Policy,* ed. by Laurence H. Meyer (Boston, Massachusetts: Kluwer-Nijhoff, 1981).

Blomqvist, Å. G., "Empirical Evidence on the Two-Gap Hypothesis: A Revised Analysis," *Journal of Development Economics* (Amsterdam), Vol. 3 (July 1976), pp. 181-93.

Booth, Anne, "The Economic Impact of Export Taxes in ASEAN," *Malayan Economic Review* (Singapore), Vol. 25 (April 1980), pp. 36-61.

Braverman, Avishay, and Joseph E. Stiglitz, "Sharecropping and the Interlinking of Agrarian Markets," *American Economic Review* (Nashville, Tennessee), Vol. 72 (September 1982), pp. 695-715.

Bürkner, Hans-Paul, "The Portfolio Behaviour of Individual Investors in Developing Countries: An Analysis of the Philippine Case," *Oxford Bulletin of Economics and Statistics,* Vol. 44 (February 1982), pp. 127-44.

Chandavarkar, Anand G., "Some Aspects of Interest Rate Policies in Less Developed Economies: The Experience of Selected Asian Countries," *Staff Papers,* International Monetary Fund (Washington), Vol. 18 (March 1971), pp. 48-112.

Chenery, Hollis B., and Alan M. Strout, "Foreign Assistance and Economic Development," *American Economic Review* (Nashville, Tennessee), Vol. 56 (September 1966), pp. 679–733.

Chesworth, D., "Statutory Minimum Wage Fixing in Tanganyika," *International Labor Review* (Geneva), Vol. 96 (July 1967), pp. 43–66.

Clower, Robert W., and M. Bruce Johnson, "Income, Wealth, and the Theory of Consumption," in *Value, Capital, and Growth: Papers in Honour of Sir John Hicks*, ed. by J.N. Wolfe (Edinburgh: Edinburgh University Press; Chicago: Aldine Publishing Co., 1968).

Corden, W.M., *Trade Policy and Economic Welfare* (Oxford: Clarendon Press, 1974).

de Melo, Jaime A.P., "Distortions in the Factor Market: Some General Equilibrium Estimates," *Review of Economics and Statistics* (Cambridge, Massachusetts), Vol. 59 (November 1977), pp. 398–405.

Dougherty, Christopher, and Marcelo Selowsky, "Measuring the Effects of the Misallocation of Labour," *Review of Economics and Statistics* (Cambridge, Massachusetts), Vol. 55 (August 1973), pp. 386–90.

Dowling, J.M., and Phitsanes Jessadachatr, "The Supply Response of Sugar Cane in Thailand," *Malayan Economic Review* (Singapore), Vol. 24 (October 1979), pp. 74–88.

Due, John F., "Value-Added Taxation in Developing Economies," in *Taxation and Development*, ed. by Nian-Tzu Wang (New York: Praeger, 1976).

Feldstein, Martin S. (1974a), "Incidence of a Capital Income Tax in a Growing Economy with Variable Savings Rates," *Review of Economic Studies* (Edinburgh), Vol. 41 (October 1974), pp. 505–13.

——— (1974b), "Tax Incidence in a Growing Economy with Variable Factor Supply," *Quarterly Journal of Economics* (Cambridge, Massachusetts), Vol. 88 (November 1974), pp. 551–73.

———, "The Welfare Cost of Capital Income Taxation," *Journal of Political Economy* (Chicago), Vol. 86, No. 2, Part 2 (April 1978), pp. S29–S51.

———, and C. Horioka, "Domestic Saving and International Capital Flows," *Economic Journal* (London), Vol. 90 (June 1980), pp. 314–29.

Fields, Gary S., "Rural-Urban Migration, Urban Unemployment and Underemployment, and Job-Search Activity in LDCs," *Journal of Development Economics* (Amsterdam), Vol. 2 (June 1975), pp. 165–87.

———, "Place-to-Place Migration in Colombia," *Economic Development and Cultural Change* (Chicago), Vol. 30 (April 1982), pp. 539–58.

Flemming, J.S., "A Reappraisal of the Corporation Income Tax," *Journal of Public Economics* (Amsterdam), Vol. 6 (July–August 1976), pp. 163–69.

Friedman, M., *A Theory of the Consumption Function* (Princeton: Princeton University Press, 1957).

Fry, Maxwell J., "Money and Capital or Financial Deepening in Economic Development?" *Journal of Money, Credit and Banking* (Columbus, Ohio), Vol. 10 (November 1978), pp. 464–75.

——— (1980a), "Saving, Investment, Growth and the Cost of Financial Repression," *World Development* (Oxford), Vol. 8 (April 1980), pp. 317-27.

——— (1980b), "Money, Interest, Inflation and Growth," *Journal of Monetary Economics* (Amsterdam), Vol. 6 (October 1980), pp. 535-45.

Galbis, Vicente (1979a), "Money, Investment, and Growth in Latin America, 1961-1973," *Economic Development and Cultural Change* (Chicago), Vol. 27 (April 1979), pp. 423-43.

——— (1979b), "Inflation and Interest Rate Policies in Latin America, 1967-76," *Staff Papers,* International Monetary Fund (Washington), Vol. 26 (June 1979), pp. 334-66.

———, "Interest Rate Management: The Latin America Experience," *Savings and Development* (Milan), Vol. 5, No. 1 (1981), pp. 5-44.

Gandhi, Ved P., "Unemployment in Developing Countries: Can Tax Incentives Help?" (unpublished, International Monetary Fund, February 3, 1981).

Goode, Richard, "Taxation of Saving and Consumption in Underdeveloped Countries," *National Tax Journal* (Columbus, Ohio), Vol. 14 (December 1961), pp. 305-22.

Gothoskar, S.P., and T.R. Venkatachalam, "Household Saving and Investment in India," *Margin* (New Delhi), Vol. 12, No. 1 (October 1979), pp. 28-40.

Gupta, K.L., "Personal Saving in Developing Nations: Further Evidence," *Economic Record* (Melbourne), Vol. 46 (June 1970), pp. 243-49.

———, and M. Anisul Islam, *Foreign Capital, Savings, and Growth: An International Cross-Section Study* (Dordrecht, Netherlands; Boston, Massachusetts: Reidel Publishing Company, 1983).

Hall, R.E., and D.W. Jorgenson, "Application of the Theory of Optimum Capital Accumulation," in *Tax Incentives and Capital Spending,* ed. by Gary Fromm (Washington: Brookings Institution, 1971).

Hansen, Bent, "Employment and Wages in Rural Egypt," *American Economic Review* (Nashville, Tennessee), Vol. 59 (June 1969), pp. 298-313.

Harberger, Arnold C., "Using the Resources at Hand More Effectively," *American Economic Review, Papers and Proceedings of the Seventy-First Annual Meeting of the American Economic Association* (Nashville, Tennessee), Vol. 49 (May 1959), pp. 134-46.

———, "The Incidence of the Corporation Income Tax," *Journal of Political Economy* (Chicago), Vol. 70 (June 1962), pp. 215-40.

Hartman, David G. (1981a), "Tax Policy and Foreign Direct Investment," NBER Working Paper No. 689 (Cambridge, Massachusetts: National Bureau of Economic Research, 1981).

——— (1981b), "Domestic Tax Policy and Foreign Investment: Some Evidence," NBER Working Paper No. 784 (Cambridge, Massachusetts: National Bureau of Economic Research, 1981).

———, "Tax Policy and Foreign Direct Investment in the United States," NBER Working Paper No. 967 (Cambridge, Massachusetts: National Bureau of Economic Research, 1982).

Hausman, Jerry A., "Income and Payroll Tax Policy and Labor Supply," in *The Supply-Side Effects of Economic Policy,* ed. by Laurence H. Meyer (Boston, Massachusetts: Kluwer-Nijhoff, 1981).

———, "Taxes and Labor Supply," NBER Working Paper No. 1102 (Cambridge, Massachusetts: National Bureau of Economic Research, 1983).

Hinrichs, H.H., "Determinants of Government Revenue Shares Among Less-Developed Countries," *Economic Journal* (London), Vol. 75 (September 1965), pp. 546-56.

House, William J., and Henry Rempel, "The Determinants of and Changes in the Structure of Wages and Employment in the Manufacturing Sector of the Kenyan Economy, 1967-1972," *Journal of Development Economics* (Amsterdam), Vol. 3 (March 1976), pp. 83-98.

International Monetary Fund, *Interest Rate Policies in Developing Countries: A Study by the Research Department of the International Monetary Fund*, Occasional Paper No. 22 (Washington, October 1983).

Jorgenson, Dale W., "Capital Theory and Investment Behavior," *American Economic Review, Papers and Proceedings of the Seventy-Fifth Annual Meeting of the American Economic Association* (Nashville, Tennessee), Vol. 53 (May 1963), pp. 247-59.

King, Mervyn A., "Taxation, Corporate Financial Policy, and the Cost of Capital: A Comment," *Journal of Public Economics* (Amsterdam), Vol. 4 (August 1975), pp. 271-79.

———,and Don Fullerton, eds., *The Taxation of Income from Capital: A Comparative Study in the United States, the United Kingdom, Sweden, and West Germany* (Chicago: University of Chicago Press, 1984).

Kotlikoff, Laurence J., and Avia Spivak, "The Family as an Incomplete Annuities Market," *Journal of Political Economy* (Chicago), Vol. 89 (April 1981), pp. 372-91.

Kotlikoff, Laurence J., and Lawrence H. Summers, "The Role of Intergenerational Transfers in Aggregate Capital Accumulation," *Journal of Political Economy* (Chicago), Vol. 89 (August 1981), pp. 706-32.

Krishna, Raj, and G.S. Raychaudhuri, "Trends in Rural Savings and Capital Formation in India, 1950-1951 to 1973-1974," *Economic Development and Cultural Change* (Chicago), Vol. 30 (January 1982), pp. 271-98.

Landau, Luis, "Saving Functions for Latin America," in *Studies in Development Planning,* ed. by Hollis B. Chenery (Cambridge, Massachusetts: Harvard University Press, 1971).

Leff, Nathaniel, "Macroeconomic Adjustment in Developing Countries: Instability, Short-Run Growth, and External Dependency," *Review of Economics and Statistics* (Cambridge, Massachusetts), Vol. 62 (May 1980), pp. 170-79.

———, and Kazuo Sato, "A Simultaneous-Equations Model of Savings in Developing Countries," *Journal of Political Economy* (Chicago), Vol. 83 (December 1975), pp. 1217-28.

Leith, J. Clark, *Foreign Trade Regimes and Economic Development: Ghana* (New York: National Bureau of Economic Research, 1974).

Lent, George E., "Tax Incentives for Investment in Developing Countries," *Staff Papers*, International Monetary Fund (Washington), Vol. 14 (July 1967), pp. 249-323.

Lewis, W. Arthur, "Economic Development with Unlimited Supplies of Labour," *Manchester School of Economic and Social Studies*, Vol. 22 (May 1954), pp. 139-91.

Lim, David, "Fiscal Incentives and Direct Foreign Investment in Less Developed Countries," *Journal of Development Studies* (London), Vol. 19 (January 1983), pp. 207-12.

———, "Tax Incentives and Resource Utilization in Peninsular Malaysian Manufacturing," in *Further Readings on Malaysian Economic Development*, ed. by David Lim (Kuala Lumpur: Oxford University Press, 1983).

Martin, Alison M., and W.A. Lewis, "Patterns of Public Revenue and Expenditure," *Manchester School of Economic and Social Studies*, Vol. 24 (September 1956), pp. 203-44.

McDonald, D., "The Determinants of Saving Behavior in Latin America" (unpublished, International Monetary Fund, April 13, 1983).

McKinnon, Ronald I., "Foreign Exchange Constraints in Economic Development and Efficient Aid Allocation," *Economic Journal* (London), Vol. 74 (June 1964), pp. 388-409.

———, *Money and Capital in Economic Development* (Washington: Brookings Institution, 1973).

McLure, C.E., Jr., "General Equilibrium Incidence Analysis: The Harberger Model After Ten Years," *Journal of Public Economics* (Amsterdam), Vol. 4 (February 1975), pp. 125-61.

Mieszkowski, Peter, "Tax Incidence Theory: The Effects of Taxes on the Distribution of Income," *Journal of Economic Literature* (Nashville, Tennessee), Vol. 7 (December 1969), pp. 1103-24.

Mikesell, Raymond F., and James E. Zinser, "The Nature of the Savings Function in Developing Countries: A Survey of the Theoretical and Empirical Literature," *Journal of Economic Literature* (Nashville, Tennessee), Vol. 11 (March 1973), pp. 1-26.

Miracle, Marvin P., "Interpretation of Backward-sloping Labor Supply Curves in Africa," *Economic Development and Cultural Change* (Chicago), Vol. 24 (January 1976), pp. 399-406.

———, and Bruce Fetter, "Backward-sloping Labor-Supply Functions and African Economic Behavior," *Economic Development and Cultural Change* (Chicago), Vol. 18 (January 1970), pp. 240-51.

Miracle, Marvin P., Diane S. Miracle, and Laurie Cohen, "Informal Savings Mobilization in Africa," *Economic Development and Cultural Change* (Chicago), Vol. 28 (July 1980), pp. 701-24.

Modigliani, Franco, and Richard Brumberg, "Utility Analysis and the Consumption Function: An Interpretation of Cross-Section Data," in *Post Keynesian Economics*, ed. by Kenneth K. Kurihara (New Brunswick, New Jersey: Rutgers University Press, 1954).

Morss, Elliott R., "Fiscal Policy, Savings, and Economic Growth in Developing Countries: An Empirical Study" (unpublished, International Monetary Fund, July 17, 1968).

Newbery, David M.G. and Joseph E. Stiglitz, *The Theory of Commodity Price Stabilization: A Study in the Economics of Risk* (Oxford: Clarendon Press; New York: Oxford University Press, 1981).

Papanek, Gustav F., "The Effects of Aid and Other Resource Transfers on Savings and Growth in Less Developed Countries," *Economic Journal* (London), Vol. 82 (September 1972), pp. 934-50.

———, "Aid, Foreign Private Investment, Savings, and Growth in Less Developed Countries," *Journal of Political Economy* (Chicago), Vol. 81 (January/February 1973), pp. 120-30.

Please, S., "Saving Through Taxation—Reality or Mirage?" *Finance & Development* (Washington), Vol. 4 (March 1967), pp. 24-32.

———, "The 'Please Effect' Revisited," International Bank for Reconstruction and Development (World Bank), Working Paper No. 82 (July 1970).

Ram, Rati, and Theodore W. Schultz, "Life Span, Health, Savings, and Productivity," *Economic Development and Cultural Change* (Chicago), Vol. 27 (April 1979), pp. 399-421.

Ranis, Gustav, and John C.H. Fei, "A Theory of Economic Development," *American Economic Review* (Nashville, Tennessee), Vol. 51 (September 1961), pp. 533-65.

Root, Franklin R., and Ahmed A. Ahmed, "Empirical Determinants of Manufacturing Direct Foreign Investment in Developing Countries," *Economic Development and Cultural Change* (Chicago), Vol. 27 (July 1979), pp. 751-67.

Rosenzweig, Mark R., "Rural Wages, Labor Supply, and Land Reform: A Theoretical and Empirical Analysis," *American Economic Review* (Nashville, Tennessee), Vol. 68 (December 1978), pp. 847-61.

———, "Neoclassical Theory and the Optimizing Peasant—An Econometric Analysis of Market Family Labor Supply in a Developing Country," *Quarterly Journal of Economics* (Cambridge, Massachusetts), Vol. 94 (February 1980), pp. 31-56.

Schultz, T. Paul, "Lifetime Migration Within Educational Strata in Venezuela: Estimates of a Logistic Model," *Economic Development and Cultural Change* (Chicago), Vol. 30 (April 1982), pp. 559-93.

Sen, Amartya K., "Peasants and Dualism with or without Surplus Labor," *Journal of Political Economy* (Chicago), Vol. 74 (October 1966), pp. 425-50.

Shaw, Edward S., *Financial Deepening in Economic Development* (New York: Oxford University Press, 1973).

Snyder, Donald W., "Econometric Studies of Household Saving Behaviour in Developing Countries: A Survey," *Journal of Development Studies* (London), Vol. 10 (January 1974), pp. 139-53.

Song, Byung-Nak, "Empirical Research on Consumption Behavior: Evidence from Rich and Poor LDCs," *Economic Development and Cultural Change* (Chicago), Vol. 29 (April 1981), pp. 597-611.

Spellman, Lewis J., "Economic Growth and Financial Intermediation," in *Money and Finance in Economic Growth and Development: Essays in Honor of Edward S. Shaw: Proceedings of the Conference Held at Stanford University*, ed. by Ronald I. McKinnon (New York: Dekker, 1976).

Starr, Gerald, "Minimum Wage Fixing: International Experience with Alternative Roles," *International Labor Review* (Geneva), Vol. 120 (September-October 1981), pp. 545-62.

Stiglitz, Joseph E., "Taxation, Corporate Financial Policy, and the Cost of Capital," *Journal of Public Economics* (Amsterdam), Vol. 2 (February 1973), pp. 1-34.

———, "The Corporation Tax," *Journal of Public Economics* (Amsterdam), Vol. 5 (April-May 1976), pp. 303-11.

Stoneman, Colin, "Foreign Capital and Economic Growth," *World Development* (Oxford), Vol. 3 (January 1975), pp. 11-26.

Sumner, Daniel, A., "Wage Functions and Occupational Selection in a Rural Less Developed Country Setting," *Review of Economics and Statistics* (Cambridge, Massachusetts), Vol. 63 (November 1981), pp. 513-19.

Sundararajan, V., and Subhash Thakur, "Public Investment, Crowding Out, and Growth: A Dynamic Model Applied to India and Korea," *Staff Papers*, International Monetary Fund (Washington), Vol. 27 (December 1980), pp. 814-55.

Tahari, Amor, "The Impact of Taxation on Saving and Consumption in Developing Countries: A Paradox?" (unpublished, International Monetary Fund, March 29, 1979).

Tanzi, Vito, "Export Taxation in Developing Countries: Taxation of Coffee in Haiti," *Social and Economic Studies* (Kingston, Jamaica), Vol. 25 (March 1976), pp. 66-76.

———, "Tax Policy in Middle-Income Countries: Some Lessons of Experience," *Bulletin*, International Bureau of Fiscal Documentation (Amsterdam), Vol. 36 (August/September 1982), pp. 411-20.

———, "Quantitative Characteristics of the Tax Systems of Developing Countries," in *The Theory of Taxation for Developing Countries*, ed. by David Newbery and Nicholas Stern (New York: Oxford University Press, 1987).

Teilhet-Waldorf, Saral, and William H. Waldorf, "Earnings of Self-Employed in an Informal Sector: A Case Study of Bangkok," *Economic Development and Cultural Change* (Chicago), Vol. 31 (April 1983), pp. 587-607.

Thimmaiah, G., "Taxation and Government Consumption," International Bureau of Fiscal Documentation, *Bulletin* (Amsterdam), Vol. 31 (December 1977), pp. 551-57.

Thirlwall, A.P., *Inflation, Saving and Growth in Developing Economies* (London: Macmillan; New York: St. Martin's, 1974).

Tolley, George S., Vinod Thomas, and Chung Ming Wong, *Agricultural Price Policies and the Developing Countries* (Baltimore: Johns Hopkins University Press, 1982).

Tun Wai, U, "A Revisit to Interest Rates Outside the Organized Money Markets of Underdeveloped Countries," *Quarterly Review*, Banca Nazionale del Lavoro (Rome), Vol. 30 (September 1977), pp. 291-312.

———, and Chorng-huey Wong, "Determinants of Private Investment in Developing Countries," *Journal of Development Studies* (London), Vol. 19 (October 1982), pp. 19-36.

Usher, Dan, "The Economics of Tax Incentives to Encourage Investment in Less Developed Countries," *Journal of Development Economics* (Amsterdam), Vol. 4 (June 1977), pp. 119-48.

Vandendorpe, A.L., and A.F. Friedlaender, "Differential Incidence in the Presence of Initial Distorting Taxes," *Journal of Public Economics* (Amsterdam), Vol. 6 (October 1976), pp. 205-29.

van Wijnbergen, S., "Interest Rate Management in LDC's," *Journal of Monetary Economics* (Amsterdam), Vol. 12 (September 1983), pp. 433-52.

Vogel, Robert C., and Stephen A. Buser, "Inflation, Financial Repression, and Capital Formation in Latin America," in *Money and Finance in Economic Growth and Development: Essays in Honor of Edward S. Shaw: Proceedings of the Conference Held at Stanford University*, ed., by Ronald I. McKinnon (New York: Dekker, 1976).

Watanabe, Susumu, "Minimum Wages in Developing Countries: Myth and Reality," *International Labor Review* (Geneva), Vol. 113 (May-June 1976), pp. 345-58.

Weisskopf, Thomas E. (1972a), "An Econometric Test of Alternative Constraints on the Growth of Underdeveloped Countries," *Review of Economics and Statistics* (Cambridge, Massachusetts), Vol. 54 (February 1972), pp. 67-78.

——— (1972b), "The Impact of Foreign Capital Inflow on Domestic Savings in Underdeveloped Countries," *Journal of International Economics* (Amsterdam), Vol. 2 (February 1972), pp. 25-38.

Williamson, Jeffrey G., "Public Expenditure and Revenue: An International Comparison," *Manchester School of Economic and Social Studies*, Vol. 29 (January 1961), pp. 34-56.

———, "Personal Saving in Developing Nations: An Intertemporal Cross-Section from Asia," *Economic Record* (Melbourne), Vol. 44 (March 1968), pp. 194-210.

World Bank, *World Development Report, 1983* (New York: Oxford University Press, 1983).

Wynn, R.F., "Foreign Capital, Trade and Savings: The Sudan 1955-71," *The Malayan Economic Review* (Singapore), Vol. 25 (October 1980), pp. 14-29.

Yap, Lorene Y.L, "Rural-Urban Migration and Urban Underemployment in Brazil," *Journal of Development Economics* (Amsterdam), Vol. 3 (September 1976), pp. 227-43.

———, "The Attraction of Cities: A Review of the Migration Literature," *Journal of Development Economics* (Amsterdam), Vol. 4 (September 1977), pp. 239-64.

4

Optimal Taxation of Financial Savings in Developing Countries

Relevance of Supply-Side Tax Policies

Liam P. Ebrill

This chapter evaluates, for the case of developing countries, the potential impact of supply-side proposals for stimulating savings. Some supply-side economists argue, in the context of developed economies, that the interaction of inflation and high marginal rates of income taxation is such as to imply a serious disincentive to savings. Thus, they recommend sharp reductions in marginal tax rates.[1] If applied to developing countries, would such reductions be either desirable or lead to a pronounced increase in savings?

In examining these issues, this chapter concentrates on savings channeled through organized financial markets. This emphasis can be justified on a number of grounds, of which three are worth special mention. First, it is often argued that, while aggregate savings are generally not very sensitive to changes in the net rate of return, that is not the case with individual components such as financial savings in organized markets, since changes in the rate of return that can be earned on any one form of savings can be expected to induce significant shifts into substitute assets. Second, organized financial markets are often central to the efficient allocation of available funds. Third, and particularly important given the supply-side perspective of our analysis, the specific disaggregation of aggregate savings employed here is useful precisely because the components can be distinguished by whether they represent savings in organized as opposed to unorganized financial markets. Since supply-side proposals for reform are typically directed at lowering high marginal rates of income taxation, the most

[1]This begs the question of whether a more direct response would be to index for inflation.

immediate effect of these proposals in developing countries will be on those savings placed in the organized rather than the unorganized money markets.

This chapter first describes the financial markets in developing countries as the backdrop against which the appropriateness of supply-side proposals are evaluated. Particular attention is devoted to the significance of financial repression, an indicator of which is the policy of institutionally setting nominal interest rates at artificially low levels. The low (indeed, negative) real rates of return that result induce asset holders to shift out of assets issued by organized financial markets into investments that are less productive, such as gold and housing. Should this effect be empirically significant, it has important implications for this study given the study's concentration on savings behavior in organized financial markets.

Given this background, what are the appropriate tax reform policies? The chapter begins with a discussion of the reform proposals of the traditional public finance theorists. It is argued that the existing optimal tax literature does not adequately accommodate the circumstances of developing countries. A modified optimal tax framework is suggested. The results of this exercise are contrasted with the recommendations of the supply-side school. The conclusion is that, while not necessarily incorrect, the proposals of the supply-side school are deficient in that they do not take account of the heterogeneity of developing countries. This is a deficiency they share with the traditional public finance literature. Specifically, the modified optimal tax framework developed in this chapter suggests that, depending on the particular country under consideration, the optimal tax treatment of financial savings runs the gamut from subsidies to substantial taxation.

All of the above treats the problem from a microeconomic perspective. It is also pointed out, however, that the ramifications of financial repression extend to macroeconomic policy, a factor that should be acknowledged in any study of tax policy in this area.

The traditional public finance literature, the supply-side approach, and the modified optimal tax framework developed here do, however, share a common theme: appropriate tax rates should depend on the sensitivity of savings behavior to changes in the rate of return.

I. Institutional Background

Any tax reform recommendations must take account of the economic environment in which the reform takes place. The financial structures of developing countries have a number of features that, although not unique to these countries, are held to be more widely experienced by them. While this is undoubtedly correct, it should also be kept in mind, as these features are introduced and discussed, that the degree to which any feature is relevant varies greatly from country to country. As argued later, this variability has important implications for tax policy.

First, financial institutions in many developing countries tend not to be well developed (cf., Miracle, Miracle, and Cohen (1980)). This has a number of implications. In particular, McKinnon (1973) argued that in developing countries, investors are constrained to using self-finance and that investments are relatively lumpy. As a result, investors must accumulate money balances prior to their investments, leading to the hypothesis that the aggregate demand for money will be greater, the larger is the share of investment in total expenditures. (This is McKinnon's complementarity hypothesis.)

Second, it has often been pointed out that in many developing countries, interest rates on assets in organized markets are often set at low nominal rates given the rate of inflation (see Galbis (1979)). A large body of literature exists in which it is argued that such institutional restraints can only result in financial repression (Shaw (1973), McKinnon (1973)).[2] The existence of these interest rate ceilings, it is held, leads to a reduced supply of financial savings to organized markets, as savers turn to alternative nonproductive investments such as property and precious metals. Depending on foreign exchange market conditions, savings may even be placed overseas. These effects, it is argued, require some type of investment rationing mechanism.

Financial repression may not only result in portfolio reallocations out of organized financial markets but may also influence short-run macroeconomic developments in many developing countries. Specifically, Leff and Sato (1980) identify a couple of macroeconomic implications. First, ex ante investment will tend to exceed ex ante savings. Second, and more important for short-run policy, interest rates cannot be used to maintain equilibrium in the savings-investment market. They argue that investment tends to be relatively more buoyant than savings with the concomitant possibility of instability. Price-level movements and foreign capital flows then become central to absorbing shocks. The general conclusion is that inflation and dependency on foreign capital inflows are structurally rooted in many developing countries.

A third distinctive feature of financial markets in some developing countries is that investors enjoy the existence of unorganized curb markets (van

[2]Tables 1 and 2 in the Annex show that financial repression varies both across countries and across time. The phenomenon is not as prevalent today as formerly. However, that only serves to emphasize the heterogeneity of developing country financial policies.

Wijnbergen (1983a) and Buffie (1984)).[3] By emphasizing the role of curb markets for portfolio allocation decisions in developing countries, van Wijnbergen questions the presumption that the alternative asset to financial holdings in organized markets must consist of nonproductive investments. Instead, it may consist of holdings of financial assets issued in unorganized money markets of the curb market type (van Wijnbergen (1983b)). This possibility alters the implications of financial repression for economic policy. For example, an increase in interest rates in organized markets may no longer result in the "free lunch" of financial flows attracted from nonproductive sources, but may instead lead to a general increase in the working cost of capital faced by firms. Further, the central governments of many developing countries exercise a major claim on savings channeled through organized money markets. If such governments invest less efficiently than the private sector, an increase in interest rates then achieves the ambiguous result of alleviating the distortion faced by savers at the expense of exacerbating the distortion associated with inappropriate government investment decisions.

A fourth and final characteristic is that many developing country governments employ compulsory savings schemes.[4] For example, Shome and Squire (1983) point out that some Asian countries such as Malaysia, Sri Lanka, and Singapore have, in varying degrees, funded social security systems.

Given that the above features are not uniformly experienced, they also serve to emphasize the heterogeneity of developing country circumstances. In view of the prominence it has attained in the economic literature, the following assessment of supply-side tax proposals will concentrate on the

[3]How important are these curb markets? Tun Wai (1977) argues that the ratio of total agricultural or rural indebtedness to the claims of the banking system on the private sector is the best index of the size of unorganized money markets relative to that of the organized money market. By that criterion, he concludes that for India, Nepal, and Pakistan the unorganized markets are larger than the organized markets. (The data he collects refers to 1969/70, 1970, and 1971, respectively.) He finds that, in general, these markets are less important in those Latin American and Middle Eastern countries for which data were available. Chandavarkar (1971) confirmed these results for India, while, of course, the importance of curb markets in Korea has long been recognized (see, for example, Williamson (1979)). On this last case, van Wijnbergen (1982) uncovered evidence, some indirect, to the effect that increased savings are mainly channeled into the curb market over time. Specifically, he discovered that wealth effects were not significant in his M2 demand equations. Since financial assets assuredly have positive wealth elasticities in the aggregate, curb markets must have been the beneficiary of increased wealth.

[4]From the perspective of this study, long-term schemes such as compulsory funded social security systems are the most important. However, as documented by Prest (1969), many countries have also resorted to shorter-term schemes.

particular role played by financial repression. An optimal tax framework will be developed that will explicitly allow for such a phenomenon. The robustness of this framework will then be assessed in light of the other structural features of developing country capital markets just discussed. The framework will also form a basis for evaluating the relevance of supply-side tax policies as they apply to savings. Even at this stage, however, there is already the sense that the heterogeneity of the financial systems of developing countries implies that tax changes based on simplistic rules of thumb are unlikely to be appropriate.

II. Evaluation of Reform Proposals

The recent supply-side literature is large. However, perhaps out of a desire to make politically feasible tax policy recommendations, the actual number of recommendations contained in that literature is quite small. Though not bearing directly on the savings issue, the best known are those associated with the Laffer curve, especially that high marginal tax rates should be sharply reduced. This type of recommendation has not been made solely with the United States in mind, however; Wanniski (1983), for example, argues for the relevance of the Laffer curve for a number of developing countries (see Ebrill (Chapter 7)).

More generally, it would appear to be in the spirit of the supply-side approach to say that they favor tax cuts aimed at stimulating (private) savings. This, of course, begs the question of the adequacy of the pre-existing level of savings. Presumably the supply-siders believe that aggregate savings are depressed in the first place due to the existence of the tax system and other distortions. In fact, there is general agreement that savings in developing countries are low in relation to investment needs.

Summary of Theoretical Literature

One way of evaluating the supply-side approach is to contrast its recommendations on savings with those of the more traditional public finance literature. In particular, there are a number of papers that address the issue of how to tax savings.[5] The orientation of this literature has been to determine whether the tax base should be income or expenditure (consumption). Among the earlier commentators on this question, Mill (1921) argued for a consumption base, not so much on efficiency as on equity

[5]This issue is logically different from that of how best to stimulate savings. However, to the extent that the literature provides qualitative results, it does provide a benchmark against which the desirability of stimulating savings can be weighed.

grounds—income taxes tend to favor those who derive their income from wealth rather than work effort. More recently, the consumption base received further support in the work of Kaldor (1955), who argued for an expenditure tax on both efficiency and equity grounds.

Even more recently optimal tax theorists sought to resolve this question by considering solely the efficiency implications. Their solution lay initially in a simple extension of the optimal commodity tax literature. Thus, Feldstein (1978) gives the static framework associated with that literature an intertemporal flavor by labeling consumption in different periods as different commodities. A two-period life-cycle model is postulated. The consumer is then assumed to allocate his endowment across leisure (which is untaxable), first-period consumption, and second-period consumption. In general, since leisure cannot be taxed, second-best theory suggests that it is optimal to violate all first-order conditions. There are circumstances in which a consumption tax is optimal—as when a compensated change in the wage rate induces the same proportional changes in consumption in the two periods.[6] This type of result suggests that in general neither a consumption tax nor an income tax will be optimal—it will in most cases be preferable to have separate tax rates on savings and consumption.

This inconclusiveness in the optimal tax literature is reinforced by more recent work. For example, Atkinson and Sandmo (1980) develop an explicit overlapping generations growth model and demonstrate that the Feldstein type of analysis can be generated within that framework if the government possesses a range of additional instruments, such as an unconstrained debt policy, to achieve the desired intertemporal allocation where the steady-state marginal product of capital equals the discount rate. They then consider the optimal tax solution in a second-best world where the government cannot attain the first-best intertemporal equilibrium. This part of their analysis is of more interest to this paper since, as pointed out above, the supply-side concern with stimulating savings is presumably predicated on a belief that the capital stock is inadequate. The Feldstein approach, however, assumes that capital markets are efficient and asks whether savings should or should not be taxed in an overall package of taxes levied with a view to raising a given amount of revenue with minimum excess burden. Unfortunately, even when it is known that the capital stock is below its "first-best" level, the effect of the recommended tax sys-

[6]This is implicitly an implication of the Ramsey Rule (Ebrill and Slutsky (1983)). Under the circumstances laid out by Feldstein (1978), a labor income tax is optimal and is equivalent to a uniform consumption tax and vice versa. Accordingly, a consumption tax is all that is required to guarantee a compensated proportionate reduction in all distortable commodities where this is precisely a statement of the Ramsey Rule.

tem remains ambiguous. Indeed, in the specific Cobb-Douglas example they consider, Atkinson and Sandmo (1980) point out that a tax on capital income is desirable, a result that depends on the shape of the aggregate savings function.

In the absence of qualitative results concerning the optimal treatment of savings, some authors have taken the more pragmatic route of parameterizing general equilibrium models and then evaluating the advisability of various tax reform proposals. For example, Fullerton, Shoven, and Whalley (1983) use a dynamic numerical general equilibrium model of the U.S. economy to determine the welfare implications of substituting a progressive consumption tax for the current income tax structure. The initial effect is that individuals consume less. The welfare changes are influenced by both the transition and the steady-state balanced growth paths. Notwithstanding the initial drop in consumption, the net effect of the tax change is welfare-enhancing. Of course, the outcome depends on the precise parameters, as is evident from the range of opinions on the magnitude of the transition costs implied by this type of tax change (Auerbach and Kotlikoff (1983), Seidman (1984)). Nonetheless, there appears to be growing interest in the proposition that, within the context of the models employed, consumption is a more appropriate base for taxation than income.

The main thrust of this chapter is not to evaluate the conclusions of the optimal tax literature concerning the appropriate treatment of aggregate savings but to determine the implications of supply-side policies for financial savings, where the latter are a component of aggregate savings. While the traditional public finance literature has not explicitly addressed the optimal tax treatment of this component, those papers concerned with determining the optimal rate of inflation are relevant. Inflation is viewed as a tax on money balances, which is a component of financial savings. Beginning with Phelps (1973) and Siegel (1978), it has been argued that a positive tax on liquidity (a positive rate of inflation) is in general desirable, on the principle that the demand for all taxable goods ought to be proportionately reduced (the Ramsey Rule). Subsequent writers have pointed out that, along lines analogous to those taken by Atkinson and Sandmo (1980) above, the economy need not be on the golden-rule path. Since inflation can affect the long-run capital intensity of the economy, its impact on this pre-existing distortion should be accommodated (Summers (1981)). Further, it is argued that account should be taken of the fact that money is costless to produce (Drazen (1979)). As might be expected, since the outcome depends both on the degree to which other distortions are recognized and on the empirical magnitude of numerous own- and cross-price derivatives, there are no unambiguous qualitative conclusions. In addition, as has already been pointed out, neither stream of the optimal tax literature (i.e., that pertaining to aggregate savings and that to money balances) is directly applicable to circumstances in the developing world.

An Optimal Tax Framework for Financial Savings in Developing Countries

Given the deficiencies of the existing optimal tax literature, an alternative, also highly simplified, optimal tax model is developed below, which incorporates certain salient features of the financial structures of developing countries as described earlier. In particular, financial repression is explicitly allowed for, in a framework in which the rate of inflation is assumed to be exogenous. The menu of financial assets available to the representative consumer consists of money for transactions purposes, financial savings deposited in organized money markets, and other savings.[7] Financial repression is allowed for in the form of pre-existing distortions on both money and financial savings.

The model does not allow for the fact that money for transactions purposes is costless to produce. This is not a serious problem since our purpose is to determine the optimal tax treatment of financial savings other than money (M1), given a rate of inflation and a degree of financial repression, rather than to determine the optimal rate of inflation. Nor, since it uses a static framework, does the model allow for the possibility of a further distortion due to the typical economy being below the golden-rule path. However, while such an effect will in general alter the magnitudes of the optimal tax changes, it is unlikely to change their direction. This point will be discussed in greater detail.

The important notations used in the model are defined below.

C_0 = consumption of leisure;
C_1 = consumption of current goods and services;
C_2 = consumption stream associated with nonfinancial savings;
C_3 = consumption stream associated with financial savings other than financial savings for transactions purposes;
C_4 = consumption stream associated with financial savings for transactions purposes (M1);
B = government's net revenue requirement;
t_i = ad valorem tax rate on C_i;
$\bar{t}_i$ = pre-existing proportional distortion on C_i, $i = 3, 4$;
P_i = market price of C_i;
θ_i = share of tax in total price of C_i;
α = share of financial savings (C_3) mediated through the government;

[7] Other savings can include savings held abroad.

η_{ij} = compensated elasticity of demand for C_i with respect to P_j;
μ = multiplier on the government's budget constraint; and
λ = private marginal utility of income.

The underlying methodology of this type of exercise is well known (cf., Atkinson and Stiglitz (1980)). Accordingly, where possible, the explanation below will concentrate on aspects of the formulation that are unique to the problem at hand. Specifically, there are five commodities, including leisure (C_0), where leisure is untaxable. Of the other commodities, C_4 is a proxy for the consumption stream a typical consumer obtains from financial wealth held for transactions purposes. The underlying stock that provides this consumption stream is assumed to be M1. C_3 refers to the remainder of financial savings. It is assumed that organized money markets act as intermediaries, so that these savings are productively invested. Accordingly, C_3 is best viewed as a proxy for the consumption stream that results from that investment. As for the investment itself, a proportion, α, is financed by the government via borrowing. This proportion is assumed to be subject to government manipulation, implying that the private sector is a residual investor. C_2 refers to the consumption stream that results from the disposition of the remainder of aggregate savings. It might be useful to view this in terms of the "consumption" of owner-occupied housing, works of art, and so on. Finally, C_1 is a variable representing the aggregate of current consumption. Given this structure, it is clear, as pointed out above, that this exercise does not accommodate the intertemporal investment dimensions of the problem or the fact that M1 is costless to produce. It is not a true general equilibrium exercise. Instead, the very fact that the variables should be viewed as proxies indicates the illustrative nature of the framework. However, this illustrative nature can be defended on the grounds that the model may nonetheless yield useful qualitative insights.

The market environment assumed for this exercise, in common with most other optimal tax exercises, presumes competitive behavior on the part of private firms and consumers. The formulation of the consumer's problem requires some elaboration. Since the paper is concerned with economic efficiency rather than equity, the general equilibrium structure is set in the context of a representative price-taking individual who has a twice continuously differentiable, monotonic, strictly quasi-concave, utility function $U(C_0, C_1, C_2, C_3, C_4)$. The consumer's maximization problem is

$$\underset{C_0, \ldots, C_4}{Max}\ U(C_0, C_1, C_2, C_3, C_4)$$

$$\text{s.t. } \sum_{i=1}^{4} P_i C_i = P_0(\bar{C}_0 - C_0) + (1 - \alpha)\bar{t}_3 C_3,$$

where $\bar{C}_0 - C_0$ is labor supplied and the other variables are as defined above. The last term in the budget constraint requires explanation. The widespread use of interest rate ceilings is in the present context modeled as a pre-existing tax on C_3 ($\bar{t}_3$). Some of the implicit revenue from this tax accrues to elements of the private sector, to the extent that the government only borrows some of the available financial savings. This quantity is gauged by the final term above. However, in order to avoid unnecessary complications, it is assumed that the representative consumer responds to the gross rather than the net price of C_3—that is, this income is modeled as lump-sum income.[8] Accordingly, the consumer's first-order conditions are

$$\frac{\partial U}{\partial C_i} = \lambda P_i, \qquad i = 0, \ldots, 4.$$

Consider the government's maximization problem. The nature of the optimal tax exercise is critically dependent on the constraints placed on the range and flexibility of policy instruments at the disposal of the authorities. In the case under consideration, two constraints are important. The first, already mentioned, is that interest rates on financial assets are institutionally fixed and that the rate of inflation is not readily amenable to control. The net effect of this is modeled as pre-existing taxes on both C_3 and C_4. The second constraint comes from the assumption that the consumption stream associated with investment in owner-occupied housing etc. (C_2) is not taxed. (This could be due to administration costs.) The government's objective is then to raise a required amount of revenue, some of which is levied by the pre-existing "inflation taxes," given that the only variables under its control are the tax rates on C_3 and C_1, the latter being a consumption tax.[9] This can be expressed as follows:

$$\underset{t_1,\, t_3}{Max}\; U(C_0, C_1, C_2, C_3, C_4) \tag{1}$$

$$\text{s.t. } t_1C_1 + t_3C_3 + \alpha\bar{t}_3C_3 + \bar{t}_4C_4 = B\colon \mu,$$

where $\bar{t}_4 = \bar{t}_3 + \partial$, $\partial > 0$, constant, in recognition of the fact that the inflation tax on C_4 is greater than that on C_3 given that cash balances pay a zero nominal interest rate. Differentiating, and substituting for the con-

[8] This treatment avoids the complications associated with the existence of profit income influencing firm behavior at the margin (Munk (1978)). It also avoids complications that might arise from noncompetitive producer behavior.

[9] Note that all variables are defined in real terms. The economy is assumed to be in an initial equilibrium where there is a positive underlying rate of inflation with all relative prices being constant. The tax changes are assumed not to affect the underlying rate of inflation.

sumer's first-order conditions, the following first-order conditions are immediate:

$$\lambda \sum_{i=0}^{4} P_i \frac{\partial C_i}{\partial P_1} + \mu \left[C_1 + \sum_{i=1,3} t_i \frac{\partial C_i}{\partial P_1} \right.$$
$$\left. + \left(\alpha \bar{t}_3 + \bar{t}_3 \frac{\partial \alpha}{\partial C_3} \right) \frac{\partial C_3}{\partial P_1} + \bar{t}_4 \frac{\partial C_4}{\partial P_1} \right] = 0 \tag{2a}$$

$$\lambda \sum_{i=0}^{4} P_i \frac{\partial C_i}{\partial P_3} + \mu \left[C_3 + \sum_{i=1,3} t_i \frac{\partial C_i}{\partial P_3} \right.$$
$$\left. + \left(\alpha \bar{t}_3 + \bar{t}_3 \frac{\partial \alpha}{\partial C_3} \right) \frac{\partial C_3}{\partial P_3} + \bar{t}_4 \frac{\partial C_4}{\partial P_3} \right] = 0. \tag{2b}$$

Note the inclusion of a term in $\partial\alpha/\partial C_3$ (<0) in recognition of the fact that a reduction in C_3 (say) may in general be expected to result in the government increasing its share of financial savings. A more complete exercise in an intertemporal framework would employ a broader government budget constraint incorporating, in addition, the optimal trade-off between borrowing and taxation. This is not attempted here.[10]

Differentiating the individual's budget constraint with respect to P_i, $i = 1, 3$, respectively, and substituting, allows one to re-express equations (2a) and (2b) as follows:

$$-\lambda \left[C_j - \left\{ (1-\alpha) - \frac{\partial \alpha}{\partial C_3} \right\} \bar{t}_3 \frac{\partial C_3}{\partial P_j} \right] + \mu \left[C_j + \sum_{i=1,3} t_i \frac{\partial C_i}{\partial P_j} \right.$$
$$\left. + \left(\alpha + \frac{\partial \alpha}{\partial C_3} \right) \bar{t}_3 \frac{\partial C_3}{\partial P_j} + \bar{t}_4 \frac{\partial C_4}{\partial P_j} \right] = 0. \quad j = 1, 3 \tag{3}$$

Substitute for the Slutsky equation into total demands $\partial C_i/\partial P_j$, where I refers to private income and S_{ij} is the compensated substitution effect of commodity i with respect to a change in the price of commodity j. Further, assume that the general equilibrium income effect associated with $\partial C_3/\partial P_j$ can be set equal to zero. Equation (3) becomes

$$\lambda \left[C_j - \left\{ (1-\alpha) - \frac{\partial \alpha}{\partial C_3} \right\} \bar{t}_3 S_{3j} \right] +$$

[10]Note that such a framework would also make the consumer's maximization problem more dynamic.

$$\mu C_j \left[\sum_{i=1,3} t_i \frac{\partial C_i}{\partial I} + \left(\alpha + \frac{\partial \alpha}{\partial C_3} \right) \bar{t}_3 \frac{\partial C_3}{\partial I} + \bar{t}_4 \frac{\partial C_4}{\partial I} \right]$$

$$= \mu \left[C_j + \sum_{i=1,3} t_i S_{ij} + \left(\alpha + \frac{\partial \alpha}{\partial C_3} \right) \bar{t}_3 S_{3j} + \bar{t}_4 S_{4j} \right].$$

$$j = 1, 3 \quad (4)$$

These equations are analogous to the first-order conditions of the traditional optimal commodity tax literature with the caveat that the equations here incorporate terms in the pre-existing distortions, $\bar{t}_i$ (e.g., Sandmo (1976)). To this point, they lack qualitative content as far as the optimal tax rates are concerned. To alleviate this, some structure can be placed on the magnitude of some of the substitution terms by considering the context of this exercise. Specifically, given the level of aggregation, the utility function is assumed to be separable between C_1 and C_i, $i = 2, 3, 4$. The net effect of this assumption is that $S_{1j} = 0$ for $j = 3, 4$. Using symmetry ($S_{ij} = S_{ji}$) and expressing in terms of elasticities, equation (4) becomes, respectively,

$$\nu = \theta_1 \eta_{11} \tag{5}$$

$$\nu = \left[\left\{ \frac{\lambda(1 - \alpha) + \mu\alpha}{\mu} \right\} \bar{\theta}_3 + \theta_3 \right] \eta_{33} + \bar{\theta}_4 \eta_{34} + \frac{\mu - \lambda}{\mu} \frac{\partial \alpha}{\partial C_3} \bar{\theta}_3 \eta_{33}, \tag{6}$$

where

$$\nu = \frac{\lambda - \mu}{\mu} + \left[\sum_{i=1,3} t_i \frac{\partial C_i}{\partial I} + \left(\alpha + \frac{\partial \alpha}{\partial C_3} \right) \bar{t}_3 \frac{\partial C_3}{\partial I} + \bar{t}_4 \frac{\partial C_4}{\partial I} \right]$$

and can be assumed to be negative by the negative definiteness of the substitution matrix. θ_1, θ_3, $\bar{\theta}_3$, $\bar{\theta}_4$ are the relevant shares.[11]

It is clear from equation (6) that the traditional Ramsey Rule, calling for compensated proportional reductions in those markets that are distortable, must be altered in light of the terms in pre-existing distortions. The Ramsey Rule is a statement about quantities. The concern here is with prices. What are the optimal tax rates t_1 and t_3? By equation (5), given the zero cross-price effects between C_1 and other distortable commodities, the

[11]Care should be taken in interpreting θ_3 and $\bar{\theta}_3$. $\theta_3 = t_3/P_3$, while $\bar{\theta}_3 = \bar{t}_3/P_3$, where P_3 is inclusive of the pre-existing distortion. Thus, for the new (derivative) distortions, the shares are in terms of original prices, whereas, for the pre-existing distortions, they are expressed in terms of final prices.

inverse elasticity rule holds—the larger the absolute value of η_{11} the smaller the value of θ_1 (and hence, t_1).

The determination of t_3, the optimal tax rate on financial savings, is of greater interest for this paper. The magnitude (and sign) of t_3, as is clear from equation (6), are influenced by a number of factors in addition to own- and cross-price elasticities. These factors are all a function of the pre-existing distortions, $\bar{\theta}_3$ and $\bar{\theta}_4$. The term in $\bar{\theta}_4$ is obvious. To the extent that the cross-price effect between C_3 and C_4 is nonzero, any change in the price of C_3 will interact with the pre-existing distortion on C_4. This interaction should be allowed for, and is elaborated on below.

To see how the pre-existing distortions on C_3 affect θ_3, collect the terms in $\bar{\theta}_3$. These are

$$\left[\frac{\lambda(1-\alpha)+\mu\alpha}{\mu}+\frac{\mu-\lambda}{\mu}\frac{\partial\alpha}{\partial C_3}\right]\eta_{33}\equiv\left[\gamma+\frac{\mu-\lambda}{\mu}\frac{\partial\alpha}{\partial C_3}\right]\eta_{33}. \tag{7}$$

The first term is a weighted average of the distortion on C_3 where the weights are the shares of C_3 invested by the private sector and the government, respectively. The weights are valued at λ, the private marginal utility of income, and μ, the social marginal utility of income, respectively. This reflects the fact that the cost of the distortion varies depending on whether it is mediated through the private or the public sector.

The second term reflects the impact of changes in the share of C_3 mediated through the government sector. It is negative, since $\partial\alpha/\partial C_3 < 0$ and $\mu > \lambda$ where the latter is due to the excess burden associated with government intervention. Thus, this term mitigates the effects associated with θ_3. The intuition is that $\bar{\theta}_3$ is a pre-existing distortion. The larger in absolute value is the magnitude of $\partial\alpha/\partial C_3$, the more will this distortion or tax be used to finance governnment activities, thereby reducing the need on the part of the government to rely on other taxes.[12]

Some further insight into the value of t_3 can be gained by appealing to homogeneity, namely,

$$\sum_{j=0}^{4}\eta_{ij}=0. \tag{8}$$

Given that $\eta_{31}=0$ by assumption, and substituting, it follows that equation (6) can be re-expressed as

[12]This immediately raises the issues of why the government does not absorb all of C_3 from the outset ($\alpha = 1$). It is assumed that there are some constraints on the government and that, further, the authorities may well view interest rate ceilings as a device for subsidizing private investment.

$$\nu = -\left[\left(\gamma + \frac{\mu - \lambda}{\mu}\frac{\partial\alpha}{\partial C_3}\right)\bar{\theta}_3 + \theta_3\right](\eta_{32} + \eta_{30})$$

$$+ \left[\bar{\theta}_4 - \left(\gamma + \frac{\mu - \lambda}{\mu}\frac{\partial\alpha}{\partial C_3}\right)\bar{\theta}_3 - \theta_3\right]\eta_{34}. \quad (9)$$

The value of θ_3 (i.e., t_3) remains, in general, ambiguous. However, one of the terms in equation (9), namely that in η_{34}, can be assumed to be small. Thus $\bar{\theta}_4 > \bar{\theta}_3$ and, accordingly, the coefficient of η_{34} may not be large. Further, the absolute magnitude of η_{34} itself may be small. This is the elasticity of financial savings to a change in the rate of return on transactions money. Some analysts, by modeling the transactions demand for money as being a function solely of the level of income, implicitly assume that this elasticity is zero. If this term is ignored, equation (9) reduces to

$$\left[\left(\gamma + \frac{\mu - \lambda}{\mu}\frac{\partial\alpha}{\partial C_3}\right)\bar{\theta}_3 + \theta_3\right] = -\frac{\nu}{\eta_{32} + \eta_{30}}. \quad (10)$$

This expression shows that the magnitude, indeed the sign, of θ_3 depends critically on the magnitudes of $\bar{\theta}_3$ and η_{32}.

From the above, it is clear that, even given a number of (plausible) assumptions concerning the magnitudes of some cross-price effects, the optimal tax treatment of financial savings will depend on the circumstances of the individual country under consideration. Specifically, the above limited exercise suggests two obvious polar cases as a mechanism for summarizing and highlighting the possibilities.

Case I: Absence of Financial Repression

In the absence of financial repression, $\bar{\theta}_3 = 0$ which, together with the assumption that $\eta_{34} = 0$, implies that equations (5) and (6) can be expressed as

$$\nu = \theta_i \eta_{ii} \qquad i = 1, 3, \quad (11)$$

which is a modified Ramsey Rule. To elaborate, as pointed out above, the Ramsey Rule requires that all distortable outputs be reduced proportionately.[13] In general, in a world of nonzero cross-price elasticities, this rule

[13]To be more precise, the Ramsey Rule specifies a reduction along the tangent plane approximation to the compensated demand curve for the good in question due to the distortions. This approximate reduction will equal an actual reduction if the derivatives of the compensated demand curves are constant or if the approximation is taken for small distortions in the neighborhood of zero revenue requirements.

does not hold if there are pre-existing distortions. Pre-existing distortions imply that the output of the goods associated with those distortions has already been reduced. Accordingly, when introducing new distortions, account must be taken of how these affect the equilibrium quantities of the predistorted commodities. Ceteris paribus, the size of a new distortion will tend to be larger if the commodity on which it is levied is a substitute for the goods with the pre-existing distortions. The new distortion will tend to cause demand to shift back into the predistorted goods. This argument holds in reverse for goods that are complements. If the new distortion is to be placed on a good with a pre-existing distortion, the new distortion is by this line of reasoning reduced since any good is the perfect complement of itself.

Turning to the case at hand, since $\bar{\theta}_3$, the pre-existing distortion on financial savings, is zero, one does not have to be concerned, at least within the context of the model, about prior direct reductions in the equilibrium quantity of financial saving. As for the other pre-existing distortion, that on cash balances, $\bar{\theta}_4$, since the cross-price effects between the demand for cash balances and the demand for both financial savings C_3 and consumption C_1 are assumed to be insignificant, one cannot use changes in the "price" of either of the latter two, that is, changes in θ_3 or θ_1, to mitigate the effects of the pre-existing distortion on cash balances. It is in this sense that the outcome is a modified Ramsey Rule. There is no guarantee that the demand for all distortable commodities will be proportionately reduced. Rather, the rule is that the demand for both consumption C_1 and financial savings C_3 be proportionately reduced irrespective of the prior reduction in the demand for cash balances, since the latter is unaffected by the new distortions.

Proceeding from a statement of the optimal outcome in terms of quantities to one in terms of prices, it can be seen from equation (11) that the optimal tax rates depend inversely on the own-price elasticities. Concentrating on the optimal tax treatment of financial savings and using the adding up condition implied by homogeneity, equation (10) becomes

$$\nu = -(\eta_{32} + \eta_{30})\,\theta_3. \tag{12}$$

Thus, the statement that the optimal tax on financial savings depends on the own-price elasticity for financial savings has been restated in terms of cross-price elasticities. In particular, the magnitude of the cross-price elasticity between financial savings, C_3, and savings mediated through unorganized markets, C_2, summarized by η_{32}, is important. For large η_{32}, θ_3 should be small.

The intuition of this result is clear. The efficiency losses associated with the taxation of savings in organized markets are the larger the greater is the sensitivity of savings flows to changes in the relative rates of return to be earned in organized and unorganized money markets.

Case II: Existence of Financial Repression

The optimal tax treatment of consumption, C_1, is unaffected by the existence of financial repression. Since the cross-price elasticity between consumption and financial saving, η_{13}, is taken to be zero, changes in θ_1 have no effect on the demand for financial savings and therefore cannot mitigate the effects of the distortion implied by financial repression.

As for the treatment of financial savings itself, equation (10) now applies. In particular, if the degree of financial repression is large (θ_3 is large) and if the capacity of the government to borrow at the margin at subsidized rates is limited ($\partial\alpha/\partial C_3$ is small), then the pre-existing distortion on C_3 becomes of paramount importance. As a result, θ_3 could easily be negative—a subsidy rather than a tax is appropriate.[14] The intuition for this result lies in the fact that the distortion associated with the existence of financial repression with the concomitant shifting of savings into other assets is such as to imply that the government should counteract it in spite of the revenue loss.

This is an important case since it may apply to many developing countries. If the further constraint of precluding the use of subsidies is imposed, this case implies the interesting result that consumption ($\theta_3 = 0$) is more appropriate than income as a tax base.

Evaluation of Limitations of Optimal Tax Framework

Some further general comments on the relevance and completeness of the above optimal tax modeling exercise are in order. It has already been noted that the model is not a true general equilibrium intertemporal framework. Neither does the model recognize that cash is effectively costless to produce. However, accommodating these discrepancies within a more complete framework is unlikely to change the qualitative results to a great extent. It remains to be considered whether there are other, more significant, discrepancies between the optimal tax framework presented above and the description of the financial structures of developing countries presented in the previous section.

A first observation is that the model has nothing to say about the public

[14]A parallel result can be found in Nellor (1983). In that paper, while considering the positive question of how precisely to counter inflation, he points out that capital income subsidies (or their equivalent in terms of other tax instruments) may well be necessary.

policy implications of whether the alternative asset to organized money market assets consists of precious metals, property, investments held abroad, and so on, or of an unorganized money market asset such as that created by Korea's curb markets. In analytical terms, this appears to be a re-emergence of the question of whether an economy is or is not on its golden-rule path. What individuals view as savings and what constitutes capital from the point of view of society as a whole are not necessarily synonymous. Investments in such activities as land speculation increase the probability that a given country's capital stock lies below its golden-rule level. This can be modeled in a more complete optimal tax framework as a pre-existing distortion and, while the outcome is not certain (cf., Atkinson and Sandmo (1980)), it would appear to increase the probability that financial savings should be subsidized. Note that this effect is over and above those direct effects described above associated with financial repression.[15]

A further institutional feature not incorporated in this exercise is the compulsory savings schemes employed by some governments (Datta and Shome (1981)). Introducing this element into the framework above would excessively complicate matters. Given the short-term illiquidity of assets implied by forced investments in funded social security programs, these savings are not perfect substitutes for other forms of savings. That would require the introduction of a new variable into the utility function. This variable would be quantity-constrained, which has implications for the market behavior of other variables (cf., Neary and Roberts (1980)).

The role of forced savings, on the presumption that they are productively invested, is analogous to the role discussed above of curb markets. Their primary influence may not be on the marginal first-order conditions but rather on the discrete issue of whether the economy is or is not on its golden-rule path. The intuitive implications, though they should be expressed with reservations, again seem clear. For example, a country with a large stock of forced savings and no financial repression is more likely to be a country where financial savings should be taxed.

The above reservations modify the analytical framework. More fundamental is the reservation that financial repression also influences the short-run macroeconomic performance of economies. This is a problem that cannot be solved by recommending a specific tax rate—what is required is

[15]The optimal outcome depends, of course, not only on the nature of the alternative asset but also on its institutional context. In the case where, for example, one of the alternative assets consists of investments held abroad, the attitude of the authorities toward external capital flows is important. For our purposes, the influence of this type of consideration will be captured in the magnitude of the relevant compensated price elasticity.

greater flexibility of the price system, particularly nominal interest rates, rather than second-best tax reform policies.

Relevance of Supply-Side Tax Policies

What are the implications of the above analysis for supply-side policies in developing country circumstances? This depends on the interpretation of what constitutes supply-side policies. Using the interpretation mentioned earlier, viz., that it concerns, in this context, the use of tax policy to stimulate savings, supply-side policies would appear to have a role to play. For example, recommendations to reduce the top marginal income taxes or to exempt completely interest income from taxation would counter some of the effects associated with financial repression.

There is a more general lesson, however. The model and the reservations presented above imply that the optimal tax treatment of financial savings depends critically on the degree of financial repression, which, as shown in Tables 1 and 2 in the Annex to this chapter, varies widely both across countries and over time. Accordingly, there is no single recommended policy such as reducing marginal tax rates. Each country has to be considered individually. This all implies that global supply-side proposals must be carefully evaluated and tailored to what is desirable. Thus, the appropriate tax policy depends not only on the degree to which financial repression and compulsory savings schemes exist but also on whether these latter distortions, and in particular financial repression, are themselves amenable to elimination.

The chapter has so far examined the merits of proposals for tax reform merely in analytical terms. There were few unambiguous qualitative results, since optimal tax rates depend on the magnitudes of various own- and cross-price elasticities. One must look at the empirical literature to see if the recommended tax reforms, which aim to reduce or eliminate the taxation on savings, will actually stimulate savings. Note that this is a somewhat different issue from the one discussed above. The tax reform discussion goes beyond a concern for stimulating the quantity of savings. Many of the recommended reforms are desirable insofar as they mitigate the effects of pre-existing distortions, such as those associated with financial repression. Such a goal could quite easily be attained without a substantial change in the quantity of savings. The topics are, of course, related since, abstracting from the macroeconomic effects, the optimal tax rates depend critically on the own-price elasticity of financial savings (or, which is effectively the same quantity, on the cross-price elasticities between financial and other forms of saving). The empirical results are summarized in Ebrill (Chapter 3). Given data inadequacies, that literature only allows one to make the general statement that financial savings may be price-sensitive. Point estimates are not possible.

III. Conclusions

The main conclusions of this chapter may be summarized as follows. First, when considering the question of the optimal treatment of financial savings in developing countries, a number of factors must be considered. In particular, the degree of financial repression is an important variable.

Second, having determined the particulars of any given case, in general, a number of policy options must then be evaluated. The best reform proposals within the limited context of tax/price policy will probably involve the abolition of financial repression. Should that be precluded, there remains the second-best type of policy recommendations such as those contained in the specific optimal tax framework developed in this paper. A useful benchmark case is one where financial repression exists and outright subsidization of savings is not feasible. In that case, there are grounds for arguing for a consumption as opposed to an income tax.

Third, the precise magnitude of the optimal tax rates depends on the empirical evaluation of the relevant price elasticities. Given the data inadequacies in most developing countries, the existing empirical literature can only indicate that financial savings may be price-sensitive. It cannot afford useful point estimates of the relevant price elasticities.

Fourth, one must recognize that the existence of financial repression in many developing countries has macroeconomic implications. This modifies the optimal tax results. Specifically, the macroeconomic circumstances in the absence of financial reform call for a flexible tax policy.

Fifth, evaluated against all of the above, the recommendations of supply-side economists appear not so much to be wrong as to be inflexible to local conditions. There are occasions where the recommendations are appropriate, but, as a blanket solution to savings problems in developing countries, they are deficient because they do not allow for the heterogeneity of developing country conditions.

ANNEX

Financial Repression in Developing Countries

Tables 1 and 2 document the extent of financial repression in a sample of developing countries. The data in Table 2 were obtained as follows.

Real Rate of Return (r). This variable consisted of correcting the nominal rate of

Table 1. Selected Developing Countries: Estimated Real Rates of Interest on Savings Deposits

	Year	Real Interest Rate
India	1969	−0.30[1]
Malaysia	1969	4.50[1]
Malaysia	1981	2.30[2]
Argentina	1976	−56.80[3]
Argentina	1981	11.85[2]
Brazil	1974	−1.10[3]
Brazil	1981	−11.50[2]
Ecuador	1976	−1.50[3]
Guatemala	1976	−1.50[3]
Mexico	1976	−3.50[3]
Peru	1976	−22.80[3]
Venezuela	1976	0.30[3]
Ghana	1981	−43.20[2]
Korea	1981	6.00[2]
Turkey	1981	14.40[2]

[1]From Anand G. Chandavarkar, "Some Aspects of Interest Rate Policies in Less Developed Economies: The Experience of Selected Asian Countries," *Staff Papers*, International Monetary Fund (Washington), Vol. 18 (March 1971), pp. 48–112.

[2]From International Monetary Fund, *Interest Rate Policies in Developing Countries*, a Study by the Research Department of the International Monetary Fund, Occasional Paper No. 22 (Washington, October 1983). The real interest rate estimates are derived estimates obtained by the formula $r = (1 + i)/(1 + \pi) - 1$, where r is the real rate of interest, i is the corresponding nominal rate, and π is the expected rate of inflation where this was assumed to equal the actual rate of inflation recorded in the relevant year.

[3]From Vicente Galbis, "Inflation and Interest Rate Policies in Latin America, 1967–76," *Staff Papers*, International Monetary Fund (Washington), Vol. 26 (June 1979), pp. 334–66.

return (i) in the sample countries for expected inflation (π). The nominal rates of return for the selected countries are defined as follows.

Ghana. Deposit rate on six-month deposits at commercial banks. Source: Bank of Ghana, *Annual Reports* (Accra), various issues.

Jamaica. Deposit rate on time deposits held for more than six months but less than nine months at commercial banks. Source: National Planning Agency, *Economic and Social Survey: Jamaica* (Kingston), various issues.

Korea. Deposit rate on six-month time deposits. Source: National Bureau of Statistics, *Korea Statistical Yearbook* (Seoul), various issues.

Singapore. Deposit rate on six-month deposits. Source: Department of Statistics, *Yearbook of Statistics* (Singapore), various issues.

Where a change in the institutionally mandated rate occurred within a calendar year, an average rate for that year is presented. Expected inflation is gauged by actual changes in the annual rate of inflation as measured by series 64 in International Monetary Fund, *International Financial Statistics Yearbook, 1983*. The formula employed is $r = (1 + i)/(1 + \pi) - 1$.

Table 2. Selected Developing Countries: Nominal (i) and Real (r) Interest Rates on Time Deposits, 1954–82

(In percent)

	Ghana		Jamaica		Korea		Singapore	
	i	r	i	r	i	r	i	r
1954	...	...	...	...	7.0	−22.2	...	...
1955	...	...	...	...	10.0	−34.6	...	...
1956	...	...	...	...	10.0	−9.5	...	...
1957	...	...	...	...	10.0	−10.0	...	...
1958	...	...	...	...	10.0	14.1	...	...
1959	...	...	...	...	9.0	5.0	...	...
1960	...	...	...	...	8.0	−2.6	...	...
1961	...	...	...	...	10.0	1.7	...	...
1962	...	...	...	...	12.0	5.6	...	...
1963	...	...	3.50	1.6	12.0	−6.7	...	...
1964	...	...	3.00	1.1	12.0	−13.7	...	...
1965	2.500	−19.0	4.00	1.1	25.0	10.8	...	...
1966	2.630	−9.4	4.25	2.3	30.0	15.9	...	...
1967	3.000	11.7	4.25	1.3	30.0	17.2	...	...
1968	2.830	−4.9	4.50	−1.3	27.6	14.9	5.75	4.9
1969	3.250	−3.7	4.40	−1.7	23.5	9.9	5.75	6.0
1970	2.830	−0.2	6.00	−1.6	22.8	12.2	5.75	5.5
1971	7.750	−1.5	7.00	1.6	22.0	12.3	5.75	3.7
1972	7.750	−2.2	6.00	0.6	15.0	1.1	5.25	3.3
1973	6.750	−9.2	8.00	−8.2	12.6	5.3	7.00	−15.3

Table 2 (*continued*). Selected Developing Countries: Nominal (*i*) and Real (*r*) Interest Rates on Time Deposits, 1954–82

(In percent)

	Ghana		Jamaica		Korea		Singapore	
	i	*r*	*i*	*r*	*i*	*r*	*i*	*r*
1974	5.500	−10.7	10.50	−13.1	15.0	−19.1	8.00	−11.8
1975	7.825	−17.0	9.00	−7.1	15.0	−9.1	4.96	2.2
1976	7.825	−30.9	10.00	0.1	15.5	2.9	4.34	6.5
1977	7.852	−50.2	8.00	−3.2	16.0	6.4	4.98	1.5
1978	7.825	−37.7	7.00	−20.7	16.0	3.9	5.55	0.8
1979	12.375	−27.2	7.00	−16.9	18.6	−0.2	7.40	3.2
1980	12.375	−25.1	9.00	−14.2	20.6	−6.3	10.92	2.2
1981	12.375	−48.1	9.00	−3.1	16.8	−3.0	8.40	0.2
1982	19.250	−2.5	9.00	2.1	8.0	3.2	6.55	2.6

Note: . . . = not available.
Sources: As cited in the text of this Annex.

REFERENCES

Atkinson, A.B., and A. Sandmo, "Welfare Implications of the Taxation of Savings," *Economic Journal* (London), Vol. 90 (September 1980), pp. 529-49.

Atkinson, A. B., and Joseph E. Stiglitz, *Lectures on Public Economics* (New York: McGraw-Hill, 1980).

Auerbach, Alan J., and Laurence J. Kotlikoff, "National Savings, Economic Welfare, and the Structure of Taxation," in *Behavioral Simulation Methods in Tax Policy Analysis*, ed. by Martin Feldstein (Chicago: University of Chicago Press, 1983).

Buffie, Edward F., "Financial Repression, the New Structuralists, and Stabilization Policy in Semi-Industrialized Economies," *Journal of Development Economics* (Amsterdam), Vol. 14 (April 1984), pp. 305-22.

Chandavarkar, Anand G., "Some Aspects of Interest Rate Policies in Less Developed Economies: The Experience of Selected Asian Countries," *Staff Papers*, International Monetary Fund (Washington), Vol. 18 (March 1971), pp. 48-112.

Datta, Gautam, and Parthasarathi Shome, "Social Security and Household Savings: Asian Experience," *Developing Economies* (Tokyo), Vol. 19 (June 1981), pp. 143-60.

Drazen, Allan, "The Optimal Rate of Inflation Revisited," *Journal of Monetary Economics* (Amsterdam), Vol. 5 (April 1979), pp. 231-48.

Ebrill, Liam P., and S.M. Slutsky, "The Ramsey Rule, Production Efficiency, and Intermediate Goods" (New Orleans, Louisiana: Murphy Institute of Political Economy, Tulane University, 1983, mimeographed).

Feldstein, Martin, "The Welfare Cost of Capital Income Taxation," *Journal of Political Economy* (Chicago), Vol. 86, No. 2, Part 2 (April 1978), pp. S29-S51.

Fullerton, Don, John B. Shoven, and John Whalley, "Replacing the U.S. Income Tax with a Progressive Consumption Tax: A Sequenced General Equilibrium Approach," *Journal of Public Economics* (Amsterdam), Vol. 20 (February 1983), pp. 3-23.

Galbis, Vicente, "Inflation and Interest Rate Policies in Latin America, 1967-76," *Staff Papers*, International Monetary Fund (Washington), Vol. 26 (June 1979), pp. 334-66.

Kaldor, Nicholas, *An Expenditure Tax* (London: Allen & Unwin, 1955).

Leff, Nathaniel H., and Kazuo Sato, "Macroeconomic Adjustment in Developing Countries: Instability, Short-Run Growth, and External Dependency," *Review of Economics and Statistics* (Cambridge, Massachusetts), Vol. 62 (May 1980), pp. 170-79.

McKinnon, Ronald I., *Money and Capital in Economic Development* (Washington: Brookings Institution, 1973).

Mill, John Stuart, *Principles of Political Economy*, ed. by W.J. Ashley (London: Longmans, 1921).

Miracle, Marvin P., Diane S. Miracle, and Laurie Cohen, "Informal Savings Mobilization in Africa," *Economic Development and Cultural Change* (Chicago), Vol. 28 (July 1980), pp. 701-24.

Munk, Knud Jørgen, "Optimal Taxation and Pure Profit," *Scandinavian Journal of Economics* (Stockholm), Vol. 80, No. 1 (1978), pp. 1-19.

Neary, J.P., and K.W.S. Roberts, "The Theory of Household Behaviour Under Rationing," *European Economic Review* (Amsterdam), Vol. 13 (January 1980), pp. 25-42.

Nellor, D.C.L., "Tax Policy, Regulated Interest Rates, and Saving" (unpublished, International Monetary Fund, August 8, 1983).

Phelps, Edmund S., "Inflation in the Theory of Public Finance," *Swedish Journal of Economics* (Stockholm), Vol. 75 (March 1973), pp. 67-82.

Prest, A.R., "Compulsory Lending Schemes," *Staff Papers*, International Monetary Fund (Washington), Vol. 16 (March 1969), pp. 27-52.

Sandmo, Agnar, "Optimal Taxation—An Introduction to the Literature," *Journal of Public Economics* (Amsterdam), Vol. 6 (July-August 1976), pp. 37-54.

Seidman, Laurence S., "Conversion to a Consumption Tax: The Transition in a Life-Cycle Growth Model," *Journal of Political Economy* (Chicago), Vol. 92 (April 1984), pp. 247-67.

Shaw, Edward S., *Financial Deepening in Economic Development* (New York: Oxford University Press, 1973).

Shome, Parthasarathi, and Lyn Squire, "Alternative Mechanisms for Financing Social Security," World Bank Staff Working Paper No. 625 (Washington, 1983).

Siegel, Jeremy J., "Notes on Optimal Taxation and the Optimal Rate of Inflation," *Journal of Monetary Economics* (Amsterdam), Vol. 4 (April 1978), pp. 297-305.

Summers, Lawrence H., "Optimal Inflation Policy," *Journal of Monetary Economics* (Amsterdam), Vol. 7 (March 1981), pp. 175-94.

Tun Wai, U, "A Revisit to Interest Rates Outside the Organized Money Markets of Underdeveloped Countries," *Quarterly Review*, Banca Nazionale del Lavoro (Rome), Vol. 30 (September 1977), pp. 291-312.

van Wijnbergen, Sweder, "Stagflationary Effects of Monetary Stabilization Policies: A Quantitative Analysis of South Korea," *Journal of Development Economics* (Amsterdam), Vol. 10 (April 1982), pp. 133-69.

——— (1983a), "Credit Policy, Inflation and Growth in a Financially Repressed Economy," *Journal of Development Economics* (Amsterdam), Vol. 13 (August-October 1983), pp. 45-65.

——— (1983b), "Interest Rate Management in LDC's," *Journal of Monetary Economics* (Amsterdam), Vol. 12 (September 1983), pp. 433-52.

Wanniski, Jude, *The Way the World Works* (New York: Simon and Schuster, rev. and updated ed., 1983).

Williamson, Jeffrey G., "Why Do Koreans Save 'So Little'?" *Journal of Development Economics* (Amsterdam), Vol. 6 (September 1979), pp. 343-62.

5

Income Taxes and Investment

Some Empirical Relationships for Developing Countries

Liam P. Ebrill

There has been growing interest in the issue of how supply-side policies might be used to affect the growth rates of developing countries. In particular, it has been suggested that taxes may well be powerful instruments of development policy. Central to this position is the presumption that tax policy can influence the level of investment. In a neoclassical framework, this presumption is sustained by the argument that taxes can be employed to reduce the cost of capital where the latter is viewed as the principal determinant of the level of fixed business investment. This chapter is written in the tradition of that neoclassical analysis. As a preliminary to answering the question of how best to direct tax policy so as to stimulate investment, one objective of this chapter is to quantify the impact of existing tax systems on the cost of capital in a selection of developing countries.

Of course, other (nonneoclassical) factors such as liquidity and acceleration effects and the availability of foreign exchange may be important determinants of investment behavior. Indeed, the available empirical evidence for developing countries indicates that these latter factors are of great importance (for example, Billsborrow (1977), Sundararajan and Thakur (1980), and Tun Wai and Wong (1982)). Accordingly, in the empirical work presented below, some of these nonneoclassical elements are accommodated. This permits an evaluation of the relative importance of a variety of factors in the determination of capital formation in developing countries. Since there are a number of potential influences on investment, care is taken to ensure that the countries studied below are chosen with a view to covering a broad range of developing country experience.

This chapter first presents the theory behind the cost-of-capital approach. Subsequent sections consider the relevance of this approach for developing countries, show how the cost of capital in these countries may be sensitive to changes in anticipated inflation, discuss the estimates of the cost of capital for the selected sample of countries, and present cross-section regression results on the determination of investment levels in developing countries.

I. The Theoretical Framework

Background to Cost-of-Capital Calculations

We begin with some comments that concentrate on the salient features of all cost-of-capital calculations.

The most obvious tax influencing the cost of capital facing corporations is the corporate income tax. The manner in which this tax exercises its influence is complicated. Corporate taxes are levied on corporate income after the allowable costs incurred in the process of generating revenue have been deducted. These costs are relatively easy to calculate as far as outlays on labor and raw materials are concerned. They are much more difficult to calculate, however, for capital inputs, because capital is a durable good whose rate of depreciation is difficult to gauge.

In much of the earlier theoretical work it was assumed that corporate taxes were, by and large, borne by capital.[1] This assumption is accurate if the deduction accorded capital is inadequate. Proceeding from the assumption that capital bears corporate taxes, authors then analyzed the general equilibrium implications of such taxes. This work, exemplified by Harberger (1962), was very important not only because of its specific conclusions concerning the impact of the corporate income tax but also because of its demonstration that general equilibrium effects of taxes could and should be documented. (For a review of the original Harberger model and more recent extensions, see McLure (1975) and Ballentine and McLure (1980).)

Recent literature, which concentrates less on the general equilibrium effects of corporate taxes and more on the issue of how the corporate income tax actually affects the cost of capital, is more relevant for our purposes.[2] Stiglitz (1973) points out that the effects of a statutory corporate income tax rate on the cost of capital cannot be viewed in isolation from other elements of the tax system such as specific provisions of the corporate tax code and the coexistence of the corporate tax with a personal income tax

[1]For an exception to this, consider Krzyzaniak and Musgrave (1963).

[2]Some important examples are Stiglitz (1973) and (1976), King (1975), and Flemming (1976).

structure. In general, a tax system which, between its interest deductibility provisions and its depreciation allowances permits a deduction whose present value is equal to the cost of a capital investment, is equivalent to a tax system with an immediate write-off provision. This, in turn, implies that such a tax system would be equivalent to a pure profits tax in the sense that, within the context of the model, no marginal conditions are affected. The ability to accommodate the full range of possible tax structures suggested by this literature is what makes the cost-of-capital formula specified below a useful device.

For institutional reasons, the effects of corporate income taxes are frequently complicated by inflation. There is a tendency in many tax systems to tax the nominal rather than the real income of capital. As a result, the tax system interacts with changes in the expected rate of inflation. For corporate taxes, this interaction is frequently the product of some combination of the following factors: the taxation of nominal capital gains and nominal interest income, the use of depreciation allowances based on historic cost, the full deductibility of nominal interest expense, and the requirement that inventory valuations be determined on a first in, first out (FIFO) basis. In a general equilibrium context, this problem is compounded by the fact that tax systems rarely treat all capital assets in the same manner. For example, owner-occupied and rental housing frequently receive a favorable tax treatment. In the case of the former, not only is there no taxation of the implicit rental income that accrues to the owner-occupier but also some amount of mortgage interest payments and property tax payments can sometimes be deducted against other income tax liabilities. This implies that one of the effects of an increase in the rate of inflation is for investors to shift their demand from corporate equity to owner-occupied housing. Thus, while changes in the expected rate of inflation might not be expected to result in large changes in total investment, there could be significant changes in the composition of that aggregate.

Any country's corporate tax system could be modified to accommodate the effects of inflation. A common solution is to allow some form of accelerated depreciation allowances. Although such allowances will counter the effect of a given expected rate of inflation, the system nonetheless remains sensitive to changes in inflation. These and other aspects of this general problem are discussed in Feldstein (1980a, 1980b, and 1980c), and Ebrill and Possen (1982a and 1982b). Again, the cost-of-capital formula derived below is general enough to permit a consideration of these issues.

When empirically estimating the incentive effects of taxation on business investment, deriving a cost-of-capital estimate is by no means the only possible route to take. A more traditional approach takes as its starting point the actual taxes paid as a proportion of income. The presumption is that marginal tax rates in a given industry are not far from the ratio of actual taxes to capital income in that industry. This may not be too likely given that actual tax revenues may be the product of inframarginal supernormal profits due to the existence of noncompetitive market structures. Examples of well-known articles that rely on this approach are Harberger (1966), Shoven (1976), Fullerton and others (1981), and Fullerton and Gordon (1983).

The use of cost-of-capital calculations is actually quite new (King and Fullerton (1984)). Based on the neoclassical framework developed by Hall and Jorgenson (1971), they have come to be used with increased regularity (e.g., Hall (1981), Jorgenson and Sullivan (1981)). The underlying methodology of the approach used below is to consider a "hypothetical project" of a dollar invested in a particular asset to be used by a representative firm. The firm is assumed to be maximizing its value to the shareholders. Given the specifics of the tax code, the cost-of-capital formula is then derived permitting an evaluation of the impact of various tax provisions at both the corporate and the shareholder level on the actual cost of capital and, hence, on the incentive to invest.

Relevance of the Cost-of-Capital Approach to Developing Countries

The cost-of-capital calculation is concerned with the investment climate facing corporations. That its usefulness is limited by the fact that the corporate sectors in developing countries are often small is not necessarily true. First, the corporate sector, although small, could well be important at the margin (Bhagwati (1978)). Second, and more important, the cost of capital facing the corporate sector may serve as an excellent proxy for the cost of capital facing unincorporated businesses. It is sufficient for both sectors to determine their tax bases in a similar fashion. For example, in countries where historic cost depreciation is the convention, that convention will usually apply to both corporations and unincorporated businesses, and, further, will be reflected in the cost-of-capital calculation.[3]

A related issue is that the cost-of-capital calculation presumes the existence of competitive capital markets. The reality in many developing countries is much different. Capital markets are commonly either nonexistent

[3]Note that the cost-of-capital calculation can similarly be viewed as a proxy for the cost of capital facing foreign investors. Although no account is taken of the home (developed) countries' costs of capital, the relative attractiveness of any developing country as a location for foreign investment can be derived from its relative cost-of-capital ranking. A caveat to this is, of course, the fact that there may be variations in the magnitude of nonfinancial restrictions to foreign investment flows across developing countries.

or fragmented. This does not, in and of itself, negate the relevance of the cost-of-capital calculation. Even in the absence of well-developed markets, the distinction between debt and equity continues to be maintained both in the practice of financing marginal investments and in the specifics of many developing countries' tax codes. Interest payments, whether on a bank loan or a bond, are often deductible against corporate tax liabilities while retained earnings are not. Further, capital gains, dividends, and interest payments frequently receive separate treatments at the personal income tax level. However, this reservation does suggest that liquidity variables may have an important role to play in determining investment flows.

Difficulties in the Use of Cost-of-Capital Calculations

The cost-of-capital approach is not without its problems. First, as pointed out by Bradford and Fullerton (1981), since the method is concerned with expected future tax liabilities (statutory corporate and personal income tax rates are normally assumed to remain constant), the choice of a discount rate is critical. Second, effective tax rate estimates are a function of the assumptions made concerning how anticipated inflation affects nominal interest rates. We assume below that all *gross* nominal returns rise with the rate of anticipated inflation.[4]

To these caveats raised by Bradford and Fullerton (1981), the most serious of which is the second, might be added a few further considerations. The value of depreciation allowances to the representative firm is gauged by the discrepancy, positive and/or negative, that exists over time between the depreciation allowances and economic depreciation, all expressed in present value terms. It is traditional to assume that economic depreciation is exponential, though there is evidence to suggest that this is not so (Feldstein and Rothschild (1974)). To the extent that economic depreciation is not exponential, one is valuing depreciation allowances against the wrong benchmark. Nonetheless, we will continue to assume that economic depreciation follows a path of exponential decay since alternative assumptions have their own difficulties.

Finally, a number of assumptions are needed to ensure that the cost-of-capital approach can be viewed as providing a general equilibrium framework in which a country's tax system can be evaluated. Implicitly, authors

[4]Although this may appear to be a partial equilibrium assumption, it is consistent with the empirical results reported for the United States by Feldstein and Summers (1978). The assumption is suspect when it is applied to those developing countries where interest rates are regulated. Indeed, as shall be seen below, the empirical results appear to be influenced by this effect.

seem to assume a closed economy framework with fixed aggregate stocks of capital and labor. This allows one to take many variables, such as the underlying marginal productivity of capital, as constant. One can also ignore the effects of many other taxes. For example, general taxes on gross output may then be consistently presumed to be borne by capital and labor in the aggregate in line with their factor shares in gross domestic product (GDP) and, accordingly, such taxes do not affect the allocation of investment funds between the corporate sector and other sectors of any given economy. This permits one to concentrate on the implications of the interactions between the personal and corporate tax systems of developing countries. However, the assumptions necessary for this general equilibrium interpretation to hold may not be realistic. The economies of many developing countries are quite open. When this is combined with the common adoption of overvalued exchange rates and a relatively heavy reliance on trade taxes, the concomitant disequilibrium in the traded goods market can influence investment flows. Thus, as pointed out in the introduction, additional factors such as foreign exchange availability should be accommodated.

It is clear, then, that cost-of-capital calculations should be interpreted with great care. However, they continue to have the great advantage over alternative techniques of being based on a theoretical rather than on an ad hoc foundation. Even if the absolute values of the calculations are subject to error, they will still be useful if the rankings of tax effects across countries are accurate, thereby affording some insight into the sensitivity of investment to changes in the level of the cost of capital. Further, the technique has the advantage of allowing calculation to be made on the basis of statutory tax rates, where these are generally accessible. Given data availability in developing countries, this advantage is particularly valuable.

Derivation of the Cost-of-Capital Formula

Before discussing the derivation of the cost-of-capital formula (equation (4), below), we introduce the following summary of the notation that will be used throughout.

π = the anticipated rate of inflation;
i = nominal rate of interest;
δ = rate of economic depreciation;
s = real interest rate, net of tax;
n = share of marginal investment financed by new issues;
h = share of marginal investment financed by borrowing;
τ = corporate tax rate;
τ^* = corporate tax rate corrected for tax holidays;

M_G = effective tax rate on capital gains;
M_D = tax rate on distributions;
M = personal income tax rate;
a = exponential rate, historic cost, depreciation allowances;
G = share of investment qualifying for initial investment allowance;
ρ' = gross real cost of capital;
ρ = net real cost of capital;
ρ^* = net real cost of capital of "pioneer" firms;
$D(t)$ = nominal income stream in period t from an additional \$1 of investment; and
$V(t)$ = stock market value of a share of the "representative" firm in period t.

As the procedure for deriving the actual formula for the cost of capital is well known, it will only be summarized here. See Agell (1983) for a more detailed discussion of the mechanics since his basic formula, with some modifications, will be used below.

The cost-of-capital calculation is derived from a model of the marginal investment decision facing a corporate firm. The marginal investment, financed in period 0 at least in part by retained earnings, yields a dividend stream $D(t)$ where

$$D(t) = \left\{(1 - \tau)[\rho' - ih] - (\delta - \pi)h - \left(\frac{s + \pi}{1 - M_D}\right) n - (\delta - \pi)n\right\} e^{-(\delta-\pi)t} + \tau a e^{-at}. \quad (1)$$

Thus, dividends net of corporate taxes are calculated by deducting payments associated with debt and the issue of new shares from the gross yield of a marginal investment and adding the tax value of depreciation allowances. To elaborate, the term in $(\delta - \pi)h$ reflects the fact that that portion of the investment which is debt-financed is amortized at a rate which reflects the rate of economic depreciation, δ, adjusted for the anticipated rate of inflation, π. Following Agell (1983), new share issues can be treated without loss of generality as a special debt instrument. These new shares must yield for their shareholders a competitive net of personal income tax return, where this is gauged by $(s + \pi)n/(1 - M_D)$, and, as with regular debt, their share in the marginal investment is amortized at a rate measured by $(\delta - \pi)n$.

This dividend stream is reflected in the value of shares, $V(0)$, as follows:

$$V(0) = \int_0^\infty \frac{(1 - M_D)}{(1 - M_G)} D(t) e^{-\frac{(s+\pi)t}{(1-M_G)}} dt, \qquad (2)$$

where this expression is a solution to the differential equation resulting from the equilibrium condition that the rate of return required by equity holders equals the sum of net of tax dividend payments and capital gains.

The firm is assumed to be maximizing its value to its existing equity holders. Given that assumption, the capital market will be in equilibrium if, at the margin, the equity holders are indifferent as to whether or not the marginal investment is undertaken; that is, equity holders will be indifferent between having the firm pay out dividends and having it make the marginal investment. This equilibrium condition can be expressed as follows:

$$(1 - M_D)(1 - h - n - \tau G) = (1 - M_G)V(0), \qquad (3)$$

that is, the forgone dividend payment, net of personal income tax, must equal the capital gain, net of capital gains tax, associated with the investment. Substituting equations (1) and (2) into (3) yields

$$\rho = ih + \frac{(s + \pi)n}{(1 - \tau)(1 - M_D)}$$

$$+ \frac{(s + \pi)}{(1 - \tau)(1 - M_G)} \left[1 - h - n - \tau G - \frac{\tau(a - (\delta - \pi))}{\frac{s + \pi}{1 - M_G} + a} \right]$$

$$- \frac{\tau G(\delta - \pi)}{(1 - \tau)} - \pi, \qquad (4)$$

where the major differences between this expression and Agell's corresponding equation (5) are (1) the fact that interest deductibility of debt against corporate tax liabilities is permitted by all the countries selected below is already incorporated in the formula and (2) it is assumed from the outset that no relative price changes take place. This last assumption implies that the anticipated rate of general inflation is equal to the expected rate of change in the price level of capital goods.

Having introduced the cost-of-capital calculation and having discussed the caveats relevant to its use, we now proceed to its estimation and evaluation for a sample of developing countries.

II. Empirical Results

The sample used in this chapter consists of 31 countries chosen with a view to covering a broad range of developing country experience.

Derivation of Cost-of-Capital Estimates

The parameters in the cost-of-capital formula given above are of three different types, namely,

(1) macrovariables (π, i, s), which are exogenous to the representative firm;
(2) microvariables (δ, n, h), which are specific to the firm; and
(3) tax variables (τ, τ^*, M_G, M_D, M, a, G).

Consider the specific parameter values for each of these categories in turn, noting that the values for the first two categories are chosen not only because they are reasonable in their own right but also because they are consistent with Agell's (1983) results.

The nominal rate of interest is presumed to rise pari passu with the rate of inflation (the Fisher assumption) so that

$$i = i_r + \pi, \tag{5}$$

where i_r is the real rate of interest.[5] The real rate of interest is set at 2 percent a year. Further, the shareholder's required real rate of return, s, is also equal to the real rate of interest, implying $s = 2$ percent.

Turning to a consideration of the microvariables, it is assumed that the rate of economic depreciation may be set equal to 0.1225. This estimate is the same as that derived by Hulten and Wykoff (1981) for "general industrial equipment" using U.S. data. Data availability precludes obtaining accurate estimates of n, the share of new financing in the marginal investment, and h, the analogous share for debt. Accordingly, in line with Agell's (1983) benchmark case, $n = 0.10$ and $h = 0.30$ are the chosen values.

Finally, a few comments on the most important tax parameters are in order. The corporate tax rate corrected for tax holidays, τ^*, is based on the

[5]Taken at face value, this assumption would appear to be violated in those countries where interest rates are institutionally fixed at an artificially low rate. However, to the extent that the resultant financial disintermediation results in the creation of secondary financial markets, such as the curb markets of Korea, this problem is ameliorated—the interest rates in such markets are likely to be responsive to changes in inflation. Further, as shall be seen below, the regression results will be altered in an attempt to accommodate those cases where the assumption is most likely to be seriously in error.

most generous tax holiday available. There is no guarantee that these terms are available to all start-up firms. The method for correcting the statutory tax rate for tax holidays is presented in Agell (1983). Some of the cases provide for partial tax holidays. The determination of the corrected corporate tax rates for two of these cases is presented in Annex I of this chapter.

The capital gains tax rates are effective tax rates—the statutory tax rates have been corrected for the fact that capital gains are levied on a realization rather than an accrual basis. Account is also taken of the fact that some countries have separate deductions against capital gains liabilities.

As in Agell (1983), the personal income tax rate on dividends is based on the marginal tax rate of the typical investor where the investor is assumed to have a taxable income equal to ten times the per capita 1981 GDP of the country under consideration. Finally, where necessary, the straight-line depreciation allowance formulas have been converted to an equivalent declining-balance formula characterized by the value of the parameter a.[6]

Consideration of Estimates for Sample

In his study, Agell (1983) concluded that the tax structures of the Association of South East Asian Nations (ASEAN) countries were not a major source of investment disincentives. Does this conclusion hold true for the more extended sample employed here? An answer to this question can be found in Table 1 in which are presented, for the complete sample of 31 countries, estimates of the cost of capital, ρ, at a zero rate of inflation; the anticipated rate of inflation, π; and the cost of capital both for ongoing firms, ρ, and pioneer firms, ρ^*, at these anticipated rates of inflation. The cost-of-capital estimates are derived along the lines laid out in the previous section.[7] The expected rate of inflation is estimated by taking an annual average of the actual rate of inflation experienced by the countries over the period 1970–80. This is an admittedly crude measure, particularly so given

[6]Since some countries index their depreciation allowances, the cost-of-capital formula is somewhat altered. The manner of the alteration is described in Annex I of this chapter.

[7]An important reservation to these estimates should be noted, namely, that they do not incorporate many specific tax incentives such as regional and industry-specific grants. For these and other reasons mentioned above, too much stock should not be placed in the absolute values of the estimates. Rather, it is hoped that the ranking implied by the calculations is accurate. The data sources for the tax variables were the relevant country issues of Price Waterhouse and Company's *Doing Business* series and the relevant supplements of the International Bureau of Fiscal Documentation. The relevant tax parameters were those in force in the early 1980s.

Table 1. Selected Developing Countries: Cost of Capital at Zero and Actual Rates of Inflation

(In percent)

	ρ at Zero Rate of Inflation	Anticipated Inflation Rate π	ρ at Anticipated Inflation Rate	ρ^* at Anticipated Inflation Rate
Argentina	0.46	130.8	−5.85	7.59
Brazil	2.50	36.7	2.80	2.80
Chile	0.80	185.6	−14.44	−14.44
Colombia	2.84	22.0	6.93	6.93
Côte d'Ivoire	−3.30	13.2	−2.13	0.98
Ecuador	2.47	14.4	−5.91	−5.91
Egypt	1.23	11.5	2.18	2.18
Ghana	−2.15	34.8	19.90	19.29
India	3.59	8.5	3.34	2.53
Indonesia	2.40	20.5	−1.80	2.60
Israel	3.15	39.7	8.40	8.40
Jamaica	1.53	17.0	5.39	4.23
Kenya	1.28	11.0	3.36	3.36
Korea	2.91	19.8	7.82	6.60
Malaysia	1.50	7.5	−0.30	0.85
Mexico	0.69	19.3	1.65	1.65
Morocco	2.79	8.1	6.29	3.81
Nigeria	1.72	18.2	6.74	6.74
Pakistan	1.92	13.5	4.53	4.53
Papua New Guinea	1.29	8.8	4.11	4.11
Paraguay	2.87	12.4	3.43	3.43
Philippines	1.90	13.2	0.88	0.98
Senegal	2.75	7.6	2.96	2.40
Singapore	−2.90	5.1	−3.20	1.00
Sudan	6.00	15.8	14.33	5.97
Syrian Arab Rep.	3.93	11.4	8.07	8.07
Thailand	2.00	9.9	1.60	1.11
Trinidad and Tobago	0.86	18.5	1.36	2.25
Tunisia	2.78	7.7	5.09	5.09
Venezuela	2.89	12.1	5.07	5.07
Zaïre	2.74	32.2	4.25	3.67

Note: π, the anticipated inflation rate, is assumed to equal the average annual rate of inflation as measured by the implicit gross domestic product deflator for the period 1970–80.

Sources: The data for π were obtained from World Bank, *World Development Report, 1982* (New York: Oxford University Press, 1982), and *World Development Report, 1983* (New York: Oxford University Press, 1983). Other data sources are described in the sections on "Derivation of Cost-of-Capital Formula" and "Consideration of Estimates for Sample."

the possibility that price controls may have been in force in some of the countries.

The conclusion must be that, contrary to Agell, the actual cost of capital facing some countries in this sample is such that the interaction between their respective tax systems and the rate of inflation is the source of investment disincentives—any value greater than 2 percent implies a positive tax wedge. For several countries, the disincentive effects are pronounced.

A comparison of the cost of capital calculated at the anticipated rates of inflation with the corresponding cost of capital at a zero rate of inflation shows that the estimates are sensitive to changes in inflation. The latter set of estimates also demonstrate that, while many countries may have a high nominal rate of corporate income tax, the deductions are such as to leave the cost of capital relatively unaffected at low rates of inflation. Indeed, the large number of values less than two imply that the tax system in many countries subsidizes the cost of investment at low inflation rates. The generous deductions implied by this outcome may have been a response to the higher actual rates of inflation experienced by these countries.

Consider the final column of Table 1, which presents estimates of the cost of capital for start-up or "pioneer" investments. An interesting feature is that for some countries, tax holidays appear to increase the cost of capital. This is not as strange as it first appears. First, if the tax system is such that, in the absence of tax holidays, the tax wedge is negative, then a tax holiday tends to remove this implicit subsidy. This effect can also be observed in Agell's work. Second, the effective tax rate on corporate capital is the product of an interaction between the corporate and personal income taxes. In some cases, one observes that taxes at the corporate level tend to be very low, even negative, due to accelerated depreciation allowances, while the treatment of capital income at the personal level involves high tax rates. As a result, a tax holiday at the corporate level implies an increase in the tax burden on corporate capital.

However, while the calculations imply that there are circumstances under which a tax holiday can increase the tax burden, a couple of reservations should be noted. First, as mentioned in an earlier section, the cost-of-capital calculation is set in a world where the representative firm is presumed to know its future tax liabilities with certainty. In the real world, notwithstanding the fact that in present value terms it implies an increase in taxes, a firm might well opt for the certainty of a tax benefit now. Second, and more important, the cost-of-capital formula is symmetric—if the incentives are sufficiently great, it requires the government to pay the firm. In reality, most tax systems do not make such payments. This reduces the potential mentioned above for a tax holiday to result in an increase in the cost of capital.

Even with these reservations, the results in Table 1 are still of interest. They imply that tax holidays do not have a major impact on the cost of capital. This surprising result appears to be due to the fact that most corporate taxes have generous allowances built into them. Another way of expressing this is that the cost of capital is not very responsive to changes in the corporate tax rate. A similar lack of sensitivity occurs when other tax parameters are altered. Where sensitivity does exist it is in the specification of the special provisions. In particular, the interaction between inflation and the historic cost depreciation and investment allowances is of critical importance. Indeed, the only possibility for a negative cost of capital arises when depreciation and investment allowances are so generous as to provide a subsidy. In contrast, reduction of the tax parameters merely reduces the degree to which corporate capital is taxed. It is fortunate that the source of the sensitivity lies in these allowances since their value can be determined with a fair degree of accuracy for any given class of capital equipment.

Regression Results

In this section, regression results based on the cross-section of countries in the sample are presented so as to cast some light on the quantitative impact of the cost of capital on investment flows in the sample of developing countries. Given obvious data inadequacies and difficulties in quantifying nontax determinants of investment, too much weight should not be assigned to these results. Since the results are based on cross-section data drawn from a range of countries rather than on time-series data for individual countries, care must be taken in interpreting the coefficients. It is assumed here that the observations can be interpreted as reflecting the behavior of a representative country; that is, were they all to face the same economic circumstances (e.g., the same cost of capital), every country would exhibit exactly the same response (e.g., the same level of investment). Accordingly, all differences in investment behavior across the sample of countries may be ascribed to differences in their economic circumstances, and the coefficients are, therefore, properly interpreted as gauging long-term effects.

The share of gross domestic investment (*GDI*) in *GDP* for 1980, designated as *GDI/GDP*, was selected as a dependent variable, a choice dictated by data availability. Unfortunately, the variable includes a number of extraneous components. For example, it includes government investment. This component is unlikely to be responsive to market-determined rates of return. It may be possible to assume that it does not vary systematically across the sample. On the basis of the available empirical evidence, this may not be an overly strong assumption. For example, Sundararajan and Thakur (1980) find evidence of some short-term crowding out between public and private investment for the case of India, while for Korea they find these two components to be strong complements. Tun Wai and Wong (1982), testing data drawn from a number of countries, find evidence of financial crowding out for some (e.g., Malaysia and Mexico) but not to the same degree for others.

In an attempt to circumvent this potential problem, estimates of central government fixed capital formation[8] were chosen as a proxy for government investment and were netted out of *GDI*. The resultant alternative dependent variable is referred to as *GDIP/GDP*.[9]

The dependent variable also includes noncorporate private investment and residential housing. It was argued above that the former poses no serious problems as long as the tax bases for the corporate and noncorporate sectors are similarly defined in the sample countries. The latter, however, could weaken the link between the dependent variable and the cost of capital. Thus, to the extent that the increase in the cost of capital is induced by increases in the expected rate of inflation, investors will have an incentive to substitute assets such as owner-occupied housing for corporate assets. Accordingly, if the cost of capital is an insignificant variable in the regressions below, it may be due to this effect. As a final comment on the specification of this variable, it should be noted that the conventional theoretical justification for employing it—rather than a measure of the private capital stock—comes from the presumed existence of adjustment costs in attaining a desired level of the capital stock (Lucas (1967), Gould (1968), Treadway (1969)).

Turning to a consideration of the independent variables, two alternative estimates of the cost of capital can be used. The first of these, designated ρ, gives estimates of the cost of capital faced by ongoing firms and is presented in Table 1, above. The second, for which no explicit estimates are presented below, substitutes the cost of capital faced by "pioneer" firms where such provisions exist.

As mentioned at the beginning of this chapter, other variables could influence the level of investment activity in developing countries. A few proxies for these variables are also included as additional regressors. The annual average real growth rate of exports over the period 1970–80, designated as ΔX, is included as a proxy for foreign exchange availability—the more rapid the growth rate, the more likely will funds be available for investment. Note that, to the extent that this is the correct interpreta-

[8]Note that this does not include capital formation by public enterprises which may respond to changes in the cost of capital and should, therefore, be part of the dependent variable.

[9]The data used in the regressions are presented in Annex II of this chapter.

tion of the role of this variable, it is measuring a supply rather than a demand effect. Accordingly, it must be argued that the single equation regression results presented below represent a reduced form. Note further that this variable can also be interpreted as an accelerator variable. A more accurate proxy for accelerator effects is provided by the annual average growth rate in *GDP* (ΔGDP).

As mentioned above, the cost-of-capital estimates presume that nominal interest rates rise in line with inflation. As pointed out earlier, this is not always so. The rigidity of nominal interest rates in reality, which can be ignored if inflation rates are not too high, may well be a problem for some of the countries in the sample, notably, Argentina and Chile, both of which experienced annual inflation rates well in excess of 100 percent. The large and negative cost-of-capital estimates recorded for both of these countries—suggesting a positive correlation between inflation and investment—could be very misleading. Indeed, there may be an independent negative correlation between inflation and investment. As McKinnon (1973) observes, the capital market in these countries may be in disequilibrium. As a result of pursuing low interest rate policies, investment funds are rationed with realized investment being less than desired. As a practical matter, this financial repression tends to be more severe the higher the rate of inflation (Galbis (1979)). Accordingly, this suggests that the anticipated rate of inflation, π, may act as a useful proxy for the presence or absence of financial disintermediation and, thus, for the availability of investable funds.

On the matter of the available supply of investable funds, there is a frequently expressed concern that the government sector might "crowd out" private investors. To accommodate this possibility, an additional regressor is defined, namely, the current account balance (without grants), designated hereafter as *CAB*. This specification of a crowding out variable was chosen rather than some measure of an overall surplus or deficit on the presumption that borrowing on the capital account is productively invested, where this investment, as suggested above, is assumed to be neither a substitute nor a complement for private investment.

Since the share of gross domestic investment in *GDP* can be expected to be influenced by the level of economic development, the 1980 per capita gross national product, *Y*, of the sample of countries is included as an independent variable. The final independent variable is the share of fuels, minerals, and metals in merchandise exports (*Min*). This variable is a proxy for the natural resource endowments of the countries under consideration where the relative abundance of these endowments might be expected to influence the investment climate, particularly from the point of view of foreign investors.

We turn now to consider a selection of the more important regression results.

$$GDI/GDP = \underset{(6.6)}{14.66} - \underset{(-2.3)}{0.32\rho} + \underset{(5.2)}{1.48\Delta GDP} + \underset{(2.8)}{0.002Y} - \underset{(-0.8)}{0.02Min.} \qquad (6)$$

$$\bar{R}^2 = 0.619 \qquad F = 13.6 \qquad N = 31$$

The regression is run in linear form. The t-ratios are presented in parentheses below the relevant coefficient. $\bar{R}^2$ refers to the adjusted R squared, F to the F ratio, and N to the number of observations.

In this regression, the signs of most of the variables are as expected. The accelerator variable, ΔGDP, is positive and significant. Further, Y, per capita gross national product has a positive and significant coefficient implying that one cannot reject the plausible hypothesis that the more developed the country, the greater the share of *GDP* devoted to *GDI*. The sign of the coefficient of the share of natural resources in exports is not significant given the value of the t-ratio for that variable.

The coefficient of the cost-of-capital variable is negative as predicted, and significant. It is not possible to reject the hypothesis that the interaction between the tax systems of these countries and their anticipated rates of inflation can influence the level of investment. The elasticity value, calculated at the means of the variables, is −0.044. Such a value implies, for example, that if the cost of capital were increased from 3.0 to 4.0, a 33 percent increase, the share of *GDI* in *GDP* would fall by 1.5 percent—a substantial effect.[10]

In view of the potential for the existence of financial repression in some of the countries in the sample, consider the outcome if π, the anticipated rate of inflation, is introduced as a regressor. Specifically, consider:

$$GDI/GDP = \underset{(7.29)}{18.14} - \underset{(-3.49)}{0.53\rho} + \underset{(3.65)}{1.09\Delta GDP} + \underset{(3.35)}{0.002Y} - \underset{(-2.54)}{0.068\pi.} \qquad (7)$$

$$\bar{R}^2 = 0.686 \qquad F = 17.4 \qquad N = 31$$

It appears from this equation that inflation has a significant and strong negative impact on the level of investment (the value of the elasticity is −0.039, which is large given the potential for large changes in inflation).

[10]Unfortunately, there is no obvious way of expressing this elasticity in terms of changes in the underlying parameters such as a change in the corporate tax rate, τ. This is because the impact is country-specific, depending on other specifics such as depreciation allowances. To see this, consider equation (4). The derivative of this equation with respect to τ is ambiguous—if the tax system of a given country subsidizes investment through its special provisions, a reduction in the corporate tax rate could *increase* the cost of capital.

Note, further, that the cost-of-capital variable is still significant but that its coefficient has increased significantly in magnitude, suggesting that any elasticity estimates should be treated with caution.[11]

Consider the outcome if *GDIP/GDP*, the share of gross investment net of gross governmental fixed capital formation in *GDP*, is the dependent variable.[12] The analogous regression equation to equation (7) above is

$$\underset{}{GDIP/GDP} = \underset{(4.60)}{13.24} - \underset{(-3.37)}{0.60\rho} + \underset{(3.46)}{1.20\Delta GDP} + \underset{(3.10)}{0.002Y} - \underset{(-1.96)}{0.061\pi}. \tag{8}$$

$$\bar{R}^2 = 0.654 \qquad F = 15.2 \qquad N = 31$$

It is clear that, at least for this set of regressors, the change in the dependent variable makes little difference.

Both of the above regression equations are potentially affected by simultaneous equation bias. Thus, it could be argued that the greater the share of *GDI* in *GDP*, the more rapid the growth rate of *GDP*. To alleviate the statistical problems posed by this chain, ΔGDP can be replaced with ΔX where the latter variable, as was pointed out above, is a proxy for both accelerator effects and foreign exchange constraints. Also, to test for the possibility that governments may be crowding out private investors, *CAB*, the governmental current account balance of the countries in the sample, is also introduced into the regression equation. The results corresponding to equations (7) and (8) are, respectively:

$$GDI/GDP = \underset{(12.99)}{22.85} - \underset{(-2.75)}{0.48\rho} + \underset{(3.30)}{0.43\Delta X} + \underset{(3.21)}{0.002Y}$$

$$- \underset{(-4.47)}{0.11\pi} + \underset{(0.94)}{0.13\,CAB} \tag{9}$$

$$\bar{R}^2 = 0.657 \qquad F = 12.50 \qquad N = 31$$

[11]The volatility of the regression coefficients indicates that the independent variables may be multicollinear. Indeed, as can be seen from the correlation matrix presented in Table 3 in Annex II, the simple correlation between ρ and π is -0.51, which is consistent with the change in the coefficient value of ρ when π is included in the regression (Rao and Miller (1971)). As an aside, note that the negative correlation between ρ and π, a cross-section result, is not inconsistent with the fact that, within any given country, the cost of capital tends to increase with increases in anticipated inflation. As can be seen from Table 3, the positive correlation is due to the inclusion of Argentina and Chile whose cases, as pointed out on page 129, are extreme.

[12]Depending on the criteria used by public enterprises in their investment decisions, it might have been preferable to net out the gross investment by public companies. Lack of data precluded this possibility.

$$
\begin{aligned}
GDIP/GDP = {} & \underset{(9.93)}{18.42} \underset{(-3.03)}{- 0.56\rho} + \underset{(4.05)}{0.56\Delta X} + \underset{(3.34)}{0.002Y} \\
& \underset{(-4.31)}{-0.11\pi} + \underset{(0.05)}{0.007\ CAB.}
\end{aligned} \tag{10}
$$

$\bar{R}^2 = 0.686 \qquad F = 14.13 \qquad N = 31$

It is clear that this measure of crowding out has no effect on the results. Again, the cost of capital and the inflation variables both continue to be significant with the coefficient of the latter having increased substantially.

All of the above indicates that the cost of capital may have a significant impact on investment levels in developing countries. However, it should also be noted that the other variables, and, in particular, ΔX and π, both of which are proxies for a number of important nonneoclassical effects, are also significant. This raises the question of which is the most promising path for policy to take. Further, there is also the possibility that the results are sensitive to the choice of countries in the sample. As a partial test of this possibility, the regressions were rerun with Argentina and Chile excluded. These two countries were chosen on account of their high rates of inflation and the concomitant possibility that the resulting financial disintermediation has not been adequately accounted for by the inclusion of π as a regressor. The analogous regression equations to (7) and (8) are

$$
GDI/GDP = \underset{(16.35)}{25.58} \underset{(-1.64)}{- 0.28\rho} + \underset{(4.12)}{0.46\Delta X} + \underset{(4.55)}{0.003Y} \underset{(-4.36)}{- 0.37\pi} \tag{11}
$$

$\bar{R}^2 = 0.761 \qquad F = 23.28 \qquad N = 29$

$$
GDIP/GDP = \underset{(10.94)}{19.95} \underset{(-1.90)}{- 0.37\rho} + \underset{(4.56)}{0.59\Delta X} + \underset{(3.89)}{0.003Y} \underset{(-2.93)}{- 0.29\pi} \tag{12}
$$

$\bar{R}^2 = 0.737 \qquad F = 20.60 \qquad N = 29$

It is clear that some of the coefficient estimates are volatile. In particular, the cost-of-capital coefficient is reduced in magnitude and is no longer as significant. Further, the magnitude of the impact of inflation on investment levels has increased—the elasticity of the effect in equation (11) is 0.25. A potential reason for this volatility can be seen in the correlation matrix where the correlation coefficient between π and ρ is now positive at 0.43. This not only reinforces the impression that the observations on Argentina and Chile are extreme outliers but also suggests that there is still some multicollinearity between the regressors. This multicollinearity might be responsible for the reduction in the significance of the cost-of-capital variable, though, as pointed out above, the reason could also lie in the fact that the dependent variable includes investments made in noncorporate assets such as owner-occupied housing. Be that as it may, these results should temper any strong policy conclusions concerning the effectiveness of tax reform proposals. Indeed, they suggest, if anything, that more attention should be paid to the role of inflation since increases in anticipated inflation appear to affect adversely the level of investment via a number of channels; that is, not only do increases in anticipated inflation interact with the tax system to increase the cost of capital but they may also directly affect the level of investment by inducing financial disintermediation. In addition, given the significance of ΔX, the growth rate of exports, the results also suggest that policymakers should concentrate on alleviating distortions which might result in foreign exchange shortages.

Finally, it should be noted that the regressions were rerun, replacing ρ with ρ^*. The results, not presented here, suggested a weaker link between the cost of capital and investment levels. This is not surprising given some of the assumptions underlying the specification of ρ^* (see p. 126, above).

III. Conclusions

The tentative nature of the results must be emphasized. The regressions are based on cross-sectional data, whereas tax reform proposals for any given country should more properly be based on empirical work (time series) drawn from that country. However, even given these reservations, the results are suggestive. Thus, it could well be the case that to concentrate on taxes as the primary source of economic inefficiency in a developing country's economic system is too narrow. The regression results indicate that investment levels are influenced by a number of other factors and, in particular, by the rate of inflation and the availability of foreign exchange as gauged by ΔX. This lends support to the approach adopted in World Bank's *World Development Report, 1983,* where it is argued that if one takes a broad definition of price distortions, then one observes a strong negative correlation between this index and the economic performance of developing countries. Further, if concern should properly be directed at this broader measure, then, as pointed out by Tanzi (1982), given the nature of the political process in many developing countries, radical reform may not be easy to implement; that is, not only are the simplistic tax reform proposals of the pure supply-side approach inadequate but the appropriate reform proposals may not be politically feasible. For example, given the underdeveloped institutional framework in place in many developing countries, the admonition that they reduce their rates of inflation sharply may be extremely difficult to implement.

Even though this all suggests that supply-side based tax reform proposals are only of limited use, this is not to say that they should be ignored. The results do suggest that the provisions of developing country tax structures may well interact with their respective personal tax systems and changes in anticipated inflation to influence investment activity. This implies that the effective tax on capital may be subject to arbitrary changes, which is hardly desirable. Therefore, given the particular sensitivity of the cost-of-capital calculations to the specification of the depreciation allowances, an obvious tax reform proposal would be to recommend the indexation of such allowances. An alternative strategy, which has the merits of being administratively more simple, would be to disallow the deductibility of interest payments on debt and to permit the expensing of all investment. The resulting corporate tax structure would define its tax base in terms of a company's cash flow and would be neutral as far as changes in inflation are concerned. (Of course, such a cash flow tax would require some modification to assist start-up companies, etc., which are likely to run losses at the outset.) At a minimum, the authorities of those countries in which indexation is not allowed should be aware of the interactions that recur between tax systems and inflation.

ANNEX I

Examples of Calculation of Effective Corporate Taxation Rates for Economies with Partial Tax Holidays

India

An investment in period 0 yields a nominal income stream which depreciates over time at rate

$$\int_0^\infty e^{-(\delta-\pi)}dt. \tag{1a}$$

India applies a statutory rate, τ, to the income stream so that 25 percent of profits are exempt for eight years, yielding a present value of expected tax payments equal to

$$T = \int_0^8 3/4\tau e^{-(\delta-\pi)t}e^{-(s+\pi)t}dt + \int_8^\infty \tau e^{-(\delta-\pi)t}e^{-(s+\pi)t}dt, \tag{2a}$$

where nominal tax payments are discounted by the required nominal rate of return.

The effective tax rate, τ^*, is that tax rate which, if applied to the same income stream at a uniform rate from period 0, would yield the same present value of expected tax payments. Thus, set

$$\int_0^\infty \tau^* e^{-(\delta-\pi)t}e^{-(s+\pi)t}dt = T, \tag{3a}$$

and solve for τ^*. It follows that

$$\tau^* = 3/4\tau + 1/4\tau e^{-(s+\delta)8}, \tag{4a}$$

where $s + \delta = 0.225$ and τ is taken to equal 55 percent. Hence, $\tau^* = 46.5$ percent.

Korea

Korea grants a complete tax holiday for four years followed by a halving of corporate tax liabilities for a subsequent two years. Following a procedure analogous to that above yields

$$\int_0^\infty \tau^* e^{-(\delta+s)} dt = 1/2 \int_4^6 \tau e^{-(\delta+s)t} dt + \int_6^\infty \tau e^{-(\delta+s)t} dt, \tag{5a}$$

which implies, for $\delta + s = 0.225$ and $\tau = 0.396$, that $\tau^* = 0.196$.

Cost-of-Capital Formula with Indexed Depreciation Allowances

Indexed depreciation allowances imply that the term measuring the tax value of depreciation allowances in equation (1), namely, $\tau a e^{-at}$ should be replaced by $\tau a e^{-(a-\pi)\tau}$. If the additional assumption of $\delta = a$ is made, then substituting the resulting modified equation (1) together with equation (2) into equation (3) results in

$$\rho = ih + \frac{(s+\pi)n}{(1-\tau)(1-M_D)} + \frac{(s+\pi)}{(1-\tau)(1-M_G)}[i - h - n - \tau G] - \frac{\tau G(\delta - \pi)}{1-\tau} - \frac{\pi}{1-\tau}. \tag{4'}$$

This is the expression which is relevant for the case of countries such as Argentina. Note that some countries, notably Israel and Mexico, allow indexation of depreciation allowances but the enabling legislation for this was so recent that it does not enter the cost-of-capital calculations in this chapter.

ANNEX II

Table 2. Selected Developing Countries: Data for Regression Analysis

	$\frac{GDI}{GDP}$	ΔX	*Min*	ΔGDP	*Y*
Argentina	26	9.3	2	2.2	2,390
Brazil	22	7.5	11	8.4	2,050
Chile	18	10.9	59	2.4	2,150
Colombia	25	1.9	4	5.9	1,180
Côte d'Ivoire	28	4.6	5	6.5	1,150
Ecuador	25	7.5	46	8.8	1,270
Egypt	31	−0.7	47	8.1	580
Ghana	5	−8.4	16	−0.1	420
India	23	3.7	8	3.6	240
Indonesia	22	8.7	69	7.6	430
Israel	22	9.6	2	4.1	4,500
Jamaica	16	−6.8	31	−1.1	1,040
Kenya	22	−1.0	21	6.5	420
Korea	31	23.0	1	9.5	1,520
Malaysia	29	7.4	29	7.8	1,620
Mexico	28	13.4	39	5.2	2,090
Morocco	21	2.1	44	5.6	900
Nigeria	24	2.6	91	6.5	1,010
Pakistan	18	1.2	7	4.7	300
Papua New Guinea	27	2.0	46	2.3	780
Paraguay	29	7.1	1	8.6	1,300
Philippines	30	7.0	18	6.3	690
Senegal	15	1.2	29	2.5	450
Singapore	43	12.0	27	8.5	4,430
Sudan	12	−5.7	4	4.4	410
Syrian Arab Rep.	25	6.8	74	10.0	1,340
Thailand	27	11.8	12	7.2	670
Trinidad and Tobago	28	−2.8	91	5.1	4,370
Tunisia	28	4.8	52	7.5	1,310
Venezuela	25	−6.7	98	5.0	3,630
Zaïre	11	2.2	56	0.1	220

Note: The variables are defined as follows:

GDI/GDP = share of gross domestic investment in gross domestic product for 1980;
ΔX = average annual growth rate of exports over the period 1970–80;
Min = share of fuels, minerals, and metals in merchandise exports in 1979;
ΔGDP = average annual growth rate of gross domestic product over the period 1970–80; and
Y = per capita gross national product in 1980.

In regression equations (8), (10), and (12), the estimates of gross fixed capital formation of central government (the most recent year available), and in regression equations (9) and (10), *CAB*, the current account balance of consolidated central government as a share of *GDP* (data for 1980 or the most recent year available), were obtained from International Monetary Fund, *Government Finance Statistics Yearbook, 1982* (Washington, 1982) and Fund staff estimates.

Sources: *GDI/GDP, ΔX, Min, ΔGDP*, and *Y* were obtained from World Bank, *World Development Report, 1982* (New York: Oxford University Press, 1982), and *World Development Report, 1983* (New York: Oxford University Press, 1983).

Table 3. Correlation Matrix

	ρ	ΔX	Y	CAB	π
		$N = 31$			
ρ	1.0				
ΔX	−0.45	1.0			
Y	−0.23	0.20	1.0		
CAB	−0.35	0.03	0.22	1.0	
π	−0.51	0.22	0.20	0.02	1.0
		$N = 29$			
	ρ	ΔX	Y	CAB	π
ρ	1.0				
ΔX	−0.40	1.0			
Y	−0.17	0.17	1.0		
CAB	−0.36	0.01	0.21	1.0	
π	0.43	−0.20	0.17	−0.34	1.0

Note: $N = 29$ refers to the correlation matrix when Argentina and Chile were excluded.

REFERENCES

Agell, Jonas, "Subsidy to Capital Through Tax Incentives in the ASEAN Countries: An Application of the Cost of Capital Approach Under Inflationary Situations," *Singapore Economic Review* (Singapore), Vol. 28 (October 1983), pp. 98–128.

Ballentine, J. Gregory, and Charles E. McLure, Jr., "Taxation and Corporate Financial Policy," *Quarterly Journal of Economics* (Cambridge, Massachusetts), Vol. 94 (March 1980), pp. 351–72.

Bhagwati, Jagdish, *Foreign Trade Regimes and Economic Development: Anatomy and Consequences of Exchange Control Regimes* (Cambridge, Massachusetts: Ballinger Publishing Co., 1978).

Billsborrow, Richard E., "The Determinants of Fixed Investment by Manufacturing Firms in a Developing Country," *International Economic Review* (Osaka, Japan), Vol. 18 (October 1977), pp. 697–717.

Bradford, David F., and Don Fullerton, "Pitfalls in the Construction and Use of Effective Tax Rates," in *Depreciation, Inflation, and the Taxation of Income from Capital,* ed. by Charles R. Hulten (Washington: Urban Institute Press, 1981).

Ebrill, Liam P., and Uri M. Possen (1982a), "Inflation and the Taxation of Equity in Corporations and Owner-Occupied Housing," *Journal of Money, Credit, and Banking* (Columbus, Ohio), Vol. 14 (February 1982), pp. 33–47.

——— (1982b), "The Interaction of Taxes and Inflation in a Macroeconomic Model," *Quarterly Journal of Economics* (Cambridge, Massachusetts), Vol. 97 (May 1982), pp. 231–50.

Feldstein, Martin (1980a), "Inflation, Tax Rules and the Stock Market," *Journal of Monetary Economics* (Amsterdam), Vol. 6 (July 1980), pp. 309-32.

——— (1980b), "Inflation, Tax Rules, and the Prices of Land and Gold," *Journal of Public Economics* (Amsterdam), Vol. 14 (December 1980), pp. 309-17.

——— (1980c), "Inflation and the Stock Market," *American Economic Review* (Nashville, Tennessee), Vol. 70 (December 1980), pp. 839-47.

———, and Michael Rothschild, "Towards an Economic Theory of Replacement Investment," *Econometrica* (Evanston, Illinois), Vol. 42 (May 1974), pp. 393-424.

Feldstein, Martin, and Lawrence Summers, "Inflation, Tax Rules and the Long-Term Interest Rate," *Brookings Papers on Economic Activity: 1* (1978), Brookings Institution (Washington), pp. 61-110.

Flemming, J.S., "A Reappraisal of the Corporation Income Tax," *Journal of Public Economics* (Amsterdam), Vol. 6 (July-August 1976), pp. 163-69.

Fullerton, Don, and Roger H. Gordon, "A Reexamination of Tax Distortions in General Equilibrium Models," in *Behavioral Simulation Methods in Tax Policy Analysis*, ed. by Martin Feldstein (Chicago: University of Chicago Press, 1983).

Fullerton, Don, A. Thomas King, John B. Shoven, and John Whalley, "Corporate Tax Integration in the United States: A General Equilibrium Approach," *American Economic Review* (Nashville, Tennessee), Vol. 71 (September 1981), pp. 677-91.

Galbis, Vicente, "Money, Investment, and Growth in Latin America, 1961-1973," *Economic Development and Cultural Change* (Chicago), Vol. 27 (April 1979), pp. 423-43.

Gould, J.P., "Adjustment Costs in the Theory of Investment of the Firm," *Review of Economic Studies* (Edinburgh), Vol. 35 (January 1968), pp. 47-55.

Hall, Robert E., "Tax Treatment of Depreciation, Capital Gains, and Interest in an Inflationary Economy," in *Depreciation, Inflation, and the Taxation of Income from Capital*, ed. by Charles R. Hulten (Washington: Urban Institute Press, 1981).

———, and D.W. Jorgenson, "Application of the Theory of Optimum Capital Accumulation," in *Tax Incentives and Capital Spending*, ed. by Gary Fromm (Washington: Brookings Institution, 1971).

Harberger, Arnold C., "The Incidence of the Corporation Income Tax," *Journal of Political Economy* (Chicago), Vol. 70 (June 1962), pp. 215-40.

———, "Efficiency Effects of Taxes on Income from Capital," in *Effects of Corporation Income Tax*, ed. by Marian Krzyzaniak (Detroit: Wayne State University Press, 1966).

Hulten, Charles R., and Frank C. Wykoff, "The Measurement of Economic Depreciation," in *Depreciation, Inflation, and the Taxation of Income from Capital*, ed. by Charles R. Hulten (Washington: Urban Institute Press, 1981).

Jorgenson, Dale W., and Martin A. Sullivan, "Inflation and Corporate Capital Recovery," in *Depreciation, Inflation, and the Taxation of Income from Capital*, ed. by Charles R. Hulten (Washington: Urban Institute Press, 1981).

King, Mervyn A., "Taxation, Corporate Financial Policy, and the Cost of Capital: A Comment," *Journal of Public Economics* (Amsterdam), Vol. 4 (August 1975), pp. 271-79.

———, and Don Fullerton, eds., *The Taxation of Income from Capital: A Comparative Study in the United States, the United Kingdom, Sweden, and West Germany* (Chicago: University of Chicago Press, 1984).

Krzyzaniak, Marian, and R.A. Musgrave, *The Shifting of the Corporation Income Tax: An Empirical Study of Its Short-Run Effect upon the Rate of Return* (Baltimore: Johns Hopkins University Press, 1963).

Lucas, Robert E., Jr., "Adjustment Costs and the Theory of Supply," *Journal of Political Economy* (Chicago), Vol. 75 (August 1967), Part 1, pp. 321-34.

McKinnon, Ronald I., *Money and Capital in Economic Development* (Washington: Brookings Institution, 1973).

McLure, C.E., Jr., "General Equilibrium Incidence Analysis: The Harberger Model After Ten Years," *Journal of Public Economics* (Amsterdam), Vol. 4 (February 1975), pp. 125-61.

Rao, Potluri, and Roger LeRoy Miller, *Applied Econometrics* (Belmont, California: Wadsworth Publishing Co., 1971).

Shoven, John B., "The Incidence and Efficiency Effects of Taxes on Income from Capital," *Journal of Political Economy* (Chicago), Vol. 84 (December 1976), pp. 1261-83.

Stiglitz, Joseph E., "Taxation, Corporate Financial Policy, and the Cost of Capital," *Journal of Public Economics* (Amsterdam), Vol. 2 (February 1973), pp. 1-34.

———, "The Corporation Tax," *Journal of Public Economics* (Amsterdam), Vol. 5 (April-May 1976), pp. 303-11.

Sundararajan, V., and Subhash Thakur, "Public Investment, Crowding Out, and Growth: A Dynamic Model Applied to India and Korea," *Staff Papers*, International Monetary Fund (Washington), Vol. 27 (December 1980), pp. 814-55.

Tanzi, Vito, "Is There a Quest for Public Sector Efficiency in Developing Countries?" paper presented at the Thirty-Eighth Congress of the International Institute of Public Finance (Copenhagen, 1982, mimeographed).

Treadway, A.B., "On Rational Entrepreneurial Behaviour and the Demand for Investment," *Review of Economic Studies* (Edinburgh), Vol. 36 (April 1969), pp. 227-39.

Tun Wai, U, and Chorng-huey Wong, "Determinants of Private Investment in Developing Countries," *Journal of Development Studies* (London), Vol. 19 (October 1982), pp. 19-36.

World Bank, *World Development Report, 1982* (New York: Oxford University Press, 1982).

———, *World Development Report, 1983* (New York: Oxford University Press, 1983).

6

Determinants of Income Tax Evasion

Role of Tax Rates, Shape of Tax Schedules, and Other Factors

Somchai Richupan

Supply-side tax policy is based on the presumption that high rates of income tax and more progressive income tax rate schedules encourage income tax evasion and therefore the lowering of tax rates and the progressivity of tax schedules will reduce tax evasion. This chapter reviews[1] the theoretical literature on factors affecting tax evasion, in particular the role of the level of tax rates and the shape of the tax schedule. It also reviews empirical studies that have focused on the determinants of tax evasion. The chapter will reveal that there is a lack of consensus on these issues. In addition, it will show how the literature has ignored the macro-nontax factors that affect tax evasion. Finally, the chapter hypothesizes the reasons for the higher level of tax evasion in developing countries than in developed countries.

A related activity to tax evasion is tax avoidance. From the legal point of view, the two activities are distinct in that the former is illegal whereas the latter is not. However, from the economist's point of view, tax evasion and tax avoidance have similar effects on government revenue, taxpayer's after-tax income, and fiscal equity. Tax evasion and tax avoidance are not independent of each other, and have the potential for substitute and/or complementary relationships. For example, given a progressive tax structure, a taxpayer who successfully engages in tax avoidance will find that the marginal tax savings to be obtained from further tax evasion is now reduced. Costs incurred in obtaining information on avoidance opportunities may provide insights into possible evasion practices. For a full under-

[1]Since this chapter is based on a study prepared in June 1984, literature published after the date is not incorporated in the review.

standing of an individual's or a society's tax resistance behavior, both tax evasion and tax avoidance should be analyzed simultaneously. This chapter, however, does not attempt to undertake such an analysis, since the focus of the chapter is on the tax resistance behavior of taxpayers in developing countries where, because of low tax administrative capability, tax evasion is more prevalent than tax avoidance.[2]

Section I of the chapter discusses the standard models of tax evasion. Section II reviews other theoretical studies pertaining to tax evasion. Section III analyzes empirical studies on the factors affecting tax evasion. Section IV discusses the limitations of the literature. Section V reviews the policy measures for deterrence of tax evasion. Section VI explores the role of nontax factors and evaluates the relative extent of tax evasion in developing country circumstances. Finally Section VII presents some concluding remarks.

I. Standard Models of Tax Evasion

Mathematical models for analyzing tax evasion follow two approaches: the expected utility maximization approach developed by Allingham and Sandmo (1972) and the expected income maximization approach developed by Srinivasan (1973). This section discusses the standard models of these two approaches.

Expected Utility Maximization Approach

Allingham and Sandmo (1972) assume that tax declaration is a decision under uncertainty. The taxpayer has a choice between two main strategies: (1) to declare his actual income, or (2) to declare less than his actual income. If he chooses the first option, he will have to pay the full amount of the tax. However, if he chooses the second option, he can pay less than the full amount, but he will have to face the probability of being detected and penalized. His problem is to maximize the expected utility derived from his income after tax and penalty (if any). Allingham and Sandmo assume that the taxpayer's behavior conforms to the von Neumann-Morgenstern axiom for behavior under uncertainty. The cardinal utility function of the taxpayer has income as its only argument and the marginal utility is assumed

[2]For further discussion on the choices between tax evasion and tax avoidance, see Cross and Shaw (1981).

to be everywhere positive and strictly decreasing so that the individual is risk averse.[3] The taxpayer's objective function is

$$E(U) = (1 - p)[U(W - \theta X)] + p[U(W - \theta X - \Pi(W - X))], \quad (1)$$

where W is the taxpayer's actual income which is exogenously given and is known to the taxpayer but not to the tax authority; θ is a constant tax rate, $\theta > 0$; X, the income reported to the tax authorities, is the taxpayer's decision variable, $X > 0$; p is the probability that the evasion will be detected; Π is the penalty rate on unreported income, $\Pi > 0$; U is the utility from disposable income; and $E(U)$ is the expected utility. The taxpayer chooses his declared income (X) so as to maximize his expected utility [$E(U)$].

Under the assumption of decreasing absolute risk aversion,[4] Allingham and Sandmo show that the sign of $\partial X/\partial\theta$ is indeterminate, which means that the effect of the tax rate on the reported income is indeterminate. Allingham and Sandmo explain that this indeterminate effect is the result of the interaction between the substitution and the income effects. The substitution effect is negative because an increase in the tax rate makes it more profitable to evade taxes on the margin. The income effect is positive because an increased tax rate makes the taxpayer less wealthy, and, under decreasing absolute risk aversion, this tends to reduce evasion.

The effect of a penalty rate on the reported income, $\partial X/\partial\Pi$ is shown to be unambiguously positive, which implies that an increase in the penalty rate will always increase the reported income. The effect of the probability of detection is also shown to be unambiguously positive, which implies that an increase in the probability of detection will always lead to a larger income being declared.

Expected Income Maximization Approach

The expected income maximization approach of Srinivasan (1973) assumes that the objective of the taxpayer is to maximize his expected

[3]A risk averter is defined as one who, starting from a position of certainty, is unwilling to take a bet even when the bet is actuarially fair. Thus, he is more unwilling to take a bet if the bet is unfair to him. The utility function of a risk averter is strictly decreasing. For proof, see Arrow (1971).

[4]The absolute risk aversion is a measure of the insistence of an individual for more-than-fair odds as a prior condition to engaging in betting, at least when the bets are small. The measure of absolute risk aversion is developed by Arrow (1971) and by Pratt (1964).

The assumption of decreasing absolute risk aversion means that the willingness of an individual to engage in a bet increases as his wealth increases. This is reflected in the decreasing odds demanded for engaging in the bet. This assumption is supported by everyday observation. For example, it is observed that an individual increases the holding of risky assets as his income or wealth increases. For further discussion on this assumption, see Arrow (1971).

income after taxes and penalties. Thus, the taxpayer's problem is to maximize the following expected income function:

$$A(y) = \Pi[y - T(y) - \lambda P(\lambda)y] + (1 - \Pi)\{y - T[(1 - \lambda)y]\}, \quad (2)$$

where y is an individual's true income; $T(y)$ is the tax based on true income; λ is the proportion by which income is understated; $P(\lambda)$ is the penalty multiplier—thus, $P(\lambda)\lambda y$ is the penalty on the understated income λy; Π is the probability of detection; and $A(y)$ is the expected income after taxes and penalty.

Srinivasan assumes that $T(y) > 0$, $0 < T'(y) < 1$, and $T''(y) \geq 0$ for all $y > 0$, which means that the tax is a positive, increasing, and convex function of income. He also assumes that $P(\lambda) \geq 0$, $P'(\lambda) > 0$, and $P''(\lambda) \geq 0$, which means that the penalty multiplier is a positive, increasing, and convex function of the proportion by which income is understated, λ.

Srinivasan denotes the optimum proportion of understated income by λ^* and shows that $\partial\lambda^*/\partial\Pi < 0$, which means that the optimum proportion of understated income, (λ^*), decreases as the probability of detection (Π) increases. The higher the probability of detection, the lower the proportion of income being evaded. He also shows that $\partial\lambda^*/\partial y$ is >0 if T'' is positive. This means that given a progressive tax function, and a probability of detection, Π, independent of income, y, the richer the person, the larger the optimal proportion by which he will understate his income. Under a progressive tax structure, as income increases, the proportion of underreported income also increases. This result is true only when the probability of detection is independent of income. If the probability of detection is an increasing function of income and the tax rate is proportional, then the proportion of understated income will decrease as income increases.

Comparison of the Two Models

The two models are different in the assumptions concerning the objective function (including the utility specification), the tax rate, and the penalty rate (Table 1). The objective function of Allingham and Sandmo's model is an expected utility function, whereas in Srinivasan's model it is an expected income function. Allingham and Sandmo's utility function implies that the taxpayer is risk averse, while the expected income function of Srinivasan implies that the taxpayer is risk neutral. Allingham and Sandmo assume a proportional tax rate, but Srinivasan allows the tax rate to be either proportional or progressive. Allingham and Sandmo's penalty rate is proportional, but Srinivasan's penalty rate is a positive, increasing, and convex function of the proportion of unreported income (λ).

Table 1. Comparison of the Assumptions of the Allingham and Sandmo Model and the Srinivasan Model of Tax Evasion

Allingham and Sandmo's Model	Srinivasan's Model
1. Assumptions concerning the utility function	*1. Assumptions concerning the utility function*
The taxpayer's behavior conforms to the von Neumann-Morgenstern axiom for behavior under uncertainty.	None.
The taxpayer's cardinal utility function has income as its only argument.	
The marginal utility is everywhere positive and strictly decreasing, which implies that the individual is risk averse.	
2. Assumptions concerning income	*2. Assumptions concerning income*
Actual income, W, is exogenously given and is known to the taxpayer but not to the government's tax collector.	Implicitly, actual income, Y, is exogenously given and is known to the taxpayer but not to the government's tax collector.
The taxpayer chose X, the declared income, so as to maximize his utility function.	The taxpayer chose λ, the proportion by which income is understated, so as to maximize his expected income.
3. Assumptions concerning the tax rates	*3. Assumptions concerning the tax rates*
Tax is levied at a constant rate, θ.	The tax paid is a function of income and $T(X) > 0$.
	The marginal tax rate is positive and strictly less than unity, that is, $0 < T'(Y) < 1$.
	$T''(Y) \geq 0$, which means that the tax rate could be either proportional or progressive. If $T''(Y) = 0$ for all Y, we get a constant marginal tax rate, which together with $T(0) = 0$ will yield a proportional tax rate. If $T''(Y) > 0$, then it will correspond to a progressive tax structure.

In Allingham and Sandmo's model, the assumption of decreasing marginal utility (which implies risk aversion) is so crucial to the model that if it had not been made the model would not have an optimal solution.[5] The assumptions of constant tax and penalty rates are also used throughout the derivation. However, it is not easy to analyze the effects of comparing Allingham and Sandmo's assumptions concerning tax and penalty rates

[5]The second order condition for maximization is satisfied only if a decreasing marginal utility, which implies risk aversion, is assumed.

Table 1 (*continued*). Comparison of the Assumptions of the Allingham and Sandmo Model and the Srinivasan Model of Tax Evasion

Allingham and Sandmo's Model	Srinivasan's Model
4. *Assumptions concerning the probability of detection* Tax evasion may be detected at a probability of P.	4. *Assumptions concerning the probability of detection* Tax evasion may be detected at a probability of Π.
5. *Assumptions concerning the penalty rate* If the tax evasion is detected, the penalty is at the rate of Π and is imposed on the undeclared income $(W - X)$.	5. *Assumptions concerning the penalty rate* The penalty multiplier, $P(\lambda)$, is a positive, increasing, and convex function of λ, that is, for all $\lambda > 0$. $P(\lambda) \geq 0$ (5.1) $P'(\lambda) > 0$ (5.2) $P''(\lambda) \geq 0$ (5.3) This penalty multiplier $P(\lambda)$ is imposed on the undeclared income λy.
6. *Assumptions concerning the objective function* The objective function is the expected utility function of the taxpayer, which is specified to be $E(U) = (1 - P)U(W - \theta X) + P[U(W - \theta X - \Pi(W - X))]$.	6. *Assumptions concerning the objective function* The objective function is the expected income function of the taxpayer, which is specified to be $A(Y) = \Pi[y - T(y) - \lambda P(\lambda)y] + (1 - \Pi)\{y - T[(1 - \lambda)y]\}$.

Sources: Compiled from Michael G. Allingham and Agnar Sandmo, "Income Tax Evasion: A Theoretical Analysis," *Journal of Public Economics* (Amsterdam), Vol. 1 (November 1972), pp. 323–38, and T.N. Srinivasan, "Tax Evasion: A Model," *Journal of Public Economics* (Amsterdam), Vol. 2 (November 1973), pp. 339–46.

with Srinivasan's assumption because to do so would involve reformulation of the model. Thus, such effects are not analyzed here.

The indeterminate effect of the tax rate is based on an additional assumption, namely, the decreasing absolute risk aversion. This assumption is crucial to the result because if the absolute risk aversion had been assumed to be either constant or increasing, the tax rate would have had a negative effect on the declared income. Nevertheless, the decreasing absolute risk aversion seemed to be the most attractive assumption because it is supported by everyday observation. The effects of the penalty rate and the probability of detection are free from the assumption of decreasing absolute risk aversion. Thus, whether the absolute risk aversion is assumed to be decreasing, constant, or increasing, the effects of both the penalty rate and the probability of detection on the declared income remain positive.

In Srinivasan's model, the assumptions of the nonregressivity of the tax rates ($T''(Y) \geq 0$), and the convexity of the penalty function [$P''(\lambda) \geq 0$], are important to the model because without either of them there is no guarantee that the model will have an optimum solution.

Based on the tax rate assumption, Srinivasan's model is more general than Allingham and Sandmo's model because it allows one to analyze a situation where there is a proportional tax rate as well as a progressive tax rate, while Allingham and Sandmo's model deals with the proportional tax rate only. Based on the penalty rate assumption, Srinivasan's model is also more general than Allingham and Sandmo's model because it allows one to analyze a situation where the penalty rate is progressive as well as where it is proportional, while Allingham and Sandmo deal only with proportional penalty rates. The significance of the difference in these two assumptions lies in the fact that Srinivasan's model is built of tax and penalty *functions*, whereas Allingham and Sandmo's model is built of tax and penalty *rates*. The key words are *functions* as opposed to *rates*. A model with tax and penalty *functions* is more flexible than a model with tax and penalty *rates* because the former allows one to manipulate different rate structures whereas the latter does not.

However, based on the objective functions, the model of Allingham and Sandmo is more general than that of Srinivasan because it allows the taxpayer to have his own utility function and because it takes account of the taxpayer's risk-bearing behavior while Srinivasan's model does not. Allingham and Sandmo's expected utility approach allows them to assume that the taxpayer is risk averse, which is more realistic than the risk-neutral assumption implicit in Srinivasan's model. However, since Allingham and Sandmo's utility function has only one argument—which is income—then, in terms of the coverage of the relevant factors affecting the taxpayer's utility, Allingham and Sandmo's model is not different from that of Srinivasan. And because Allingham and Sandmo's utility function has income as its only argument, ceteris paribus, the qualitative result of the two approaches would have been the same if the taxpayer's utility function had been a monotonic transformation of the expected income. However, as assumed by Allingham and Sandmo, the taxpayer's utility function is not a monotonic transformation of the expected income. This explains the differences in the qualitative results of the two models.

II. Theoretical Studies on Factors Affecting Tax Evasion

The Effect of the Tax Rate

It is frequently claimed that high tax rates induce tax evasion. This section reviews the theoretical literature to see whether there are grounds for such a claim. The effect of the tax rate on tax evasion is discussed in Allingham and Sandmo (1972), Yitzhaki (1974), McCaleb (1976), Sandmo (1981), and Koskela (1983a). As stated in the preceding section, Allingham and Sandmo (1972) have shown that the effect of the tax rate on tax evasion is indeterminate. However, their result is based on the assumption that the penalty is imposed on the understated income. The effect of the tax rate when the penalty is imposed on the evaded tax is discussed in Yitzhaki (1974), who uses the same model as Allingham and Sandmo to show that if a penalty is imposed on the evaded tax as is the case for Israel, Thailand, and a number of other countries, the indeterminacy disappears and the tax rate has a negative effect on tax evasion. Yitzhaki's result contradicts the general belief that high tax rates stimulate tax evasion. His economic explanation of this result is that once the penalty is imposed on the evaded tax, the ordinary tax rate as well as the penalty rate increases proportionally with θ. Therefore, there is no substitution effect and we are left with a pure income effect, which is positive. As the tax rate increases, the taxpayer increases his reported income and reduces the amount of tax evasion.

Based on Allingham and Sandmo's model, McCaleb (1976) shows that the effect of tax rates on tax payment, $\partial(\theta X)/\partial\theta$, can be either positive, zero, or negative, which implies that an increase in the tax rate may cause the tax payment to increase, remain the same, or decrease.

Sandmo (1981) also shows that on purely theoretical grounds, one cannot easily prove the popular claim that high rates of tax stimulate activities in the hidden economy. This conforms with the results of his first paper which he co-authored with Allingham (Allingham and Sandmo (1972)).

Koskela (1983a) found that if the penalty rate is imposed on the amount of income evaded, a compensated increase in the tax rate will increase tax evasion. However, if the penalty rate is imposed on the evaded tax, a compensated increase in the tax rate will reduce tax evasion. The compensated increase in the tax rate is an increase in the tax rate that is accompanied by a lump-sum transfer so that either the expected tax revenue of the government or the expected utility of the taxpayer remains unchanged. Like Allingham and Sandmo, Koskela uses the expected utility approach and assumes a decreasing absolute risk aversion. However, he explains that when the penalty rate is imposed on the undeclared income, the increase in the lump-sum transfer neutralizes the negative income effect on tax evasion and we are left with the positive substitution effect, which increases tax evasion as tax rate increases. On the other hand, if the penalty rate is imposed on the evaded tax, then the amount of penalty will increase proportionally with the tax; thus, there is no substitution effect and the increase in the tax rate has only a negative income effect on tax evasion. This income effect is now stronger than in the case where the penalty is imposed on the undeclared income because the evaded tax also increases as a result of the increase in the tax rate. Koskela's result does not provide grounds for the popular claim that an increase in the tax rate stimulates tax evasion. In the first place, Koskela, like Yitzhaki (1974), produced just the opposite result, that is, if the penalty is imposed on the evaded tax, an increase in the tax rate reduces tax evasion. In the second place, where Koskela provides grounds for stating that an increase in the tax rate increases tax evasion, it is under the condition that the tax rate increase is accompanied by an increase in the lump-sum transfer (in the form of tax exemptions) from the government to the taxpayer in an amount such that either the government's expected tax revenue or the taxpayer's expected utility remains unchanged. However, such a condition is not part of the claim.

To summarize, the theoretical literature does not support the claim that an increase in the tax rate will lead to an increase in tax evasion. Theoretical investigation shows that if the penalty rate is imposed on the evaded tax, an increase in the tax rate will lead to a reduction in tax evasion rather than to an increase as claimed. If the penalty rate is imposed on the understated income, the tax rate has an indeterminate effect on tax evasion. Only under the conditions that the penalty rate is imposed on the understated income and that such an increase in the tax rate is accompanied by a compensatory increase in the lump-sum transfer so that the expected tax revenue of the government remains unchanged will the increase in the tax rate lead to an increase in tax evasion. However, the second condition is not a part of the claim because the purpose of increasing the tax rate is to raise more revenue and not to keep the tax revenue unchanged.

The Effect of the Shape of the Tax Rate Schedule

Given the ability of an individual to pay tax, it is believed that a progressive tax rate schedule will generate more tax revenue than a proportional tax rate schedule. However, such a belief is based on the assumption that tax evasion does not exist. If tax evasion exists, it is uncertain whether a progressive tax rate schedule will generate more tax revenue. However, in recent years it has been popularly claimed that a progressive tax rate schedule stimulates tax evasion and consequently will yield less tax revenue to the government than a proportional tax rate schedule. Therefore, it is useful to investigate whether such a claim has theoretical grounds.

The effect of the shape of the tax rate schedule on tax evasion is considered in Srinivasan (1973), Nayak (1978), and Koskela (1983b). Srinivasan, assuming a progressively increasing penalty multiplier and a probability of detection, Π, independent of the level of income, y, shows that a progressive tax function that yields the same revenue as the proportional tax function in the absence of understatement of income will yield less expected revenue and penalties in the presence of understatement of income. Nayak, using a model along the lines of Srinivasan and assuming that the penalty is a progressive function of the fraction of income understated, λ, finds that a regressive tax function, which yields the same total tax revenue as a proportional tax function in the absence of understatement of income, will yield a larger expected revenue in the presence of the optimum understatement of income.

The results of the analyses of Srinivasan and Nayak imply that if the progressive, proportional, and regressive tax rate structures, which are designed to generate the same amount of revenue in a situation where tax evasion does not exist, are enforced in a situation where tax evasion does exist, a regressive tax rate structure will yield the highest tax revenue. The analyses also show that a proportional tax rate structure will yield higher revenue than a progressive tax rate structure.

Koskela (1983b), using the expected utility maximization approach and assuming a general tax function, shows that given the decreasing absolute risk aversion, the direction of the change in the fraction of income reported when the actual income increases is ambiguous for progressive and regressive taxation. However, when the taxation is linear progressive,[6] the nondecreasing relative risk aversion is a sufficient, but not a necessary, condition for the negative relationship between the fraction of income not being declared and the actual income. When the taxation is linear regressive,[7] the nonincreasing relative risk aversion is a sufficient, but not a necessary,

[6]A linear progressive tax is a linear tax function with a negative lump-sum tax, for example, $t(x) = -r + tx$. Note that here, progressivity is measured in terms of the average tax rate rather than the marginal tax rate.

[7]A linear regressive tax is a linear tax function with a positive lump-sum tax, for example, $t(x) = r + tx$. As in the case of the linear progressive tax, here too the regressivity is measured in terms of the average tax rate rather than the marginal tax rate.

condition for the positive relationship between the fraction of income not being declared and the actual income.

The intuitive explanation of the ambiguity is that under the progressive and regressive tax rates, the substitution effect and the income effect work in opposite directions. In the case of progressive taxation, on the one hand, the fraction of income reported tends to decrease as the actual income increases due to the substitution effect because it is more profitable to evade taxes. On the other hand, a rise in the income reported induced by an increase in the actual income raises the average taxes and thus makes the taxpayer worse off. This income effect tends to increase the fraction of income reported as the actual income increases. Thus, the effect is ambiguous. In the case of regressive taxation, on the one hand, the fraction of income reported tends to increase as the actual income increases due to the substitution effect because, at a lower marginal tax rate, it is less profitable to evade tax. On the other hand, a rise in the fraction of income reported, induced by an increase in the actual income, lowers the average taxes and thus makes the taxpayer better off. This income effect tends to decrease the fraction of income reported as the actual income increases. The end results depend on the size of the parameters which are unknown on a priori grounds. If the marginal tax rates are constant, then there is no substitution effect because there is no change in the relative prices, and the fraction of income not being declared depends on the behavior of the average taxes and the relative risk aversion. Thus, Koskela concluded that, given any hypothesis on the relative risk aversion, the linear regressive tax rate schedule, and not the linear progressive tax rate schedule, tends to induce a rise in the fraction of income not being declared when the actual income increases.

At first glance, it seems that Koskela's conclusion contradicts the conclusions of Srinivasan, as well as those of Nayak. However, a closer examination indicates that the two sets of conclusions are not contradictory. Srinivasan and Nayak deal with the aggregate revenue under progressive, proportional, and regressive tax rate structures, while Koskela deals with the effect of the change in the actual income of a single taxpayer on the fraction of income that he reported. In Srinivasan and Nayak's analyses, there is a restriction that the three tax rate structures will yield the same amount of revenue to the government, whereas there is no such restriction in Koskela's analysis. Koskela shows that under the linear progressive tax rate structure, an increase in the actual income would lead to a reduction in the fraction of income not being declared, whereas under the linear regressive tax structure, an increase in the actual income will lead to an increase in the fraction of income not being declared. This is where the seeming contradiction arises because it implies that under the linear regressive tax rate structure, as the income of an individual increases, the fraction of income reported decreases, which tempts one to think that the amount of revenue will be reduced. This is not necessarily the case because it depends on the relative change in the fraction of income reported with respect to the relative change in the actual income. Only if the percentage reduction of the income reported is greater than the percentage increase of the actual income will there be a decrease in the total tax revenue to the government. The tax rate does not have any effect here because, first, the marginal tax rate is imposed on the marginal income and, second, under the linear regressive tax rate structure, the marginal tax rate is constant. Thus, as long as there is an increase in the absolute amount of reported income, there will always be an increase in the revenue no matter how much the fraction of income reported changes.

The regressive, the linear progressive, and the linear regressive tax rate schedules will not be discussed further because they exist only in theory and are not likely to be implemented. We will now consider the progressive and the proportional tax rate schedules because the former exists in most countries and the latter appears frequently in the tax policy literature and may replace the former.

Based on the two types of tax rate schedules, although Srinivasan's results are not exactly comparable with those of Koskela, they do suggest the same area of policy concerns, although they suggest them differently. According to Srinivasan, a progressive tax should not be implemented because it yields less revenue in the presence of tax evasion. However, Koskela's result suggests that whether a progressive tax will yield more or less revenue is uncertain because it is not certain whether the fraction of income reported will increase or decrease when the actual income increases. The source of the differences lies in the assumption concerning the risk-bearing behavior of the taxpayer. Srinivasan's assumptions imply that the taxpayer is risk neutral, while Koskela assumes that the taxpayer has a decreasing absolute risk aversion. If the assumption of a risk-neutral taxpayer were incorporated in Koskela's analysis, there would be no income effect, leaving only a positive substitution effect of an increase in income on tax evasion; thus, as income increases tax evasion will increase because it is more profitable to evade tax at a higher rate of tax. Consequently, under the progressive tax rate structure, an increase in income will lead to a decline in the fraction of income reported. In that case, there will be no differences in the policies suggested by Srinivasan and Koskela.

Thus, it can be concluded that the popular claim that a progressive tax rate schedule stimulates tax evasion and consequently will yield less tax revenue to the government than the proportional tax rate schedule has theoretical support. However, such support is based on the assumption that the taxpayer is risk neutral. If the taxpayer is assumed to have a decreasing absolute risk-aversion behavior, then the claim has no theoretical support.

The Effect of the Penalty Rate

The penalty is incorporated in the tax system to discourage tax evasion. It is generally believed that the effect of a penalty is to deter tax evasion. This section will survey the literature to see whether such a belief has theoretical grounds.

The effect of the penalty rate on tax evasion is discussed in Allingham and Sandmo (1972), Singh (1973), McCaleb (1976), Sandmo (1981), and Koskela (1983b). In Section I we have shown that Allingham and Sandmo (1972) demonstrated that an increase in the penalty rate will always increase the fraction of actual income declared. Singh (1973), using the maximization of expected income approach, shows that the higher the penalty rate, the lower the magnitude of tax evasion.

McCaleb (1976) finds that an increase in the penalty rate will lead to an increase in the tax payment. This result is based on the assumption that all policy parameters, namely, the tax rate (θ), the penalty rate (Π), and the probability of detection and conviction (P) are independent. However, if the probability of detection and conviction (P) depends negatively on the penalty rate (Π), then the effect of an increase in the penalty rate on the amount of unreported income and on the amount of tax is indeterminable. McCaleb states that the reason for assuming that the probability of detection and conviction depends on the penalty rate is because it is likely that the probability of conviction by a judge or jury may vary inversely with the severity of the punishment.

Sandmo (1981)[8] also shows that an increase in the penalty rate will lead to a decrease in the supply of hours worked in the informal market, which implies that the proportion of unreported income will decrease and the proportion of reported income will increase.

Koskela (1983b), using the expected utility maximization approach and assuming a general tax function (i.e., the structure of the tax rate could be either progressive,[9] proportional, or regressive[10]), as well as the endogenous probability of detection, found that a penalty is a deterrent to tax evasion.

[8]Care should be taken in comparing Sandmo's results with those of the others because Sandmo's labor supply specification deals with compensated changes.

[9]A progressive tax rate is defined to be a function in which $t'' > 0$, and $t - t'(x) < 0$ (i.e., the average tax is less than the marginal tax).

[10]A regressive tax is one in which $t'' < 0$, $t - t'(x) > 0$ (i.e., the average tax is greater than the marginal tax).

To summarize, theoretical results indicate that the penalty has a negative effect on tax evasion except in cases where the probability of detection is a negative function of the penalty. In such cases, the effect of the penalty on tax evasion is indeterminate. Thus, it can be concluded that, generally, the belief that the penalty is a deterrent to tax evasion has theoretical support.

The Effect of the Probability of Detection

The effect of the probability of detection on tax evasion is discussed in Allingham and Sandmo (1972), Srinivasan (1973), Singh (1973), McCaleb (1976), Christiansen (1980), Sandmo (1981), and Koskela (1983b).

Allingham and Sandmo (1972) have shown that the effect of an increase in the probability of detection is to increase the reported income. Srinivasan (1973) also shows that an increase in the probability of detection will lead to a decrease in the optimal proportion of understated income. On the basis of the tax structure of India, Singh (1973) shows that at a constant penalty rate, the higher the value of probability of detection (Π), the lower the proportion of income understated (λ). This means that an increase in the probability of detection is a deterrent to tax evasion.

McCaleb (1976) shows that an increase in the combined probability of detection and conviction would lead to an increase in the tax payment. Christiansen (1980) discussed the relative effectiveness of the penalty rate and the probability of detection as deterrents of tax evasion, which implies that an increase in the probability of detection reduces tax evasion. Koskela (1983b), assuming an endogenously determined probability of detection, shows that an increase in the probability is a deterrent to tax evasion. He assumes that the probability of detection depends positively, but linearly, on the ratio of the undeclared income to the actual income, that is, $P = P(W - X)/W$; $P' > 0$, $P'' = 0$. The reasons for assuming that P is endogenously determined and is a function of X and W is because the tax authorities might base their audit and investigation policy on a statistical hypothesis that in the absence of any knowledge about the actual income, a person with a low reported income is more likely to be an evader than a person with a higher reported income; thus, the former is more likely to be subject to audit and investigation than the latter. Moreover, the authorities may have some crude indication from the general observation that the actual income of some specific taxpayers in certain sectors has increased but the reported income is unchanged. This will lead to an audit of the taxpayer's account, which suggests that P is related to W.

To summarize, all theoretical analyses indicate that an increase in the probability of detection will lead to a decrease in tax evasion.

The Effect of Fiscal Inequity

So far, we have focused our attention on four factors, namely, the tax rate, the progressivity of the tax system, the penalty rate, and the probability of detection. All these four factors were analyzed within the framework of the conventional tax evasion models. However, these models have been criticized for being overly simplified because they view tax evasion as only a special form of gambling, namely, the gambling for extra income in light of the likelihood of detection and penalties imposed on detected tax evaders. This view takes account of only one element in the relationship between the government and the taxpayer. According to Spicer and Lundstedt (1976), the relationship between a taxpayer and his government contains at least three elements—the element of coercion, the element of internalized norm or role expectation, and the element of exchange. The conventional tax evasion model takes account of only the coercive element of the relationship. The element of exchange is discussed below. The element of internalized norm is not considered in this paper since it belongs to the realms of human psychology and sociology rather than economics.

In the element of exchange, a taxpayer is seen as exchanging purchasing power in the market in return for government services. Thus, the taxpayer's behavior is affected by his satisfaction or lack of satisfaction with his terms of trade with the government. Tax evasion is seen partly as an attempt by the taxpayer to adjust his terms of trade with the government in response to dissatisfaction stemming from a perceived inequity in his terms of trade when compared with other taxpayers. Thus, another factor affecting tax evasion is the perceived relative inequity in the taxpayer's terms of trade with the government. This idea has been developed further by Spicer and Becker (1980) as the link between (horizontal) fiscal inequity and tax evasion. In this context, the taxpayers' utility functions are assumed to be interdependent so that the utility derived from extra income accrued through tax evasion depends on the taxpayer's sense of equity regarding his relationship with the government. If the taxpayer perceives himself to be a victim of inequity, his anger increases the marginal utility that he derives from an extra dollar of tax evasion income and hence increases tax evasion. On the other hand, if he perceives himself to be the beneficiary of fiscal inequity, his guilt feelings reduce his marginal utility of income from tax evasion and hence decrease evasion. Proponents of this hypothesis acknowledge that it is not possible for the taxpayer to assess the exact value of what he pays and what he receives from the government in return. However, they argue that it seems reasonable to assume that the taxpayer has general impressions and attitudes concerning his own and others' terms of trade with the government. As far as evidence is concerned, a number of survey research and simulation studies have reported positive correlations between the perception of fiscal inequity and tax evasion.[11]

III. Empirical Studies on Factors Affecting Tax Evasion

Empirical studies on tax evasion take two approaches: the simulation approach and the survey approach. These two approaches are discussed below.

Simulation or Experimental Approach

Arguing that theoretical models of optimal evasion, though yielding interesting insights, are often beset by key, ambiguously signed derivatives, Friedland and others (1978) conduct a tax evasion study using the game-simulation approach. They simulate taxpaying situations and conduct experiments on 15 subjects. Their objectives are to find out (1) how sensitive income tax evasion is to changes in tax rates; (2) which socioeconomic variables are related to tax evasion; (3) whether the decisions to evade tax and the extent of tax evasion are separate and distinct decisions; and (4) whether large fines are a more effective deterrent than frequent audits. Their subjects are seven male and eight female Israeli undergraduate psychology students whose average age is 25. Regression and correlation analyses based on data from the experiments indicate that the relation between underreporting and the tax rate can be experimentally determined (at $t =$ 25 percent, the incidence of underreporting occurred 50 percent of the time, and at $t = 50$ percent, the incidence occurred 80 percent of the time). The decision to evade tax (P) and the extent to which taxes are underreported (X) are distinct and separate decisions. Large fines with a small probability of detection are a more effective deterrent than small fines with a large probability of detection. Women are more likely to evade, but understate a much smaller fraction of their income than men, and those who habitually buy lottery tickets are not more likely to evade than those who do not. However, lottery ticket buyers conceal much more income when they do evade.

Spicer and Becker (1980) use a simulation approach to test the relationship between tax evasion and perceived fiscal inequity. Their hypothesis is that tax evasion increases for victims of fiscal inequity but decreases for beneficiaries of fiscal inequity. Their experiment is conducted on 57 sub-

[11]See, for example, Strümpel (1969), Spicer and Lundstedt (1976), and Spicer and Becker (1980).

jects, 21 of whom are male and 36 female. Inequity is simulated by providing some participants with false information regarding relative tax rates. The result is that the perceived high-tax group has an evasion rate of 33 percent, the perceived medium-tax group a rate of 25 percent, and the perceived low-tax group a rate of 12 percent. A regression analysis based on data from the experiments indicates that the perceived relative tax rates, sex, and age are significant in explaining the variation in the percentage of tax evaded, but the income is not significant. This regression result supports the hypothesis that perceived inequity is another factor that affects tax evasion and that the amount of taxes evaded increases for victims of fiscal inequity but decreases for beneficiaries of fiscal inequity.

Survey Approach

The survey approach is less restrictive than the theoretical model and the simulation approach in that it allows the investigator to consider a wider range of factors. However, the survey approach is subject to sampling biases and sampling errors as well as to the problem of the reliability of the responses. Factors affecting the tax evasion examined in the survey studies can be classified into four types, namely, factors related to the degree of sanctions, administrative capabilities, fiscal inequity, and social norms. Spicer and Lundstedt (1976) investigate these four types of factors. In particular, their hypotheses are (1) tax evasion is less likely when sanctions against it are perceived to be severe; (2) tax evasion is less likely when the probability of detection is perceived to be high; (3) tax evasion is more likely when a taxpayer perceives his terms of trade with the government to be inequitable compared with other taxpayers; and (4) the more tax evaders a taxpayer knows, the more likely he is to evade taxes himself. Spicer and Lundstedt conduct a survey on 130 households selected from two suburbs in a large metropolitan area in central Ohio. From the survey data, a "tax resistance scale," a tax evasion index, and an inequity index are constructed. The scale measures a relative propensity to evade taxes rather than tax evasion itself. The tax evasion index provides a way to assess the extent to which a taxpayer evades taxes. The inequity index measures the perceived fiscal inequity. Regression analyses indicate that the inequity index and the number of tax evaders known personally (a proxy of factors related to social norms) are significantly and positively related to tax evasion. The perceived probability of detection is significant in the equation using tax resistance as a dependent variable but not in the one using tax evasion. The perceived severity of sanctions is not significant in any equation.

Spicer and Lundstedt find that the level of family income is negatively related to tax resistance and that the proportion received in wages, salaries, and pensions is positively related. The first finding is in conflict with Srinivasan's theoretical result[12] and with Mork's (1975) finding, which is reviewed below. The second finding contradicts the general belief that tax evasion opportunities decrease as the proportion of income received in wages, salaries, and pensions increases. Spicer and Lundstedt explain that these discrepancies may have arisen because those with higher incomes or smaller proportions of wage income have greater opportunities to resort to tax avoidance—which is legal—and, therefore, the motivation to undertake risky acts of tax evasion is reduced. They also find that age is significant and negatively related to tax resistance, whereas the experience with tax audits is significant but positively related to tax resistance.

Mork (1975) uses interview data from the Norwegian Occupational Life History Study, which are compiled by the Institute of Applied Social Research in Oslo. This data source, which is composed of 3,479 observations, is extraordinarily extensive and includes data on the 1970 income of the interview respondents. The income data from the survey are then compared with the assessed income[13] and pension-giving income[14] from the income tax return of each respondent. These income data are tabulated by income classes, and the average reported assessed income (X_1) and the average reported pension-giving income (X_2) for each class are then divided by the interview income (W) obtaining X_1/W and X_2/W. If we consider the interview income (W) as actual income, then X_1/W and X_2/W are the proportion of income reported in the context of the standard tax evasion models. Mork found that as income moves to the higher brackets, the proportion of income reported is smaller. Thus, Mork concludes that empirical evidence indicates that as income increases the proportion of income reported decreases. This, in the framework of Allingham and Sandmo (1972), implies that the relative risk aversion is a decreasing function of income. This result is consistent with Srinivasan's theory but inconsistent with Spicer and Lundstedt's survey result.

Enrick (1963), using the survey approach, investigates U.S. taxpayers' income tax consciousness or awareness. In particular, his purposes are to

[12]Which indicates that $\partial\lambda^*/\partial y > 0$; λ^* being the optimal proportion by which income is understated.

[13]Assessed income is full income (including capital income) minus legal deductions, such as interest payments and cost incurred in connection with one's occupation, but it does not exclude "special deductions," which are a part of income made tax free because of illness, infirmity, etc.

[14]Pension-giving income is roughly the income from active work, whether the worker is employed by someone else or is his own employer.

examine (1) how accurately individuals estimate their own tax liabilities, apart from the particular day near April 15 when a final return must be filed; (2) if they tend to make errors in estimation, in what direction are these likely to fall; and (3) whether the withholding has a demonstrable effect on the accuracy or inaccuracy of estimation. Enrick argues that the study of tax consciousness or awareness is important because if we do not know peoples' tax consciousness it does not make much sense to claim that we know the extent to which changes in their tax burden will affect their behavior. In Enrick's survey, first, without referring to his income tax return, each participant is asked to guess and write down the total amount of federal income tax he thought he had paid in the previous year and then after looking it up, write down the actual amount he paid. Enrick's survey result indicates that the respondents do not accurately know the amount of federal income taxes they paid. In addition, a slight tendency to underestimate rather than overestimate the amount of tax paid is noted. And finally, there is no demonstrable effect of withholding on the degree of income tax awareness. Schmölders[15] conducts a similar study for the Federal Republic of Germany but reports a moderate degree of tax overestimation. According to Enrick, the difference between his result and that of Schmölders is possibly due to the difference in questionnaire technique. The German taxpayer is asked to estimate his tax burden as a percent of gross income. The taxpayer's error is then evaluated based on statistical data on average income taxes paid by various craft, business, and professional groups of taxpayers. Enrick argues that by being asked only one figure, the respondent may possibly have felt inclined to exaggerate his tax burden. In Enrick's study, the taxpayers are asked both the estimated and the actual tax paid in juxtaposition.

IV. Limitations of the Literature

In order to put the literature in perspective, this section further clarifies the nature of tax evasion and highlights the scope and limitations of the literature.

Forms of Tax Evasion

There are four possible cases of tax evasion: (1) providing false values of the socioeconomic variables that enter into the determination of the tax base such as underreporting income or claiming nonexistent dependents; (2) intentionally misinterpreting the law so that the tax liability is mini-

[15]As reported in Enrick.

mized; (3) doing both (1) and (2); and (4) failing to file a tax return. The first case includes actions such as underreporting or unreporting of income, claiming nonexistent dependents, claiming fictitious expenditures, and engaging in any other illegal activities that have the effect of reducing the tax base (net income). The second case includes actions such as intentionally applying wrong tax rates, intentionally claiming unentitled tax credits, and engaging in any other illegal activities that would lead to the reduction of the legal tax liability.[16] The theoretical literature covers only the first case and part of the third case, which involve underreporting of net income. It does not cover tax evasion under the second case, the remaining part of the third case, and the fourth case. Thus, the scope of the literature is rather limited.

Types of Income Evaded

In general, taxation is evaded on two types of income: income derived from illegal activities and income derived from legal activities. For the former, the decision to evade taxes arises because the activities are illegal and need to be kept a secret; therefore, the income derived therefrom is not reportable. This decision may seem to be independent of tax policy and tax administrative parameters but is actually not.[17] For the latter, the decision to evade the taxes stems from the expected utility maximization or the expected income maximization behavior of the taxpayer. In this case, the decision to evade taxes is affected by tax policy and tax administrative parameters. The literature reviewed deals with tax evasion of income apparently derived from legal activities without reference to that derived from illegal activities.

Individual Versus Aggregate Tax Evasion Behavior

Tax evasion behavior is similar to consumption behavior in the sense that it can be analyzed either at the individual or micro-level, or at the aggregate or macro-level. Literature on the theoretical and empirical anal-

[16]Without reporting net income differently from the true income.

[17]The tax laws of most countries make no distinction between legal and illegal or even criminal activities. In many countries, there are ways to pay tax on illegal income (essentially, by reporting "laundered" income) that in practice makes the decision whether or not to evade as dependent on "administration parameters," that is, the quality of enforcement and penalties, as it is in the case of legal income.

ysis of tax evasion reviewed in the previous sections is at the micro-level,[18] because it deals with the decision making of individual taxpayers rather than the aggregate pattern of tax evasion in the economy as a whole. Thus, it cannot directly provide an answer to the question why tax evasion in one country differs from that in another. It can only provide some indirect suggestions explaining the differences.

Types of Factors Affecting Tax Evasion

Two types of factors affect tax evasion: tax and nontax. The former are factors within the tax system, such as the tax rate, the tax base, the tax structure, the penalty system, the probability of detection, and the probability that the penalty will be applied once evasion is detected. Nontax factors arise outside the tax system and influence the decision of an individual to evade tax. Nontax factors are of two types: micro-nontax factors and macro-nontax factors. Micro-nontax factors pertain to the individual taxpayer, such as sex or educational background, which influence his decision to evade tax. Macro-nontax factors relate to the characteristics of the economy as a whole, such as the price policy and the incomes policy of the economy. Whereas tax factors are more relevant to tax evasion on income derived from legal activities and nontax factors are more relevant to evasion on income derived from illegal activities, both factors have certain influences on evasion of both types of income. On the one hand, tax factors, such as excessively high tax rates and overly progressive tax rate schedules, may constitute a cause for illegal activities from which the income derived is not reportable. On the other hand, nontax factors may constitute a cause for tax evasion on income derived from legal activities. For example, an excessive government expenditure leakage through corruption may influence the taxpayer's decision to evade tax by underreporting income from legal activities.

Theoretical literature reviewed in this paper deals only with tax factors, but not with nontax factors, while empirical literature deals with tax and micro-nontax factors. Macro-nontax factors are not covered in the literature. Thus, the literature is limited in the sense that it takes account of only a part of the whole range of factors that affect tax evasion.

To summarize, the literature reviewed in Sections I, II, and III is limited

[18]Although, in analyzing the effects of tax rate schedules on tax evasion Srinivasan (1973) and Nayak (1978) deal with the total government tax revenue from income taxes, their primary concern is not the aggregate tax evasion. Their approaches are still micro-approaches because they derived the total tax revenue by integrating overall individual taxpayers rather than relating one aggregate variable to other aggregate variables within the system of the aggregate economy.

insofar as (1) it deals only with tax evasion through underreporting of income; (2) it covers evasion of legal income only; (3) it is a micro analysis; and (4) it takes account of only some of the factors that affect tax evasion.

V. The Role of Tax Factors

The Tax Rate

The effectiveness of the tax rate as a policy instrument for the deterrence of tax evasion depends on the relationship between the tax rate and tax evasion, that is, whether the high tax rate is a cause of tax evasion. Unfortunately, such a relationship has not been definitely established one way or the other. On the one hand, it is generally believed that a high tax rate is the main cause of tax evasion. Such a belief is supported by observations, reports, and studies of experts and committees on taxation as well as by statements of tax policymakers. For example, Kaldor (1956), in his well-known report on Indian tax reform, states that the incentive to evade taxes depends on the marginal rates of taxation, because these govern the gains from evasion as a percent of the sum evaded. Kaldor's statement is reinforced by the Direct Taxes Administration Enquiry Committee (1960) of India, which finds that high personal income tax rates are one of the major reasons for tax evasion. The Committee observes in its report that many witnesses state that the prevailing high rates of taxation are one of the main causes for tax evasion and that the high rates of tax in the high-income brackets are said to be tolerated only because of the considerable evasion that takes place. Moreover, the then Finance Minister of India, in his budget speech, stated that he had come to the conclusion that in India, the tax rate of direct tax at top levels encouraged large-scale evasion. Tanzi (1983a, p. 5), in discussing the erosion of tax bases in developing countries, states that, "High tax rates, of course, make the problem of evasion worse." Herschel (1978), in commenting on the relationship between tax evasion and tax avoidance, states that both of them can be considered as alternative means of facing extremely high tax rates. This implies that high tax rates are one source of tax evasion. In addition, a simulation study by Friedland and others suggests that beyond some rate of tax, the fraction of reported income becomes very elastic with respect to the tax rate and that the positive relationship between the decision to underreport is increased as the tax rate increases. Moreover, survey data used by Mork (1975) indicate that taxpayers in higher-income brackets who pay tax at higher rates tend to have a higher proportion of underreported income. Furthermore, in an analysis of individual tax returns, Clotfelter (1983) finds that higher tax rates tend to stimulate tax evasion.

On the other hand, as reviewed in Section II, the results of theoretical analyses do not directly confirm the belief that a high tax rate is the cause of tax evasion. Such theoretical results are supported by the experience of tax administrators, tax committees, and some empirical observations. For example, tax administrators in many developing countries believe that, as far as farmers, traders, and professionals are concerned, tax evasion exists at all income levels and not only in the high-income brackets where the marginal tax rate is high. Moreover, the Working Group on Central Direct Taxes Administration of the Administrative Reforms Commission of India (1969), which investigated the causes of tax evasion by studying the amounts of detected concealed incomes, reported that an increase in the rate of taxation was not followed by an increase in tax evasion, nor did a decrease in the rates bring about a higher tax responsiveness. Furthermore, the experience of tax administration in India suggests that lower tax rates do not secure better tax compliance; for example, during 1970/71 to 1978/79 when the marginal tax rates were steeply reduced, income tax collection as a proportion of national income in the nonagricultural sector was also reduced. All these are evidence that there is no relation between high tax rates and tax evasion.

The empirical results for both sides of the argument are sketchy and indirect, which indicate that further such studies are needed before making a definitive conclusion regarding the effect of the tax rate on tax evasion. Thus, one may conclude that the effectiveness of the tax rate as a policy measure for the deterrence of tax evasion is unclear.

The Penalty Rate and the Probability of Detection

Unlike the tax rate, the theoretical result of the effect of the penalty rate on tax evasion is much clearer. According to the tax evasion model, a penalty has a negative effect on tax evasion[19] except when the probability of detection is a function of the penalty; in such a case, the effect of a penalty on tax evasion is indeterminate. For the probability of detection, the message from the theoretical result is even clearer because all theoretical analyses, without any exception, indicate that an increase in the probability of detection is a deterrent to tax evasion. The next legitimate question is, if both the probability of detection and the penalty rate are deterrents to tax evasion, what is their relative effectiveness? A number of theoretical analyses have addressed this issue, which are reviewed below chronologically.

Singh (1973) finds that, at a given proportion of underreported income,

[19] The literature has focused only on penalties that are in the form of a percentage of either the tax bill or the tax evaded. No account is taken of nonmonetary sanctions.

there is a negative relationship between the penalty rate and the probability of detection. He also finds that, for India, if the penalty rate is at 200 percent of the evaded income, then the probability of detection must be one third for the proportion of underreported income to be zero, that is, no evasion at all. McCaleb (1976) argues on theoretical grounds alone that the penalty rate and the probability of detection are superior instruments to tax rates in generating increased tax payments through the reduction of tax evasion because the tax rate gives indeterminate results, whereas both the penalty rate and the probability of detection give a definite result. Further, he argues that if the implementation cost is also taken into account, then the penalty rate is superior to the probability of detection. Thus, he draws a general conclusion that only the penalty rate on unreported income is a preferred instrument on the grounds of both certainty of the effect and the cost of implementation. Christiansen (1980) finds that, given a constant expected gain from tax evasion, if the penalty is increased and the probability of detection is adjusted downward accordingly, risk averters will always reduce their tax evasion. This implies that a high penalty rate is a more effective deterrent to tax evasion than the high probability of detection. Further, if the penalty rate is "small enough," then an increase in the penalty rate will increase tax evasion. However, if the initial penalty rate is "large enough," an increase in the penalty rate will reduce tax evasion. This indicates that when the penalty rate is initially low, then an increase in the probability of detection is more effective than an increase in the penalty rate. When the penalty rate is high enough, then an increase in the penalty rate is more effective than an increase in the probability of detection.

Koskela (1983b), introducing cost of detection into his model, finds that provided the ratio of the marginal cost of detecting tax evasion is "small," large penalties seem to be more effective deterrents to tax evasion than high probability of detection. He explains that an intuitive interpretation of this result is that an increase in the penalty rate and a decline in the probability of detection that results in a constant expected gain from a given tax evasion induces a greater loss for the taxpayer in the case of detection. Greater risk will thereby be involved and tax evasion will decline assuming that the taxpayers are risk averse. Further, he demonstrates that a high penalty rate is a more effective deterrent to tax evasion than large lump-sum fines. This is because the lump-sum fine does not vary with the amount of undeclared income and thus leaves more incentive to risk-taking than the penalty rate, which varies with the declared income. Friedland and others (1978) report that their simulation study indicates that a high penalty rate with a low probability of detection is a more effective deterrent than a low penalty rate with a high probability of detection.

To summarize, at least in theory, both the probability of detection and the penalty rate are effective deterrents of tax evasion and the penalty rate is relatively more effective than the probability of detection.[20]

Factors Relating to Tax Administration

The Withholding Scheme

Evidence from the Tax Compliance Measurement Program (TCMP)[21] indicates that the wage and salary income which is under a withholding scheme has a high rate of compliance or a low rate of evasion.[22] Moreover, statistics in many developing countries indicate that a sizable amount of income tax is collected from wages and salaries and is deducted at the source. (For example, in Thailand 78 percent of individual income taxes is collected from wages and salaries; the corresponding figures are 73 percent for Cyprus, 70 percent for Indonesia, and 67 percent for Turkey.) This indicates that a tax withholding scheme is an effective means of preventing tax evasion. However, the problem with the withholding scheme is that it cannot be applied to many types of income because, for the withholding scheme to be effective, there must be a relatively small number of easily identifiable payers of the income. Many types of income, for example, rental income, income of professionals, and income from small businesses, do not lend themselves to withholding schemes because there are more payers than receivers of such income. However, capital income, such as dividend and interest paid by banks, does lend itself to withholding schemes because there are a lot fewer payers of such income than receivers. Agricultural income of farmers, whose products are mainly for export or for further processing by domestic factories (for example, sugarcane in Thailand and rubber in Indonesia) also lends itself to withholding schemes. However, care should be taken in introducing withholding schemes on these types of income because if the schemes are not correctly instituted and administered, the withholding tax becomes the final tax and acts more like an export tax or a sales tax on agricultural products rather than as an income tax on farmers. This is because the tax is based on turnover rather than on income and the tax does not vary with the income of the taxpayer. Farmers who experience losses still have to pay this tax.

[20]Note that this is a theoretical result. In many countries, high penalties contained in legal codes are never applied in practice and have little or no deterrent effect.

[21]For further discussion on the TCMP, see Henry (1983).

[22]The 1976 TCMP result reported a 99 percent "Voluntary Compliance Level" (VCL) for income from wages and salaries. The VCL is defined as the ratio of the reported tax to the sum of the reported and the unreported taxes.

The Self-Enforcement Tax System

Economists have attempted to design an interlocking tax system in such a way that it will rely on the self-interest of taxpayers to encourage them to provide information to the tax department. Kaldor (1956), in his well-known report on India, suggests that the five taxes, namely, the income tax, the capital gains tax, the wealth tax, the personal expenditure tax, and the gift tax be filed in a single comprehensive return and should be assessed simultaneously. Kaldor explains that the advantage of filing a comprehensive single return and simultaneous assessment is that the taxes are self-checking in character for two reasons: first, concealment or understatement of items in order to reduce liability in some taxes may increase liability in other taxes, and, second, the information furnished by a taxpayer in order to prevent overassessment of his own liabilities automatically reveals the receipts and gains made by other taxpayers. Higgins (1959) carries Kaldor's idea further by introducing a self-enforcing incentive tax system for developing countries. Higgins's system includes (1) a personal income tax (including capital gains), (2) a corporation income tax, (3) a general sales or turnover tax, (4) a wealth tax, (5) a tax on excess inventory, and (6) a personal expenditure tax. Theoretically, the Kaldor-Higgins system is self-checking because personal expenditure is defined as the excess of income over savings, and savings are equal to the increase in net wealth. Thus, taxpayers who underreport their expenditure by overstating their savings increase their wealth tax liability. A seller of a property who understates his capital gains hurts the buyer because the buyer cannot claim the full amount of the investment, thereby forcing him to declare higher expenditures and increasing his expenditure tax liability. The excess inventory tax is designed to discourage underreporting of sales, thus helping to enforce sales and income tax. However, the system is not practical and cannot be implemented. Goode (1981, p. 266), commenting on some economic aspects of tax administration states:

> These proposals appear so unrealistic that a detailed critique is not worthwhile. In my opinion, their authors exaggerated the proclivity of taxpayers to refined calculations, the capacity of tax departments to use the great mass of data that would be generated, and the receptivity of governments to fiscal innovations. I suspect that most tax administrators will regard the idea of a self-enforcing tax system as fantastical. Even if put into operation, the proposed systems would not prevent evasion in cases in which both parties to a transaction omit it from their records or understate its amount. Both parties could evade the related taxes, and as no conflict of interest would arise between them, neither would have an economic incentive to report correctly.

Other Administrative Factors

Other tax administrative measures that can possibly prevent tax evasion include the simplification of tax laws and procedures, taxpayer education, the publicizing of names of tax law offenders, and the honesty of the tax enforcing department. These measures are practiced in a number of countries with varying degrees of success.

VI. The Role of Nontax Factors in Developing Countries

Nontax Factors[23]

As pointed out in Section IV, the theoretical models of tax evasion deal only with micro-analysis of tax evasion and account only for tax factors affecting tax evasion, while some empirical studies under review account for tax and micro-nontax factors but not macro-nontax factors. Such models and studies do not directly or fully explain why tax evasion varies from one country to another. We now consider several macro-nontax factors that can affect tax evasion in developing country circumstances. No attempt is made here to establish the relative importance of the various macro-nontax factors.

Micro-nontax factors are relevant only to the micro-analysis of tax evasion behavior but are not relevant when macro-tax evasion behavior (such as intercountry comparison of tax evasion behavior) is considered because their effects tend to be canceled when the variables are aggregated. Macro-nontax factors are relevant to both micro-analysis and macro-analysis of tax evasion behavior. Since the focus here is on the intercountry comparison of tax evasion, only macro-nontax factors will be explored.

Price Control Policies

Price control tends to generate black markets and tax evasion, irrespective of whether the control is in the goods and services market, the factor market, the money market, or the foreign exchange market. In the goods and services market, price control imposed on any good or service usually leads either to the understatement of sale receipts in the accounts that are prepared for the inspection of the tax authorities, or to the disappearance of such goods or services from the regular market; they can be purchased only in the black market at higher prices. In the factor markets, price control usually leads to the declaration of false prices of the factor being con-

[23] Tanzi (1983b) lists four causes of underground economy, namely, taxes, regulations, prohibition, and bureaucratic corruption.

trolled. For example, rent control usually leads to tax evasion either through the understatement of rental income in the tax return of the landlord, or through an unreported amount of premium[24] (which is usually substantial) that the landlord receives in cash before renting the property at the controlled rent. In an economy where the minimum wage is artificially set higher than the equilibrium wage, one is likely to find overstatements of wages paid in the tax returns of employers, unreported employment on the part of employees, and even illegal manufacturing plants because the plant owners could not register their plants since all or almost all employees receive salaries lower than the minimum wage. In the money market, the ceiling imposed on the interest rates often drives funds from the officially organized market to the unorganized market because interest rates in the organized market are closely controlled, while it is not possible to enforce such interest ceilings on loans in the unorganized market. The result is that a sizable amount of interest income from loans in the unorganized market is not taxed because it has not been reported to the tax authorities. In the foreign exchange market, if exchange rates are fixed artificially and differently from equilibrium rates, then a black market for foreign exchange is likely to develop. Such a market is not only illegal in itself but it also facilitates the operation of other illegal activities such as drug trafficking, smuggling, and illegal trade in arms and ammunition by making available foreign currencies needed for such activities, which otherwise would be available only through official channels.

Government Rules and Regulations

The preponderance of rules and regulations imposed by the government tends to increase tax evasion. This is because in an economy where there are too many and too complicated rules and regulations governing business practices, it is generally difficult, often not profitable, and sometimes impossible to do business legally. Thus, businesses have to find some ways to get around such rules and regulations and often have to do business illegally. For example, rules laid down to restrict trade—such as import quotas, import licensing, and import prohibitions—often lead to the problem of smuggling, which in itself is an evasion of customs duties and which generates other black markets. Once the black markets are started, tax

[24]For example, in India, rent controls have given rise to a system called "pugree," in which a substantial amount of money is received by the landlord, in cash, before the property is rented at the controlled rent. Pugree is a premium paid illegally to the landlord, outside the books of account at the time of change of tenancy of the property. The payment is usually made out of unaccounted money.

evasion follows automatically. Other examples of rules and regulations governing business practices are prohibitions, rationing, forced sales of commodities to the government or to the marketing board, town and city planning regulations, factory acts, permits to produce certain goods, and licenses required to start a shop.

Public Sector Salaries

Public officials have certain responsibility and authority which can either be used for providing public services or be abused for private benefit. If the salaries of such officials are not commensurate with their responsibility and authority, the temptation for them to abuse such authority and responsibility is high. Moreover, if their salaries are so low that they cannot maintain a reasonable standard of living, it is likely that they will find ways to supplement their income via legal or illegal means. If illegal means are used by officials other than tax officials, these are likely to have an indirect effect on increasing tax evasion. If such means are used by tax officials, these are likely to have both indirect and direct effects in increasing tax evasion.

Government's Expenditure Policy

Taxes finance government expenditures, which in turn are expended for the well-being of taxpayers. This is the justification for taxes and government expenditures. However, when taxpayers start to question the justification for either the size or the pattern of expenditures, or both, then they are unwilling to pay taxes, at least in the amount for which they are liable. For example, taxpayers may see no justification for the large size of the budget because they do not see why the government has to be so luxurious, or why they have to pay tax to support public servants who live much more lavishly than they do. Or, taxpayers may disagree with the government's spending policies such as defense spending or spending on welfare. In such a case, they will be unwilling to pay tax and such an unwillingness leads them to find ways of reducing their tax liability through legal or illegal means. This leads to either tax avoidance or tax evasion. Such evasion is based purely on political considerations.

Other Factors

Other nontax factors affecting tax evasion are, for example, the level of education of the population and the stage of development of the economy. The level of education of the population influences tax evasion in two ways. First, a better educated population is more likely to have a better understanding of the tax system and its purposes; thus, the chance that they will violate tax laws because of ignorance or because not enough attention is paid to the tax system, is reduced. Second, a well-educated population is more likely to know how the tax system works and thus can reduce its tax liabilities through utilization of various relief provisions available in the tax laws, thereby reducing the necessity to evade tax.

The stage of development of the economy can indirectly affect tax evasion. In developing countries, economic activities are conducted in a manner that does not lend itself to easy tax enforcement. In such countries, the agricultural sector is relatively large, the share of the self-sufficient economy in the total economy is high, the share of the nonmonetized economy to total gross domestic product is high, and small and scattered production units are more prevalent. Such circumstances hinder the effectiveness of the tax enforcement mechanism and create greater temptation and opportunity for tax evasion.

It would seem that not only the validity of the above argument concerning tax and nontax factors affecting tax evasion but also the extent to which such factors influence tax evasion can be tested empirically by using the regression technique. Such tests would enable us to explain why and how tax evasion differs between developing and developed countries. However, the absence of a well-defined and generally accepted measurement of tax evasion[25] prevents us from making such a test. Thus, we have to rely on qualitative evaluation of such factors and we will do so for the developing countries in the next subsection.

Tax Evasion Under Developing Country Circumstances: Some Explanations

We have investigated both tax and nontax factors that affect tax evasion. We can now evaluate them with a view to shedding some light on the extent of tax evasion in developing country circumstances.

Until recently, the rate structures of the income tax in most developing countries have been highly progressive with respect to the absolute amount of income. Such high progressivity is likely to lead to high tax evasion, since, as has been shown, a progressive tax rate structure encourages tax evasion. The high progressivity of the income tax in developing countries is a result of historical developments in the tax systems of these countries.

The income tax laws of most developing countries are adapted from the tax laws of well-developed societies. As a result, on the one hand, one can

[25]For a review of the techniques for measurement of tax evasion, see Richupan (1984a and 1984b).

find a very sophisticated income redistribution scheme as well as built-in stabilizing measures in most of the tax laws—regardless of the stage of development of the countries. On the other hand, one also finds generous exemptions and relief for the promotion of development. The combination of generous exemptions and relief while there is pressing need for revenue to finance development and income redistribution concerns have led most developing countries to enforce highly progressive income tax systems.

Penalty rates in developing countries are quite varied. Some countries have rather high rates, while others have low rates. In many developing countries, only fixed fines are imposed, which are often out of date. With high rates of inflation, unless fixed fines are changed frequently, they become obsolete very rapidly. Many developing countries do not distinguish between penalties and interest, and charge only penalties without charging interest on the evaded tax. The penalties are charged as a percentage of either the evaded income or the evaded tax without any time dimension. Thus, the absence of interest charged on the evaded tax further weakens the effect of penalties. Since high penalty rates are rarely enforced, the deterrent effects of penalty rates in developing countries are likely to be low and therefore tax evasion is likely to be high.

The probability of detection depends on the efficiency of tax administration. Since tax administration in the developing countries is relatively inefficient, the probability of detection is likely to be low. Thus, tax evasion is likely to be high.

Price control is normally implemented because of equity considerations and is generally designed either to make goods or services that are subject to such control available to the public at the controlled low prices or to guarantee a certain minimum income level (in the case of the price of labor—the minimum wage). Price control is practiced more frequently in developing countries than in developed countries because of the greater need in developing countries to take into account equity considerations in conducting public policy. This is because, in general, personal income is more unevenly distributed in developing countries.[26] In the goods and services market, one generally finds that prices of essential goods are controlled either because of shortage of supply due to low productive capacity (in the case of goods domestically produced and consumed), or because of higher prices in foreign markets (in the case of domestically produced goods for domestic consumption as well as for export), or because of the lack of foreign exchange (in the case of imported goods). These occur-

[26]See, for example, Sen (1980).

rences are more frequent in developing countries than in developed countries. Thus, price controls are more prevalent in developing than in developed countries. In the factor market, rent control and the minimum wage are widely practiced in developing countries. In the money market, interest rates in the organized market are relatively inflexible, but the unorganized or parallel money market is very popular, whereas such a market is insignificant in developed countries. In the foreign exchange market, most developing countries use some form of fixed exchange rates, while the exchange rates in the major industrial countries are floating. Furthermore, most developing countries often experience balance of payments deficits and foreign exchange shortages because their foreign exchange earnings depend mainly on exports of primary products that fluctuate greatly either because of weather conditions or because of the fluctuation in the world market prices, over which they have no control. Fixed exchange rates, coupled with a high frequency of balance of payments deficits, lead to a black market for foreign exchange, which in turn leads to tax evasion.

On the extent to which the government regulates the economy through rules and regulations, there are no a priori reasons for stating whether it is more or less widely practiced in the developed or the developing countries. However, in some specific areas, for example, in import control, one can find a higher frequency of controls in developing countries than in developed countries, because foreign currency shortages occur more often in the developing countries.

In developing countries, there is often a large gap between the salaries of public employees and the income level needed for a reasonable standard of living, while such a gap is rarely observed in developed countries. This gap usually leads to either legal or illegal supplementary income. The unexplainable supplementary income of public officials contributes directly or indirectly to higher tax evasion.

Concerning the level of education and the stage of economic development, it is obvious that these are lower in developing countries than in developed countries. Thus, tax evasion due to these factors is likely to be higher in the former than in the latter.

To summarize, the developing country circumstances are characterized by a highly progressive nominal tax structure, ineffective penalty deterrents, low probability of detection, impaired horizontal fiscal equity, prevailing price controls in all markets, a moderate degree of government rules and regulations, a large gap between public sector salaries and a reasonable standard of living, low level of taxpayer education, and low stage of development. Since such circumstances stimulate tax evasion, it is likely to be higher in developing countries than in developed countries.

VII. Conclusions

This chapter has reviewed the theoretical and empirical literature concerning factors affecting tax evasion behavior and the policy measures for the deterrence of such behavior. Since only tax factors are analyzed in the literature, for the sake of completeness, the chapter has also explored nontax factors in a separate section and has evaluated developing country circumstances concerning such tax and nontax factors.

Theoretical and empirical studies dealing with the effect of tax rates on tax evasion give contradictory and inconclusive results. Theoretical studies indicate that such effects are indeterminate if the penalty is a function of the evaded income, negative if the penalty is a function of the evaded tax, and positive only if the penalty is imposed on the evaded income and the increase in the tax rate is accompanied by a reduction in the lump-sum transfer in such a way that the government's revenue remains unchanged. On the other hand, empirical studies suggest that such an effect is positive without any condition on the revenue of the government. However, both the theoretical and the empirical studies indicate that the effects of the penalty and the probability of detection on tax evasion are negative. In addition, theoretical studies indicate that in a situation where tax evasion exists, a regressive tax structure tends to generate the highest government revenue and a proportional tax structure tends to generate higher revenue than a progressive structure. On the effect of fiscal inequity, empirical studies confirm the belief that tax evasion is high among victims of fiscal inequity and low among beneficiaries of fiscal inequity.

On policy measures for the deterrence of tax evasion, both the theoretical and the empirical studies suggest that the penalty rate is more effective than the probability of detection. Among administrative measures for the prevention of tax evasion, withholding schemes seem to hold the greatest promise.

The nontax factors explored are price distortion, the extent of government rules and regulations governing business practices, the extent to which the public sector salaries are lower than the level required for a reasonable standard of living, the faith in the government's expenditure policy, as well as the level of education of the population and the stage of development of the economy. Evaluations of both tax and nontax factors in developing countries suggest that such factors appear to exist in developing countries to such a degree that they create circumstances that are highly conducive to tax evasion. Thus, the particular circumstances of developing countries leads one to question whether supply-side tax policy by itself will be able to discourage income tax evasion in these countries.

REFERENCES

Allingham, Michael G., and Agnar Sandmo, "Income Tax Evasion: A Theoretical Analysis," *Journal of Public Economics* (Amsterdam), Vol. 1 (November 1972), pp. 323-38.

Arrow, K.J., *Essays in the Theory of Risk-Bearing* (Chicago: Markham Publishing Company, 1971).

Christiansen, Vidar, "Two Comments on Tax Evasion," *Journal of Public Economics* (Amsterdam), Vol. 13 (June 1980), pp. 389-93.

Clotfelter, Charles T., "Tax Evasion and Tax Rates: An Analysis of Individual Returns," *Review of Economics and Statistics* (Cambridge, Massachusetts), Vol. 65 (August 1983), pp. 363-73.

Cross R.B., and G.K. Shaw, "The Evasion-Avoidance Choice: A Suggested Approach," *National Tax Journal* (Columbus, Ohio), Vol. 34 (December 1981), pp. 489-91.

Enrick, Norbert Lloyd, "A Pilot Study of Income Tax Consciousness," *National Tax Journal* (Columbus, Ohio), Vol. 16 (June 1963), pp. 169-73.

Friedland, Nehemiah, Shlomo Maital, and Aryeh Rutenberg, "A Simulation Study of Income Tax Evasion," *Journal of Public Economics* (Amsterdam), Vol. 10 (August 1978), pp. 107-16.

Goode, Richard, "Some Economic Aspects of Tax Administration," *Staff Papers*, International Monetary Fund (Washington), Vol. 28 (June 1981), pp. 249-74.

Henry, James S., "Noncompliance with U.S. Tax Law—Evidence on Size, Growth, and Composition," in *Income Tax Compliance: A Report of the ABA Section of Taxation, Invitational Conference on Income Tax Compliance* (Reston, Virginia, March 1983), pp. 15-112.

Herschel, Federico J., "Tax Evasion and Its Measurement in Developing Countries," *Public Finance* (The Hague), Vol. 33, No. 3 (1978), pp. 232-68.

Higgins, Benjamin, *Economic Development: Principles, Problems, and Policies* (New York: Norton, 1959).

India, *Report of the Direct Taxes Administration Enquiry Committee, 1958-59* (New Delhi: Government of India Press, 1960).

India, Administrative Reforms Commission, *Report of the Working Group on Central Direct Taxes Administration,* January 1968 (New Delhi: Government of India Press, 1969).

Kaldor, Nicholas, *Indian Tax Reform: Report of a Survey* (New Delhi: Department of Economic Affairs, Ministry of Finance, 1956).

Koskela, Erkki (1983a), "A Note on Progression, Penalty Schemes and Tax Evasion," *Journal of Public Economics* (Amsterdam), Vol. 22 (October 1983), pp. 127-33.

——— (1983b), "On the Shape of Tax Schedule, the Probability of Detection, and the Penalty Schemes as Deterrents to Tax Evasion," *Public Finance* (The Hague), Vol. 38, No. 1 (1983), pp. 70-80.

McCaleb, Thomas S., "Tax Evasion and the Differential Taxation of Labor and

Capital Income," *Public Finance* (The Hague), Vol. 31, No. 2 (1976), pp. 287-94.

Mork, Knut Anton, "Income Tax Evasion: Some Empirical Evidence," *Public Finance* (The Hague), Vol. 30, No. 1 (1975), pp. 70-76.

Nayak, P.B., "Optimal Income Tax Evasion and Regressive Taxes," *Public Finance* (The Hague), Vol. 33, No. 3 (1978), pp. 358-66.

Pratt, John W., "Risk Aversion in the Small and in the Large," *Econometrica* (Evanston, Illinois), Vol. 32 (January-April 1964), pp. 122-36.

Ratti, Ronald A., and Parthasarathi Shome, "The General Equilibrium Theory of Tax Incidence Under Uncertainty," *Journal of Economic Theory* (New York), Vol. 14 (February 1977), pp. 68-83.

Richupan, Somchai (1984a), "Income Tax Evasion: A Review of the Measurement Techniques and Some Estimates for the Developing Countries" (unpublished, International Monetary Fund, July 23, 1984).

——— (1984b), "Measuring Tax Evasion," *Finance & Development* (Washington), Vol. 21 (December 1984), pp. 38-40.

Sandmo, Agnar, "Income Tax Evasion, Labour Supply, and the Equity-Efficiency Tradeoff," *Journal of Public Economics* (Amsterdam), Vol. 16 (December 1981), pp. 265-88.

Schmölders, G., *Das Irrationale in der Öffentlichen Finanzwirtschaft* (Hamburg: Verlag Rowohlt, 1960).

Sen, Amartya, "Levels of Poverty: Policy and Change," World Bank Staff Working Paper No. 401 (Washington, 1980).

Singh, Balbir, "Making Honesty the Best Policy," *Journal of Public Economics* (Amsterdam), Vol. 2 (July 1973), pp. 257-63.

Spicer, Michael W., and Lee A. Becker, "Fiscal Inequity and Tax Evasion: An Experimental Approach," *National Tax Journal* (Columbus, Ohio), Vol. 33 (June 1980), pp. 171-75.

Spicer, Michael W., and S.B. Lundstedt, "Understanding Tax Evasion," *Public Finance* (The Hague), Vol. 31, No. 2 (1976), pp. 295-305.

Srinivasan, T.N., "Tax Evasion: A Model," *Journal of Public Finance* (Amsterdam), Vol. 2 (November 1973), pp. 339-46.

Strümpel, B., "The Contribution of Survey Research to Public Finance," in *Quantitative Analysis of Public Finance*, ed. by Alan T. Peacock (New York: Praeger, 1969).

Tanzi, Vito (1983a), "Tax Systems and Policy Objectives in Developing Countries: General Principles and Diagnostic Tests" (unpublished, International Monetary Fund, November 28, 1983).

——— (1983b), "The Underground Economy: The Causes and Consequences of this Worldwide Phenomenon," *Finance & Development* (Washington), Vol. 20 (December 1983), pp. 10-13.

United States, Internal Revenue Service, Office of the Assistant Commissioner (Planning and Research), *Taxpayer Compliance Measurement Handbook* (September 1977).

Yitzhaki, Shlomo, "A Note on Income Tax Evasion: A Theoretical Analysis," *Journal of Public Economics* (Amsterdam), Vol. 3 (May 1974), pp. 201-202.

7

Evidence on the Laffer Curve

The Cases of Jamaica and India

Liam P. Ebrill

This chapter evaluates the appropriateness of the tax reform proposals advocated by the so-called popular supply-side approach to economic policy in developing countries. The particular focus here is on the Laffer curve itself; that is, on the highly publicized proposition that it is possible for nominal tax revenue to increase when tax rates are reduced. The analysis attempts to determine whether examples of the Laffer curve exist in developing countries.

Section I of the chapter begins with a summary of the more important tenets of the popular supply-side approach as they apply to tax reform, followed by a discussion of those instances in which supply-side policies are held to have been successfully applied in developing countries. It is argued that some of the claims of the supply-side approach have yet to be demonstrated. Section II discusses in greater detail the cases of Jamaica and India, two developing countries in which, for whatever reason, tax changes (including some reforms) of relevance to the Laffer curve proposition had been implemented even before 1985 when this study was completed. An attempt is made to evaluate these (pre-1985) tax changes. Finally, in Section III, it is argued that, given the limited nature of the data available, the empirical tests lack sufficient discriminatory power to permit a definitive resolution of whether any given set of observations is consistent with the Laffer curve. If, as is likely, the quality of the data available for the two cases examined is typical of that for developing countries, the most important conclusion must be that assertions to the effect that developing countries are operating in regions of the Laffer curve, where tax rate reductions would lead to revenue increases, should be treated with caution.

I. The Supply-Side Approach

The literature on the popular supply-side approach to economic policy is by now voluminous. It is not the intent to summarize here the content of that literature and its relationship to the traditional public finance literature, since that has already been done elsewhere.[1] Rather, this chapter focuses on those elements of the popular supply-side approach that bear most directly on the issue of the Laffer curve.

Summary of Theoretical Discussion

Briefly, the proposition of the Laffer curve takes as its starting point the simple notion that tax revenue is zero if the tax rate is either zero or 100 percent, with a smooth relationship between tax rates and tax revenues connecting these two polar points.[2] The existence of such a relationship suggests that if tax rates are sufficiently high—that is, if tax rates are in what the supply-siders refer to as the "prohibitive range"—then a reduction in tax rates could lead to an increase in tax revenues.

On what does the existence of the Laffer curve depend? Borrowing from Blinder (1981), consider the specific example of a proportional tax on labor income. If w is the gross wage rate and $w(1 - t)$ the net tax wage rate, if $S(w(1 - t))$ is the supply of labor function, with $S(0) = 0$ by assumption, and if $D(w)$ is the demand function for labor, it can be shown that, for $G(t)$ continuous and differentiable, revenue responds to variation in the marginal tax rate as

$$\frac{dG}{dt} = wS(.)\left[1 + \frac{t}{1+t} \cdot \frac{\eta_S(1 - \eta_D)}{\eta_S - \eta_D}\right], \tag{1}$$

where G is revenue and η_i, $i = S, D$, refers to the relevant elasticities of labor supply and demand. Given the assumptions, equation (1) yields the Laffer curve. It follows that the revenue-maximizing tax rate t^* can be found by setting equation (1) equal to zero, yielding

$$t^* = \frac{\eta_S - \eta_D}{-\eta_D(1 + \eta_S)}, \tag{2}$$

[1]See Gandhi (Chapter 1). Readers interested in examining some of the original sources are referred to Meyer (1981); Bartlett (1982); Federal Reserve Bank of Atlanta (1982); Fink (1982); Hailstones (1982a, 1982b); Raboy (1982); Canto, Joines, and Laffer (1983); Wanniski (1983); and Roberts (1984); and also to the other publications listed in the Selected Bibliography in Appendix II.

[2]We leave aside here the issue of whether this concept should be credited to Laffer. Current conventional wisdom maintains that the basic concept has many antecedents. Bartlett (1982) accords the honor of first discovery of the Laffer curve to Ibn Khaldun, a fourteenth century Arabic philosopher.

where $\eta_D < 0$. As pointed out by Blinder, even if both elasticities are as high as 2, t^* is still as high as two thirds.

Proponents of the supply-side approach believe that the relevant elasticity values are very high. There is considerable variation among the supply-siders, however, when it comes to defining the economic environment, and hence the relevant elasticities, in which the tax reduction is set.

Some establish a traditional neoclassical framework of a closed general equilibrium framework with flexible prices and full employment. They implicitly conduct a balanced-budget incidence exercise—whatever tax revenue is raised is reinjected back into the economic system via government expenditures. In such an environment, aggregate income effects can only occur if the pattern of government expenditures differs substantially from the pattern of expenditures that would have resulted in the absence of government intervention. Even then, the income effects are not likely to be large. The appropriate focus of tax policy analysis then becomes the examination of the magnitude of the substitution effects that are the inevitable outcome of the relative price movements induced by tax changes. For Laffer-style propositions to be correct, compensated elasticities of substitution would have to be sufficiently high. The argument of supply-siders presumably is that such is the case because many of the tax rates currently in force in many countries are very high. Even though a reduction in tax rates leads to a reduction in revenue per unit, the concomitant reduction in price (increase in net wages) leads to such an increase in the demand for the commodity (supply of labor) as to imply an increase in tax yield in the aggregate. An excellent example of work founded on such neoclassical microeconomic grounds is Canto, Joines, and Laffer (1983).

Some supply-siders have argued for higher elasticity values by implicitly changing the base for the tax. This change is to counter the criticism of those who argue that the large elasticities required to generate Laffer-type effects are most unlikely to exist for broadly based taxes. For example, Blinder (1981), in his critique of the Laffer curve, argues that it would be much better to apply supply-side analysis to narrowly based taxes.[3] In response, some supply-siders have emphasized the role of tax evasion. Thus

[3]An example of a Laffer-type effect is the case of New Hampshire liquor taxes. It is argued that a reduction in that state's liquor tax rate could well lead to an increase in tax revenue because an incentive would then be provided to consumers to come in from out of state, notably from Massachusetts, to purchase alcohol. The essence of this argument is that New Hampshire alcohol and out-of-state alcohol are close substitutes, implying highly elastic behavior on the part of purchasers. More generally, this example suggests that, the smaller geographically is the taxing jurisdiction, the greater are the possibilities for Laffer curve effects associated with changes in the level of taxation of a mobile factor. This could be important in a developing country context.

it may be the case that, although labor supply in the aggregate is not very elastic, the supply of labor to the official market economy (as opposed to the underground economy) is much larger. This is precisely one of the effects advanced by Bartlett (1982) in support of tax rate reductions: marginal tax rate reductions provide an incentive for labor to exit from the underground economy, thereby increasing tax revenue.

This last argument is perfectly consistent with a neoclassical framework. Some, though by no means all, supply-side economists rely in addition on short-run macroeconomic considerations. Specifically, if an economy is experiencing excess unemployment, tax cuts stimulate the economy—presumably by the way they influence consumer expectations and liquidity—so much that revenues increase. This appears to be the characterization of the Laffer curve contained, for example, in Roberts (1984, p. 27). Note that income effects again play a role, though here they are due to changes in aggregate demand, changes that are precluded in a neoclassical framework.[4] The nature of the elasticities implied by this analysis is markedly different from that envisaged by other authors.[5] Representative empirical work on the possibilities for revenue-increasing tax reductions in developed countries is discussed in the Annex to this chapter.

Irrespective of the precise mechanism underlying the Laffer curve, there is a consensus among the supply-side economists as to the appropriate direction of tax reform. Since reductions in marginal tax rates lead to revenue increases only if tax rates are very high, the preferred reform involves reductions in the highest marginal tax rates on income (see, for example, Canto, Joines, and Laffer (1981) and Wanniski (1983)).

Although it is clearly a supply-side concept, there is no sense in which

[4]A similar, though more neoclassical, characterization of the Laffer curve can be found in Bartlett (1982). With reference to the economy of Hong Kong, he argues that a reduction in tax rates led to an acceleration in growth rates and, thus, to revenue increases (an income effect).

[5]A further potential short-run macroeconomic effect has been pointed out to me. To the extent that a tax cut stimulates economic activity, the resultant increase in the transactions demand for money could allow the government to finance some of its expenditures through money creation. As an aside, one might also note a particular supply-side perspective that applies to those at lower income levels. It is argued that the various unemployment and social security compensation schemes in many developed countries have tended to make it unprofitable for the unemployed to seek work. At the microeconomic level, accordingly, this line of reasoning says that the discrete decision to work or not to work is influenced by tax-induced or unemployment-compensation-induced income effects. Given the low level, both relative and absolute, of social welfare payments in most developing countries, however, it is unlikely that these effects would be important in the context of this chapter. They are therefore not treated in what follows.

the Laffer curve encompasses the entirety of the supply-side approach. If it did, it would imply that increasing government revenue was an important objective of supply-side economists. That objective would obviously run counter to other goals of the supply-side program, most notably a reduction in the size of the government sector. In more general perspective, concern is focused on improving the production efficiency of economic systems.[6]

In essence, then, the primary concern of supply-siders is to ensure that, whatever the degree of government intervention in the workings of private markets, government intervention should occur in the most efficient manner possible. The Laffer curve is important since, if Laffer effects do exist in any given economy, they are extreme examples of inefficient intervention.

Summary of Empirical Evidence

The bulk of the empirical evidence advanced by supply-siders to support their position is concerned with economic policy in the United States (for a summary of this and related material, see the Annex to this chapter). Empirical analysis considering developing countries is scarcer and such results as exist are superficial, frequently based on a simple correlation between some change in a country's tax structure and the subsequent economic performance of that country. A supply-side writer who has devoted considerable attention to circumstances in developing countries is Wanniski (1983). He argues that many developing countries have adopted extremely progressive income tax structures where this is presumably a source of major disincentives. Leaving aside the question of how one can interpret the effective progressivity of a nominal tax structure given the plethora of deductions and exemptions as well as the low monetary income levels in many developing countries, consider how Wanniski utilizes the income tax information. In particular, consider his discussion of the effects of tax policy changes in India (Wanniski (1983, p. 258, et seq.)). He ascribes the "extraordinary quiescence" that descended on India, after a period of political turmoil, to the tax changes introduced by Finance Minister Subrama-

[6]To quote Wanniski from evidence he presented before the U.S. Congress Task Force on Tax Policy (U.S. Congress (1981, p. 41)):

> "To the supply-sider, the producer is the active participant. . . . The government . . . regulates the marketplace in the interests of all producers. . . . The supply-sider is not per se a tax cutter. If the supply-sider believes the efficiency of production will be enhanced over time by more public roads . . . he will urge that they be financed by borrowing or taxing away a greater share of the producer's production."

nian in 1975. These tax changes were very much in the supply-side mode in that they involved reductions in the highest marginal income tax rates (cut to 77 percent from 85 percent), corporate tax rates, and wealth tax rates. Further rate reductions and bracket changes were made in April 1976 as a result of unexpected revenue buoyancy. These in turn, it is argued, stimulated even more dramatic economic growth. As implied above, the trouble with this type of reasoning is that it is suggestive but perhaps overly simplistic.

Kwon (1984) has examined the case of Korea. Working at an aggregate level, he concluded that the behavior of tax revenues over time as tax rates were increased is not inconsistent with the existence of a Laffer curve. However, he also concluded that Korean income tax rates do not appear to be such as to have placed Korea over the Laffer "hill."

In the remainder of this chapter a few examples of tax changes in developing countries—changes of the supply-side type—are examined. Specifically, the next section considers the effects of reductions in top marginal income tax rates on income tax revenues in Jamaica and India.

II. Supply-Side Effects and the Personal Income Tax

An obvious problem with any empirical test of the existence of Laffer curve effects in developing countries is the paucity of the data available. What are the minimal requirements that such data should satisfy, given that the approach being used here is to consider countries on a case-by-case basis?

Empirical Methodology

First, and trivially, the examples selected should be of cases in which top marginal tax rates have been changed. The tax rate reductions undertaken by Jamaica and India satisfy this criterion. Second, because attention is focused on the behavior of those facing the highest marginal tax rates, a breakdown of taxable income and taxes paid by income level both before and after the tax change is required. Data of this type are available for India, but for Jamaica all that is available is a breakdown of the number of pay-as-you-earn (PAYE) taxpayers by income level for the relevant years. Third, it is essential that any exercise of this type control for other factors that might influence the outcome. This requirement exposes the greatest weakness of the study. With the exception of the influence of inflation and growth, it proved impossible to control for these other factors. For the case of inflation, over time, as nominal incomes increase, there is a tendency for tax revenues to increase more than proportionately because of the progressive nominal structure of most income taxes (including those of Jamaica and India). This effect should be netted out of any revenue change consequent on a marginal tax change.

The significance of the interaction of inflation with the tax system depends on the underlying distribution of income. In the absence of detailed data on this distribution, it is assumed here that incomes are distributed in the form of the Pareto distribution, whose cumulative distribution is given by

$$F(w) = 1 - \left(\frac{w}{w^*}\right)^{-\alpha}, \qquad w \geq w^* > 0, \tag{3}$$

where F refers to the cumulative distribution, w refers to income level, and w^* represents the lowest value of w for which this distribution is relevant. The exponent is typically assumed to be greater than or equal to 2 (Atkinson (1973)). The shape of the distribution can be found in Figure 1. Although not representative of the whole distribution of income, this distribution may be an accurate representation of the upper tail of the earnings distribution. Such an argument is made by Lydall (1968). Clearly, the

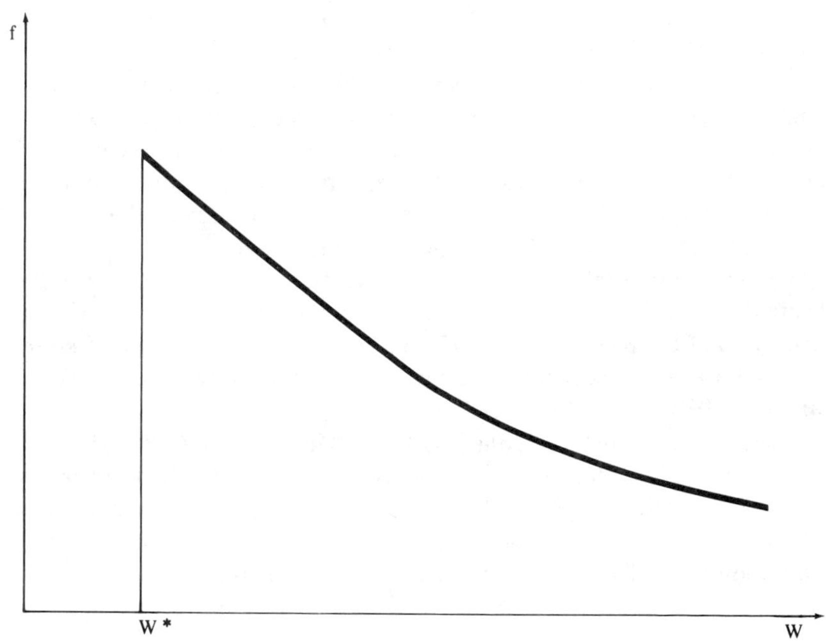

Figure 1. Pareto Distribution of Earnings

upper tail of the income distribution is of great concern to this study. A positive rate of inflation implies, other things being equal, that the whole distribution shifts to the right.[7] What does this imply about the number of taxpayers in each given nominal income tranche? Given that the distribution is not uniform, there will be a tendency for the number of taxpayers in each income tranche to increase at a more rapid rate than the rate of inflation.

To refine this statement somewhat, note that an alternative way to measure the effect of inflation is to hold the distribution constant and to reduce the nominal income values. Thus, the elasticity of the number of taxpayers in any given income slice to the rate of inflation is the same as the elasticity of the area to the left of any given income level, w, to a reduction in that income level. Given the specification of the cumulative distribution, that area, $A(w)$, is

$$A(w) = w^{*\alpha} w^{-\alpha}, \tag{4}$$

from which it follows

$$\frac{w}{A} \cdot \frac{dA}{dw} = -\alpha. \tag{5}$$

Equation (5) is the elasticity of the relevant area for increases in w. Hence, if $\alpha = 2.5$ say, a 10 percent increase in the rate of inflation will, other things being equal, cause a 25 percent increase in the number of taxpayers in each income slice in the upper tail. (The choice of α cannot be confirmed empirically here, though Lydall (1968) reports estimated values can often exceed 2.) A similar line of reasoning can be used to describe the changes in the number of taxpayers as a result of economic growth.

The importance of this result is that, for a given tax system, α is also the elasticity of tax revenues; that is, the elasticity of both the number of taxpayers and of tax revenue in response to uniform increases in nominal income is, for a given tax structure, equal. The analysis draws on Hutton and Lambert (1979).

To see this relationship, define Y to be total income and $R(Y)$ to be total tax revenue. The definition of the tax elasticity is then given by $\eta = Y \cdot R'(Y)/R(Y)$. Let $t(w)$ be the tax payable on income level w, with $(0 \leq w \leq \infty)$, and let $f(w)$ be the frequency density of that income for a population level. Then the elasticity can be re-expressed as

[7]The analysis could as easily consider the case of real growth. Note that the implicit assumption is being made at this stage that, whatever the source of nominal income growth, it is affecting all income levels uniformly. This assumption is dictated by data inadequacies.

$$\eta = \frac{\int_0^\infty wt'(w)f(w)dw}{\int_0^\infty t(w)f(w)dw}. \tag{6}$$

Substituting for the Pareto distribution, it follows by differentiating equation (3) that

$$f(w|w > w^*) = \alpha w^{*\alpha} w^{-\alpha-1},$$

from which it follows

$$\eta = \frac{\int_{w^*}^\infty wt'(w)\, \alpha w^{*\alpha} w^{-\alpha-1}\, dw}{\int_{w^*}^\infty t(w)\, \alpha w^{*\alpha} w^{-\alpha-1}\, dw}$$

$$= \frac{\int_{w^*}^\infty t'(w)\, w^{-\alpha}\, dw}{\int_{w^*}^\infty t(w)\, w^{-\alpha-1}\, dw}. \tag{7}$$

From integrating the numerator by parts, it follows that

$$\eta = \alpha, \tag{8}$$

which is also the elasticity of the number of taxpayers. Hence, for $\alpha = 2.5$, a 10 percent increase in the rate of inflation will, other things being equal, yield a 25 percent increase in tax revenue in each income slice in the upper tail of the distribution. Discrepancies are, of course, possible. In particular, contrary to assumption, nominal incomes for the relevant income groups might not rise in line with inflation. Finally, note that the result that $\eta = \alpha$ greatly alleviates any problems that might arise because the distribution data available for Jamaica are in numbers of taxpayers.

The value of α is determined by the distribution of income based on cross-section data. Presumably, this value, therefore, already reflects the decisions of income earners in response to the given tax structure. On the assumption that all individuals have the same preferences concerning the work-leisure trade-off, the value of α then incorporates the disincentive effects that individual taxpayers face as they move into higher tax brackets in response to nominal increases in income.

The analysis has to be modified to account for the fact that the tax structure has changed. In particular, top marginal tax rates have been reduced. One way of accommodating this reduction is to interpret α as the elasticity of the tax base. The product of the change in the tax base and the average change in tax rates can then be used to calculate the approximate change in tax revenue and, hence, to evaluate the Laffer curve hypothesis.

With the preceding subsection as background, we now consider the specifics of the two cases selected.

Jamaica

The structure of the progressive Jamaican personal income tax is presented in Table 1. This structure has been subject to a number of changes, which can be classified into two types. First, the Jamaican authorities made some attempt to adjust the income tranches for inflation—this was the primary motivation for the changes that became effective January 1, 1975. It is clear, however, that the effects of inflation were not fully accommodated by these changes. Thus, nominal per capita gross domestic product (GDP) increased from J$626 in 1970 to J$2,195 in 1980, a period of negligible real growth which indicates a high rate of nominal income growth. Second, the highest marginal tax on incomes was increased from 60 percent to 80 percent. This presumably represents a deliberate attempt to increase tax revenues by raising the tax rates faced by wealthier individuals in Jamaica.

The above is purely descriptive. Before examining the disincentive effects implied by this tax structure, or indeed whether this tax system might imply that Jamaica is operating in the prohibitive region of its Laffer curve, it is important to determine the effective tax rates implied by Table 1. To do so, one first might ask what is the economic incidence of an income tax on earned income. This paper adopts the traditional assumption that the tax is borne by labor, a view consistent with the incidence analysis of a general factor tax in a closed economy framework with fixed aggregate supplies. Use of this assumption, however, may not be entirely appropriate. It is not correct if aggregate factor supplies are endogenous, as they would be in the long run (Feldstein (1974a, 1974b)) or if the economy is open. The latter consideration could be important for Jamaica and should, therefore, be kept in mind. For example, if the net impact of a progressive income tax is for skilled labor to emigrate, some of the burden of the tax may well be shifted to other factors. (This might be particularly true if labor is heterogeneous with specific skills and if some of the commodities

Table 1. Jamaica: Rates of Income Taxation

Before January 1, 1975		On January 1, 1975		Before January 1, 1980		After January 1, 1980	
Taxable income (In Jamaica dollars)	Tax rate (In percent)	Taxable income (In Jamaica dollars)	Tax rate (In percent)	Taxable income (In Jamaica dollars)	Tax rate (In percent)	Taxable income (In Jamaica dollars)	Tax rate (In percent)
1-500	15						
501-1,000	20	1-1,000	20				
1,001-1,500	26	1,001-2,000	25				
1,501-3,500	32½	2,001-3,500	30				
3,501-4,500	35	3,501-5,500	35	0-5,000	30		
4,501-7,000	37½-45	5,501-7,500	42½	5,001-7,000	35	0-7,000	30
7,001-8,000	50	7,501-9,500	50	7,001-10,000	40	7,001-10,000	40
8,001-11,000	56½	9,501-12,500	57½	10,001-12,000	45½	10,001-12,000	45
Above 11,000	60	Above 12,500	60	12,001-14,000	57	12,001-14,000	50
				14,001-20,000	60	Above 14,000	57½
				20,001-30,000	70		
				Above 30,000	80		

Sources: Jamaica, Ministry of Finance and Planning, budget speeches (Kingston), various issues; and *Report of the Commissioner of Income Tax* (Kingston), various issues.

consumed in the country are nontraded commodities. For example, consider the impact of the emigration of doctors on the quality of the health care of those who remain.)

The issue of the effective burden of an income tax raises some practical questions as well. For example, how burdensome is a tax system such as that delineated above, given that per capita GDP in 1980 was only J$2,195 (at an official exchange rate of J$1.7814 per U.S. dollar this equals US$1,232). Further, the tax schedule applies only to reported income after deductions, exemptions, and allowances. Given that it is generally conceded that tax evasion is widespread and that, further, tax administration has been weak in Jamaica, the disincentive effects are by that token substantially altered.[8] This topic will be discussed further below.

The Jamaican personal income tax system is of particular interest to this study because of the tax reforms that became effective January 1, 1980. As can be seen from Table 1, the highest marginal tax rates were significantly reduced, from 80 percent to 57½ percent. This reduction is precisely the type of rate realignment recommended by supply-siders. Did it have the predicted supply-side effect, namely, an increase in tax revenues? Consider Table 2, which presents the data for the partial test outlined in the previous section. The table documents the recent trend in the number of PAYE taxpayers by income class.[9] While this does not provide direct evidence on income tax revenue, the analytical results presented above suggest that the trends in the number of taxpayers in each income class can be illuminating.

To draw on the earlier analysis, any evaluation of the relevance of the Laffer curve to Jamaican circumstances, which are characterized on the basis of trends in the numbers of taxpayers, depends on the interaction of a number of factors; the underlying rates of inflation and real growth, the underlying distribution of incomes, and the changes in tax rates. Inflation, in Jamaica, as measured by changes in the consumer price index, was 27 percent in 1980 and 12.5 percent in 1981 (calendar years). The corre-

[8]As evidence of the extent of the tax administration problem, the *Report of the Commissioner of Income Tax for Years Ended 31st March, 1981 and 31st March, 1982* notes that the prospects for remedying the tax evasion situation were unlikely to improve as long as resources for the task continued to be inadequate and sanctions against evasion remained weak (Jamaica (1982)).

[9]PAYE data are easy to use because tax collections and tax liabilities tend to be contemporaneous. Further, for Jamaica, they are a pre-eminent source of individual income tax revenue. The *Report of the Commissioner of Income Tax for 1981 and 1982* notes that in 1982 PAYE was responsible for 92 percent of gross individual income tax receipts (Jamaica (1982)).

Table 2. Jamaica: PAYE Employees Classified by Income Groups

Income Groups (In Jamaica dollars)	Number of PAYE Employees 1979	Number of PAYE Employees 1980	Percentage Change	Number of PAYE Employees, 1981	Percentage Change
2,300-2,500	4,588	3,384	−26	2,535	−25
2,501-3,500	22,602	20,399	−10	12,040	−41
3,501-5,000	26,799	31,409	17	24,326	−23
5,001-7,000	23,557	26,008	10	41,057	56
7,001-9,000	15,109	16,896	12	16,291	−4
9,001-11,000	8,869	9,830	11	10,041	2
11,001-12,000	2,920	3,094	6	3,214	4
12,001-16,000	6,193	7,175	16	7,541	5
16,001-20,000	1,956	3,043	56	3,495	15
20,001-30,000	917	1,682	83	2,003	19
30,001-50,000	212	387	83	376	−3
Above 50,001	43	117	272	93	−21
Total	113,765	123,424	9	123,012	0

Source: Jamaica, *Report of the Commissioner of Income Tax for Years Ended 31st March, 1981 and 31st March, 1982* (Kingston, 1982).

sponding growth rates in real GDP were −5.4 percent and 2.0 percent, respectively.[10]

The actual income categories for which the Laffer curve hypothesis can be most readily evaluated are those in which income exceeds J$20,000. Thus, for incomes in the range of J$16,000–20,000, marginal tax rates were reduced by 2½ percentage points, whereas for the income ranges J$20,000–30,000 and above J$30,000, the reductions were 12½ and 22½ percentage points, respectively. If the hypothesis is correct, a significant proportion of the increase in the number of taxpayers (hence in the tax base) earning above J$20,000 may be credited to the income tax changes, which presumably provided a sufficient incentive to induce a sharp increase in the supply of work effort to the organized market. For the Laffer curve to apply, however, this increase would have to exceed the increase that would normally be expected because of fiscal drag. For incomes in excess of J$20,000, it can be calculated that the tax base increased by 87 percent between 1979 and 1980.[11] This increase, however,

[10]These estimates were obtained from International Monetary Fund (1983).

[11]Note that there are absolute decreases in the number of taxpayers in the lowest income classes in both years. This confirms the view that inflation and/or growth combined with changes in basic allowances, tends to shift the whole distribution. Of course, the Pareto distribution cannot be applied to the whole income distribution. For that task, a log-normal distribution would be more appropriate.

has to be seen in light of an inflation rate of 27 percent in that year. If nominal incomes in those income categories increased by a like amount, and if the Pareto distribution is a correct characterization of the underlying income distribution, then a value of $\alpha = 2.5$ would result in an increase in the tax base of 67.5 percent owing solely to the effects of fiscal drag.[12]

The evidence to this point suggests that the Jamaican tax base responded buoyantly to the tax rate reductions. Assuming $\alpha = 2.5$, the base grew by approximately 29 percent more than would have been anticipated. Further, this occurred in a year of negative GDP growth. What happened to tax revenue, the primary concern of the Laffer curve? Using 1979 weights, the average reduction in marginal tax rates for the relevant income groups was approximately 20 percent, indicating that tax revenue did increase relative to what collections would have been had the tax system remained unchanged and tax revenues had increased only as a result of the effects of fiscal drag.

Although these data are consistent with the existence of a Laffer curve in Jamaica, the reservations about such an interpretation should be kept in mind. It is based on little evidence and on just one year's observation. Indeed, referring back to Table 2, it is clear that the buoyancy of the tax base in the following year, a year of 12½ percent inflation, fell below what would have been predicted by the framework developed here. More important, the exercise above is cast as if the tax reductions occurred in a vacuum, which, of course, was not the case. The increase in the number of taxpayers in the target year may have been due to other factors, such as a simultaneous drive to enhance tax administration and a coincidental growth in government employment. The 1980 *Economic and Social Survey* notes that a significant part of the larger-than-expected tax collections from individuals on the PAYE system represented payments of arrears in income tax (Jamaica, National Planning Agency (1980)).

A further reason for caution in interpreting these results as evidence of the Laffer curve is that PAYE taxpayers are not the most suitable group to consider when looking for Laffer curve effects. Thus, as pointed out earlier, the significant factor may not be the aggregate elasticity of labor supply but rather the elasticity of labor supply to organized markets. Elaborating, reductions in marginal tax rates might not result in increased work

[12]Ideally, one would test the validity of assuming that the upper tail of the income distribution conforms to the Pareto distribution by using a χ^2 test. Unfortunately, there are insufficient observations for such a test. Note also that lack of data precludes an independent verification of the magnitude of α for Jamaica, or, indeed, for India below, though in both cases the true value of α would have to differ significantly from that assumed here to alter the interpretation of the data.

effort. Instead, they might yield increased tax revenue because of reduced tax evasion.[13] This effect, which enhances the observed elasticity of labor supply to organized markets, is less likely to be relevant in the case of PAYE taxpayers. Those paying income taxes under PAYE schemes typically have little control either over the income they report or over the hours they work. If Laffer-type effects exist in Jamaica, these effects are more likely to be observed when other taxpayers are included. As noted in the *Report of the Commissioner of Income Tax for 1981 and 1982,* delinquency and tax evasion are so extensive that in excess of 80 percent of the self-employed are assumed to be "dodging their responsibilities" (Jamaica (1982, p. 18)).

India

Because the case of India was cited by Wanniski (1983), it is appropriate to consider the example of the marginal income tax reductions introduced in that country in 1975.[14] As rationalized in the budget speech for 1974/75, the reductions in marginal income tax rates were a response to recommendations made by the Direct Taxes Enquiry Committee. The existing high rates were held to be a major cause of tax evasion. The magnitude of the reductions can be gauged from Table 3. As for the revenue loss implied by these reductions, the Minister for Finance argued

> The reduction in the rates of income-tax on personal income would ordinarily have resulted in a loss of about Rs. 60 crores in a full year and Rs. 36 crores in the financial year 1974-75. I am, however, not taking any loss into account for budgetary purposes as I expect that the reduction in the rates of taxes will lead to better tax compliance, and full disclosures of incomes by all taxpayers.[15]

At face value, the Minister's optimism appears to have been justified—the yield of the income and corporation taxes was later revised from Rs 1,370 crores to Rs 1,460 crores (India (1976, p. 5)). This upward revi-

[13]In this context, the tax cuts might also have enhanced revenue by reducing the incentives for tax avoidance techniques in the form of awarding nontaxable perquisites.

[14]Major income tax reforms, including a substantial reduction of top marginal income tax rates, were introduced in the 1985/86 budget, and the early indications are of substantial increase in income tax collections. However, an analysis of the reasons underlying these revenue trends remains to be carried out. It has not been undertaken in this chapter either.

[15]See India (1975, pp. 187–88). A crore is a unit of ten million. There are some discrepancies between Wanniski's account and the measures proposed by the budget speech. Specifically, Wanniski refers to reductions in annual taxes on large holdings, whereas the Minister proposed wealth tax increases in general.

Table 3. India: Rates of Income Taxation, 1973/74 and 1974/75

1973/74		1974/75	
Income (In rupees)	Tax rate	Income (In rupees)	Tax rate
Below 5,000	0	Below 6,000	0
5,001-10,000	11.00	6,001-10,000	13.2
10,001-15,000	18.70	10,001-15,000	16.5
15,001-20,000	26.15	15,001-20,000	22.0
20,001-25,000	34.50	20,001-25,000	33.0
25,001-30,000	46.00	25,001-30,000	44.0
30,001-40,000	57.50	30,001-50,000	55.0
40,001-60,000	69.00	50,001-70,000	66.0
60,001-80,000	80.50	Above 70,000	77.0
80,001-100,000	86.26		
100,001-200,000	92.00		
Above 200,000	97.75		

Sources: Data for 1973/74 were obtained from Anupam Gupta, *Impact of the Personal Income Tax* (New Delhi: National Institute of Public Finance and Policy, 1978); and data for 1974/75 were obtained from Kailash C. Khanna, "India: The Finance Bill, 1974," *Bulletin*, International Bureau of Fiscal Documentation (Amsterdam), Vol. 28 (April 1974), pp. 143-46. The surcharge has been included.

sion is only evidence, however, of buoyancy at the aggregate level. As was the case with Jamaica, a more disaggregated approach is necessary. Such a breakdown of income tax receipts by income class for fiscal years 1972/73 and 1975/76 (unfortunately, these were the only two years for which data were available) is presented in Table 4. Applying the framework developed above for Jamaica, nominal national income (a proxy for the tax base) increased by 55 percent between fiscal year 1972/73 and fiscal year 1975/76. During the same period, as can be seen from Table 4, total income assessed increased by 30 percent, whereas the tax payable increased by only 27 percent. At this level, it would appear that the supply-side view was not vindicated.

When one considers the breakdown in greater detail, a clearer picture emerges. First, a sharp drop in tax revenue occurred in the lowest income classes where this may be ascribed to the increase in the basic exemption. Second, the increase in the basic exemption also implies tax revenue reductions in the higher gross income tranches. Note that this may well be an inframarginal tax reduction for many taxpayers—taxpayers may find their taxes reduced and yet face the same marginal tax rates. (This is not to deny that there are grounds, based on equity considerations, for introducing this type of tax reduction—grounds that may be all the more relevant in an inflationary environment.)

Table 4. India: Classification of the Tax Payable by Assessees According to Income Class

Income (In rupees)	Number of Assessees 1972/73	Number of Assessees 1975/76	Percentage Change	Total Income Assessed (In thousands of rupees) 1972/73	Total Income Assessed (In thousands of rupees) 1975/76	Percentage Change	Total Tax Payable (In thousands of rupees) 1972/73	Total Tax Payable (In thousands of rupees) 1975/76	Percentage Change
Below 5,000	193,547	55,144	−72	838,614	188,990	−77	14,172	13,652	−4
5,001-7,500	775,715	661,569	−15	4,723,772	4,206,137	−11	128,274	95,920	−25
7,501-10,000	368,500	529,829	44	3,172,975	4,547,482	43	185,861	192,894	4
10,001-15,000	367,666	514,001	40	4,458,580	6,236,169	40	370,121	437,440	18
15,001-20,000	158,879	237,186	49	2,730,230	4,075,961	49	303,047	426,495	41
20,001-25,000	87,227	127,322	46	1,913,090	2,835,629	48	262.710	371,179	41
25,001-30,000	52,844	74,094	40	1,439,533	2,026,970	41	246,417	319,770	30
30,001-40,000	57,489	81,957	43	1,979,265	2,817,788	42	373,008	531,798	43
40,001-50,000	30,621	44,381	45	1,364,970	1,979,749	45	284,655	408,822	44
50,001-60,000	17,403	25,507	47	949,898	1,394,372	47	210,898	308,592	46
60,001-70,000	11,668	16,999	46	753,310	1,097,824	46	176,365	249,842	42
70,001-100,000	18,109	27,094	50	1,498,032	2,245,859	50	378,420	535,446	41
100,001-200,000	13,057	22,685	74	1,752,792	3,030,834	73	526,964	843,829	60
Above 200,000	6,245	8,554	37	8,506,048	10,351,019	22	4,673,453	5,608,908	20
Total	2,158,970	2,426,322	12	36,111,110	47,061,783	30	8,134,365	10,344,587	27

Sources: India, Central Statistical Organization, *Statistical Abstract* (New Delhi), various issues.

Third, as can be seen from Table 5, which presents summary data based on Table 4, the increase in total tax payable tends to decline as income levels increase. More important, average assessed income per assessee and average tax payable per assessee both decline in absolute terms for incomes in excess of Rs 50,000. These declines were even more pronounced for incomes in excess of Rs 100,000. A comparison of Tables 4 and 5 reveals the source of this behavior: income and revenue growth rates of the highest income group (those with incomes above Rs 200,000) were sluggish, both in comparison with the corresponding growth rates registered in most other income classes and with the underlying growth in national income. If in addition it is assumed that income is Pareto distributed, with $\alpha = 2.5$, one would expect above-average increases in these categories.

The data on India, at least for the years selected, therefore, do not support the Laffer curve hypothesis.[16] The "revenue performance" of the highest income group was quite poor. This is, of course, the income group that might be expected to exhibit the most pronounced Laffer-type effects because taxpayers in this bracket experienced the greatest reduction in marginal tax rates (20.75 percentage points).

Just as caution was required in interpreting the data for Jamaica, so it is required in this case. For example, the low income growth registered by the highest income group might be due to income and price (e.g., rent control) policies. This possibility raises the obvious point that, for the Laffer curve to exist, individuals must be able to earn more income. Nonetheless, the conclusion of this section must be that strong supply-side effects are not readily observable in India. Again, one should remember that such a conclusion concentrates on the revenue implications of cuts in marginal tax rates to the exclusion of any consideration of efficiency or equity effects.

III. Overview and Conclusions

This chapter represents an attempt to evaluate empirically whether Laffer curve effects are to be found in developing countries. Jamaica and India, which have reduced their top marginal tax rates, were selected for the exercise. Empirical tests rarely afford definitive resolutions of intellectual disputes, but the prospects of their doing so in this instance appear

[16]This assessment receives support in Acharya and others (1985). Their report cites work by Bagchi and Rao (*Economic and Political Weekly*, Bombay, September 4, 1982) in which they concluded that the tax compliance effects of rate reductions were much lower than had been presumed in the budgets (see above). Bagchi and Rao's methodology relies on obtaining independent estimates of assessable income in years after tax reduction and their results further belie the optimism generated by the aggregate data discussed earlier.

Table 5. India: Trends in Tax Base and Taxes Paid, 1972/73 and 1975/76
(In thousands of rupees, unless otherwise stated)

	Assessees					
	Number (In thousands)	Percent total	Total Income Assessed	Total Tax Payable	Average Assessed Income/ Assessee	Average Tax/ Assessee
			All income levels			
1972/73	2,159	100.0	36,111	8,134	16.8	3.76
1975/76	2,426	100.0	47,061	10,345	19.4	4.26
Percentage change	12.4	—	30.3	27.2	15.5	13.40
			Income levels above Rs 50,000			
1972/73	66	3.0	13,460	5,966	203.9	90.4
1975/76	100	4.1	18,120	7,547	181.2	74.6
Percentage change	52.0	—	34.6	26.5	−11.1	−17.5
			Income levels above Rs 100,000			
1972/73	19	0.9	10,259	5,200	539.9	273.7
1975/76	31	1.3	13,382	6,453	431.7	208.2
Percentage change	63.1	—	30.4	24.1	−20.0	−23.9

Sources: India, Central Statistical Organization, *Statistical Abstract* (New Delhi), various issues.

particularly poor. The data are hardly adequate. Although there was some evidence of tax revenue buoyancy in Jamaica, the opposite was found in India. Because the testing techniques used depended on a number of critical assumptions and lacked discriminatory power, however, in both cases the results could easily be rationalized using non-Laffer curve explanations. For Jamaica, one could appeal to the possibility of a once-and-for-all gain from improved tax administration; for India, the existence of other market imperfections might have played a role.

A paper such as this, which considers the Laffer curve as it applies to marginal income tax reductions, focuses on a narrow aspect of supply-side economics. Taking a broader perspective, the supply-side approach is concerned with the disincentive effects of tax distortions irrespective of their source (cf., Chapter 9). This broader concern was touched on when it was argued that the effects of the marginal tax rate reductions extend beyond the revenue effects. Even if Laffer-type effects are not in evidence, removal of tax distortions may nonetheless induce significant supply responses.

Moreover, although the reduction of top marginal tax rates may yield some revenue increase or, at least, a negligible revenue decline, the real significance of the result most likely lies in its implications for economic efficiency and equity. Thus, for Jamaica, the 387 taxpayers in the income group of J$30,001–50,000 (Table 2) might have been expected to pay approximately J$7 million in taxes in fiscal year 1980/81. This amount must be seen in the context of total individual income tax payments in the year of J$924 million (Jamaica, Ministry of Finance and Planning (1981)). The J$7 million refers to total revenue, which implies that any change in revenue associated with marginal tax changes will be correspondingly smaller. (A caveat is that the revenue implications for the highest income group cannot be derived because of the open-ended nature of the income levels in that group; although this group is certain to have "outliers," particularly if the analysis is extended to non-PAYE taxpayers, the force of the point in this paragraph is unlikely to be altered.)

ANNEX

Summary of Empirical Evidence: Developed Countries

The bulk of the empirical evidence advanced by supply-side economists to support their position is concerned with economic policy in the United States. Much of this work concerns the revenue effects associated with the Kennedy tax cuts implemented in 1962 and 1964. These tax cuts are felt to be particularly suitable as a test of the supply-side approach, since they involved reductions in the highest marginal tax rates on earned income as well as reductions in the corporate profits tax. Much of the evidence cited in support of the supply-side position is anecdotal. Most argue that the tax cut was stimulative and that the resultant surge in economic activity resulted in significant revenue buoyancy.[17] However, to the extent that the revenue increase was due to a surge in macroeconomic activity it does not necessarily sustain the argument that the Kennedy tax cuts led to the large gains in microeconomic efficiency sought by some supply-side economists.[18]

There have been more rigorous attempts to evaluate the Kennedy tax cuts. Consider, for example, the research by Canto, Joines, and Laffer (1981). On the assumption that the exogenous policy variables bear a constant relationship to the endogenous variables and that the structure of the complete model is stable, they used univariate time-series analysis to identify the stochastic process generating,

[17]For a summary of the opinions of various authorities on the impact of the Kennedy tax cuts, see Bartlett (1982).

[18]An important related point is that the nature of the income tax change was such that it resulted in an increase in the elasticity of that tax. This point is discussed further in Tanzi and Hart (1972).

for example, the income tax revenue series. The forecast errors that result when these univariate models are applied to the post-sample period (i.e., the period after the Kennedy tax cuts became effective) may then be regarded as estimates of the revenue changes resulting from those tax cuts. There are a number of conclusions. In particular, the authors found that their time-series estimates showed smaller revenue losses than those predicted at the time by the U.S. Treasury. This result is of interest since, given that the Treasury utilized a Keynesian framework for its revenue loss projections, the time-series discrepancy may be due to relative price effects. However, this interpretation is predicated on the Treasury model having exhaustively captured all effects associated with the tax cuts other than the relative price changes.[19]

Taking an alternative approach to the evaluation of actual tax changes such as the Kennedy tax cuts, Fullerton (1982) used an empirical U.S. general equilibrium model to plot the Laffer curve for various elasticity values of factor supply in the United States. He concluded that, although Laffer effects were conceivable in the context of the U.S. income tax system, they were unlikely given the conventional wisdom concerning the relevant elasticities of labor supply. Mackenzie (Chapter 2) has modeled the effects of a tax reduction on aggregate supply within the context of a simple macroeconomic model and found the aggregate demand effects to be more pronounced than the aggregate supply effects. Grieson and others (1977) reported a more positive result. They found the possibility of an inverse relationship between tax rates and tax revenue for local government in New York. This finding lends support to the hypothesis that Laffer effects are likely to be most pronounced where the tax base is narrowly defined, and substitution possibilities are thus increased. As a final example of research on the extent of Laffer effects in developed countries, consider Stuart's (1981) study of Sweden. Using a two-sector model with parameter values to fit Sweden, he found that the peak of the Laffer curve occurs at a marginal tax rate of approximately 70 percent. This result can be contrasted with actual marginal tax rates in force in Sweden—rates as high as 80 percent—and he concluded that tax rate reductions were in order. (A weakness of this latter study is that the parameterization was done within a Cobb-Douglas framework. This not only imposes the strong restriction that labor-supply elasticities be constant but it may also imply larger labor-supply elasticities than actually occur.)

REFERENCES

Acharya, Shankar N., and others, *Aspects of the Black Economy in India,* Report of a Study by the National Institute of Public Finance and Policy (New Delhi: Ministry of Finance, 1985).

Atkinson, A.B., "How Progressive Should Income Tax Be?" in *Essays in Modern Economics: The Proceedings of the Association of University Teachers of Eco-*

[19] The interpretation is also predicated on the accuracy of the assumptions required for the application of the univariate time-series analysis.

nomics, Aberystwyth, 1972, ed. by Michael Parkin and A.R. Nobay (London: Longman, 1973).

Bartlett, Bruce R., *Reaganomics: Supply Side Economics in Action* (New York: Quill, updated ed., 1982).

Blinder, Alan S., "Thoughts on the Laffer Curve," in *The Supply-Side Effects of Economic Policy,* ed. by Laurence H. Meyer (Boston, Massachusetts: Kluwer-Nijhoff, 1981).

Canto, Victor A., Douglas H. Joines, and Arthur B. Laffer, "Tax Rates, Factor Employment, and Market Production," in *The Supply-Side Effects of Economic Policy,* ed. by Laurence H. Meyer (Boston, Massachusetts: Kluwer-Nijhoff, 1981).

———, *Foundations of Supply-Side Economics: Theory and Evidence* (New York: Academic Press, 1983).

Federal Reserve Bank of Atlanta and Emory University Law and Economics Center, *Supply-Side Economics in the 1980s: Conference Proceedings* (Westport, Connecticut: Quorum Books, 1982).

Feldstein, Martin S. (1974a), "Incidence of a Capital Income Tax in a Growing Economy with Variable Savings Rates," *Review of Economic Studies* (Edinburgh), Vol. 41 (October 1974), pp. 505–13.

——— (1974b), "Tax Incidence in a Growing Economy with Variable Factor Supply," *Quarterly Journal of Economics* (Cambridge, Massachusetts), Vol. 88 (November 1974), pp. 551–73.

Fink, Richard H., ed., *Supply-Side Economics: A Critical Appraisal* (Frederick, Maryland: University Publications of America, 1982).

Fullerton, Don, "On the Possibility of an Inverse Relationship Between Tax Rates and Government Revenues," *Journal of Public Economics* (Amsterdam), Vol. 19 (October 1982), pp. 3–22.

Grieson, Ronald E., William Hamovitch, Albert M. Levenson, and Richard D. Morgenstern, "The Effect of Business Taxation on the Location of Industry," *Journal of Urban Economics* (New York), Vol. 4 (April 1977), pp. 170–85.

Gupta, Anupam, *Impact of the Personal Income Tax* (New Delhi: National Institute of Public Finance and Policy, 1978).

Hailstones, Thomas J. (1982a), *A Guide to Supply-Side Economics* (Richmond, Virginia: Robert F. Dame, Inc., 1982).

——— (1982b), ed., *Viewpoints on Supply-Side Economics* (Richmond, Virginia: Robert F. Dame, Inc., 1982).

Hutton, John P., and Peter J. Lambert, "Income Tax Progressivity and Revenue Growth," *Economics Letters* (Amsterdam), Vol. 3, No. 4 (1979), pp. 377–80.

India, Ministry of Finance, *Budget for 1974/75* (New Delhi, 1975).

———, *Budget for 1975/76* (New Delhi, 1976).

International Monetary Fund, *International Financial Statistics Yearbook, 1983* (Washington, 1983).

Jamaica, *Report of the Commissioner of Income Tax for Years Ended 31st March, 1981 and 31st March, 1982* (Kingston: Government Publications, 1982).

———, Ministry of Finance and Planning, *Financial Statements and Revenue Estimates for 1981/82* (Kingston, 1981).

———, National Planning Agency, *Economic and Social Survey: Jamaica, 1980* (Kingston: Government Publications, 1980).

Khanna, Kailash C., "India: The Finance Bill, 1974," *Bulletin*, International Bureau of Fiscal Documentation (Amsterdam), Vol. 28 (April 1974), pp. 143-46.

Kwon, Ohchul, "Taxes, Tax Revenues, and the Laffer Curve for a Developing Country Like Korea," *International Tax Journal* (New York), Vol. 10, No. 4 (May 1984), pp. 269-72.

Lydall, H.F., *The Structure of Earnings* (Oxford: Clarendon Press, 1968).

Meyer, Laurence H., ed., *The Supply-Side Effects of Economic Policy* (Boston, Massachusetts: Kluwer-Nijhoff, 1981).

Raboy, David G., ed., *Essays in Supply Side Economics* (Washington: Institute for Research on the Economics of Taxation, 1982).

Roberts, Paul C., *The Supply-Side Revolution: An Insider's Account of Policymaking in Washington* (Cambridge, Massachusetts: Harvard University Press, 1984).

Stuart, Charles E., "Swedish Tax Rates, Labor Supply, and Tax Revenues," *Journal of Political Economy* (Chicago), Vol. 89 (October 1981), pp. 1020-38.

Tanzi, Vito, and Thomas P. Hart, "The Effect of the 1964 Revenue Act on the Sensitivity of the Federal Income Tax," *Review of Economics and Statistics* (Cambridge, Massachusetts), Vol. 54 (August 1972), pp. 326-28.

U.S. Congress, House, Committee on the Budget, *Supply-Side Economics: Hearing Before the Task Force on Tax Policy of the Committee on the Budget, House of Representatives,* 97th Congress, 1st Session, March 10, 1981 (Washington: Government Printing Office, 1981).

Wanniski, Jude, *The Way the World Works* (New York: Simon and Schuster, rev. and updated ed., 1983).

8

Relationship Between Income Tax Ratios and Growth Rates in Developing Countries

A Cross-Country Analysis

Luis A. Mañas-Antón

This chapter presents some empirical evidence on the interrelationship between output growth and the reliance of the tax system on income taxes in developing countries, using cross-country and pooled cross-country time-series samples.

Output growth is influenced by many factors, in addition to the structure of the tax system, and these need to be controlled to isolate the net effect of income taxes. The main sources of output growth will first be identified according to the Dennison growth accounting tradition. Then, drawing on the development economics literature, the main determinants of these sources will be analyzed and used as explanatory variables in the final reduced-form equation for growth rates.

The proposition that income taxes have a negative effect on output growth is one of the central arguments in the old controversy in the theory of public finance about the choice between a consumption or an income-based tax system (Hall (1968), Tanzi (1969), Goode (1976), Meade (1978), Pechman (1980)). In recent years, this controversy has been rekindled by the emergence of the supply-side approach, which emphasizes the significant negative effects of high income taxes on savings, productive investment, labor supply, and, consequently, growth (Boskin (1978), Canto, Joines, and Laffer (1983)).[1]

[1]This is one of the major propositions associated with the supply-side school. See Gandhi (Chapter 1).

The theoretical arguments used by the supply-siders are similar in substance to those of the neoclassical economists writing on taxation and, among others, include the following:

- Taxation of capital incomes (through personal and corporate income taxes, capital gains taxes, and so on) distorts the marginal conditions for intertemporal consumption, providing an incentive to substitute current consumption for future consumption, or savings (Atkinson and Stiglitz (1980), Feldstein (1983)).
- Taxation of labor incomes (through personal income tax) distorts the marginal conditions for static labor-leisure decisions, providing an incentive to substitute leisure for labor. This effect is particularly significant for a highly skilled labor force whose incentives to work are easily eroded by high and progressive income tax rates.
- Taxation of labor incomes (through personal income tax—especially at highly progressive rates) seriously distorts the marginal conditions for human capital formation decisions (such as investment in education or training). However, when taxes on labor incomes are proportional and the only costs of human capital formation are forgone earnings, that is, all other costs are fully expensed (or tax deductible), taxes on labor incomes tend to be neutral (see Boskin (1975)). In other words, proportional labor taxes lead to the same investment in human capital as do lump-sum taxes.

These arguments suggest that if two countries were compared that were identical in all respects except that the share of capital income taxes in total taxes was higher for one than for the other, the latter would grow faster, as its savings rate would be higher. Alternatively, if they were identical except that the share of labor income taxes in total taxes was higher for one than for the other, the growth rate for the former would be smaller, provided its higher share of labor income taxes was the result of a progressive rate structure. Combining these arguments for capital and labor income taxes suggests that the higher the share of direct tax revenue, the lower the growth rate, all else being equal.[2]

[2]The skeptic can raise some doubts about the validity of this proposition in the context of the neoclassical growth theory according to which income tax may influence the aggregate level of real variables in the steady-state but not of their growth rates which are dependent only on exogenous variables such as the labor supply growth rate. Even in neoclassical models, however, growth rates can still differ in the transition path to the steady-state. If we assume that developing countries are in such a situation, these models will imply, under a wide range of specifications, that countries that provide disincentives to capital accumulation and/or technological progress, say, through high and progressive income taxes, could well grow slower.

In the end, however, the existence and size of the negative effect of income taxes on capital accumulation and growth must be substantiated by empirical evidence.[3] This chapter attempts to shed some light on the issue by focusing on the empirical analysis of cross-section data from developing countries.[4]

The remainder of this chapter is divided into three sections and an annex. Section I examines the strategy for empirical testing and derives a general regression equation for the growth rate. Section II analyzes the empirical results from the final model. Section III summarizes the findings of the paper. The Annex describes the sources of data and includes some additional regression equations.

I. Strategy of the Empirical Analysis

The empirical analysis in this paper is based on a final regression equation in which output growth, as the dependent variable, is explained by a relatively short list of exogenous determinants for which data are readily available in developing countries. The approach taken for deriving such a regression equation is the growth accounting approach in the Dennison (1962) tradition.

As a first step, the aggregate production possibilities of a country were assumed to be characterized by the inequality:

$$Y(t) \leq A(t)\, F[K(t), H(t)], \tag{1}$$

where real output (Y) in period t is limited by the state of the technology (A), physical capital (K), and human capital (H). The aggregate production function, $F(\ )$, has constant returns to scale and the usual neoclassical properties.

Rewriting expression (1), we derive:

$$Y(t) \equiv \gamma(t)\, A(t)\, F[K(t), H(t)] \qquad 0 < \gamma(t) \leq 1, \tag{2}$$

[3]In recent years, there has been some effort in this direction using different techniques or data sets. For instance, using time-series data, see Boskin (1978), Howrey and Hymans (1980), Giovannini (1985); using simulations of general equilibrium models, see Auerbach and Kotlikoff (1983), Kotlikoff (1984), and the references therein; and pairing similar countries with different levels of taxation, see Marsden (1983).

[4]This approach has been interestingly applied to other macroeconomic and fiscal hypotheses in relation to developing countries in recent papers by Kormendi and Meguire (1985). For developed countries, Tanzi (1969) provides case studies and cross-country comparisons of growth rates and the structure of the individual income tax.

where $1 - \gamma$ measures the difference between the current output level and the level attainable on the production possibilities frontier. Expression (2) is tautologically true unless γ or A have restrictions.

The growth accounting identity is, then, obtained from the logarithmic derivative of (2) (suppressing all time arguments):

$$\hat{Y} \equiv \hat{\gamma} + \hat{A} + \alpha\hat{K} + (1 - \alpha)\hat{H}, \tag{3}$$

where growth rates are indicated by circumflex accents and α is the elasticity of output with respect to capital and is equal to the share of capital in total output when factors are paid the value of their marginal product.

In identity (3), following the Dennison tradition, output growth is decomposed into four different sources: (1) physical capital growth, $\hat{K}$; (2) human capital growth, $\hat{H}$; (3) technical change, $\hat{A}$; and (4) change in the efficiency in the use of resources, $\hat{\gamma}$. This expression can be seen as a closing identity of a general model in which each of the growth sources is determined endogenously.

The next step was to derive the basic determinants of each of these sources of growth as a function of a short list of observable exogenous variables. Because reasonably consistent and reliable data had to be readily available for these variables for the period of analysis, the number of these potential exogenous variables was rather limited.

The final step in the process was to obtain the reduced-form equation for output growth, $\hat{Y}$, ready to be used in empirical estimation.

We will start now by examining various determinants of the sources of output growth identified in identity (3) above.

Physical Capital (K)

The change in the capital stock during a given period is equal to investment (I), net of depreciation (δK):

$$\hat{K}_t = \frac{\Delta K_t}{K_t} = \frac{I_t - \delta K_t}{K_t} \qquad 0 < \delta < 1. \tag{4}$$

Denoting the ratio of investment to output as i and the capital-output ratio as u, equation (4) can be rewritten as:

$$\hat{K}_t = \frac{i_t}{u_t} - \delta. \tag{5}$$

From a national accounting perspective, the investment-output ratio is identically equal to domestic savings plus net foreign investment divided by gross domestic product (GDP).[5]

A review of the available literature suggests that the following factors potentially influence capital accumulation.[6]

Reliance on Income Taxes (TI)

The theoretical justification for the inclusion of reliance on income taxes has already been provided in the introductory section.[7] The empirical analysis in this paper makes use of two measures of a country's reliance on income taxes: TI/T—the share of income tax revenue in total tax revenue (the focus of the analysis) and TI/Y—the share of income tax revenue in GDP. According to supply-side advocates, these two variables should be negatively related to output growth. Part of this effect is likely to come through lower physical capital accumulation from the taxation of capital income.[8]

Capital income is taxed under both individual and corporate income taxes. It is difficult to disentangle their different potential effects on output growth empirically, since the systems of integrating these taxes are varied (in our sample of countries they range between complete nonintegration, in, for example, India, to virtual full integration, as in Greece).[9] Nonetheless, the study will derive some regression results using separate ratios of individual and corporate income taxes to total tax revenue (TII/T and TCI/T, respectively), in spite of the difficulties in the interpretation of their coefficients.

[5]In the absence of interventions, the quantities observed ex post for these variables reflect the interaction of demand and supply of investable funds in the market. However, for our purpose, we are interested in understanding the exogenous factors ("shift parameters") that determine the position of these demand and supply schedules. Unfortunately, the empirical importance of capital market interventions in developing countries cannot be ignored, especially the widespread existence of nominal interest rate ceilings. (These are documented in Galbis (1979) and International Monetary Fund (1983).)

[6]For a thorough survey of the literature on these issues, both theoretical and empirical, see Ebrill (Chapter 3).

[7]In that section we abstracted from open economy considerations. These considerations do not change the essence of our testable proposition. Investment decisions of foreign economic agents (usually firms) depend on the relative tax treatment of the generated income (among several other factors). Relatively high corporate income tax rates could be expected to decrease foreign investment and, thus, accumulation of capital in a country.

[8]This argument ignores the positive effect that government expenditures may have on physical capital accumulation.

[9]For some considerations on the choice of integration systems, see Prest (1985).

Inflation (INF)

Inflation can have a negative effect on capital accumulation in two main ways. First, it is usually associated with greater uncertainty about the returns on current savings as well as those future relative prices that are important for returns on investment. This increased and, generally, uninsurable uncertainty discourages the accumulation of productive capital (see Mirman (1971)).[10] The second negative impact of inflation arises because nominal interest rates in developing countries are often set by the government at artificially low rates (Galbis (1979)). The adverse effect of such a policy on savings and investment is exacerbated by high rates of inflation, since they lead to highly negative real interest rates for savers which, by reducing the flow of savings, constrain investment.

On the other hand, in some models (see, e.g., Fischer (1979)) inflation is assumed to have positive effect on capital accumulation by virtue of the Tobin-Mundell effect: high anticipated inflation leads to shifts in portfolios away from real money balances and toward real capital.

The relative strength of positive and negative effects of inflation on capital accumulation will need to be determined empirically.

Demographic Variables (AGE)

For explaining savings behavior, life-cycle models stress the importance of the humped shape of earnings profiles and the desire of individuals for a smooth consumption pattern over their lifetimes. These two factors together imply that individuals will accumulate assets in their most productive years to pay for debts incurred when young and for retirement. Thus, we would expect that the percentage of the population that is within the working age, say, 15–65 years of age (*AGE*), might increase savings.[11]

Level of Government Activity (PEX, KPEX)

It is important to separate the effects of the structure of taxation on capital accumulation from the effects of the level of government activity. There are sharp differences of view on these latter effects; according to supply-siders they are substantial and negative, while according to some development economists they may be substantial and positive in developing countries.

[10] High mean inflation (or money growth) is very closely correlated with a high standard deviation of monetary shocks, as calculated by Kormendi and Meguire (1985).

[11] For example, countries with a large percentage of the population below working age (as in many African countries) will be expected to have, ceteris paribus, lower savings ratios.

The level of government activity can best be measured in expenditure terms rather than revenue terms (Kotlikoff (1984)). The ratio of government expenditure to the value of output (PEX) is included as another explanatory variable in the regression for investment. The possible effect on investment of the composition of government expenditure is captured by including the ratio of government capital expenditure to output ($KPEX$). As Blejer and Khan (1984) point out, the sign of the overall effect on capital accumulation will depend on the strength of real and financial "crowding out" effects and on the substitutability or complementarity of government capital expenditure with private investment.

Per Capita Income (YPC)

Finally, standard neoclassical models predict that, in the transition to the steady-state, the lower is the level of income per capita, the faster will be the approach to the steady-state path and, hence, the faster will be output growth. Per capita income is, therefore, also added to the list of variables.

Human Capital (H)

Human capital (H) can be viewed as the product of the number of workers and an index of the average human capital per worker (h). The number of workers in an economy depends on the total population (N) and the labor participation rate (PR):

$$H_t = N_t \cdot PR_t \cdot h_t. \tag{6}$$

Taking percentage changes:

$$\hat{H}_t = \hat{N}_t + \hat{PR}_t + \hat{h}_t. \tag{7}$$

Data on the first two components ($\hat{N}$ and $\hat{PR}$) are readily available and their sum, denoted as labor change (LC), is taken in this paper as an explanatory variable in the final equation. The coefficient on labor change is expected to be positive.

The average human capital component ($\hat{h}$) depends on the education and training of individuals. Since the expected rates of labor taxes are relevant exogenous parameters for human investment decisions, especially when the tax rate structure is progressive and education costs cannot be fully expensed (as is usually the case with individual income taxes), TI/T and TI/Y can affect growth negatively through their effect on human capital accumulation as well. This negative effect of tax variables is particularly reinforced by such factors as the possibility of international mobility of human capital (especially in the case of highly skilled labor) or of labor shifting to nontaxed sectors of the economy (either underground or non-market—household or subsistence—activities). Another potentially important determinant of human capital formation is the degree of public subsidization of marginal human capital investment. A good proxy for it would be the ratio of public expenditure on education to GDP (*EDU*), but there are many problems of availability and homogeneity of cross-country data on this variable; hence, this variable will not be used in the empirical analysis below.

Based on the discussions on physical and human capital, above, the capital accumulation component of equation (3) can now be written as equation (8), which makes it a function of the explanatory variables analyzed in the preceding paragraphs:

$$\alpha\hat{K} + (1 - \alpha)\hat{H} = \Psi\,(TI/T \text{ or } TI/Y,\ INF,\ AGE,\ PEX,\ KPEX,\ YPC,\ LC), \tag{8}$$

where

TI/T = the share of income taxes in total tax revenues;
TI/Y = the share of income taxes in GDP;
INF = inflation;
AGE = the share of the population at working age;
PEX = the ratio of government expenditure to the value of output;
$KPEX$ = the ratio of government capital expenditure to value of output;
YPC = per capita income; and
LC = the change in labor (change in total population plus the change in participation rate).

Technological Progress (*A*)

The economics of technological progress is an area of economic theory that is not well developed yet, perhaps because of its intrinsic theoretical difficulties (see Kamien and Schwartz (1982) for an introduction to these problems). Nevertheless, there are some tentative conclusions that may be drawn upon.

Technological advances in developing countries do not usually come from major breakthroughs in original research, but from adopting and using effectively already established technologies. Thus, it seems likely that countries with lower levels of development (measured by per capita GDP) may have a faster introduction of new technology. Growing contact with more developed countries should also be positively correlated with increased technological progress and, hence, with higher growth. This growing contact might be measured by the outward orientation of a country's development, specifically by a variable such as growth in the ratio of exports to GDP (*XGW*). This variable is also important for measuring the country's capacity to increase foreign capital goods imports—another crucial factor for technological advance by a developing country.

Finally, a variable such as lagged growth rate (growth rate in the 1960s or *G*60) is included, to represent the increase in know-how, learning by doing, and so on associated with a faster path of development in previous periods.[12]

Changes in the Gap Between Actual and Potential Output (γ)

Economies do not usually function on their production possibilities frontier for several reasons. On the one hand, rigidities and inefficiencies may lead to a lower-than-potential level of output, while on the other hand, cyclical oscillations may lead to short-run unemployment of resources.

In the first situation, growth can be related to the rate of removal of the inefficiencies. For many developing countries, obstacles to free trade (such as tariffs, quotas, or exchange and trade controls) are a very important reason for this gap between attainable and actual output. Again, growth in the ratio of exports to GDP (*XGW*) can be used as a proxy for these opening policies.[13]

The second consideration, the existence of cyclical oscillations, implies that a large component of short-run changes in output would not be explainable with the set of variables determining long-run growth. Hence, for our empirical work, we would like to clean our data of these cyclical oscillations. There are different ways to accomplish this. We have chosen to take long-period averages (for five and ten years), and hope that the influences of cyclical fluctuations will cancel out over that period of time, which will allow our set of regressors to explain a major portion of the variance of the growth variable, the primary focus of our study.

Summing up, we can now put all the parts together by expanding equa-

[12]The relation between export performance and economic growth has been a subject of intense debate in the development literature (see Feder (1983), Balassa (1985) among many others). These studies have usually shown a positive contribution to growth arising from increased integration in world markets.

[13]Since trade liberalization is usually closely associated with removal of other policy distortions as well, the variable *XGW* will also pick up some of the influence on output of the reforms in other policies.

tion (3) to obtain a final equation that links growth with a list of explanatory variables described above.

$$\hat{Y} = f(TI/., INF, AGE, PEX, KPEX, YPC, LC, XGW, G60, \ldots), \tag{9a}$$

where

$$TI/. = TI/T \text{ or } TI/Y.$$

II. Empirical Analysis

Econometric Methodology

The empirical analysis below is based on equation (9a), which links long-term output growth of a country, $\hat{Y}$, to a partial list of general explanatory variables.[14] Additional general variables (unobservable or unavailable for the period studied) and idiosyncratic factors are combined in a random error term, ϵ_i, that is expected to have the usual properties. Linearizing equation (9a) (i.e., taking a first order approximation to the function $f(.)$), we obtain a readily estimable equation:[15]

$$\hat{Y}_i = \beta_1 + \beta_2\, TI/T + \beta_3\, INF_i + \beta_4\, AGE_i + \beta_5\, PEX_i + \beta_6\, KPEX_i + \beta_7\, YPC_i + \beta_8\, LC_i + \beta_9\, XGW_i + \beta_{10}\, G60 + \epsilon_i \tag{9b}$$

$$i = 1, \ldots, N.$$

Since the analysis is cross-country, growth in all the countries included in the sample is assumed to be well described by equations (1) to (9b).[16] Thus, countries whose growth had other country-specific and directly identifiable determinants over the period studied were excluded (such as members of the Organization of Petroleum Exporting Countries or countries involved in prolonged strife, for example, Angola, Nicaragua, and Zimbabwe).

[14]The econometric exogeneity of the variables is based on two considerations: (1) some variables are predetermined before the sample period (*G60*, *YPC*, *AGE*, or *LC*) and (2) other variables are taken to be choice variables for economic policymakers (tax structure, *TI/.*; inflationary financing, *INF*; and public sector participation in the economy, *PEX* and *KPEX*).

[15]*TI/T* is used initially as the tax structure variable.

[16]Cross-sectional data pooled with time series is also used.

The data for the study have been taken from the Fund's *International Financial Statistics Yearbook* (*IFS*), *Government Finance Statistics Yearbook* (*GFS*), and *World Tables* published by the World Bank (for a complete description and comments, see the Annex). The final sample includes observations for 39 developing countries for the 1973–82 period. The relevant data are given in Tables 1 and 2.

The main cross-section regressions use ten-year (1973–82) averages as regressors. Five-year averages were also used, with two observations for each country. By pooling these time-series and cross-section data, the sample size was doubled at the expense of increased standard deviation of the random error (because of additional short-run noise in output growth).

In estimating empirical regression equations, some variables given in equation (9b) may turn out to be irrelevant and, thus, could be deleted from the regression with consequent lower variance in the estimation of the remaining coefficients. This increased precision has to be weighed against the possibility of biased estimation from imposing inexact linear restrictions.[17] For solving this trade-off problem, the choice of the benchmark specification is done by using the Akaike information criterion (*AIC*), that is, by minimizing among all the possible linear specifications the expression:

$$AIC = -(2/N) \ln (L(.)) + (2/N) K_i,$$

where

$L(.)$ = likelihood function evaluated at the restricted maximum likelihood estimates;
K_i = number of regressors; and
N = number of observations.

The *AIC* (Akaike (1974)) is based on the Kulback-Leibler measure of information. This criterion has been shown to have high relative accuracy in applied work (see Geweke and Meese (1981)).

Regression Results and Checks for Robustness

In order to select a benchmark specification, regressions are estimated for all possible subsets of the list of explanatory variables (subset regressions). The specification that minimized the *AIC* (henceforth called

[17]This is a very general econometric problem, the choice of a specific model nested on a general model, for which there is no easy solution. As Judge and others (1980), remark: "the appropriate parameterization of a linear statistical model is a hard and important problem, and [that] despite the productive efforts of many, it remains just that" (p. 442).

benchmark specification) is given in equation (10) in Table 3[18] and includes five explanatory variables (*TI/T*, *LC*, *AGE*, *XGW*, and *INF*), all of them with expected (or plausible) signs. These five variables are able to explain almost 50 percent of the growth variance; variance that, as we saw from Tables 1 and 2, is very high in our sample. All variables are significantly different from zero at the usual 5 percent level. The F-statistic, $F = 6.49$, rejects the null hypothesis of no explanatory power for the regression as a whole at better than the 1 percent level.

The estimated equation for the most general model (all nine independent variables contained in equation (9b)) is reported as equation (11) in Table 3. The results are very similar with those of equation (10): all variables common to both equations have the same signs and the coefficients are stable. As expected, the inclusion of four additional variables decreases the precision in the estimation of the other ones although the $\bar{R}^2$ of the second equation (equation (11)) is slightly lower than that of the first (equation (10)): all the t-ratios decrease and it cannot be rejected at the 5 percent significance level that the coefficients of *TI/T* and *AGE* are equal to zero, but neither can it be rejected that they are equal to their previous values.

Before focusing on the income tax variables, we shall briefly comment on the results of some of the other regressors.

None of the government expenditure variables appears in the benchmark specification (equation (10)). In the most general regression (equation (11)), total public expenditure over GDP has a negative sign that is nonsignificant (as does total tax revenue over GDP—see equation (A1) in the Annex). Government capital expenditure (*KPEX*) has a positive sign in equation (11) but it is not significantly different from zero either.[19]

Labor force change (*LC*), inflation (*INF*), and export growth (*XGW*) have highly significant coefficients in all specifications given in Table 3. The coefficient of labor force change (*LC*) is higher than one, probably because of the absence of some nonquantifiable and excluded variables that pick up the human capital accumulation effort.[20] In the case of inflation (*INF*), the negative effects on resource allocation seem to outweigh

[18]The same model would have been chosen using several other criteria such as Mallow's C_p or $\bar{R}^2$.

[19]For this variable it would be interesting to try to distinguish between infrastructure expenditure and other types of public investment (as suggested by Blejer and Khan (1984)). Unfortunately, data are not readily available to test for this.

[20]*EDU*, total government expenditure on education over *GDP*, was included but it was not significant. In any case, this variable is not very reliable since local governments are often in charge of education and their data are patchy and incomplete.

Table 1. Selected Developing Countries: Data on Nonfiscal Variables, 1973–82[1]

(In percent unless otherwise indicated)

	GDP Growth Rate	Labor Force Growth Rate	Inflation Rate	Percent of Population in 15–65 Age Group	Growth in Export/GDP	Growth Rates 1960s	GNP Per Capita (In U.S. dollars)
Burma	5.3	2.4	11.5	55.7	4.78	2.6	151
Malawi	2.7	3.0	10.6	50.4	2.01	5.3	205
India	4.1	2.0	9.5	55.5	5.00	4.5	220
Tanzania	3.8	3.5	17.3	51.7	−6.03	6.0	273
Sri Lanka	5.0	1.7	10.9	57.0	3.73	4.9	231
Pakistan	6.0	3.1	14.0	50.6	10.36	7.1	278
Ghana	0.9	2.9	59.1	51.1	−14.37	2.2	470
Kenya	4.7	4.1	13.7	48.1	−0.09	5.9	400
Yemen Arab Rep.	8.1	1.9	20.4	52.7	19.68	5.0	284
Zambia	1.1	2.8	12.8	50.8	−2.36	5.0	688
Bolivia	3.7	2.4	24.9	52.9	0.91	4.8	541
Thailand	7.3	2.4	11.9	52.9	3.15	8.2	525
Philippines	6.2	2.7	14.0	52.2	1.49	5.2	600
Papua New Guinea	3.6	2.6	9.5	54.9	7.38	6.7	776
Morocco	5.1	3.1	10.1	49.5	2.09	5.3	734
Guatemala	4.9	3.3	12.0	52.7	−0.49	5.7	1,004
Peru	3.0	2.7	42.3	52.8	5.27	4.8	1,142
Brazil	6.8	2.9	48.3	54.8	2.90	6.1	898
Dominican Rep.	5.8	2.9	11.2	50.3	1.10	5.6	1,002
Mauritius	6.0	1.5	17.7	58.0	−1.64	1.6	893
Colombia	4.9	2.3	24.2	55.5	−0.52	5.3	1,123
Tunisia	5.3	2.5	6.9	52.5	6.72	5.2	1,259
Costa Rica	4.1	2.5	15.6	50.4	5.58	6.1	1,284
Turkey	4.5	2.2	38.4	55.4	7.07	5.8	1,071
Syrian Arab Rep.	8.6	3.7	13.0	48.2	−1.17	6.5	1,009

Jordan	8.5	2.4	12.1	50.9	13.81	5.0	1,038
Paraguay	9.2	3.4	14.8	51.5	−1.31	7.9	1,020
Korea	8.3	1.7	17.9	58.1	8.22	8.6	1,245
Malaysia	7.9	2.9	7.2	53.5	5.12	6.4	1,592
Panama	5.1	2.8	7.9	54.4	2.10	7.2	1,682
Mexico	6.8	3.1	20.6	50.7	5.19	7.7	1,944
Portugal	4.3	1.0	20.8	62.5	1.64	6.4	2,327
Chile	2.9	1.7	185.0	59.6	10.57	4.2	2,665
Argentina	1.3	1.8	158.5	63.5	3.07	4.1	2,478
South Africa	3.8	2.4	12.1	57.0	2.23	6.2	2,209
Uruguay	3.8	0.7	63.7	63.0	0.61	1.7	1,807
Malta	11.2	2.2	8.2	63.9	5.71	4.7	3,167
Cyprus	2.7	0.6	9.0	61.5	3.19	5.7	3,628
Greece	3.5	1.0	18.0	64.1	6.61	7.5	3,139
Mean	5.1	2.4	26.5	54.6	3.43	5.51	
σ	2.3	0.8	36.9	4.5	5.53	1.6	

Sources: International Monetary Fund, *International Financial Statistics Yearbook, 1984* (Washington); and World Bank, *World Tables, 1980* (Washington).

[1]See the introduction to the Annex for the exact definition of each variable and the specific sources of data.

Table 2. Selected Developing Countries: Data on Fiscal Variables, 1973–82[1]

	In Percent of Total Tax Revenue			In Percent of GDP	
	Income tax	Individual income tax	Corporate income tax	Public expenditure	Public capital expenditure
Burma	0.14	. . .	. . .	0.15	0.03
Malawi	0.42	0.16	0.27	0.27	0.10
India	0.25	0.12	0.12	0.13	0.02
Tanzania	0.31	0.05	0.18	0.28	0.09
Sri Lanka	0.24	0.04	0.11	0.28	0.09
Pakistan	0.15	0.09	0.05	0.17	0.03
Ghana	0.23	0.11	0.12	0.15	0.03
Kenya	0.38	0.06	0.34	0.23	0.05
Yemen Arab Rep.	0.07	0.03	0.03	0.31	0.13
Zambia	0.49	0.19	0.19	0.34	0.06
Bolivia	0.15	0.08	0.06	0.13	0.01
Thailand	0.18	0.08	0.10	0.17	0.04
Philippines	0.26	0.12	0.13	0.13	0.02
Papua New Guinea	0.62	0.30	0.32	0.34	0.05
Morocco	0.23	0.07	0.14	0.32	0.11
Guatemala	0.01	0.01	—	0.12	0.04
Peru	0.22	0.05	0.16	0.18	0.04
Brazil	0.18	0.01	0.07	0.18	0.02
Dominican Rep.	0.22	0.07	0.14	0.17	0.07
Mauritius	0.27	0.15	0.13	0.26	0.05
Colombia	0.30	0.14	0.15	0.12	0.04
Tunisia	0.18	0.08	0.08	0.30	0.09
Costa Rica	0.17	0.17	—	0.21	0.03
Turkey	0.50	0.39	0.06	0.24	0.07
Syrian Arab Rep.	0.20	. . .	. . .	0.41	0.17

Jordan	0.11	0.03	0.07	0.53	0.16
Paraguay	0.13	0.02	0.11	0.11	0.02
Korea	0.28	0.13	0.12	0.16	0.03
Malaysia	0.38	0.09	0.31	0.27	0.06
Panama	0.27	. . .	. . .	0.32	0.07
Mexico	0.41	0.18	0.22	0.17	0.04
Portugal	0.17	0.07	0.03	0.34	0.05
Chile	0.19	0.11	0.07	0.33	0.05
Argentina	0.07	. . .	. . .	0.18	0.03
South Africa	0.56	0.22	0.32	0.23	0.03
Uruguay	0.08	0.03	0.05	0.24	0.02
Malta	0.50	0.26	0.23	0.38	0.06
Cyprus	0.24	0.14	0.06	0.26	0.05
Greece	0.15	0.10	0.04	0.33	0.06
Mean	0.25	0.10	0.12	0.24	0.06
σ	0.14	0.09	0.10	0.09	0.04

Note: There may be some apparent inconsistencies because of rounding; . . . = data not available; — = negligible.

Sources: International Monetary Fund, *Government Finance Statistics Yearbook, 1984* (Washington), and *International Financial Statistics Yearbook, 1984* (Washington).

[1]See the introduction to the Annex for the exact definition of each variable and the specific sources of data.

Table 3. Regression Results (OLS)[1]

Benchmark regression (TI/T)

$$\hat{Y} = \underset{}{-18.22^{*}} - \underset{(-2.24)}{4.98^{*}\ TI/T} + \underset{(3.3)}{2.42^{**}\ LC} + \underset{(2.69)}{0.347^{*}\ AGE} + \underset{(3.74)}{0.2^{**}\ XGW} - \underset{(-3.79)}{0.033^{**}\ INF} \quad (10)$$

$RSS = 102.6$; $N = 39$; $F(5, 33) = 6.49 > F_{0.99} = 3.63$; $AIC = 2.938$; $R^2 = 0.49$; $\bar{R}^2 = 0.41$

General model regression

$$\hat{Y} = -16.12 - \underset{(-1.62)}{4.11\ TI/T} + \underset{(2.82)}{2.27^{**}\ LC} + \underset{(1.79)}{0.30\ AGE} + \underset{(2.77)}{0.19^{**}\ XGW} - \underset{(-3.16)}{0.031^{**}\ INF} + \underset{(0.87)}{4.26.10\ YPC} + \underset{(-0.05)}{0.013\ G60} \quad (11)$$

$$- \underset{(-0.6)}{4.08\ PEX} + \underset{(0.85)}{14.28\ KPEX}$$

$RSS = 96.25$; $N = 39$; $F(9, 29) = 3.89 > F_{0.99} = 3.08$; $AIC = 2.981$; $R^2 = 0.51$; $\bar{R}^2 = 0.36$

Pooled cross-country time-series regression

$$\hat{Y} = -10.27 - \underset{(-2.23)}{4.97^{*}\ TI/T} + \underset{(2.56)}{1.56^{*}\ LC} + \underset{(2.16)}{0.25^{*}\ AGE} + \underset{(2.18)}{0.09^{*}\ XGW} - \underset{(-4.70)}{0.036^{**}\ INF} \quad (12)$$

$RSS = 493.26$; $N = 78$; $F(5, 72) = 5.64 > F_{0.99} = 3.29$; $AIC = 6.482$; $R^2 = 0.28$; $\bar{R}^2 = 0.23$

Benchmark regression (TI/Y)

$$\hat{Y} = -19.0 - \underset{(-2.08)}{22.1^{*}}\, TI/Y + \underset{(3.12)}{2.33^{**}}\, LC + \underset{(2.66)}{0.36^{*}}\, AGE + \underset{(3.87)}{0.22^{**}}\, XGW - \underset{(-3.58)}{0.032^{**}}\, INF \quad (13)$$

$RSS = 107.23$; $N = 39$; $F(5, 33) = 5.95 > F_{0.99} = 3.63$; $AIC = 3.05$; $R^2 = 0.47$; $\bar{R}^2 = 0.38$

Source: Author's calculations based on ordinary least squares (OLS) method, where

$\hat{Y}$ = output growth;
TI/T = ratio of income taxes to total tax revenue;
TI/Y = ratio of income tax to GDP;
LC = labor force change;
AGE = share of population of age 15–65 in total population;
XGW = growth of ratio of exports to GDP;
INF = inflation (rate of change of consumer price index);
RSS = residual sum of squares;
N = sample size; and
AIC = Akaike information criterion.

[1] *t*-values are given in parentheses. Marginal significance levels higher than 5 percent and 1 percent are represented by one and two asterisks, respectively.

any possible Tobin-Mundell effect. However, if countries are divided according to whether they have high or low inflation rates (more or less than 25 percent rate of inflation), the negative relation is only significant for the high-inflation countries. For the growth in exports to GDP ratio (*XGW*), our results corroborate other empirical analyses that have used different methodology and data sets (see Balassa (1985) and references therein).

Turning to income tax variables, in the benchmark specification (equation (10)) the coefficient of *TI/T* (the ratio of income taxes to total tax revenue) has a negative sign and is significantly different from zero at the 5 percent significance level. This would seem to give support to the hypothesis of negative correlation between reliance on income taxes and output growth. In fact, the sign of the coefficient for this variable is consistently negative for all the regressions that we ran, although the marginal significance levels are sometimes higher than the usual standard of 5 percent. For instance, this is the case in equation (11).

The stability of the sign and value of the *TI/T* coefficient can be checked further by pooling cross-section and time-series data (two five-year averages for each country). Assuming the same slope and intercept coefficients for the two periods, we obtained equation (12) from ordinary least squares (OLS) estimation. The value of the *TI/T* coefficient is very close to the one estimated in the benchmark specification (equation (10)) of −4.97 compared with −4.98. Taking the two periods separately and performing a Chow test for stability of coefficients, we accept their equality in the two periods at a 1 percent significance level.

When *TI/Y* (the ratio of income taxes to GDP) is included in the regression equation instead of *TI/T*, the previous results remain basically unaffected (see equation (13)). The *TI/Y* coefficient is also negative and significant at the 5 percent level (although with a *t*-ratio lower than for *TI/T*).

The equations given in Table 3, therefore, show that the presumption that the rate of output growth is negatively correlated with the income tax ratio is not rejected by the sample data. Further regressions were run to check if this conclusion holds for subsamples of countries at different levels of development as well. For this purpose, the 39 countries were ordered by gross national product (GNP) per capita and divided into two subsamples of low-income and middle-income countries (with 20 and 19 observations, respectively). The GNP per capita of US$1,000 was used as a cut-off point. Equations (A2) and (A3) in the Annex show that the coefficients for *TI/T* are negative with values (*t*-values in parentheses) equal to −6.47 (−2.61) for low-income countries and −4.69 (−1.35) for middle-income countries. The conclusion is now supported for low-income countries, but is not supported for middle-income countries.

Regressions were also run to check whether the results obtained for total income taxes held for individual and corporate income taxes as well. These substituted total income taxes in the numerator of TI/T by its components: taxes on individual income (TII) and taxes on corporate income (TCI). The regression results reported in the Annex (equations (A4) and (A5)) show that the coefficients remained negative but had low t-values (in parentheses), TII (-1.55) and TCI (-1.34), thereby suggesting that the negative relationship between growth rate and individual or corporate income tax ratios cannot be asserted with much confidence.

Output growth for Malta was almost three standard deviations away from the mean; thus, this country seemed to be very influential in the OLS estimation results. As a sensitivity check, the observation for Malta was deleted and equation (10) was re-estimated. Equation (A6) in the Annex is the re-estimated benchmark specification that shows the relative insensitivity of the coefficients to deleting this possible outlier.

The main conclusion from all these regression exercises is that the sign and size of the TI/T coefficient are robust but the t-ratios are not very high in all cases and that the point estimates of equation (10) can be taken as a good description of the information contained in the sample. This description would be applicable to all economies whose structure could be summarized by equations (1)-(9b). Thus, the estimated equation could also be expected to hold out-of-sample: that is, for different periods and/or countries.

III. Concluding Remarks

The regression analysis that examined the empirical relationship between growth rates in developing countries and the reliance of their tax structures on income taxes had three main results.

1. The sign of the relationship between the ratio of income taxes to total tax revenue and the growth rate of output was found to be consistently negative in all specifications. The coefficient was found to be significantly different from zero (5 percent level) in the benchmark regression equation, but this result did not hold in all specifications. The results from pooling time-series (five-year averages) and cross-section data corroborated the conclusions obtained from the benchmark regression equation—the coefficients for TI/T were almost identical.

2. The coefficient was also negative and statistically significant when TI/T was substituted by TI/Y (the ratio of income taxes to GDP) as a measure of a country's reliance on income taxation.

3. However, when the ratios of individual and corporate income taxes to

total tax revenue were considered, their coefficients were negative, but statistically insignificant in both cases.

In summary, the tentative conclusion that can be drawn from this chapter is that while there is some evidence supporting a negative relationship between output growth rates and the reliance of a country on income taxes, this relationship cannot be asserted with much confidence. This conclusion is, of course, subject to many limitations: cross-country regression analysis can be easily criticized (see Ebrill (Chapter 3, pp. 61-62)), the model specification may be inadequate and will need to be further checked for robustness, and so on. These limitations will have to be overcome in future empirical work on the subject on which the present study is no more than a first step.

ANNEX

Definition of the Variables, Sources of Data, and Additional Regression Equations

Definition of the Variables and Sources of Data

Unless otherwise stated, variables are arithmetic averages of annual observations for the period 1973-82. In a few cases, data were not available in the 1984 issues of the *International Financial Statistics Yearbook* (*IFS*) and the *Government Finance Statistics Yearbook* (*GFS*) for starting and ending years of the period considered. For those cases, averages were taken for the available data within 1973-82. The variables have been defined as follows (*IFS* and *GFS* along with line numbers indicated in parentheses or World Bank, *World Tables,* 1980):

$\hat{Y}$ = growth of real GDP (*IFS* 99 b.p.);
LF = labor force growth (the sum of population growth (*IFS* 99z) and the change in the activity rate—data for 1970 and 1981 were obtained from *World Tables*);
INF = change in the consumer price index (*IFS* 64);
AGE = share of population between the ages 15 and 65 in total population (average of data for 1970 and 1980 in *World Tables*);
XGW = growth of share of exports (*IFS* 90c) in GDP (*IFS* 99b);
YPC = per capita GNP in 1972 (*World Tables,* estimation);
$G60$ = growth rate during the 1960s (*World Tables*);
TI/Y = taxes on income, profits, and capital gains (*GFS* A-IV.1) over current GDP (*IFS* 99b);
TI/T = taxes on income, profits, and capital gains (*GFS* A-IV.1) over total tax revenue (*GFS* A-IV);
TII = taxes on individual income (*GFS* A-IV.1.1) over total tax revenue;
TCI = taxes on corporate income (*GFS* A-IV.1.2) over total tax revenue;

PEX = total government expenditure (*GFS* 7) over GDP;
$KPEX$ = capital expenditure (*GFS* 9) over GDP; and
T/Y = total tax revenue over GDP.

Additional Regression Equations[21]

TOTAL TAX REVENUE (POOLED DATA)

$$\hat{Y} = \underset{}{-10.14} - \underset{(-2.17)}{5.02^{*}\, TI/T} + \underset{(0.08)}{0.57\, T/Y} - \underset{(-4.60)}{0.036^{*}\, INF} + \underset{(2.52)}{1.56^{*}\, LC}$$

$$+ \underset{(1.99)}{0.24^{*}\, AGE} + \underset{(2.11)}{0.08^{*}\, XGW} \qquad \text{(A1)}$$

$RSS = 493.2$; $N = 78$; $F(6, 71) = 4.63$; $AIC = 6.5$; $R^2 = 0.28$

LOW-INCOME COUNTRIES ONLY

$$\hat{Y} = -3.8 - \underset{(-2.61)}{6.47^{**}\, TI/T} - \underset{(-1.09)}{0.028\, INF} + \underset{(0.81)}{0.17\, AGE} + \underset{(2.28)}{0.13^{*}\, XGW}$$

$$+ \underset{(0.41)}{0.52\, LC} \qquad \text{(A2)}$$

$RSS = 27.69$; $N = 20$; $F(5, 14) = 4.1$; $AIC = 1.98$; $R^2 = 0.59$; $\bar{R}^2 = 0.45$

MIDDLE-INCOME COUNTRIES ONLY

$$\hat{Y} = -24.26 - \underset{(-1.35)}{4.69\, TI/T} - \underset{(-3.44)}{0.035^{**}\, INF} + \underset{(2.42)}{0.41^{*}\, AGE} + \underset{(2.02)}{0.23^{*}\, XGW}$$

$$+ \underset{(3.61)}{3.63^{**}\, LC} \qquad \text{(A3)}$$

$RSS = 41.42$; $N = 19$; $F(5, 13) = 5.3$; $AIC = 2.8$; $R^2 = 0.67$; $\bar{R}^2 = 0.54$

INDIVIDUAL INCOME TAX ONLY

$$\hat{Y} = -15.8 - \underset{(-1.55)}{5.4\, TII} - \underset{(-3.41)}{0.03^{**}\, INF} + \underset{(2.33)}{0.31^{*}\, AGE} + \underset{(2.75)}{2.02^{**}\, LC}$$

$$+ \underset{(3.77)}{0.22^{**}\, XGW} \qquad \text{(A4)}$$

$RSS = 110.2$; $N = 39$; $F(5, 33) = 5.53$; $AIC = 3.13$; $R^2 = 0.46$; $\bar{R}^2 = 0.37$

[21]Values in parentheses are *t*-values.

CORPORATION INCOME TAX ONLY

$$\hat{Y} = -17.8 - \underset{(-1.34)}{4.7}\ TCI - \underset{(-3.40)}{0.031^{**}}\ INF + \underset{(2.40)}{0.32^{*}}\ AGE + \underset{(3.00)}{2.3^{**}}\ LC + \underset{(3.61)}{0.21^{**}}\ XGW \qquad (A5)$$

$RSS = 112.1; N = 39; F(5, 33) = 5.33; AIC = 3.18; R^2 = 0.45; \bar{R}^2 = 0.36$

EXCLUDING MALTA

$$\hat{Y} = -16.95 - \underset{(-2.07)}{4.65}\ TI/T^* - \underset{(-3.71)}{0.033^{**}}\ INF + \underset{(2.53)}{0.33^{*}}\ AGE + \underset{(3.45)}{0.19^{**}}\ XGW + \underset{(2.78)}{2.18^{**}}\ LC \qquad (A6)$$

$RSS = 103.92; N = 38; F(5, 32) = 5.71; AIC = 3.05; R^2 = 0.47; \bar{R}^2 = 0.39$

REFERENCES

Akaike, Hirotugu, "A New Look at the Statistical Model Identification," *I.E.E.E Transactions on Automatic Control* (New York), Vol. AC-19 (December 1974), pp. 716–23.

Atkinson, Anthony B., and Joseph E. Stiglitz, *Lectures on Public Economics* (New York: McGraw-Hill, 1980).

Auerbach, Alan J., and Laurence J. Kotlikoff, "National Savings, Economic Welfare, and the Structure of Taxation," in *Behavioral Simulation Methods in Tax Policy Analysis,* ed. by Martin Feldstein (Chicago: University of Chicago Press, 1983).

Balassa, Bela, "Exports, Policy Choices, and Economic Growth in Developing Countries After the 1973 Oil Shock," *Journal of Development Economics* (Amsterdam), Vol. 18 (May–June 1985), pp. 23–35.

Blejer, M.I., and Mohsin S. Khan, "Government Policy and Private Investment in Developing Countries" (unpublished, International Monetary Fund, February 2, 1984).

Boskin, Michael J., "Notes on the Tax Treatment of Human Capital," in *Conference on Tax Research, 1975,* sponsored by the Office of Tax Analysis, Department of the Treasury (Washington: Government Printing Office, 1975).

_____, "Taxation, Saving, and the Rate of Interest," *Journal of Political Economy* (Chicago), Vol. 86, No. 2, Part 2 (April 1978), pp. S3–S27.

Canto, Victor A., Douglas H. Joines, and Arthur B. Laffer, *Foundations of Supply-Side Economics: Theory and Evidence* (New York: Academic Press, 1983).

Dennison, E., *The Sources of Economic Growth in the United States and the Alternatives Before Us* (New York Committee for Economic Development, 1962).

Feder, Gershon, "On Exports and Economic Growth," *Journal of Development Economics* (Amsterdam), Vol. 12 (February-April 1983), pp. 59-73.

Feldstein, Martin S., "Incidence of a Capital Income Tax in a Growing Economy with Variable Savings Rates," *Review of Economic Studies* (Edinburgh), Vol. 41 (October 1974), pp. 505-13.

______, *Capital Taxation* (Cambridge, Massachusetts: Harvard University Press, 1983).

Fischer, Stanley, "Anticipations and the Nonneutrality of Money," *Journal of Political Economy* (Chicago), Vol. 87 (April 1979), pp. 225-52.

Fullerton, Don, and Jonathan Skinner, "Cost Price Effects and Capital Taxation," National Tax Association—Tax Institute of America, *Proceedings of the Seventy-Seventh Annual Conference on Taxation* (Columbus, Ohio, 1985).

Galbis, Vicente, "Inflation and Interest Rate Policies in Latin America, 1967-76," *Staff Papers,* International Monetary Fund (Washington), Vol. 26 (June 1979), pp. 334-66.

Geweke, John, and Richard Meese, "Estimating Regression Models of Finite but Unknown Order," *International Economic Review* (Osaka, Japan), Vol. 22 (February 1981), pp. 55-70.

Giovannini, A., "Saving and the Real Interest Rate in LDCs," *Journal of Development Economics* (Amsterdam), Vol. 18 (August 1985), pp. 197-218.

Goode, Richard B., *The Individual Income Tax* (Washington: Brookings Institution, rev. ed., 1976).

Hall, Robert E., "Consumption Taxes Versus Income Taxes: Implications for Economic Growth," National Tax Association, *Proceedings of the Sixty-First Annual Conference on Taxation* (Columbus, Ohio, 1968).

Howrey, E. Philip, and Saul H. Hymans, "The Measurement and Determination of Loanable-Funds Saving," in *What Should Be Taxed: Income or Expenditure?* ed. by Joseph A. Pechman (Washington: Brookings Institution, 1980).

International Monetary Fund, *Interest Rate Policies in Developing Countries: A Study by the Research Department of the International Monetary Fund,* Occasional Paper No. 22 (Washington, October 1983).

Judge, George G., W.E. Griffiths, R. Carter Hill, and Tsoung-Chao Lee, *The Theory and Practice of Econometrics* (New York: John Wiley, 1980).

Kamien, Morton I., and Nancy L. Schwartz, *Market Structure and Innovation* (Cambridge, Massachusetts: Cambridge University Press, 1982).

Kormendi, Roger C., and Philip G. Meguire, "Macroeconomic Determinants of Growth: Cross-Country Evidence," *Journal of Monetary Economics* (Amsterdam), Vol. 16 (September 1985), pp. 141-63.

Kotlikoff, Laurence J., "Taxation and Savings: A Neoclassical Perspective," *Jour-*

nal of Economic Literature (Nashville, Tennessee), Vol. 22 (December 1984), pp. 1576–1629.

Marsden, Keith, "Links between Taxes and Economic Growth: Some Empirical Evidence," World Bank Staff Working Paper No. 605 (Washington, 1983).

Meade, J.E., *The Structure and Reform of Direct Taxation* (London: Allen & Unwin, 1978).

Mirman, Leonard J., "Uncertainty and Optimal Consumption Decisions," *Econometrica* (Evanston, Illinois), Vol. 37 (January 1971), pp. 179–85.

Modi, Jitendra R., "Major Features of Corporate Profit Taxes in Selected Developing Countries," *Bulletin,* International Bureau of Fiscal Documentation (Amsterdam), Vol. 41 (February 1987), pp. 65–74.

Pechman, Joseph A., ed., *What Should Be Taxed: Income or Expenditure?* (Washington: Brookings Institution, 1980).

Prest, A.R., *Public Finance in Developing Countries* (New York: St. Martin's Press, 3rd ed., 1985).

Sandmo, A., "The Effect of Uncertainty on Saving Decisions," *Review of Economic Studies* (Edinburgh), Vol. 37 (July 1970), pp. 353–60.

Tanzi, Vito, *The Individual Income Tax and Economic Growth: An International Comparison* (Baltimore: Johns Hopkins University Press, 1969).

——, "Quantitative Characteristics of the Tax Systems of Developing Countries," in *The Theory of Taxation for Developing Countries,* ed. by David Newbery and Nicholas Stern (New York: Oxford University Press, 1987).

Theil, Henri, *Principles of Econometrics* (New York: John Wiley, 1971).

Yusuf, Shahid, and R. Kyle Peters, "Capital Accumulation and Economic Growth: The Korean Paradigm," World Bank Staff Working Paper No. 712 (Washington, 1985).

PART III

Tax Policy for Efficiency and Growth: Aspects of Basic Supply-Side Tax Policy

9

Tax Structure for Efficiency and Supply-Side Economics in Developing Countries

Ved P. Gandhi

Supply-side economists stress minimizing the distortions that taxes, in general, and high and progressive taxes, in particular, inject into market decisions and believe that reforming the tax structures, in general, and lowering the rates of taxes, in particular, would encourage savings and production by allowing the economic incentives of a free market to work.[1] As the problems of developing countries frequently are the result of insufficient savings and production, it would appear, prima facie, that the tax policy prescriptions of supply-siders, viz., low and less progressive taxes, could be highly relevant to them. This argument provides the background for the present paper.

The purpose of this paper is not to discuss the validity of factor and output elasticity (growth) optimism of the popular supply-side economists; this has been examined in the preceding chapters and by other authors.[2] Instead, this paper attempts to identify the relationships that the tax policy prescriptions of supply-side economics bear with those of the traditional and modern literature on taxation. In addition, it seeks to establish what

[1]As described in Chapter 1, basic supply-side economists focus on all aspects of the tax system, while the popular supply-side economists primarily focus on the levels and progressivity of marginal income tax rates. An empirical study frequently quoted in support of the validity of the proposition that lower taxes will encourage economic growth in developing countries is that of Marsden (1983a and 1983b). The Annex to this chapter describes and reviews the methodology underlying this study.

[2]In particular, see Boskin (1973, 1978, 1982); Howrey and Hymans (1980); King (1980); Rosen (1980); Hausman (1981a, 1981b); Keleher (1982); Keleher and Orzechowski (1982); and Evans (1982, 1983).

the tax system of developing countries would look like if supply-side (disincentive) effects of taxation and efficiency in the allocation of resources were the major concerns of tax policymakers. The discussion in the chapter covers both tax design (establishing a new tax system) and tax reform (revising the existing tax system).

This chapter therefore has five objectives. First, it defines the efficiency objective of a tax system, reviews the importance of this objective among multiple objectives of taxation in the literature, and describes the broad theoretical characteristics of a tax system based on efficiency considerations (Section I). Second, after reviewing selected literature on taxation, it attempts to throw light on those elements of a tax structure, or the structure of tax bases, that would minimize distortions and thus would be consistent with the efficiency objective (Section II). Third, it seeks to define a rate design, or the structure of tax rates (including its progressivity), that would be least distortionary and thus would be consistent with the efficiency objective (Section III). Fourth, it examines the differences between a popular supply-side economist and a modern optimal tax economist (Section IV). Finally, the chapter concludes with some thoughts on the implications of the popular supply-side approach to tax reform in developing countries.

I. Supply-Side Objectives of the Tax System—in Theory

Supply-side economists stress that "neutrality" in taxation is the most desirable of all objectives of taxation, but, if for some practical reason this objective is unattainable, a second-best aim should be to minimize the distortionary substitution and excise effects of taxation. In fact, as was mentioned in Chapter 1, few tax economists would disagree with the importance attached to the neutrality objective or the reduction of distortionary effects of taxation.[3] In theoretical literature, this objective is labeled as the

[3]"Neutrality" in the strictest sense will require that neither relative prices of goods and services nor relative factor rewards should be affected by tax rates or other provisions of the tax system. A less stringent definition of neutrality will involve effective tax rates to be such that they will avoid diversions of labor, savings, investments, etc., to uses that are suboptimal. For a fuller discussion of this subject, see section on "A Neutral Tax System," below. Even some popular supply-siders have emphasized the objective of neutrality. See Kemp (1981, p. 68), Raboy (1982, p. 58), and Ture (1982, p. 17).

"efficiency" objective of taxation.[4] In this paper, therefore, the two terms, neutrality and efficiency, will be used interchangeably.

Conflicts Among Multiple Objectives of Taxation

Traditional tax theory, taking a cue from political reality, considered taxation as an instrument with multiple objectives: to raise adequate revenue with administrative ease, to correct externalities and play a sumptuary role, to redistribute income and wealth and, since Keynes, to stabilize aggregate demand and support other macroeconomic objectives. As the history of economic thought reveals, it is not that the traditional tax literature ignored the supply-side effects (distortionary economic effects) of taxation that so concern supply-side economists, but that it frequently treated efficiency and equity as two separate criteria. The traditional tax literature discussed them sequentially offering little or no guidance on how they could or should be combined.[5] When the two conflicted, the traditional theory tended to allow the objective of equity and fairness in taxation take precedence over neutrality and efficiency.

For example, while Adam Smith's famous canons of taxation (equity, certainty, convenience, and collection cost) did not include a supply-side objective and he ultimately argued in favor of the ability-to-pay principle ("The subjects of every state . . . ought to contribute . . . as nearly as possible, in proportion to their respective abilities"), he was, nevertheless, well aware of the effects of high taxes on output and government revenues via the behavior of taxpayers. As he wrote, "high taxes, sometimes by diminishing the consumption of the taxed commodities and sometimes by encouraging smuggling, afford a smaller revenue to government than what might be drawn from more moderate taxes."[6]

[4]That productive efficiency or ensuring the efficient allocation of resources is desirable frequently goes unquestioned. However, there may be exceptional situations where productive inefficiency rather than efficiency may be "optimal" on certain distributive and allocative grounds. Such situations are described in Dasgupta and Stiglitz (1972) and Mirrlees (1972). They, of course, involve high administrative and informational costs. See Sandmo (1976, p. 48).

[5]See, for example, Musgrave (1959) and Samuelson (1969). The conflict between equity and efficiency in taxation has been well known in literature and has been frequently repeated by economists since the time of Adam Smith. Much of the recent optimal taxation literature, in fact, is devoted to developing a framework for dealing with both simultaneously rather than separately.

[6]Smith (1950, Volume II, pp. 310 and 367). The Laffer curve of supply-side economics seems to draw its inspiration from this quotation from Smith.

Alfred Marshall did not have much to say on the objectives of a good tax system, yet he argued that high excise taxes on necessities were better than many other taxes because, given their low elasticity of demand, they have the least effect on consumer welfare: "If therefore a given aggregate taxation has to be levied ruthlessly from any class it will cause less loss of consumers' surplus if levied on necessaries than if levied on comforts."[7]

Arthur Pigou considered a tax system based on the principle of least aggregate sacrifice (i.e., on distributional considerations) to be ideal, but he, too, was very conscious of the "announcement effects" of high tax rates on the supply of work effort, savings, and risk-undertaking. He was particularly concerned about the significance of these effects on savings.[8]

Henry Simons had all the attributes of becoming the first supply-side tax economist. A strong advocate of reducing the role of government, he disliked selective consumption taxes because they interfered with the free private allocation of resources. He also disliked general consumption taxes because they were easy to collect and were likely to lead to irresponsible government expenditure. Nonetheless, he, too, ended up favoring progressive taxation, essentially on the "moral" ground of reducing inequality. He was, of course, quite concerned about the economic effects of progression on the supply of capital, but accepted the trade-off between equity and growth, finally asserting that the dangers of infringement of taxes on incentives were much exaggerated.[9]

It must, therefore, be recognized that tax policy has been and will remain an instrument of achieving multiple objectives. Many leading traditional theorists on public finance have struggled with the multiplicity of objectives of taxation but, while recognizing the likely economic (relative price) effects of taxation, concluded that equity was the more important objective in designing a tax system.[10] Once that was accepted, the traditional literature on taxation concentrated on the search for a proper tax base (i.e., the measures of ability to pay—income, expenditure, wealth) and a proper rate structure (i.e., the measures of equality of sacrifice—progressivity, proportionality, regressivity).[11]

[7]Marshall (1948, p. 467) quoted in D. Walker (1970, p. 365).

[8]Pigou (1962, p. x). The optimal taxation literature, in fact, traces its origin to Pigou's "announcement effects" in estimating the deadweight losses of various taxes. Indeed, Pigou is said to have posed the "Ramsey problem" to Ramsey and helped to develop the efficiency rules relating to taxation.

[9]Simons (1938, pp. 18–19) and (1950).

[10]Some theoreticians, such as Rawls (1971), believed only in the equity objective.

[11]See Goode (1976, especially Chapters 2 and 4).

A Neutral Tax System

The relevant question that this chapter must address is the following. If the multiple objectives of taxation are to be foresaken and if neutrality or efficiency is to be the paramount objective of taxation (i.e., if the primary aim is to cause minimal distortions to the choices of economic agents), what is an ideal tax system? A clue to the answer to this question is provided by the theory of the first-best and the second-best taxation, succinctly developed primarily in the recent literature on optimal taxation.

General Theory of the First-Best Taxation

The theory of first best claims that, in the absence of market failures,[12] all taxes, except lump-sum taxes and those levied on inelastic bases that an individual cannot alter by any of his actions, should be considered distortionary.[13] All taxes, other than those mentioned above, increase rather than reduce distortions in one or more of the following: (1) the relative prices of commodities; (2) the relative rewards of factors of production; (3) the relative values of present versus future consumption; and (4) the relative rewards of work versus leisure.

Government activities should, therefore, as a first-best solution, be primarily financed not through taxes (except via a poll tax or a tax on inelastic bases which alone are consistent with Pareto optimum), but through user prices.[14]

This view of taxation depends on five main assumptions. (1) Choices made by individuals are better than other choice mechanisms, since all

[12]Market failures, defined as the inability of markets to achieve an efficient allocation of resources, generally arise in cases of goods where (1) private costs and benefits are different from social costs and benefits; (2) prices are higher than marginal costs due to the failure of competition or the existence of monopolies; or (3) benefits of outputs are shared by all individuals, irrespective of whether or not they pay.

[13]Any system of taxation will have an income effect, but a tax is said to be distortionary (or to cause "excess" burden) if it creates distortions in compensated demands. For details of this argument see Atkinson and Stiglitz (1980) and Tresch (1981).

[14]These prices, sometimes called benefit taxes, can be based on the voluntary exchange principle, enunciated by Wicksell and Lindahl. This is particularly valid for "impure" public goods, which do not suffer from the "free rider" problem, that is, where consumers can be identified and preferences can be determined. "Pure" public goods should, on the other hand, be financed through nondiscriminatory and nondistortionary poll taxes. All pure public or nonmarket goods, of course, have a revelation problem requiring the use of demand-revealing mechanisms that are nondistortionary. For some of these mechanisms, see Vickrey (1961, pp. 8–37) and Mueller (1979, pp. 72–84). For any redistribution beyond that implicit in Pareto-optimal taxation, the theory of first best recommends lump-sum transfers only.

individuals are rational economic beings and have the relevant information needed for making rational decisions. (2) Product and factor markets are perfectly competitive, factors are perfectly mobile, and pretax market prices reflect true social opportunity costs. Implicit in this assumption is the belief that the cost of and benefits from consumption or production are wholly internalized—there are no externalities or spillovers. (3) Individual behavior is affected by prices (taxes being, of course, elements of prices); that is, there are neither social and institutional constraints nor any uncertainty influencing individual economic behavior. (4) Government expenditures have no desirable effect on relative prices; they certainly cannot compensate for the distortionary effects of taxation on relative prices and at the same time provide "merit goods" that may be desirable on social welfare grounds. (5) Redistribution is not a major objective of taxation; the initial distribution of income and wealth as well as the redistribution generated by market forces (and lump-sum transfers, if any) are correct and socially acceptable or else that redistribution should be achieved by policy instruments other than taxation.

The theory of first best does tolerate some taxation (and subsidies) besides poll taxes, even though it affects market-determined relative prices, but only under two conditions. The first condition is that it correct some major market failure (such as positive and negative externalities), that is, raise the level of private costs to the level of social costs or absorb the excess of private benefits over social benefits.[15] This, of course, requires that there is an agreement among one and all as to the existence and magnitudes of externalities in the economic system and that the differences between private and social costs (and benefits) can be measured to design an optimal tax (or subsidy). The second condition is that the negative tax or the subsidy bring the prices charged by decreasing-cost (i.e., increasing-return) industries to the level of long-run marginal costs and optimize output.

General Theory of the Second-Best Taxation

The theory of second best starts with the premise that (1) reality is unlikely to conform to the assumptions needed for first-best solutions; (2)

[15]An externality exists whenever the action of a given consumer (or a producer) affects, negatively or positively, the utility (or production possibilities) of some other consumer (or producer), so that the marginal social cost of his action differs from the marginal private cost of his action. The appropriate first-best policy in such a case would be to make the former individuals directly compensate the latter financially for the latter's gains and losses. However, this may not be possible if more than a few individuals are involved.

lump-sum taxes are generally infeasible, forbidden, or simply insufficient to meet revenue needs; and (3) all other taxes distort individual choices and create deadweight (welfare) losses to the consumer and/or to the producer, by placing a "wedge" between prices paid and prices received.

The basic premise of the theory of the second best, then, is that when a government must raise a given amount of revenue by imposing a distortionary tax (i.e., a tax with "excess" burden), it is generally optimal to tax all goods and factors at differentiated rates to bring about equiproportional changes in compensated demand and supplies so as to minimize excess burden (Ramsey rule).[16] That is, tax rates should not be uniform: goods and factors with relatively inelastic demand and supply should be subjected to relatively higher rates of taxation. This is the well-known inverse elasticity rule, according to which an efficient tax is one whose rate is proportional to the inverse of the price elasticity of the tax base.

The recent optimal taxation literature, which deals with direct versus indirect taxes, as well as the mix between direct and indirect taxes, is essentially an application of this theory of the second best and attempts to minimize the deadweight loss of any and all packages of distortionary but feasible taxes.[17] The design of a tax system in the second-best situation requires that, for each individual, the own- and cross-price elasticities of demand (of commodities consumed) and supply (of factor inputs) are known and that, despite the wide range of elasticities that exist between individuals, it is possible to "personalize" the tax base and the tax rates for each individual separately.

Conclusion

In sum, a tax system would seem to meet the efficiency or supply-side objective fully if it either did not affect relative prices at all (theory of first best), or if it only affected them in a unique manner, as described above (theory of second best). The tax-mix and the rate-design characterizing such a tax system, which emerge from the foregoing discussion, is summarized in Table 1.

As is apparent from Table 1, a neutral and efficiency-dictated tax system would require reforms in the tax bases as well as in the tax rates. As a

[16] The presence or absence of pure profits can complicate the optimal tax rules and raise issues concerning the number of degrees of freedom available to the government. Cf., Munk (1978).

[17] In fact, optimal taxation theory is an advance over second-best theory since it allows for nonlinear taxes, which were ruled out by Ramsey. For a brief review of optimal taxation literature, see Sandmo (1976) and Stern (1984).

Table 1. Characteristics of a Tax System Consistent with Efficiency and Supply-Side Economics

Objective(s)	Tax Base(s)	Tax Rate(s)
1. No effect on relative prices.	User prices for most public services and a lump-sum tax and/or a tax on completely inelastic base to finance pure public goods.	User prices as determined by the equilibrium of demand and supply for public services and any rate of lump-sum tax as well as tax on completely inelastic base.
2. Affect relative market prices but only to correct market failures and externalities.	Taxes on negative production and consumption externalities.	A rate of tax which will capture the degree of externality.
3. Least distortion of choices of economic agents.	Taxes on items of relatively inelastic (or less elastic) demand and relatively inelastic (or less elastic) supply of both commodities and factors of production.	Tax rate inversely related to elasticity of demand and positively related to elasticity of supply.

matter of fact, only a certain mix of taxes and a mix of (upward and downward) revisions in the rates of taxes would be consistent with efficiency-oriented tax reforms. The next two sections deal with the ingredients of a supply-side or efficiency-based tax system more fully.

II. Tax Bases for Supply-Side Economics or Efficient Tax Bases

A review of selected traditional and modern literature on taxation shows that there is agreement as to the bases that should be taxed if allocative efficiency was the only consideration of policymakers. Those taxes that either have no effect on relative prices or have no substitution effects would be considered most desirable. The next in line would be those taxes that have least distortionary effects on relative prices.

Appropriate Taxes for Efficiency Objective

A tax system geared toward efficiency or supply-side objective alone would consist of the following taxes:

- taxes for internalizing the negative externalities;
- poll tax;

- taxes on land area;
- taxes on windfall or monopoly profits;
- taxes on items with inelastic demand (such as basic necessities); and
- taxes on the ability of individuals to earn income, or on potential income. (The second-best alternatives to this proposal would be *either* a tax on accrued income of an individual coupled with taxes on the consumption of complements to leisure, *or* a tax on life-time personal expenditures.)

The rationale for taxes for internalizing the externalities and the poll tax is clear from the arguments given in Section I.[18] Taxes on land area are defensible on the assumption that land is in inelastic supply, so that the ground rent of land is a sort of economic rent. Taxes on windfall or monopoly profits are justified on the ground that they will not affect price and production decisions made by producers before the imposition of such taxes. Taxes on basic necessities are defended on the ground that these commodities tend to have inelastic demand.

A tax on ability to earn income or on potential income is also acceptable but this requires further explanation. Whereas a tax on actual earnings allows a person to favor leisure over work, a tax on potential income as determined by ability (which is inelastic in supply) is said to be nondistortionary.[19] However, ability is difficult to measure, so that a tax on potential income will be difficult to administer. Hence a tax on accrued income (including own consumption, transfers by gifts and bequests, and unrealized capital gains), though a poor second best, is considered a vast improvement over existing income tax systems, which are based on realized money incomes and which contain many tax shelters and loopholes. But a tax on accrued income, besides entailing the well-known problem of how to measure the unrealized gains, would still suffer from intratemporal and intertemporal inefficiencies: the leisure component of welfare or economic capacity would still remain tax free, resulting in intratemporal welfare loss from distortions in work-leisure choices, and savings would continue to be penalized by double taxation causing intertemporal inefficiency. (The latter would be exacerbated by inflation.)

To avoid the distorting effect of income taxes on intratemporal choices, and recognizing the difficulties of taxing leisure, taxes on consumption goods that are complements to leisure are generally recommended. To avoid the distorting effect of income taxes on intertemporal choices, the

[18]Poll tax is justified only when the assumption of no migration is made.

[19]For a detailed discussion of this point, see Kay and King (1980, Chapter 6, especially pp. 75–76), Tanzi (1980), and Millward (1983, especially Chapter 2).

exemption of savings from the tax base is favored and the levy of a flat-rate tax on the lifetime consumption of an individual (with a personal exemption or an exemption that recognizes differences in family circumstances) is considered theoretically attractive. Leisure will, nonetheless, remain untaxed even under a personal consumption or expenditure tax, producing a disincentive to work; consequently, even the proposal to replace an income tax by a personal consumption tax will not be completely satisfactory on efficiency grounds. However, the efficiency losses of an expenditure tax are stated to be much smaller than those of the present income tax, which is frequently based on realized incomes and a nonindexed tax base, and which arbitrarily discriminates among various forms of savings (e.g., in favor of owner-occupied housing and against equity investment).[20]

Efficiency or supply-side considerations would thus demand that many taxes existing in the tax systems of developing and developed countries should be eliminated.[21] There is no place, for example, in such a system for the following:

- A separate corporation income tax—for without imputation (adequate credit to the shareholder), it is an additional tax on the form of business organization, and all incomes and taxes must, in the final analysis, be imputed to individuals. In addition, a corporation income tax also tends to be nonneutral whenever (1) tax depreciation differs from economic depreciation; (2) inventory valuation in inflationary times is different from that on replacement basis (last in, first out rather than first in, first out); and (3) dividends are treated differently from interest payments. The tax can become neutral provided these differences are eliminated or the tax allows "free depreciation" and is based on cash flow rather than on profits.
- Tax loopholes, special tax preferences, or tax incentives—for they affect relative taxes and prices. (Although some of these may be defended on the grounds that they accommodate market failures, an expenditure subsidy rather than a tax expenditure is the proper vehicle for meeting this objective.)
- A wealth tax—for in the final analysis this is only an additional tax on savings and capital accumulation.

[20]Savings will be taxed over the lifetime of a consumer and, if transferred to the next generation, by taxes on inheritances. The case in favor of consumption tax is presented in Fisher and Fisher (1942), Kaldor (1955), Meade (1978), United States, Department of the Treasury (1977), Lodin (1978), and Sumner (1983). For the case against consumption tax, see Pechman (1980) and Musgrave (1983, pp. 23–24).

[21]Cf., Musgrave (1978).

- Gifts and transfer taxes—for a tax on accrued incomes would theoretically cover all receipts from gifts and transfers.
- A general sales tax—for this tends to affect consumer choices, especially as all goods and services with very different elasticities of demand and supply tend to be taxed relatively uniformly.
- A payroll tax—for it is an arbitrary additional tax on wage incomes.
- A separate capital gains tax—for capital gains are theoretically included in accrued income.

In the specific circumstances of developing countries, an efficiency-based tax system would require, in addition, the elimination of both export duties (unless they are seen as taxes on windfalls only, not affecting incentives, as shown in Chapter 11) and import duties (unless they are seen as protecting domestic industry only temporarily during which the externalities resulting therefrom can be internalized).

There will also be no case for other narrowly based taxes, such as an urban property tax or a rural land tax, which affect relative sectoral prices.

How Realistic Is Such a Tax System?

How realistic is it to institute in developing countries a tax system solely for efficiency objective, as described above?

First, the normative theorizing implicit in the strictly efficiency-oriented tax structure is based on certain assumptions that may not be valid in the special circumstances of developing countries. As mentioned earlier, it assumes that government is not, and in fact should not, be a major producer in its own right, beyond being a supplier of a few essential public goods.[22] Moreover, it assumes that all private individuals are rational and optimizing agents responding to price signals alone (where the market prices reflect true social costs) and that there are no social and institutional determinants of, and constraints on, either market prices or their behavior (which can be removed by government actions).[23] Other assumptions are that there is perfect mobility of factors of production and that income distribution is reasonably appropriate without redistributive taxation and expenditure policies of the government.

Second, an efficiency-oriented tax system (especially one that consists of taxes on basic necessities while luxuries could be exempt) will be politically unacceptable.

[22]See Shome (Chapter 12) for the potential role of governments in the process of development.

[23]See Ebrill (Chapter 3) for nonprice determinants of the behavior of economic agents.

Third, there is little resemblance between the efficient tax bases consistent with supply-side considerations and the existing tax systems of developing countries, which would suggest the introduction of a completely new tax system. But experience shows that the barriers to changing existing tax systems even modestly tend to be fundamental because of the view that old taxes are good taxes. Moreover, major tax changes profoundly affect capital values and imply sizable income and wealth redistribution (capital-based taxes may already have been capitalized and reflected in asset prices). Therefore, in a real sense, fundamental tax reform to institute a completely new tax system, however desirable that may be from the efficiency point of view, may well be just about impossible in reality.[24]

Finally, the efficiency-dictated tax system, described above, may not provide enough revenue to run a modern government, especially if a tax on potential income is found to be administratively infeasible.

To conclude: the ingredients of a tax system for efficiency or supply-side objectives are well known, as are the limitations of adopting such a system in the real world. Therefore, in making their recommendations, tax reformers of developing countries not only must take all these factors into account, they must also be aware that attempts at moving existing tax systems in the direction of meeting efficiency and supply-side objectives are likely to be gradual at best.

III. Rate Design for Supply-Side Economics or Optimal Tax Rates

If efficiency in resource allocation is the only aim of taxation, then, as Table 1 shows, there will be a variety of tax rates for the taxed commodities and for individuals. The tax system will not be progressive with respect to individual economic capacities, however measured, and even the tax on accrued incomes would tend to be proportional (flat rate) or perhaps regressive.[25] In addition, few judgments, if any, can be made on the optimal levels of tax rates that will prevail in an efficiency-oriented tax system, for they will require complete knowledge of empirical estimates of own- and cross-price elasticities of demand and supply for individual commodities and factors of production, measures of externalities associated with relevant commodities, and so on. As there is little reason to believe that such

[24] Cf., Feldstein (1976).

[25] As Pigou (1962, p. x) has concluded, "[If announcement effects are important] the order of merit among tax formulae [will be] first, poll-taxes; second, regressive income taxes; third, proportionate income taxes; fourth, progressive income taxes."

crucial parameters can be correctly estimated, there is little hope that optimal tax rates can be derived, against which existing tax rates can then be judged.[26]

A popular supply-sider will argue, and with some validity, that lowering the tax rates, in general, and income tax rates, in particular, from their existing high levels in itself is desirable.[27] According to this view, high and progressive income tax rates can simply discourage savings and investment, often without achieving their intended effects on income distribution. Lowering income tax rates and reducing their progressivity can, on the other hand, encourage savings and investment and promote productive effort to such an extent as to generate employment and incomes for the less well-off and, thereby, actually improve equity in the longer run. It can also reduce tax evasion.

The desirability of lowering income tax rates and reducing their progressivity deserves, of course, closer examination by tax reformers in all developing countries where marginal tax rates are considered high.[28] However, certain special circumstances of developing countries will have to be borne in mind.

First, given the relatively low standards of living of even the middle-income groups, a reduction of income tax rates might well encourage overall consumption in developing countries more than savings. It might encourage savings by the rich (even in the short run as anticipated by the popular supply-siders), but if economic signals implicit in other economic policies are not correct, such savings can easily flow into unproductive investments, viz., speculation in and hoarding of commodities, foreign exchange, land, housing, and other existing capital assets. The efficiency gains from income tax reforms would, thus, very much depend upon the assumptions made about other economic policy instruments.

Second, lowering income tax rates and reducing their progressivity alone may not be enough to reduce income tax evasion, since in developing countries tax evasion is determined by many factors, the nominal progressivity of tax rates, although important, being only one such factor.[29] It remains

[26]Even econometric estimates of own-price elasticities from past data are only going to be point estimates and with standard errors attached to them.

[27]The theory underlying this view is that, under certain assumptions regarding the shapes of demand and supply curves, the "excess burden" of a tax, which is not a lump-sum tax, is directly a function of the rate of tax.

[28]See Table A9 in the Statistical Appendix on the extent to which high top marginal income tax rates prevail in developing countries.

[29]A multiplicity of factors, including many nontax factors and factors relating to income tax administration, are said to be responsible for the high levels of income tax evasion found in developing countries. See Richupan (Chapter 6).

to be empirically established that an across-the-board reduction in the progressivity and levels of income tax rates would reduce tax evasion and improve tax compliance in developing countries to any great degree, at least in the short run.

Third, in developing countries income inequality is frequently a result of highly skewed land and property ownership. Furthermore, in most of them, education—which accounts for most of the inequality of human capital and which is heavily subsidized by the government—yields extremely high private returns. Higher taxation on the earnings from skewed land and property ownership and on human capital can at once reduce the private windfalls and economic rents from the ownership of such assets, and this can be politically very appealing.

Finally, the degree of progressivity of the income tax system is frequently the result of a political and social consensus, but its interaction with high levels of inflation can raise the progressivity far beyond its intended level. If inflation rates are excessive, as they often are in many developing countries, it may be desirable to adjust the tax system for inflation before tackling the degree of progressivity.

To sum up, there is no theoretical case for progressive income tax rates in a tax system dictated solely by efficiency considerations, but then there is very little of practical value that can be said from theory about the rate structure of a strictly efficient income tax. As modern taxation literature has shown, there is no optimal degree of progression. The optimal degree depends very much upon the form and shape of the social welfare function (comprising equity and efficiency objectives) as well as the form and shape of individual utility functions (as determined by factors such as ability, taste, relative income position, and so on). Consequently, little can be said even theoretically about the degree of progressivity which is of immediate policy relevance. Empirically, the degree of progressivity in taxation frequently reflects the political and social consensus on income redistribution in a given country, and the only circumstance in which it can be justified on efficiency grounds is if it captures scarcity rents or windfall gains.

The inherent conflict between equity and efficiency objectives of taxation has always been well known. Policymakers in developing countries are also aware of this conflict. To resolve it, they frequently tend to have high nominal tax rates but give liberal tax exemptions and concessions to selected taxpayers and sectors. This is obviously inadvisable as such a policy simply compounds the distortionary effects of taxation. A strategy of taxation consistent with the spirit of basic supply-side economics (i.e., removal of tax-induced distortions) would call for broadening the tax base (to reduce the scope of exemptions, tax concessions, and other deductions) while simultaneously lowering income tax rates and applying them uniformly across income categories.[30] Most tax economists would agree with such a tax policy prescription of basic supply-side economists. It would simplify the tax system, ensure horizontal equity, and curtail the powers of tax policymakers to erode the tax base in the name of supporting one or more social and noneconomic objectives. Besides, it would also strengthen tax policy as an instrument for stabilization purposes because, with fewer tax preferences and concessions, the effectiveness of tax rate cuts (and increases) as a component of macroeconomic policy would be enhanced.

IV. A Popular Supply-Side Economist Versus an Optimal Tax Economist

"Thus the policy suggestions of the supply side school are fully compatible with the spirit of the huge body of optimal taxation literature," claims a recent supply-sider.[31]

This paper may have implied that because supply-side economics attaches a great deal of importance to the objective of efficiency, there is little difference between a popular supply-side economist and a modern optimal tax economist. This is not true. There are at least five major differences.

- A popular supply-side economist is inherently an elasticity optimist and favors large reductions in tax rates; in contrast, an optimal tax economist assumes little about elasticities in relation to marginal changes in tax rates and considers them to be entirely empirical matters.
- A popular supply-side economist concerns himself little with the equity objective, horizontal or vertical; in contrast, an optimal tax economist fully concerns himself with equity (vertical, if not horizontal) and, in fact, attempts to optimize between the efficiency and equity objectives of taxation—maximizing a social welfare function by minimizing excess burdens of taxation while achieving a socially desirable redistribution of income through taxation.
- A popular supply-side economist accepts some progressivity in nominal tax rates on pragmatic grounds, though, in the extreme, he would prefer a flat-rate (or proportional) income tax; in contrast, an optimal tax economist refuses to provide a definitive conclusion on the optimal

[30]Recent reforms of income taxation in India, Indonesia, and Jamaica reflect this strategy. A report of the Treasury Department has stressed this strategy for the reform of the U.S. tax system as well. See United States, Department of the Treasury (1984).

[31]Raboy (1982, p. 59).

degree of progressivity, since, according to him, the optimal outcome is highly sensitive to the specification of the social welfare function (incorporating equity objective) and the individual utility functions (incorporating individual tastes). The most robust findings of optimal taxation on this subject have been that marginal tax rates should first increase and then decrease, with those on the highest income becoming zero—in other words, income tax rates should be regressive in the upper-income ranges.[32]

- A popular supply-side economist takes the existing tax system as given, including the dominance of income taxation; in contrast, an optimal tax economist is fully concerned with the composition of tax structure and the balance between direct and indirect taxes as well as the structures of both income and commodity taxes.[33]
- A popular supply-side economist is perhaps pragmatic enough about tax reform not to want to design the tax structure de novo or to change the status quo; in contrast, an optimal tax economist is not pragmatic at all. The design of optimal tax structures requires a great deal more information than has been, or can ever be, collected. In addition, the implementation of such structures is not even on the horizon, as an optimal tax economist frequently does not concern himself with administrative feasibility (i.e., with the potential for tax avoidance and tax evasion) nor with taxpayers' preferences or the compliance costs of his proposals about tax designs. For these reasons, the large literature on optimal taxation, though enriching, has yielded few practical policy conclusions and results commensurate with the intellectual resources devoted to it.[34]

[32]Some progressivity of income tax might, however, be acceptable to them—provided that the rate structure can be made a function of distribution of skills and abilities and there is a negative income tax at the bottom of the income scale—but the degree of progressivity will be nowhere near what will be indicated solely by the application of minimum sacrifice principle.

[33]Cf., Atkinson (1977) and Atkinson and Stiglitz (1980). On the whole, an income tax on all incomes that is approximately linear (a constant marginal tax rate with an exemption below which negative supplements are payable) is considered optimal. A linear income tax on labor incomes only and without an exemption is simply equivalent to a linear commodity tax (a proportional rate on all goods) and is very much distortionary. On the other hand, nonlinear income taxes (proportional rate income tax with an exemption) are considered preferable, given equity and efficiency considerations, over differentiated taxes on goods and services, except where there is an interaction between the supply of labor and the marginal rates of substitution between goods. This conclusion, however, ignores the problems of administration, evasion, horizontal equity, and taxpayer's preferences between taxes.

[34]One of the major policy-oriented conclusions of optimal taxation literature is that taxes on elastic tax bases should best be avoided or, at best, kept low. It is in this spirit that the case is made for lower taxation of capital incomes vis-à-vis labor incomes and of married women vis-à-vis married men.

The popular supply-side economist has, therefore, little resemblance to those who belong to the stream of recent theoretical literature on taxation. One common denominator between the two perhaps is that both view the expenditure side of the budget in an unusual manner. The optimal tax economist discusses the problem of optimal taxation on the assumption that the government has a fixed revenue requirement for an unspecified purpose that has no bearing on the utility of individuals. The popular supply-side economist also seems to discuss the problem of taxation on the implicit, if not explicit, assumption that government should provide few goods and services beyond pure public goods. That public expenditures can positively influence the utility of individuals is not an issue in either approach. This may, however, be an unrealistic assumption in the context of developing countries where certain public expenditures on social and economic infrastructure and its maintenance may be positively productive and social welfare enhancing.

V. A Tax System Dictated by Popular Supply-Side Economics: Some Implications

Taxation is in practice an instrument with multiple objectives and will continue to be so despite what economists profess. The conflict between the objectives of equity and efficiency is fundamental. A tax system based solely on efficiency grounds is unrealistic, while that designed solely for equity purposes cannot be justified on allocative grounds. The degree of progressivity will, in practice, continue to be dictated by political and social consensus rather than by the optimizing formulas of tax economists. One solid contribution of supply-side economics has been to remind us that the way out of the conflict between the equity and efficiency objectives of taxation is not to have high and progressive nominal tax rates and generous tax incentives and preferences, as most developing countries do (they achieve neither income redistribution nor desired resource reallocation), but to have as wide a tax base as possible, as well as lower nominal tax rates. Tax reforms along these lines will be consistent with supply-side economics as well as with the same or even a greater degree of income redistribution.

Whether or not rates of taxes on incomes and profits in developing countries should be lowered significantly all at once or simply be restructured to reduce the degree of progression would depend very much upon the height of the present tax rates, government revenue from the existing high tax rates, the validity of the elasticity optimism of the popular supply-side approach in the context of developing countries (i.e., whether lowering tax rates will have much effect on production), and the relevance in the particular circumstances of a developing country of the assumptions on which supply-side theory is based. Various chapters in this volume (especially in Part II) deal with many of these issues in depth, and this chapter has touched upon others. However, should a developing country be serious about adopting the popular supply-side tax policy and lowering its income tax rates significantly, it must take into account the following five considerations.

First, the lowering of income tax rates must be accompanied by reforms in the income tax base, viz., the removal of tax preferences and tax concessions. The removal of narrowly based foreign trade taxes (e.g., export duties) and certain other taxes important to their tax systems (e.g., payroll and other selective taxes) may also be equally, if not more, important on efficiency grounds. High tax rates and narrow and selective tax bases can create distortions, encourage unproductive activities, erode the revenue base, and lower the effective tax rates below the intended nominal tax rates. Tax cuts without reforms in the tax base can introduce more distortions of efficiency and equity than they correct, especially if they result in inflationary finance.

Second, tax rate reductions must be permanent or, at least, be perceived by taxpayers to be so if they are to have significant effect on savings and investment behavior. The theory of rational expectations suggests that investors change their behavior according to their expectations of the costs of capital, including their expectations of future tax rates over the lifetime of an investment. The same holds true for the behavior of savers. Besides, tax rate reductions would have to be substantial if they are to have a marked "net" effect on behavior, especially because selective tax exemptions and concessions, which may have been enjoyed by savers and investors and which may have had some positive economic effect on their behavior, may now be withdrawn from the tax structure.

Third, short-run elasticities frequently tend to be lower than long-run elasticities for a given change in prices; consequently, it would be advisable to expect the full supply-side effects of a reduction of tax rates to become evident only in the longer run.

Fourth, reducing tax rates for supply-side effects (including improving tax compliance and to further other objectives) must go hand-in-hand with government expenditure cuts and reforms of public enterprise pricing, at least in the short run, or until elasticity optimism materializes. Otherwise there will be a growing budget deficit and a likely rise in inflation (depending upon the sources of financing) with its own distortions and unintended economic consequences. For example, if people expect inflation to continue, and interest rates do not adjust with inflation, they will spend rather than save in the current period, thereby negating the effect of tax cuts on savings and investment.

Fifth, the use to which tax revenues are put in developing countries is also relevant. If a large proportion of government expenditure is directed at financing desirable human capital and social and economic infrastructure in an efficient manner, it removes supply bottlenecks, aids the development process, and provides the justification for higher tax rates. On the other hand, if government revenues go toward financing a large and unproductive civil service or nonpriority capital expenditure, they support wasteful consumption rather than capital formation.

In the final analysis, a tax structure for efficiency and supply-side economics calls for fundamental reforms in the existing tax systems of developing countries. The reforms will have to be directed at reducing the distortionary effects of their existing taxes, which would require removing most exclusions and exemptions and widening the tax base, while reducing rates of taxation. In the context of the tax structures prevalent in developing countries, this strategy would apply not only to personal income tax (which is often an unimportant source of revenue in low-income countries) but to all other direct and indirect taxes as well.

ANNEX

Relationship Between Tax Ratio and Growth Rate

A study by Keith Marsden is sometimes quoted by popular supply-siders in the United States as "evidence" in support of the relevance of supply-side tax policy to developing countries.[35] This Annex describes and critically appraises the nature of this evidence.

Marsden reviewed the experience of growth and taxation in 20 selected countries during the 1970s and concluded that those with lower taxes experienced more rapid expansion of investment, productivity, employment, and government services, and had better growth rates. The selected countries were grouped into 10 pairs with similar per capita incomes but contrasting tax levels, and their growth rates over the past decade were then compared (see Table 2). Marsden concluded from this evidence that "In all cases, the countries that imposed a lower effective average tax burden on their populations achieved substantially higher real rates of growth of gross domestic product (GDP) than did their more highly taxed counterparts."[36]

He analyzed his data further with the help of regression analyses and obtained the following two equations:

[35]Marsden (1983a). The conclusions of this paper are available in Marsden (1983b and 1984).

[36]Marsden (1983a, p. 2).

$$g = 11.281 - 0.361t \quad (1)$$
$$\quad (6.011) \quad (3.830)$$

$N = 20$; $R^2 = 0.449$

$$g = 5.267 - 0.136t + 0.316i + 0.221n \quad (2)$$
$$\quad (2.183) \quad (1.581) \quad (4.892) \quad (0.438)$$

$N = 20$; $R^2 = 0.779'$

where

g = GDP growth rate;
t = tax to GDP ratio;
i = investment growth rate; and
n = labor force growth rate.

His multivariable equation (2) had a higher R^2 but revealed a relative insignificance of the tax variable. He, therefore, tended to rely on his bivariate equation (1) and concluded that "an *increase* of one percentage point in the tax/GDP ratio *decreases* the rate of economic growth by 0.36 percent points."[37]

There are, at least, four problems with this evidence. First, some of his tax revenue data are partial and are susceptible to misleading comparisons. The tax revenue data for Japan, for example, have been understated by excluding social security taxes, while the data for Brazil have been understated by excluding all taxes collected by state and local governments.[38] As a result, both Japan and Brazil would seem to become "low-tax" countries in his sample by design, while for some other "low-tax" countries, for example, Malawi, Korea, Singapore, and Spain, the data are valid only for late 1960s and early 1970s but not necessarily for the late 1970s or for more recent years.[39] Second, his data are on total tax to GDP ratio ("effective average tax burden" on populations, as he puts it) and not on marginal income tax rates, which is the primary focus of popular supply-siders, or even the burden of direct taxes. Third, his sample of 20 countries is not randomly chosen, which is an essential requirement for drawing general and unbiased conclusions. Furthermore, the pairing of the low-tax and high-tax countries is obviously quite arbitrary and bears no relationship whatsoever to the structures of their economies or the other variables that could possibly influence their growth rates. To show how the arbitrary pairing of countries might have influenced his conclusions, Table 3

[37] Marsden (1983a, p. 8).

[38] During the 1970s, tax revenues of state and local governments in Brazil accounted for about 8 percent of GDP. See International Monetary Fund (1985, p. 81).

[39] The tax to GDP ratio in these countries for more recent years are as follows (see International Monetary Fund (1985, pp. 80–81)):

Malawi (1980)	18.14
Korea (1978)	17.27
Singapore (1983)	19.81
Spain (1983)	27.33

Table 2. Selected Industrial and Developing Countries: Comparative Performance

	Per Capita Income Groups, 1979 (In U.S. dollars)	Total Tax Revenue[1] As Percent of GDP (1970s)	Real Average Annual Growth Rates of GDP, 1970–79 (In percent)
Malawi (low tax)	200–300	11.8	6.3
Zaïre (high tax)		21.5	− 0.7
Cameroon (low tax)	500–600	15.1	5.4
Liberia (high tax)		21.2	1.8
Thailand (low tax)	500–600	11.7	7.7
Zambia (high tax)		22.7	1.5
Paraguay (low tax)	700–1,100	10.3	8.3
Peru (high tax)		14.4	3.1
Mauritius (low tax)	1,100–1,300	18.6	8.2
Jamaica (high tax)		23.8	− 0.9
Korea (low tax)	1,400–1,700	14.2	10.3
Chile (high tax)		22.4	1.9
Brazil (low tax)	1,700–2,100	17.1	8.7
Uruguay (high tax)		20.0	2.5
Singapore (low tax)	3,800–5,950	16.2	8.4
New Zealand (high tax)		27.5	2.4
Spain (low tax)	4,300–6,350	19.1	4.4
United Kingdom (high tax)		30.4	2.1
Japan (low tax)	8,800–11,950	10.6[2]	5.2
Sweden (high tax)		30.9	2.0

Source: Keith Marsden, "Taxes and Growth," *Finance & Development,* Vol. 20 (September 1983), pp. 40–43. See also Keith Marsden, "Links Between Taxes and Economic Growth: Some Empirical Evidence," World Bank Staff Working Paper No. 605 (Washington, 1983).
[1]Central government tax revenue only.
[2]Including nontax revenue but excluding social security contributions.

presents another arbitrary pairing of some of the countries selected by him, with somewhat similar per capita incomes, and the conclusion is very different. For example, now two relatively low-tax countries (Peru and Korea) have very dissimilar growth rates and the same is true of the two relatively high-tax countries (Uruguay and Brazil). On the other hand, two developing countries (Mauritius and Paraguay) now have very different tax ratios but very similar high growth rates. Obviously, no firm conclusions can be derived on the relationship between tax ratios and growth rates from such evidence.

It would have been much better for Marsden to (1) not arbitrarily select only 20 countries and (2) certainly not arbitrarily pair them. Had he carried out a regression analysis of a larger cross-section of developing countries he would have found,

Table 3. Selected Developing Countries: Comparative Performance—Information Rearranged

	Per Capita Income, 1979[1] (In U.S. dollars)	Total Tax Revenue As Percent of GDP	Real Average Annual Growth Rates of GDP, 1970–79 (In percent)
Peru	730	14.4	3.1
Korea	1,130	14.2	10.3
Uruguay	2,100	20.0	2.5
Brazil	1,780	17.1	8.7
Mauritius	1,110	18.6	8.2
Paraguay	1,070	10.3	8.3

Source: Keith Marsden, "Taxes and Growth," *Finance & Development,* Vol. 20 (September 1983), pp. 40–43. See also Keith Marsden, "Links Between Taxes and Economic Growth: Some Empirical Evidence," World Bank Staff Working Paper No. 605 (Washington, 1983).

[1]World Bank, *World Development Report, 1981,* pp. 134–35.

much as Rabushka and Bartlett did, that the overall level of taxation as well as the direct tax ratio are positively, and not negatively, correlated with growth rates.[40] To be analytically correct, he should, in fact, have carried out a multivariate analysis of growth rates based on an appropriately specified economic model such as Mañas-Antón has done in Chapter 8 in relation to income taxes.

REFERENCES

Atkinson, A.B., "Optimal Taxation and the Direct Versus Indirect Tax Controversy," *Canadian Journal of Economics* (Toronto), Vol. 10 (November 1977), pp. 590–606.

———, and Joseph E. Stiglitz, *Lectures on Public Economics* (New York: McGraw-Hill, 1980).

Boskin, Michael J., "The Economics of Labor Supply," in *Income Maintenance and Labor Supply: Econometric Studies*, ed. by Glen G. Cain and Harold W. Watts (Chicago: Rand McNally College Pub. Co., 1973).

———, "Taxation, Saving, and the Rate of Interest," *Journal of Political Economy* (Chicago), Vol. 86, No. 2, Part 2 (April 1978), pp. S3–S27.

———, "An Empirical Evaluation of Supply-Side Economics," in Federal Reserve Bank of Atlanta and Emory University Law and Economics Center, *Supply-Side Economics in the 1980s: Conference Proceedings* (Westport, Connecticut: Quorum Books, 1982).

[40]See Rabushka and Bartlett (1985, pp. 81–82).

Canto, Victor A., Douglas H. Joines, and Arthur B. Laffer, *Foundations of Supply-Side Economics: Theory and Evidence* (New York: Academic Press, 1983).

Dasgupta, Partha, and Joseph E. Stiglitz, "On Optimal Taxation and Public Production," *Review of Economic Studies* (Edinburgh), Vol. 39 (January 1972), pp. 87–103.

Evans, Michael K., "An Econometric Model Incorporating the Supply-Side Effects of Economic Policy," in *The Supply-Side Effects of Economic Policy,* ed. by Laurence H. Meyer (Boston, Massachusetts: Kluwer-Nijhoff, 1981).

———, "New Developments in Econometric Modeling: Supply-Side Economics," in *Supply-Side Economics: A Critical Appraisal,* ed. by Richard H. Fink (Frederick, Maryland: University Publications of America, 1982).

Evans, Paul, "What Does a Tax Cut Do?" in *Foundations of Supply-Side Economics: Theory and Evidence,* by Victor A. Canto, Douglas H. Joines, and Arthur B. Laffer (New York: Academic Press, 1983).

Federal Reserve Bank of Atlanta and Emory University Law and Economics Center, *Supply-Side Economics in the 1980s: Conference Proceedings* (Westport, Connecticut: Quorum Books, 1982).

Feldstein, Martin, "On the Theory of Tax Reform," *Journal of Public Economics* (Amsterdam), Vol. 6 (July–August 1976), pp. 77–104.

Fink, Richard H., ed., *Supply-Side Economics: A Critical Appraisal* (Frederick, Maryland: University Publications of America, 1982).

Fisher, Irving, and Herbert W. Fisher, *Constructive Income Taxation: A Proposal for Reform* (New York: Harper, 1942).

Goode, Richard B., *The Individual Income Tax* (Washington: Brookings Institution, rev. ed., 1976).

Hausman, Jerry A. (1981a), "The Effects of Taxes on Labor Supply," in *How Taxes Affect Economic Behavior,* ed. by Henry J. Aaron and Joseph A. Pechman (Washington: Brookings Institution, 1981).

——— (1981b), "Income and Payroll Tax Policy and Labor Supply," in *The Supply-Side Effects of Economic Policy*, ed. by Laurence H. Meyer (Boston, Massachusetts: Kluwer-Nijhoff, 1981).

Houghton, R.W., ed., *Public Finance: Selected Readings* (Baltimore: Penguin Books, 1970).

Howrey, E. Philip, and Saul H. Hymans, "The Measurement and Determination of Loanable-Funds Saving," in *What Should Be Taxed: Income or Expenditure?* ed. by Joseph A. Pechman (Washington: Brookings Institution, 1980).

International Monetary Fund, *Government Finance Statistics Yearbook, 1985,* Vol. 9 (Washington, 1985).

Kaldor, Nicholas, *An Expenditure Tax* (London: Allen & Unwin, 1955).

Kay, J.A., and M.A. King, *The British Tax System* (Oxford: Oxford University Press, 1980).

Keleher, Robert E., "Evidence Relating to Supply-Side Tax Policy," in *Supply-Side Economics: A Critical Appraisal,* ed. by Richard H. Fink (Frederick, Maryland: University Publications of America, 1982).

———, and William P. Orzechowski, "Supply-Side Fiscal Policy: An Historical Analysis of a Rejuvenated Idea," in *Supply-Side Economics: A Critical Appraisal,* ed. by Richard H. Fink (Frederick, Maryland: University Publications of America, 1982).

Kemp, Jack, "The Classical Economic Case for Cutting Marginal Income Tax Rates," in *Supply-Side Economics, Hearing Before the Task Force on Tax Policy of the Committee on the Budget, House of Representatives,* 97th Congress, 1st Session, March 10, 1981 (Washington: Government Printing Office, 1981).

King, M.A., "Savings and Taxation," in *Public Policy and the Tax System,* ed. by Gordon A. Hughes and Geoffrey M. Heal (London: Allen & Unwin, 1980).

Lodin, Sven-Olof, *Progressive Expenditure Tax—An Alternative?,* A Report of the 1972 Government Commission on Taxation (Stockholm: LiberFörlag, 1978).

Marsden, Keith (1983a), "Links Between Taxes and Economic Growth: Some Empirical Evidence," World Bank Staff Working Paper No. 605 (Washington, 1983).

——— (1983b), "Taxes and Growth," *Finance & Development* (Washington), Vol. 20 (September 1983), pp. 40–43.

——— (1984), "Low Taxes Signal a Healthy Economy," *Wall Street Journal* (December 18, 1984), p. 34.

Marshall, Alfred, *Principles of Economics: An Introductory Volume* (London: Macmillan, 9th ed., 1948).

Meade, J.E., *The Structure and Reform of Direct Taxation* (London: Allen & Unwin, 1978).

Meyer, Laurence H., ed., *The Supply-Side Effects of Economic Policy* (Boston, Massachusetts: Kluwer-Nijhoff, 1981).

Millward, Robert, and others, *Public Sector Economics* (New York: Longman, 1983).

Mirrlees, J.A., "On Producer Taxation," *Review of Economic Studies* (Edinburgh), Vol. 39 (January 1972), pp. 105–11.

Mueller, Dennis C., *Public Choice* (New York: Cambridge University Press, 1979).

Munk, Knud Jørgen, "Optimal Taxation and Pure Profit," *Scandinavian Journal of Economics* (Stockholm), Vol. 80, No. 1 (1978), pp. 1–19.

Musgrave, Richard A., *The Theory of Public Finance: A Study in Public Economy* (New York: McGraw-Hill, 1959).

———, *The Future of Fiscal Policy: A Reassessment* (Leuven, Belgium: Leuven University Press, 1978).

———, "The Nature of Horizontal Equity and the Principle of Broad-Based Taxation: A Friendly Critique," in *Taxation Issues of the 1980s,* ed. by John G. Head (Sydney: Australian Tax Research Foundation, 1983).

Pechman, Joseph A., ed., *What Should Be Taxed: Income or Expenditure?* (Washington: Brookings Institution, 1980).

Pigou, A.C., *A Study in Public Finance* (London: Macmillan, 1947, 3rd rev. ed., 1962).

Raboy, David G., ed., *Essays in Supply Side Economics* (Washington: Institute for Research on the Economics of Taxation, 1982).

Rabushka, Alvin, and Bruce Bartlett, *Tax Policy and Economic Growth in Developing Nations* (Washington: PPC/EA, U.S. Agency for International Development, 1985, mimeographed).

Rawls, John, *A Theory of Justice* (Cambridge, Massachusetts: Harvard University Press, 1971).

Rosen, Harvey S., "What Is Labor Supply and Do Taxes Affect It?" *American Economic Review, Papers and Proceedings of the Ninety-Second Annual Meeting of the American Economic Association* (Nashville, Tennessee), Vol. 70 (May 1980), pp. 171–76.

Samuelson, P.A., "Pure Theory of Public Expenditure and Taxation," in *Public Economics: An Analysis of Public Production and Consumption and Their Relation to the Private Sectors,* ed. by J. Margolis and H. Guitton (New York: St. Martin's Press, 1969).

Sandmo, Agnar, "Optimal Taxation—An Introduction to the Literature," *Journal of Public Economics* (Amsterdam), Vol. 6 (July–August 1976), pp. 37–54.

Simons, Henry C., *Personal Income Taxation: The Definition of Income as a Problem of Fiscal Policy* (Chicago: University of Chicago Press, 1938).

———, *Federal Tax Reform* (Chicago: University of Chicago Press, 1950).

Smith, Adam, *An Inquiry into the Nature and Causes of the Wealth of Nations,* ed. by Edwin Cannan (London: Methuen and Co., 6th ed., 1950).

Stern, Nicholas H., "Optimum Taxation and Tax Policy," *Staff Papers,* International Monetary Fund (Washington), Vol. 31 (June 1984), pp. 339–78.

Summers, Lawrence H., "Capital Taxation and Accumulation in a Life Cycle Growth Model," *American Economic Review* (Nashville, Tennessee), Vol. 71 (September 1981), pp. 533–44.

Sumner, Michael T., "The Incentive Effects of Taxation," in Robert Millward and others, *Public Sector Economics* (New York: Longman, 1983).

Tanzi, Vito, "Potential Income as a Tax Base in Theory and in Practice" (unpublished, International Monetary Fund, December 31, 1980).

Tresch, Richard W., *Public Finance: A Normative Theory* (Plano, Texas: Business Publications, 1981).

Ture, Norman B., "Supply Side Analysis and Public Policy," in *Essays in Supply Side Economics,* ed. by David G. Raboy (Washington: Institute for Research on the Economics of Taxation, 1982).

United States, Department of the Treasury, *Blueprints for Basic Tax Reform* (Washington: Government Printing Office, 1977).

———, *Tax Reform for Fairness, Simplicity, and Economic Growth: The Treasury Department Report to the President,* Vols. I–III (Washington: Office of the Secretary, Department of the Treasury, November 1984).

Vickrey, William, "Counterspeculation, Auctions, and Competitive Sealed Tenders," *Journal of Finance* (New York), Vol. 16 (March 1961), pp. 8–37.

Walker, D., "Direct v. Indirect Taxes," in *Public Finance: Selected Readings,* ed. by R.W. Houghton (Baltimore: Penguin Books, 1970).

World Bank, *World Development Report, 1981* (New York: Oxford University Press, 1981).

10

Rationality of Income Tax Incentives in Developing Countries

A Supply-Side Look

Fernando Sanchez-Ugarte

This chapter examines tax incentives from the supply-side point of view and analyzes whether selective tax incentives can be used by developing countries to achieve the supply-side objectives of economic efficiency and growth while maintaining equity.[1] The chapter shows that the role of tax incentives in reconciling equity and efficiency is very limited. Even though tax incentives can be designed to produce economic efficiency gains, they should not be used as substitutes for an efficient tax system to satisfy supply-side objectives. Tax incentives have a limited role to play in tax policy. First, they entail loss of government revenue. Second, efficient tax incentives are cumbersome to design—they are by nature selective and can often induce other economic distortions. Third, their effectiveness can seldom be guaranteed. In principle, they should be given to those economic agents who need them to perform the desired action. However, this is a difficult task that often leads to unwarranted economic rents to the lucky beneficiaries. Finally, tax incentives can readily fall prey to special interest groups so that the original economic motivation of the policy is easily superseded by other less objective motives.

In this paper, a tax incentive is defined as a reduction in either the tax rate, the tax base, or the tax liability, which is granted if a specified action is taken by the selected beneficiary. The beneficiary of the tax incentive is a taxpayer who is selected on the basis of certain qualifications. Typical qualifications are the type of organization (incorporated or unincorpo-

[1]See Gandhi (Chapter 1) for a detailed discussion of supply-side tax policy.

rated, business or individual); the origin of the taxpayer (national or foreign); the activity performed; and the age of the beneficiary (newcomer or established). The change in behavior sought through tax incentives may be, for instance, real (as distinct from financial) investment, production of goods for export, employment of labor, increase in the level of output, and so on.

The tax incentive reduces the base, the rate, or the overall tax liability of a given tax. For instance, a tax incentive to investment can be granted through the corporate income tax in the form of a tax holiday, which is a reduction in the tax rate; in the form of accelerated depreciation or immediate write-off of investment expenditure, which is a reduction in the tax base; or in the form of an investment tax credit, which is a reduction of the tax bill. Each form of tax incentive is different in the way it affects economic efficiency and in the extent to which it induces the desired behavior. Efficiency will be understood throughout the paper in the Pareto sense—that is, an increase in economic efficiency is attained when an individual's well-being can be increased without having to reduce that of any other individual.

This paper deals with tax incentives as they are applied in developing countries. It does not attempt to describe all tax incentives used by these countries. Rather, it singles out tax incentives for the promotion of investment, regional development, export promotion, and employment to illustrate the problems that most commonly plague tax incentives.

Section I discusses the economic efficiency criteria for tax incentives. The paper distinguishes between the "pure" and the "impure" case for tax incentives. The pure case arises from the need to counteract externalities that break the equality between marginal social benefits and costs. The impure case arises either from the practical impossibility of reaching an optimal tax structure or from the existence of one or more resource-distorting economic intervention schemes. In both cases, the use of tax incentives can be economically efficient. However, it is argued that it would be far superior to resort to tax reform or the removal of an economic intervention scheme in order to eliminate the source of the distortions than to provide tax incentives to compensate for such distortions.

Section II broadly examines the design of tax incentives in an attempt to identify the limitations of tax incentive policy as a means of pursuing various and often competing objectives with access to scarce tax revenue.

Section III analyzes the economic distortions induced by specific tax incentives and concludes that even though it is possible to design relatively more neutral tax incentives, this is a complicated task that limits considerably the applicability of tax incentive policy.

Section IV considers the effectiveness of tax incentives. An effective tax incentive is defined as one that maximizes the probability that the desired behavior is attained. This section suggests that most tax incentive schemes are ineffective. Very often they are cluttered with design flaws that convert them into mere rent-generating transactions.

Finally, Section V presents conclusions and policy recommendations and comments on the "appropriateness" of adopting a policy of selective tax rate reductions via tax incentives—a widely prevalent policy in developing countries—as opposed to effecting general tax rate reductions while broadening the tax base, as recommended by supply-siders.

I. The Economic Rationality for Tax Incentives

A pure case or "first best" for tax incentives (or subsidies) exists whenever external economies are present, that is, when, under a free market arrangement, the marginal social benefit of an activity exceeds the marginal social cost of undertaking that activity. The failure of the "invisible hand" to reach the maximization of social welfare calls for the Pigovian prescription of subsidizing such activities so that the marginal private cost equals the marginal social benefit.[2] A Pigovian tax incentive removes a distortion from the economy and is therefore by nature welfare-improving. As to how to finance the first-best subsidies, the solution lies in a nondistorting tax system for which the financing could come from either poll taxes, which do not distort, or Pigovian taxes, which remove negative externalities.

An impure case for tax incentives arises when economic policy in general or tax policy in particular is distortionary.[3] For political, social, or administrative considerations, economic policymakers often implement a tax system that is nonneutral and adopt other economic policies that lead to distortions. Ideally, the distortions should be removed by way of tax reform or reform in other economic policies, but this may not always be feasible.

However, through economic policy (e.g., tax incentives), it is possible to induce behavior that can be at the margin welfare-improving. The literature on social cost-benefit analysis, aware of this possibility, has developed criteria and methods that assess whether the undertaking of an activity or a project leads to improvement in social welfare by reducing unwanted dis-

[2]See Bator (1958) for the cases where free market failure is likely to arise.

[3]An optimal tax system would be devoid of tax incentives; by design the tax rates that apply are optimal in the sense that no other tax structure can increase economic welfare, given the government's budget constraint and the set of taxes that are considered feasible.

tortions and negative externalities and/or by inducing positive externalities.[4] In this author's opinion, this methodology can also be put to use in the design of tax incentive (or subsidy) policy.

The Pure Case for Tax Incentives

In a free market situation, economic agents do not always behave in a manner that leads to equality between private and social costs and benefits. Intervention is called for when the externalities cannot be internalized by private agents.[5] In the case of a positive externality, the intervention would consist of a subsidy (or tax incentive) to the activity. Examples of tax incentives based on such an argument follow.

Regional Distribution of Economic Activity

It can be argued that the promotion of regional development is justified on economic grounds, given that there are external economies of relocation to less developed regions and external diseconomies of concentration in already developed ones. Private agents acting on market signals will not take advantage of the external economies, resulting in an overconcentration of activities in certain areas. Tax incentives that reduce the cost of relocating to undeveloped regions, where positive externalities are generated, could increase welfare. (See also section on "Tax Incentives to Regional Development," below.)

The role of tax incentives in reaching this goal is complementary to the role of other instruments of regional economic policy, such as public investment, credit, and financial policy, which are often partly responsible for the overconcentration in major metropolitan areas of developing countries.

Risk-Taking and Savings

Arrow and Lind (1970) have shown that, owing to imperfections in the capital market, private agents do not often encounter the institutional setup that will encourage them to diversify risk to a "socially optimal" level. Under such conditions, a positive externality can be derived from inducing risk-taking by private agents. Thus, tax incentives to promote private investment in risky projects with substantial social benefits could

[4]The literature is vast. See, for example, Layard (1972), Harberger (1974), Little and Mirrlees (1974), and Boadway (1979).

[5]See, however, Coase (1960) who shows that under certain conditions external effects can be internalized by contractual arrangements reached among the affected parties.

lead to an improvement in economic well-being. However, it would be better to attain optimal diversification of risk by reducing imperfections in the capital markets.

Another argument, advanced by Sen (1967), is that the economies frequently tend to save below the level that is "socially optimal." Lack of consideration for the welfare of future generations leads to an overconsumption in the present and, in turn, to the formation of a lower-than-optimal stock of capital for the future. This external effect calls for tax incentives to private savings.

Short-Run Output Disturbances

Along the business cycle troughs, output and the level of employment are below the steady-state values. It can be argued that it is socially desirable to move the economy back to its steady-state equilibrium path. Economic policy, in general, can be used to attain such a goal. The new literature on the business cycle (Lucas (1981)) has stressed the relevance to economic behavior of economic agents' expectations about policy changes. Accordingly, an unexpected policy change will not affect economic behavior, and a policy change that is expected to be transitory will have very different effects from one that is seen to be permanent.[6] The policy prescription emerging from this literature is that rules are better than discretion, first, because a rule will be incorporated into the behavior of economic agents, and, second, because the effect of a rule can be objectively predicted.

Research and Development

Externalities are also present in basic research, which is pursued for the accumulation and advancement of general knowledge. It can be argued that since the benefits of basic research cannot be appropriated by the researcher, such research will be conducted at a suboptimal level.[7]

Applied research, on the other hand, is generally more easily marketable since the patent system allows the inventor to receive most of the di-

[6]Lucas (1981) compares the effects of alternative rules for granting tax incentives to investment; one is a tax incentive given permanently, the other a tax incentive given for a period of five years, disappearing afterward. He shows that, under certain assumptions about the interest rate and the rate of depreciation, the effect of the transitory tax incentive is 4.5 times as large as that of the permanent incentive.

[7]See Johnson (1975) for a review of the issues regarding optimal allocation of resources in research and development.

rect rewards of the invention. It is difficult, in practice, to make a clear-cut distinction between applied and basic research, and as a result the patent system does not cover all situations. A case could therefore be made for the promotion of basic research by the private sector through the use of tax incentives.

To sum up, the pure case for tax incentives exists whenever there are externalities in the economy and the decisions of the economic agents are less than socially optimal. However, as the above examples show, tax incentives can play only a complementary role to the many other conditions necessary for the activity to thrive, for example, infrastructure, a conducive environment, know-how, and entrepreneurial capacity.

The Impure Case for Tax Incentives

Governments often pursue economic policies that introduce distortions into the economic system, for example, in the areas of trade policy, tax policy, and wage policy.

The theory of the "second best" attempts to minimize the welfare cost implied by government intervention.[8] However, government policy very rarely follows second-best prescriptions. Therefore, it can be argued that a tax incentive, if properly designed, can increase economic well-being.

As will be shown below, tax incentives should not be the first choice of the policymaker; it will always be better to move to the second best through appropriate reforms in economic policy. Examples of how tax incentives can reduce distortions in the areas of trade policy, tax policy, and wage policy follow.

Economic Distortions Related to International Trade

Most countries protect domestic activities by restricting imports of selected commodities for a variety of reasons, including protection of infant industry, encouragement of self-sufficiency, and diversity in production. Johnson (1960) developed the "scientific tariff" approach, which allows trade policy to reach any desired "noneconomic" objective with the minimum of economic distortions. Most countries, however, do not follow the scientific tariff approach to determine the level and structure of trade restrictions. Hence, it is possible to reduce some of these distortions and increase economic well-being through the appropriate use of tax incentives, as the examples below illustrate.

Restrictions on international trade through tariffs, quotas, and overval-

[8]See Stern (1984) for a discussion of optimum taxation policy.

ued exchange rates reduce the supply of exports by reducing the relative price of exports charged by exporters. This, in turn, means that the social value of foreign exchange generated by any activity is higher than the market value. The literature on social accounting prices provides different methods by which the social opportunity cost of foreign exchange may be estimated.[9] Once this value has been calculated, economic efficiency recommends that private agents follow social rather than private prices, which result from the appropriate combination of taxes and subsidies. If, for instance, exports were promoted through tax incentives, there could be an improvement in social welfare. It is important to take into account the reaction of trading partners to the export subsidy. The rules established by the General Agreement on Tariffs and Trade (GATT) allow developing countries to give subsidies temporarily to exports when such subsidies do not cause serious injury to other signatory countries and allow for the drawback of domestic indirect taxes incorporated on the value of exports (Goode (1984)).

Protection in developing countries usually results in very different rates of effective protection across industries (Balassa and associates (1971)). Typically, import tariffs are highest for luxury consumption items and lower for intermediate goods and basic commodities, thereby resulting in higher effective protection for luxury consumption goods and lower protection for necessities, intermediate goods, and capital equipment. The use of tax incentives for the promotion of, for example, the capital goods industry could under certain circumstances be welfare-improving. It can be shown that if the promoted activity brings a reallocation of resources that increases income measured at international prices, economic welfare will increase [10]—for example, where the promoted activity allows the substitution of imports at a social cost below the world price of imports. However, adopting a tariff structure that minimizes the efficiency cost of a given level of protection (scientific tariff) would be preferable to granting tax incentives.

[9]The two approaches most widely advocated are the weighted average approach (Harberger (1972) and Boadway (1979)) and the international price approach (Little and Mirrlees (1974)). Under the first approach, all exports and imports are valued at the social accounting price of foreign exchange, which is derived using a weighted average of import tariffs and export taxes. Under the second approach, all tradables are valued at the international price. The two approaches are not contradictory, and the choice should be made on practical grounds.

[10]See Sanchez-Ugarte (1983, Chapter IV), where this argument is developed further.

Economic Distortions on the Savings-Investment Decision Introduced by the Tax System

Savings-investment decisions caused by nonoptimal tax systems present inherent distortions. Three distortions in particular frequently occur.

A first distortion arises from the corporation and personal income taxes, which create a difference between the social opportunity cost of capital and the social rate of time preference, both of which would be equal in a perfect capital market and under conditions of no taxation (Marglin (1963), Feldstein (1964), Sen (1967), and Harberger (1976)). Since the return on savings is taxed by the personal income tax, usually at a progressive rate, taxation creates a wedge between the rate of time preference and the rate of return on savings. On the other hand, the classical corporate income tax creates a difference between the marginal product of capital (opportunity cost of capital) and the net rate of return on savings.[11] This double distortion leads to less capital accumulation and less savings than would result in the absence of taxation.

A second distortion arises from the classical corporate income tax, which favors debt financing over equity financing and reinvestment of profits over distribution of earnings.[12] This leads to a nonoptimal financing structure. Because equity financing is taxed more heavily, the debt-equity ratio of firms is probably too large. This distortion could also lead to the underdevelopment of certain financial markets such as the stock market. The inducement to reinvest, implicit in the corporate income tax, probably favors large over small firms and old over new ones. Tax incentives can be used to reduce these distortions.

A third distortion arises from the persistence of inflation and its interaction with the income tax. This tax usually permits the deduction of nominal interest and the depreciation of assets at original cost, creating a disincentive for investment in shorter-lived assets and an incentive for the excessive use of debt financing (Auerbach (1979)). Here again, a case can be made in favor of using tax incentives to counteract, at least partially, some of these effects.

In all these instances, however, tax reform or correcting the cause of the distortions would be superior to tax incentives for offsetting the effects of the distortions. For example, transforming the income tax into a consump-

[11]According to the new view of the corporate income tax, there is no such distortion in the cost of funds (see Stiglitz (1976) and Auerbach (1983)). The first distortion still persists, however.

[12]See Auerbach (1983) for a survey of the issues regarding the corporate income tax.

tion tax, integrating the personal and corporate income taxes, or correcting income tax for inflation would result in the removal of the distortions referred to above.

Distortions in the Labor Market

The market wage rate does not always fully reflect the social opportunity cost of employing labor. Two such cases are the rural-urban disequilibrium analyzed by Lewis (1954) and the distortions identified in the Harberger-Harris-Todaro two-sector model (Todaro (1969) and Harberger (1972)). In the first case, the wage rate is determined by the average product of labor in the rural sector, while the marginal product of labor in this sector, which equals the social opportunity cost of labor, approaches zero. In the second case, the urban minimum wage is above the rural wage, leading to unemployment in the urban sector and to a social opportunity cost of labor that is intermediate between the two wage rates. In both cases, the difference between the private and social cost of labor indicates that as long as wage policy is not corrected, a subsidy or tax incentive to encourage the use of labor in the urban sector can be welfare-improving.

The basic conclusion to be derived from these examples is that even though tax incentives can be justified in terms of economic efficiency, they are never the most appropriate policy to follow in order to achieve the desired objective. Basic policy reform or the use of some other policy preferable to a tax incentive is usually possible. Furthermore, the creation of too many tax incentives can in itself be distortionary in often unpredictable ways. For example, a subsidy to investment, even though it could reduce some distortions in the investment decision-making process, would in itself distort the labor-capital choice.[13]

II. General Considerations in the Design of Tax Incentives

The social cost-benefit approach to tax incentives, developed in the previous section, suggests that a tax incentive can improve welfare when given to an activity whose private cost exceeds its social cost or when the private benefit derived from the activity falls short of the social benefit. The application of the above criteria poses few problems if the country has already calculated the social accounting prices that could be used to determine the

[13]See discussion in the section on "Tax Incentives to Investment," below, where it is argued that the relative strength of distortions calls for favoring one or the other factor of production.

level of tax incentives. A major problem arises when many activities call for tax incentives, as might be the case in many developing countries. If all needed tax incentives were to be granted according to the efficiency criteria, the fiscal requirements could be very demanding. Since public policy in developing countries must meet the needs of so many other objectives with very limited fiscal resources, objectives and instruments must be carefully selected. In this way, tax incentive policy advances social welfare to the maximum, with only a limited amount of tax revenue forgone.

Selection of Objectives

Before the policymaker selects his objectives, he must decide how much tax revenue should be allocated to tax incentives. Tax incentive policy competes with expenditure policy for the use of available tax revenue, making essential a proper evaluation of the relative social returns of using resources in support of either one of the alternative policies.[14]

The main issue at stake is whether the public or the private sector can make better use of tax revenue. If all taxes are optimal, the issue has no economic relevance because by definition the change in a marginal tax rate or the reduction of public expenditure would move the economy away from the optimum. If taxes are distortionary, however, the issue becomes relevant. It is important to compare the social return of using revenue to finance public projects against that derived from returning the revenue to finance private projects.[15]

It can be argued that when the selection process is perfect—that is, only inframarginal projects are selected—a tax incentive to investment involves no tax revenue forgone (Mutén (1982) and Goode (1984)). The additional investment generated by the tax incentive would not have taken place in its absence; similarly, the taxes left unpaid would not have been paid in the absence of the tax incentive. This argument assumes a perfection in the selection process that cannot be achieved in practice—most selection processes will pick up supramarginal projects, leading to a loss of net tax revenue. Nor is the argument valid in a dynamic context. If the tax incentive remains operative for any length of time, it will eventually cover all investment projects. Since it is impossible to make an accurate assessment of the tax revenue forgone as a result of investment incentives, a practical solu-

[14]See Mutén (1982) for a discussion of the problems of measuring the costs involved in tax incentives.

[15]Without distributional considerations, $1 of tax revenue transferred to the private domestic investor is worth $1. The relevant question therefore is whether or not the social return of the project exceeds the cost of the funds (both private and public) invested.

tion is to treat all projects as exactly marginal and presume that all tax revenue forgone is a cost.[16]

It is hard to state precisely how much tax revenue a country should allocate to tax incentives, but obviously it cannot be much. As stressed earlier, tax incentives are not substitutes for an adequate and efficient tax system. If the tax system is so distorting as to require that a large fraction of the tax revenue be rebated in order to reduce these distortions, the question is, would it not be better to reform the tax system so that it produces the desired revenue with fewer distortions? Similarly, if other distortions induced by misguided economic policy are so large as to require corrective tax incentives that give rise to substantial loss in tax revenue, then the question is again, would it not be better to reform the economic policy to minimize distortions? Furthermore, as Section IV below illustrates, tax incentives can achieve only limited results and, therefore, only a small amount of tax revenue should be allocated to them.

Once it has been decided how much revenue should be allocated to tax incentive policy, objectives should be selected so as to obtain the maximum increase in economic welfare for a given amount of revenue.

Tax incentives are not equally effective in the pursuit of all objectives. For instance, evidence indicates that tax incentives are relatively ineffective in promoting employment.[17] One reason for this is that the tax systems of developing countries usually encompass only the modern sector, which is not the major employer in the economy. Furthermore, the pursuit of a comprehensive tax incentive policy for the promotion of employment, assuming that it were effective, would imply the use of a large amount of tax revenue. For example, if a 10 percent subsidy for the use of labor by any sector were given when the share of labor income in gross domestic product (GDP) was 40 percent, the program would end up using 4 percent of GDP. Some might argue that because tax incentives should be granted only on additional employment, not as much tax revenue would be forgone. Unfortunately, there are few practical ways of granting tax incentives to incremental employment. But even if a practical way could be found, the amount of tax revenue involved in an effective program could still be very large. If unemployment were to be reduced from 10 percent to 5 percent through a 30 percent tax incentive on incremental employment, this would imply a loss of tax revenue of about 0.6 percent of GDP (assuming as above that the share of labor was 40 percent). Furthermore, the benefit of tax

[16]This criterion is based on a project that is exactly marginal without any tax incentive.

[17]See Gandhi (1981) for a detailed evaluation of the effectiveness of tax incentives in the promotion of employment in developing countries.

incentives to incremental employment may be offset partially, if not fully, by the existence of a social security or payroll tax on employers.

There are other policies that are more effective in promoting employment that do not involve forgoing such a large amount of tax revenue. For instance, a more flexible wage policy, more favorable terms of trade for the agricultural sector, and elimination of institutional barriers to employment are among the many ways of promoting employment more effectively.

In general, when the objective involved is very broad, tax incentive policy will not be as effective—the loss of revenue will be large relative to a given incentive effect. Accordingly, less benefit will accrue from applying a tax incentive scheme to promote a broad objective than from reshaping the distorting economic policies or reforming the tax system, thereby achieving the desired objective without the revenue loss. For instance, the more direct way to use the tax system to promote savings seems to be through an expenditure tax in lieu of the income tax.[18] Such a tax change can be made without losing tax revenue by choosing the rate of taxation accordingly.

To sum up, tax incentive policy can be more effective in the pursuit of narrowly based objectives such as the promotion of regional development, the promotion of selective exports, or the promotion of a specific sector. The reason is clear. A narrowly based tax incentive will have a larger inducement effect for a given amount of tax revenue forgone. Caution should be exercised, however, when narrowing down an objective so as not to create severe distortions. For instance, the selection of regions for promotion cannot be so narrow as to leave other adjacent regions out of competition. Alternatively, the selection of promoted sectors cannot be so narrow as to leave very close substitutes out of the incentive scheme.

Selection of Instruments

The selection of specific tax incentives can be judged according to two main criteria: effectiveness and efficiency. A tax incentive is effective when it induces the desired behavior. Given that an ineffective tax incentive does not change economic behavior, it leads to windfall profits or economic rents. An efficient tax incentive is one that increases economic well-being. An inefficient tax incentive is one that changes economic behavior without

[18]There are ways in which the income tax or the corporate income tax can be converted into an expenditure-type tax (see, for example, Meade (1978)). Even a general sales tax covering intermediate and capital goods can be converted into a consumption tax, the one more widely applied practical way being through the value-added tax on consumption.

actually increasing economic welfare, or worse, one that introduces distortions that lead to a decrease in welfare.

A third and very important consideration in the choice of tax incentives is ease of administration. This paper will not directly discuss this criterion unless it has some bearing on the other two. However, the proper choice of tax incentives should give adequate weight to their administration.

III. The Efficiency of Specific Tax Incentives

This section discusses some of the distortions that specific tax incentives can induce. Even though, as will be shown, tax incentives can be designed so as to avoid such distortions, most tax incentives used in developing countries do not generally meet efficiency criteria.

Tax Incentives to Investment

Tax incentives to investment are the most prevalent form of tax incentive. They are relatively easy to apply in relation to different objectives such as regional development, economic stabilization, and development of a specific sector. The efficiency of various tax incentives to investment linked to specific taxes and in connection with various objectives discussed below.

Most tax incentives to investment are given through the corporate income tax (CIT). Among the many ways of granting tax incentives through the CIT are tax holidays, accelerated depreciation, immediate write-off of investment expenditure (expensing), and the investment tax credit. The issue of tax incentive neutrality, discussed in the public finance literature, has arisen basically in connection with tax incentives affecting the CIT.[19]

There are three important ways in which tax incentives related to the CIT can be nonneutral, or distortionary, in their effects: (1) with respect to the life of the asset; (2) with respect to the type of financing; and (3) with respect to the time path of the investment project. It has been shown else-

[19]A useful criterion in the selection of efficient tax incentives is that of neutrality. According to Harberger (1980), a tax incentive to investment is neutral if it induces neither new covered investment with low rates of social yield nor other covered investments with higher rates of social yield. Neutrality is desirable for two reasons: first, it is useful to be able to predict at what level an activity is being subsidized. A nonneutral tax incentive does not permit us to know this because the level of the incentive depends on factors outside the control of economic policy. Second, by maintaining neutrality one can avoid unpredictable distortionary effects. The purpose of tax incentives is to favor certain activities relative to others, but it is important to know to what extent one activity is being favored. This cannot be left to unpredictable factors (see Sandmo (1974), Swan (1976), Boadway (1978), Auerbach (1982), and Ruane (1982)).

where (Sanchez-Ugarte (1983)) that given a classical CIT, all tax incentives to investment are nonneutral with respect to the type of financing if they are given on total investment expenditure. The CIT is avoided when the investment is entirely debt financed. More generally, the CIT is avoided on that part of the investment that is debt financed. It follows that a tax incentive given on the total investment outlay will favor debt financing over equity financing even beyond the built-in bias of the classical CIT. The solution is to grant the incentive only for the self-financed part of the investment.

Immediate write-off (expensing) of part of the asset is a neutral tax incentive with respect to the life of the asset. The investment tax credit favors short-lived projects, and accelerated depreciation will have a bias depending on how the acceleration procedure works.[20] The investment tax credit is a distortionary tax incentive; it can be shown that it reduces the cost of gross investment (whereas expensing acts on net investment) and may therefore lead to the selection of very short-lived projects with negative social returns (Sanchez-Ugarte (1983)).

A third type of tax incentive nonneutrality involves the time path of revenues along the life of the investment. The so-called tax holidays tend to favor short-run projects producing revenues at the beginning of the life of the project over long-run, slow-maturing projects. In this sense, tax holidays are nonneutral.

Neutrality, as was mentioned earlier, is an important criterion for the design of tax incentives. Nonneutral tax incentives can lead to unwanted results of unpredictable magnitude. For instance, the investment tax credit can lead to the selection of projects with negative social returns, while the tax holiday can favor very short-lived investments. Even if the tax incentive does not produce such undesirable effects, a nonneutral tax incentive implies a higher loss of revenue for a given incentive effect. For example, the difference between the cost of expensing and that of the investment tax credit for a given effect on net investment is the tax incentive given to replacement investment because the former is a subsidy on net investment, while the latter is a subsidy on gross investment.[21] Most tax

[20]In Sanchez-Ugarte (1983), a procedure is devised for making accelerated depreciation neutral with respect to the life of the asset.

[21]This point is developed in Sanchez-Ugarte (1983, Chapter I). To give an idea of what is involved in the argument, assume that the net present value of an investment project (*NPV*) is given by

$$NPV = Y - T - I, \qquad (1)$$

incentives discriminate against working capital, inventories, and human capital because they are usually given to fixed capital formation. This bias can be eliminated by granting the tax incentive over the whole investment outlay, but it is difficult to measure forms of investment different from fixed capital formation.

In addition, tax incentives to investment reduce the cost of using physical capital relative to other factors of production, labor in particular. This distortion has been noted by several public finance experts and has been pointed out as one of the many distortions that exist in developing countries in the labor employment decision. Two things should be mentioned in this respect. First, even though, as was mentioned before, the labor market distortions prevalent in developing countries call for subsidies for the use of labor, other distortions call for subsidies for the use of capital. Hence, the factor of production that should be favored by public policy will depend on the relative strength of the various distortions present in the economy.[22] It cannot be asserted prima facie that a subsidy for the use of labor is preferable to a subsidy for investment; furthermore, the adequate selection of tax incentives will vary by industry and by region so that tax incentives are best designed on a case-by-case basis.

Second, even though from the static point of view a tax incentive to investment tends to reduce the use of labor, the same result does not necessarily apply in a dynamic context. Capital deepening in the economy will

---

where Y is the present value of gross revenue, T is the present value of taxes, and I gross investment.

Under the investment tax credit (ITC) at rate c, the present value of taxes is $T = (Y - dI)t - cI$, where d is the present value of depreciation allowance and t the corporate tax rate. Subtracting depreciation to obtain net income and net investment in equation (1),

$$NPV = (Y - dI)(1 - t) + cI - I(1 - d). \tag{2}$$

With expensing at rate α, the present value of taxes becomes $T = (Y - \alpha I - (1 - \alpha)dI)t$. In order to obtain net income, we subtract depreciation from the present value of gross revenue:

$$NPV = (Y - dI)(1 - t) - \alpha(I - dI)t - I(1 - d). \tag{3}$$

Net investment is equal to $I - dI$. If $\alpha t = c$, it is clear that the cost of the ITC is larger than that of expensing at equivalent rates. The ITC costs cI, and expensing of part of the investment costs only $\alpha(I - dI)t$. It is also clear that the ITC is given on gross investment (I), whereas expensing acts on net investment $[I(1 - d)]$.

[22]For instance, it has been shown (see Sanchez-Ugarte (1983)) that under certain assumptions when the structure of industrial output is distorted by international trade restrictions, tax incentives favoring the use of capital should be granted to new industries. This can still be a valid conclusion even when labor markets are distorted.

tend to increase the productivity of labor in the steady state, and could increase the relative share of labor in total output, depending on the elasticity of substitution in production.[23]

Tax incentives have been proposed and used as an alternative to adjusting the tax system for inflation. It has been argued that an investment tax credit or accelerated depreciation can give approximately the same result as correction of the income tax for inflation, with fewer complications (Keith (1966), Aaron (1976), and Feldstein (1981)). This argument is valid for low rates of inflation (say, below 15 percent). However, when inflation rates exceed this range, the distortionary effects of inflation become larger, and the counteracting effects of tax incentives are then less effective (Sanchez-Ugarte (1983)). For instance, if accelerated depreciation is used to avoid the distortionary effects of tax depreciation at historic costs, at a high enough inflation rate and on a relatively short-lived asset, there is no rate of depreciation fast enough to avoid the effects of inflation. Instant depreciation is more than fast enough, whereas depreciation in two years is not fast enough. On the other hand, with high rates of inflation, the expected rate of depreciation becomes less predictable. Tax incentives have to be announced in advance, which gives a large margin of error favoring either investors or the government. Correcting the income tax for inflation, rather than using tax incentives, results in less distortion and is less costly.

Tax Incentives to Regional Development

Consider a tax incentive scheme for the promotion of industry in a less-developed region. The tax incentive scheme should remove the negative externalities and induce positive ones (see section on "Regional Distribution of Economic Activity," above). One positive externality might result from an increasing urban concentration in the developing region, which reduces the cost of public services and provides for certain economies of scale. If concentration in a particular region is a desired objective, this can be achieved through a tax incentive to investment on plant and equipment.

Another positive externality can be derived from the employment of labor that accompanies the new investment. However, prospective investors in the region take into consideration not only the direct cost of using labor, which in nominal terms can be cheaper in the backward areas, but also its productivity. The lack of skill of the local labor force is likely to pose a major obstacle for the new investment project. This problem can be re-

[23]This argument rests on the dynamic incidence of taxation, which is different from the static case. See Boskin (1978) for an application.

duced by simultaneously granting tax incentives for the training of the labor force in that region in the form of, for example, additional income tax deductions. Similarly, where transportation costs can also be a major problem in such areas, a tax incentive for the purchase of transportation equipment can be granted simultaneously.

Notice, however, that many developing countries promote regional development through tax incentives to investment in physical capital (Modi (1982)). As shown above, this is not always the best way to induce the desired externality.

Tax Incentives and International Trade

Tax Incentives to Imports

Reductions of and exemptions from import tariffs are a common form of tax incentive in developing countries. Tax incentives are frequently given to encourage the importation of both raw material and capital equipment, and in both cases they appear to be distortionary. The reduction of import taxes on inputs increases the effective rate of protection granted to domestic production by the import tariff structure.[24] This distortionary effect is further enhanced by the effect of import tariff reductions on capital equipment. It can be shown that import tariff reductions on capital goods lead to effective rates of protection higher than the nominal protection and higher than the traditional measure of protection, which only incorporates the effect of tariffs on intermediate goods.[25]

This form of incentive, which is widely used in developing countries, should be a matter of concern. First of all, selective import tariff reductions are often granted to individual firms, and not to all the firms in the

[24]See Sanchez-Ugarte (1983, Chapter II). This effect results from the fact that domestic value added has a higher cost than would result under a uniform tariff. For instance, if a tariff of 30 percent is imposed on a product, and 50 percent of the product produced domestically is imported without tariffs, the effective protection on that product is 60 percent.

The domestic producers can sell the product in question at 30 percent above the international price and they can import 50 percent of the components free of tariffs. This means that the 30 percent tariff is really protecting 50 percent of the product (the rest is imported), so the effective protection on this 50 percent is as high as 60 percent. See Corden (1971) where the concept of effective protection is thoroughly analyzed.

[25]The formula for effective protection that incorporates the effect of imported capital equipment is $E = t_x - t_m + v(t_m - \eta t_k)/v(1 - \eta)$, where t_x is the tariff on final output, t_m the tariff on intermediate inputs, t_k the tariff on capital equipment, v the ratio of domestic value added to gross output, and η the ratio of investment to value added. See Sanchez-Ugarte (1983) for the derivation.

industry. This distorts the structure of effective protection in unpredictable ways. Second, a high level of effective protection gives rise to great inefficiency in the use of domestic resources. Third, the reductions in, or exemptions from, tariffs on the importation of capital equipment and raw materials leave the domestic industries that produce these commodities unprotected and increase the level of protection of industries that produce consumption goods. Exports using imported raw materials, which are taxed, frequently receive duty drawbacks to reduce the cost disadvantage imposed on them by the levy of the tariff. Such duty drawbacks, however, do not extend to taxed imports of capital goods, whose cost disadvantage to exports can only be relieved by allowing duty-free importation of capital goods by export industries.

Throughout developing countries, the production of capital equipment tends to have rates of protection well below those granted to other industries. Hence, a case can be made, on efficiency grounds, for tax incentives to favor the use of domestic capital goods vis-à-vis imported ones. This implies that if tax incentives are given to investment, a higher rate should be granted to investment in domestically produced capital goods.

Tax Incentives to Exports

In discussing tax incentives for the promotion of exports, one needs to separate two issues. One is the problem of border tax adjustments, which implies that under the destination principle of taxation, indirect taxes apply where the good is consumed. This means that imports are taxed and exports are exempt. In order to avoid double taxation, an individual country should adhere to the destination principle as long as everybody else follows the same principle. This kind of tax rebate is not in any sense a subsidy to exports, but rather is a way of harmonizing indirect tax systems across international borders.[26]

On the other hand, tax incentives are frequently given to exports in developing countries to compensate for other distortions in the foreign trade sector such as protection and overvalued exchange rates. Protection changes the domestic terms of trade in favor of the production of goods that substitute for imports. This reduces the attractiveness of producing export and nontradable goods. However, protection increases the domestic price of importables relative to exportables and of nontradables. This reduces the demand for imports. Since, in the long run, the external balance

[26]The GATT rules allow such rebates, and the European Community requires that the indirect taxes of its member countries be applied according to the destination principle.

of the country has to be in equilibrium, a policy that reduces imports will also reduce exports. Moreover, the protected sector is rarely able to become an exporter because it is being isolated from foreign competition. Tax incentives are frequently used to reduce the size of these two effects. It is worth noting, however, that if all exports are subsidized to eliminate the negative effects of protection, the relative price advantage of producing import substitutes will be eliminated. This is one reason why export promotion policy is very often selective by sector. Contriving to have a protected industry that also has the capacity to export is a difficult exercise. Few countries have been successful in promoting exports, while still protecting the industrial sector.[27] An additional element is that many importing countries abide by the GATT rules for international trade and often establish countervailing duties and/or quantitative restrictions on those exports subsidized in the home country. In this case, the subsidy to exports becomes a transfer to the foreign country's treasury.

Export subsidies are often used by developing countries to compensate for the trade effects of an overvalued exchange rate. Such a policy is seldom effective as it is difficult to compensate through the government budget for the distortions resulting from inadequate exchange rate policy that tend to grow over time. Moreover, export subsidies can often lead to further efficiency losses by delaying an exchange rate adjustment.

Other Tax Incentives

Tax incentives are also given through domestic indirect taxes and are often distortionary. The incentive given to new firms in any industry will distort competition within the industry and can have a high cost in terms of tax revenue forgone. Furthermore, given that the design of indirect taxes very often takes into account distributional considerations, lower tax rates apply to goods considered to be necessities or are consumed by low-income groups, whereas higher rates apply to goods that are considered to be luxuries or are consumed by higher-income groups. Tax incentives in relation to indirect taxes have the effect of reversing the distributional bias inherent in the tax structure. On the other hand, a tax incentive given through an indirect tax will, if effective, lead to an increase in production. Hence, it does not favor a specific factor of production such as a tax incentive to investment or a tax incentive to the use of labor.

[27]An exception is Korea which has been able to increase nontraditional exports by a judicious use of fiscal and financial incentives. The key to success in the tax incentive policy has been efficiency and expediency in granting the incentives. See Rhee and others (1984).

Another form of tax incentive that has become popular in some countries (e.g., Colombia and Mexico) is the so-called tax savings certificate (TSC). This is a document issued by the government, in connection with a tax incentive scheme, which can be used for payment of various taxes. The main advantage of this document is that the amount of tax revenue transferred to the private agent is known with certainty in nominal terms. This is not generally the case with most tax incentives, the value of which depends on the future tax liability.

The TSC also has an advantage over other tax incentives linked to a specific tax in that it is more liquid and can be applied to the payment of any tax. Tax incentive recipients often have other taxes to which the certificate can be applied. The liquidity of the certificate can be increased by allowing it to be traded.

The basic advantage of the TSC is also its main disadvantage—it allows the government to grant tax incentives in amounts that can be highly disproportionate to the taxes generated by the activity in question. Moreover, it may not provide immediate liquidity to the taxpayer if the taxpayer can neither fully use it himself nor trade it for its full value.

Conclusions

Two general conclusions can be derived from the above examples as to the efficiency of tax incentives. First, tax incentives tend to induce diverse and often unpredictable distortions in the economy, a factor often overlooked in their design. Second, the best way of achieving a net positive externality (or reducing a negative one) through tax incentives is by selecting instruments that act as directly on the externality as possible. Thus, if the positive externality derives from net investment, the tax incentive should be granted on net investment; if the positive externality arises from use of labor, the incentive should act to encourage the use of this factor of production. A tax incentive is, in general, linked to a specific tax base. The policymaker should select the tax base that is most closely related to the positive external effect that he wishes to induce.

IV. The Effectiveness of Tax Incentives

Most economists and lay persons alike have doubts about the overall effectiveness of tax incentives policy in developing countries. The empirical literature has been inconclusive on the effectiveness of tax incentive policy.[28] Among the reasons why tax incentives tend to be ineffective, some of which were alluded to earlier, the following need to be stressed: too broad a spectrum of objectives pursued with limited resources; excessive selectivity in the granting process; unpredictability in the granting of the incentives; too much political influence of vested interests in the design of policy; an inadequate relationship between the objective and the instrument; and countereffective general equilibrium (or indirect) effects. For tax incentives to be effective, therefore, certain criteria must be fulfilled, and these are highlighted below.

Limiting the Objectives

The first problem stems from the authorities' wanting to pursue too many objectives with limited resources. Most developing countries tend to use tax incentives for a variety of objectives, resulting in a very diffuse impact on any one of the objectives.

The typical tax incentive scheme in a developing country contains, as the backbone of the policy, an industrial promotion program that is aimed at the development of the manufacturing industry (Sanchez-Ugarte (1983) and Modi (1987)). Such a scheme typically involves benefits for certain sectors and regions of the country, which are granted through several specific tax incentives relating to the corporate income tax, import tariffs, and other taxes. It is also common to find tax incentives for the promotion of exports, which are usually granted to nontraditional exports. Many countries also grant incentives to mineral and oil exploration and development; the tourist sector also receives tax incentives, and it is not uncommon to find additional tax incentives given to agriculture, livestock raising, forestry, and fishing.

In addition to tax incentives by sector, the specific tax legislation frequently contains reductions and exemptions directed toward promoting economic development in general. For instance, income taxes may contain accelerated depreciation or investment tax credits to promote investment; there might be incentives to induce private savings in the financial sector or the stock exchange. Other taxes may also contain built-in tax incentives. Finally, many countries also grant tax incentives or tax rate reductions in special cases, at the discretion of the tax administration authorities. Tax incentives in developing countries would be more effective and less costly if two or three narrow objectives were chosen.

[28]See, for instance, Taylor (1957), Heller and Kauffman (1963), Porter (1969), Hirschman (1967), Tanzi (1969), Joel (1971), Goodman (1972), Mahar (1976), Moore and Rhodes (1976), and Sanchez-Ugarte (1983).

Reducing the Discretionary Element

Tax incentives are effective if they induce the desired economic behavior. Developing countries typically use a long and complicated process of application and selection in order to ensure that the recipient of the tax incentive really needs it. The excessive red tape tends to nullify the desired result, because in order to apply for the incentive the firm has to have both the resources for covering the costs involved in the application process and the interest in doing so. A firm that is exactly on the margin between undertaking the activity and doing something else will not apply because it has very little to gain from doing so and much to lose.[29] On the other hand, a firm that will obtain rents in pursuing the activity will be willing to go through the selection process. Such a firm runs no risk and may in fact increase its profits on an activity that it would have undertaken even without the tax incentive. Excessive selectivity and administrative discretion defeat their own purpose, as they decrease the probability of selecting those candidates who are in greatest need of the incentive.

The arguments above suggest that the granting of tax incentives should be an automatic process and that selectivity should be exercised with great care.

Ensuring Predictability

A third reason for the ineffectiveness of tax incentives is their unpredictability. Most countries fine-tune their tax incentive policy to respond to the ever-changing economic conditions. However, these changes tend to make the policy ineffective because as long as tax incentives are not incorporated into individuals' economic calculations, they do not lead to changes in economic behavior but rather to windfall gains to the lucky recipients.

It follows that, while tax incentives do not have to be permanent, they must be predictable, so that they can be incorporated into the decision-making process of the economic agents.

Minimizing Political Influences

Tax incentives are commonly sought by vested interest groups. Governments are likely to yield to such political pressures, first, because the cost of tax incentives is borne by all taxpayers—and is therefore more easily absorbed—whereas the benefits are specific. Second, tax incentives are

[29]See Sanchez-Ugarte (1983) where this argument is developed and tested in relation to Mexico.

commonly granted at the discretion of the administrative branch of the government, so that they are not subject to the political decision-making process involved in other tax legislation. Quite often they are given by ministries other than the ministry of finance and against the will of the latter. Furthermore, it can be argued that tax incentives are an expeditious and simple instrument of effecting transfers to specific groups and have apparent redeeming social value as vehicles of economic development. They ease the transfer of resources since an actual disbursement is not involved nor are they controlled by the normal budgetary process. The result is that tax incentives are often aimed at the pursuit of political rather than economic objectives.

Economists have become increasingly aware that some fiscal measures give rise to economic rents and induce rent-seeking behavior on the part of economic agents, thereby leading to economic inefficiency. The literature touching upon this issue has concentrated on the rent-seeking behavior with respect to import tariffs and other trade restrictions (Krueger (1974) and Brock and Magee (1978)). Much of the analysis dealing with the rent-inducing effects of tariffs can be extended to tax incentives, which constitute one of the prime examples of rent-inducing fiscal measures. Even though there will always be political pressure to use tax incentives to effect transfers, the recommendations given above to limit the scope of tax incentive policy, to reduce discretionary criteria for granting incentives, and to ensure predictability will help reduce rent-seeking behavior.

Ensuring Direct Relationship Between the Instrument and the Objective

Tax incentives are not always chosen so that they act specifically on the objective they pursue. Most tax incentives are granted for investment since these types of incentives are less difficult to apply. It is hoped that at the same time as they increase investment, they will also meet other complementary objectives, such as regional development, exports, employment of labor, and import substitution. As pointed out earlier, this lack of focus can create other distortions with often unpredictable results.

The choice of instruments should therefore closely match the objective pursued.

General Equilibrium Effects

The design of tax incentives should take into account the general equilibrium effects that can easily nullify the desired incentive effect. Under certain assumptions, tax incentives for regional development tend to be capitalized on the value of land. This capitalization effect, aside from its effect on income distribution might lessen the inducement to invest in the region. Tanzi (1969), citing the case of Ecuador, shows that tax incentives to investment had a successful allocative role, redirecting investments to the manufacturing sector without actually increasing the rate of investment for the economy as a whole.

A similar phenomenon can affect tax incentives to selective exports—certain types of exports may be substituted in production for other exports thereby increasing the level of one export while reducing that of another. This phenomenon lessens the overall impact of tax incentives on total exports.

General equilibrium effects can reduce the effectiveness of tax incentives to the use of labor. In most developing countries, the tax system basically covers the modern, urban, relatively capital-intensive sector of the economy. Granting a subsidy to the use of labor by the capital-intensive industry has two effects. On the one hand, it reduces the cost of labor by the modern sector, thereby increasing the demand for labor. On the other hand, it expands the sector that is relatively capital-intensive, leading to the contraction of the sector that is labor-intensive and thus reducing the demand for labor. It is not certain which of the two effects will dominate.

The proper design of tax incentives should therefore attempt to take into account the general equilibrium effects of the specific measures taken in order to guarantee the effectiveness of tax incentive policy.

V. Concluding Remarks

It has been argued throughout this chapter, that even though the granting of tax incentives under certain circumstances might be economically rational, this policy presents severe limitations and drawbacks.

Tax incentives, even when designed to promote economic efficiency, are not necessarily the most appropriate method. Quite often, there is a more direct and effective alternative policy. The attempt by some developing countries to use a vast array of liberal tax incentives to counteract the negative effects of high marginal tax rates of narrowly based taxes and/or wrong economic policies with regard to wage rates, interest rates, exchange rates, and so on is likely to be ineffective and even counterproductive.

This chapter has shown that tax incentives often have more deleterious side effects than the distortions caused by tax and other economic policies they attempt to eliminate. Furthermore, as has been shown, it is no simple task to design effective tax incentives to produce the desired result. If the tax system is so distorting as to require more than just "fine-tuning," the suggested course of action would be to reform the tax system itself so that a second-best situation is attained. The recent optimal taxation literature has shown that it is theoretically possible to design a tax system, taking into account both economic efficiency and income distribution, even though such a system would consist of only a few feasible taxes. Tax incentives are no substitute for an efficient tax system. All tax reform efforts should, therefore, be directed at achieving the latter. Reducing the marginal tax rates while expanding the tax base, as recommended by supply-siders, would be an important component of such a strategy.

However, tax incentives exist worldwide and, even though many of them have little justification in a first- or second-best world, they are here to stay. It is, therefore, necessary to consider how to design tax incentives that are both economically efficient and effective. Efficiency can be ensured by granting tax incentives in accordance with the net social benefit generated by the promoted activity. The methodology developed for social cost-benefit analysis can be applied to the design of tax incentives in order to obtain this result.

The selection of specific tax incentives is a very important matter. Some incentives severely erode the neutrality of the tax upon which they act, in ways that are not only economically undesirable but also unpredictable.

The choice of objectives to which incentives can be applied is also important as not all objectives are attainable through tax incentive policy. Care should be taken not to select too many or too broad objectives—goals can never be reached if too little tax revenue is allocated to any one of these objectives. Tax incentive policy will be more effective if it is restricted to a few, well-defined, and very specific objectives. The first three that come to mind, though not the only ones, are regional development, selective industries (or sectors), and export promotion. More broadly based objectives—for example, the promotion of employment, the increase in the overall level of capital accumulation, or the promotion of savings—are less effective targets for tax incentives. This is not to imply that such objectives should not be pursued, but rather that there are other more effective ways of attaining them. For instance, tax reform can be a way of eliminating some of the distortions inherent in some tax systems with respect to capital accumulation, savings, or the financial structure of the economy. Similarly, other economic policy instruments, such as wage policy, are more effective in the promotion of employment than are tax incentives.

The point that needs to be stressed is that tax incentives are only marginally effective, while these economy-wide objectives need more than marginal changes. The fact that the amount of revenue allocated to tax incentives has to be small (if it is not to damage the tax system intrinsically) validates this conclusion.

Tax incentives should not be granted on a discretionary basis. It is one thing to design tax incentives with very specific objectives in mind and another to be so selective in granting them that they cannot be incorporated in the decision-making process. Automaticity and objectivity in the granting of tax incentives are essential to the success of tax incentive policy. This, in turn, means that tax incentives must be meticulously designed to match the instrument with the objective as closely as possible. It follows that tax incentive policy should, as far as possible, be independent of political considerations. One way to attain this is to shift the function of selecting tax incentives away from the administrative branch of the government and into the regular tax legislation process.

REFERENCES

Aaron, Henry J., ed., *Inflation and the Income Tax* (Washington: Brookings Institution, 1976).

Arrow, Kenneth J., and Robert C. Lind, "Uncertainty and the Evaluation of Public Investment Decisions," *American Economic Review* (Nashville, Tennessee), Vol. 60 (June 1970), pp. 364–78.

Auerbach, Alan J., "Inflation and the Choice of Asset Life," *Journal of Political Economy* (Chicago), Vol. 87 (June 1979), pp. 621–38.

———, "Tax Neutrality and the Social Discount Rate: A Suggested Framework," *Journal of Public Economics* (Amsterdam), Vol. 17 (April 1982), pp. 355–72.

———, "Taxation, Corporate Financial Policy and the Cost of Capital," *Journal of Economic Literature* (Nashville, Tennessee), Vol. 21 (September 1983), pp. 905–40.

Balassa, Bela, and associates, *The Structure of Protection in Developing Countries* (Baltimore: Johns Hopkins University Press, 1971).

Bator, Francis M., "The Anatomy of Market Failure," *Quarterly Journal of Economics* (Cambridge, Massachusetts), Vol. 72 (August 1958), pp. 351–79.

Bird, R., "Tax Incentives for Investment: The State of the Art," Canadian Tax Paper No. 64 (Toronto: Canadian Tax Foundation, 1980).

Boadway, Robin, "Investment Incentives, Corporate Taxation, and Efficiency in the Allocation of Capital," *Economic Journal* (London), Vol. 88 (September 1978), pp. 470–81.

———, *Public Sector Economics* (Cambridge, Massachusetts: Winthrop Publishers, 1979).

Boskin, Michael J., "Taxation, Saving, and the Rate of Interest," *Journal of Political Economy* (Chicago), Vol. 86, No. 2, Part 2 (April 1978), pp. S3–S27.

Brock, William A., and Stephen P. Magee, "The Economics of Special Interest Politics: The Case of the Tariff," *American Economic Review, Papers and Proceedings of the Ninetieth Annual Meeting of the American Economic Association* (Nashville, Tennesee), Vol. 68 (May 1978), pp. 246–50.

Coase, R.H., "The Problem of Social Cost," *Journal of Law and Economics* (Chicago), Vol. 3 (October 1960), pp. 1-44.

Corden, W.M., *The Theory of Protection* (Oxford: Clarendon Press, 1971).

Feldstein, M.S., "The Social Time Preference Discount Rate in Cost Benefit Analysis," *Economic Journal* (London), Vol. 74 (June 1964), pp. 360–79.

———, "Adjusting Depreciation in an Inflationary Economy: Indexing Versus Acceleration," *National Tax Journal* (Columbus, Ohio), Vol. 34 (March 1981), pp. 29-43.

Gandhi, Ved P., "Unemployment in Developing Countries: Can Tax Incentives Help?" (unpublished, International Monetary Fund, February 3, 1981).

Goode, Richard, *Government Finance in Developing Countries* (Washington: Brookings Institution, 1984).

Goodman, David E., "Industrial Development in the Brazilian Northeast: An Interim Assessment of the Tax Credit Scheme of Article 34/18," in *Brazil in the Sixties*, ed. by Riordan Roett (Nashville, Tennessee: Vanderbilt University Press, 1972).

Harberger, Arnold C., "On Measuring the Social Opportunity Cost of Labour," in *Fiscal Measures for Employment Promotion in Developing Countries* (Geneva: International Labor Office, 1972).

———, *Taxation and Welfare* (Boston: Little, Brown, 1974).

———, *Project Evaluation: Collected Papers* (Chicago: University of Chicago Press, Midway reprint, 1976).

———, "Tax Neutrality in Investment Incentives," in *The Economics of Taxation*, ed. by Henry J. Aaron and Michael J. Boskin (Washington: Brookings Institution, 1980).

Heller, Jack, and Kenneth M. Kauffman, *Tax Incentives for Industry in Less Developed Countries* (Cambridge, Massachusetts: Harvard Law School International Program in Taxation, 1963).

Hirschman, Albert O., "Desenvolvimento Industrial no Nordeste Brasileiro e o Mecanismo de Crédito Fiscal do Artigo 34/18," *Revista Brasileira de Economia* (Rio de Janeiro), Vol. 21 (December 1967), pp. 5-34.

Hirschleifer, J., "Investment Decision Under Uncertainty: Applications of the State-Preference Approach," *Quarterly Journal of Economics* (Cambridge, Massachusetts), Vol. 80 (May 1966), pp. 252-77.

Joel, Clark, "Tax Incentives in Central American Development," *Economic Development and Cultural Change* (Chicago), Vol. 19 (January 1971), pp. 229-52.

Johnson, Harry G., "The Cost of Protection and the Scientific Tariff," *Journal of Political Economy* (Chicago), Vol. 68 (August 1960), pp. 327-45.

———, *Technology and Economic Interdependence* (London: Macmillan, 1975).

Keith, E. Gordon, "Introduction and Summary," in *Foreign Tax Policies and Economic Growth: A Conference Report of the National Bureau of Economic Research and the Brookings Institution* (New York: Columbia University Press, 1966).

Krueger, Anne O., "The Political Economy of the Rent-Seeking Society,"

American Economic Review (Nashville, Tennessee), Vol. 64 (June 1974), pp. 291-303.

Layard, Richard, ed., *Cost-Benefit Analysis: Selected Readings* (Harmondsworth, England: Penguin Books, 1972).

Lewis, W. Arthur, "Economic Development with Unlimited Supplies of Labour," *Manchester School of Economic and Social Studies*, Vol. 22 (May 1954), pp. 139-91.

Little, I.M.D., and J.A. Mirrlees, *Project Appraisal and Planning for Developing Countries* (London: Heinemann Educational Books, 1974).

Lucas, Robert E., Jr., *Studies in Business-Cycle Theory* (Cambridge, Massachusetts: MIT Press, 1981).

Mahar, Dennis J., "Fiscal Incentives for Regional Development: A Case Study of the Western Amazon Basin," *Journal of Interamerican Studies and World Affairs* (Coral Gables, Florida), Vol. 18 (August 1976), pp. 357-78.

Marglin, Stephen, A., "The Opportunity Costs of Public Investment," *Quarterly Journal of Economics* (Cambridge, Massachusetts), Vol. 77 (May 1963), pp. 274-89.

Meade, J.E., *The Structure and Reform of Direct Taxation* (London: Allen & Unwin, 1978).

Modi, Jitendra R., "Narrowing Regional Disparities by Fiscal Incentives," *Finance & Development* (Washington), Vol. 19 (March 1982), pp. 34-37.

———, "Major Features of Corporate Profit Taxes in Selected Developing Countries," *Bulletin*, International Bureau of Fiscal Documentation (Amsterdam), Vol. 41 (February 1987), pp. 65-74.

Moore, Barry, and John Rhodes, "Regional Economic Policy and the Movement of Manufacturing Firms to Development Areas," *Economica* (London), Vol. 43 (February 1976), pp. 17-32.

Mutén, Leif, "Forms of Tax Incentives; Their Economic Costs and Benefits," in *Fiscal Incentives: Tax Policy as an Instrument of Economic Development* (German Foundation for International Development, Berlin, 1982).

Porter, Richard C., "The Effectiveness of Tax Exemption in Colombia," Discussion Paper No. 8 (Ann Arbor, Michigan: University of Michigan, Center for Research on Economic Development, 1969).

Rhee, Yung Whee, Bruce Ross-Larson, and Garry Pursell, *Korea's Competitive Edge: Managing the Entry into World Markets* (Baltimore: Johns Hopkins University Press, 1984).

Ruane, Frances P., "Corporate Income Tax, Investment Grants, and the Cost of Capital," *Journal of Public Economics* (Amsterdam), Vol. 17 (February 1982), pp. 103-110.

Sanchez-Ugarte, Fernando, "Tax Incentives to Investment for the Promotion of Industry: The Mexican Experience" (doctoral dissertation, Chicago: University of Chicago, December 1983).

Sandmo, Agnar, "Investment Incentives and the Corporate Income Tax," *Journal of Political Economy* (Chicago), Vol. 82 (March-April 1974), pp. 287-302.

Sen, Amartya K., "Isolation, Assurance and the Social Rate of Discount," *Quarterly Journal of Economics* (Cambridge, Massachusetts), Vol. 81 (February 1967), pp. 112–24.

Stern, Nicholas H., "Optimum Taxation and Tax Policy," *Staff Papers,* International Monetary Fund (Washington), Vol. 31 (June 1984), pp. 339–78.

Stiglitz, Joseph E., "The Corporation Tax," *Journal of Public Economics* (Amsterdam), Vol. 5 (April–May 1976), pp. 303–11.

Swan, Peter L., "Income Taxes, Profit Taxes and Neutrality of Optimizing Decisions," *Economic Record* (Melbourne), Vol. 52 (June 1976), pp. 166–81.

Tanzi, Vito, "Tax Incentives and Economic Development: The Ecuadorian Experience," *Finanzarchiv* (Tübingen), Vol. 28 (March 1969), pp. 226–35.

Taylor, M.C., *Industrial Tax-Exemptions in Puerto Rico: A Case Study in the Use of Tax Subsidies for Industrializing Underdeveloped Areas* (Madison, Wisconsin: University of Wisconsin Press, 1957).

Todaro, M.P., "A Model of Labor Migration and Urban Unemployment in Less Developed Countries," *American Economic Review* (Nashville, Tennessee), Vol. 59 (March 1969), pp. 138–48.

11

Are Export Duties Optimal in Developing Countries?

Some Supply-Side Considerations

Fernando Sanchez-Ugarte and Jitendra R. Modi

Export duties play an important role in the revenue structures of developing countries. For these countries, export duties are a useful tool for raising revenue, since compared with their enormous financing needs for social and economic development they generally have few tax bases at their disposal and also are hampered by their limited capacity for tax administration. Government budgets in a number of developing countries rely rather heavily on export duties, accounting for more than 1 percent of gross domestic product (GDP) and, with some minor exceptions, exceeding 10 percent of total tax revenue.[1] In most cases, export tax receipts are derived from high rates of taxes on one or two commodities that feature prominently in the exports of these countries. Frequently, export duties in developing countries are levied in lieu of income taxes on exporters and are justified on grounds of the ease of tax administration. They are also generally made progressive with respect to export prices, and thereby incomes earned by exporters; this is justified on grounds of equity and needs for macroeconomic stabilization. Furthermore, exports from developing countries are frequently subject to implicit export duties in the form of overvalued or multiple exchange rates, producer price ceilings, and quantitative restrictions on exports. These implicit export duties probably lead to a reduction in the level of exports even though they often do not yield fiscal revenue.

[1]The Annex to this chapter contains summary information on the levels and structure of export duties prevalent in many developing countries. For a review of the quantitative characteristics of the tax systems of developing countries, including export taxes, see Tanzi (1987).

Supply-side economists stress the negative effects of high and progressive taxes on the incentives to work, save, and invest.[2] Their argument, however, specifically relates to income taxes and not export duties, which are frequently levied in developing countries in lieu of income tax on exporters. Because export duties can have important effects on producer incentives, significant supply-side effects can occur.[3] A straightforward application of supply-side economics to export taxation would call for the reduction of high export duties existing in many developing countries to create incentives to produce and export and to generate private incomes and increase employment. In fact, from the point of view of world economic efficiency, the first-best policy would be to remove all restrictions on world trade and even remove rather than reduce export duties. Hence, the supply-side prescription of lowering or even eliminating export duties would go hand-in-hand with the economic efficiency criterion for the use of world resources.

A country might argue that there is some justification for the levy of export duties under certain circumstances. First, it might possess market power in a certain commodity market and be tempted to increase its economic well-being at the expense of the welfare of the importing countries by imposing an export duty. Second, a tax on exports can be levied to absorb windfall profits, if any, and as long as it does not affect economic behavior it could be nondistortionary. However, as this paper shows, to meet this objective, the tax has to be "unexpected" by the economic agents. Finally, export taxes can also be levied to stabilize producer incomes over time and, under certain conditions, this type of taxation can be "efficient."

Following the argumentation underlying the first justification, the paper estimates country optimal export duties for a number of developing countries by commodity and compares them with the actual effective level of export taxes that incorporates, wherever possible, the effect of both explicit and implicit export duties. The comparison shows that for most cases the actual level of export taxation is higher than the level that can be con-

[2]See Gandhi (Chapter 9) for a review of the main issues regarding the application of supply-side economics to the tax levels and structures of developing countries.

[3]There is little reference to export taxes in the public finance literature; however, there is an implicit belief by some public finance specialists that such taxes are more closely related to income (or direct) taxes than to excise (or indirect) taxes. See, for instance, Prest (1972), who argues that insofar as such taxes do not cover output assigned to the home market, they are only a partial substitute for income taxation of agricultural producers. In the international trade literature, they are treated as equivalent to import tariffs because from a general equilibrium point of view export duties and import tariffs reduce the size of the international trade sector. See Corden (1974).

sidered even *country optimal,* let alone *world optimal*. Furthermore, given the small but significant values of the supply elasticities, the paper also shows that export taxation substantially lowers exports. Finally, the paper presents information for selected developing countries that suggests that the use of export duties to stabilize producer incomes does not necessarily reduce risk and can have a detrimental effect on the incentives to produce.

Section I of the chapter describes the rationality for export duties in developing countries. Section II develops a methodology for estimating country optimal export duties and for measuring the supply-side effects of export taxation.

In Section III, an attempt is made to illustrate (it must be stressed that it is only an illustration) the application of the methodology developed in Section II to the measurement of the supply-side effects of export taxation prevalent in many developing countries. The section also notes important qualifications that must be borne in mind when interpreting the results of this exercise. The section concludes with an analysis of the impact of country-specific commodity stabilization schemes.

Section IV sums up the major findings of the study and discusses the ways in which existing export taxes could be modified from the standpoint of supply-side objectives. The chapter concludes with an annex, which presents the levels and structure of export duties in selected developing countries.

I. The Rationale for Export Taxes

Developing countries apply export taxes for many reasons,[4] among which the most important are (1) to limit exports to take advantage of the monopoly power in a certain market or to benefit from other market imperfections; (2) to raise revenue from export commodities; and (3) to stabilize producer incomes.[5] This section describes these arguments and shows that export duties used in connection with (1) may increase the welfare of the country while reducing that of the rest of the world; export duties used in connection with (2) may distort economic efficiency in general; and export duties used in connection with (3) may improve a country's economic welfare without lowering the welfare of the rest of the world.

[4]See Aguirre, Griffith, and Yücelik (1981), Goode, Lent, and Ojha (1966), Goode (1984), and Tanzi (1976), who discuss extensively the role of export duties in developing countries.

[5]Export duties are also used to promote the growth of the untaxed activities by changing the producer terms of trade against traditional exports. This rationale for export duties is not pursued here since import tariffs are more commonly employed for this purpose. See Corden (1974).

Export Duties and Market Imperfections

The literature focuses on two kinds of market imperfections: those relating to the existence of some form of monopoly power in the commodity market (the optimal tariff argument) and those arising from protectionism on the part of consuming or importing countries and from other restrictions in commodity markets.

Monopoly Power of the Exporter

The optimal export duty argument is that a given country, or a group of countries, with monopoly power in the world market of a commodity should levy an export duty to extract monopoly profits[6] and thus to obtain a net welfare gain. The export duty, however, will improve the welfare of the individual country that exerts monopoly power but not of the world as a whole. Partial equilibrium analysis shows that the level of taxation that can be considered country optimal (i.e., that will maximize the gain to an exporting country) equalizes the marginal revenue and the marginal cost of exporting the commodity as given by the inverse elasticity rule[7] (Figure 1):

$$t_k^i = 1/\eta_k^i,$$

where t_k^i is the country optimal ad valorem export duty on the f.o.b. price of the export commodity k and η_k^i is the country-specific long-run elasticity of demand for exports of the taxed commodity. The country in question does not have to be a "pure" monopolist in the export market for the optimal tariff argument to apply.

Protection by Importing Countries and Other Restrictions on Trade in Commodity Markets

Importing countries often protect domestic producers of particular commodities by restricting the volume of imports through import quotas or other means.[8] Furthermore, producing countries have signed agreements, sometimes with the participation of major consumers, to stabilize and regulate commodity markets by means of restrictions on the level of exports by assigning export quotas to producing countries or by relying on interna-

[6]Quotas can also be used instead but in that event monopoly profits accrue to individual producers rather than to the government.

[7]See Corden (1974) and Johnson (1968).

[8]For instance, domestic sugar production is protected in the European Community (EC) countries and the United States; tobacco is protected in the United States; and rice is protected in Japan.

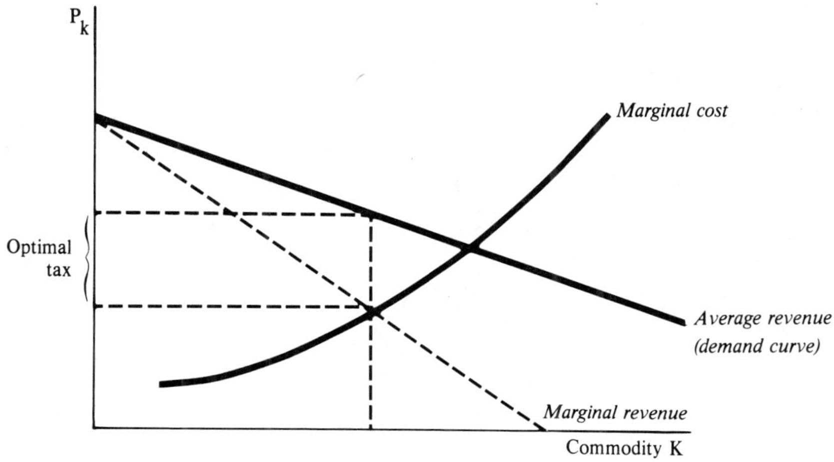

Figure 1. Country Optimal Export Duty

tional buffer stock arrangements.[9] Such trade restrictions give rise to a dual world market price structure—the commodity price in countries that have a protected market is higher than the price in the nonrestricted market—and the producers in an exporting country have an incentive to overproduce, given a positive elasticity of supply, as long as they assign a positive probability to selling extra output in the protected market.[10] The authorities of exporting countries can restrict overproduction and avoid an excessive world supply of the commodity by levying an export tax, which would efficiently achieve the desired level of production (Figure 2).

[9]Of the five international commodity agreements that were in existence in the early 1980s, only those for coffee, cocoa, and rubber are fully operational at present. An arrangement for stabilizing sugar prices through export quotas and special stock provisions lapsed after 1983, following the lack of agreement among the parties concerned. The tin agreement lapsed in October 1985 when it ran out of resources required to finance buffer stock purchases. See Singh (1977) for a discussion of the coffee and the cocoa agreements; Baldwin (1983) for the tin agreement; and Hart (1976) for the use of export taxation in connection with commodity agreements.

[10]Given that exports to the quota market are restricted, the marginal social revenue to the exporting country is equal to the free trade nonquota price. Optimality would dictate equality between the marginal social revenue and the marginal social cost. If the expected producer price (private marginal revenue) is a weighted average of the free and protected market price, the producer will tend to produce more than what is actually optimal in the hope that he can export more to the quota market. An export tax could close the gap between the private and the social marginal revenue.

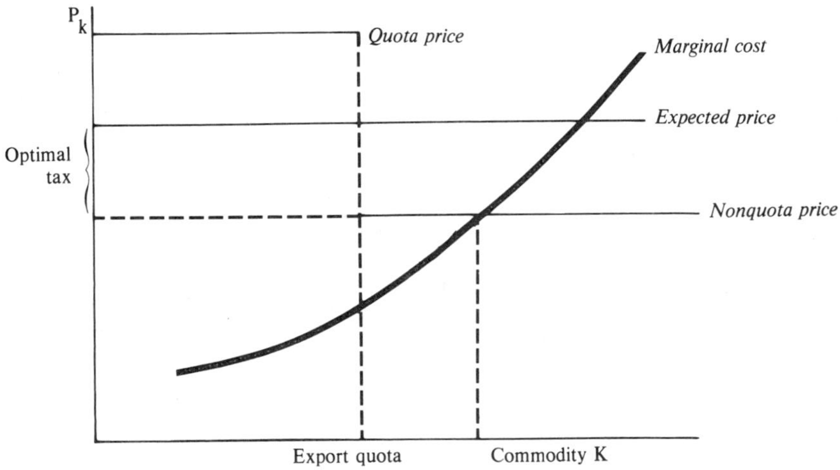

Figure 2. Export Taxation in Quota Markets

Taxes on Exports as Income Taxes

Export taxes are commonly used simply to collect revenue from export activities. Public finance literature has tended to assimilate these taxes under income or direct taxes because insofar as export taxes cannot be shifted to consumers in the international market, they obviously affect the income of domestic producers.[11] The export tax can also have an "excise" effect to the extent that the decline in the export price of a commodity relative to its domestic price reduces the level of exports (Tanzi (1976)). Whether export duties should be treated as an income tax or an excise tax is still controversial.

It might be argued that the supply of the typical export of a developing country is highly price inelastic, either because its producers are not price responsive or because the commodity is produced with the help of a sector-specific factor of production whose supply is fixed. In this case, a tax on exports can be simply considered as an income tax on an immovable factor of production and hence nondistortionary.[12] The assumptions underlying

[11]This is strictly true of export duties levied by a country that is a price taker in the world market and faces a perfectly elastic demand curve for its exports. Hence, a tax imposed on exports will, by necessity, be shifted back to producers. When exports are intermediated by traders, part of the tax burden can be borne by them as well. See Tanzi (1976).

[12]A tax on the income of an immovable factor of production is nondistortionary because it does not alter either the level of production or the level of exports of the commodity that employs the taxed factor, since the factor of production has no alternative use.

this conclusion can be questioned. With respect to the first point, there is ample empirical evidence that the supply of export commodities is affected by the producer price.[13] With respect to the second point, it can be argued that even when an export duty is fully capitalized in the price of an immovable factor of production (say, land), it still can have undesirable "excise" or supply-side effects.[14]

In the long run, an export duty imposed on an activity that employs an immovable factor of production will tend to be fully capitalized in the price of this factor of production—a result which may seem to indicate that the tax is nondistortionary.[15] The output of the taxed commodity, however, will tend to decrease because the export duty reduces the producer price of export goods compared with other goods and thus creates a distortion. It is the contraction in the level of output of the export good that reduces the price of the immovable factor of production. Furthermore, the export tax will create a "wedge" between the international price and the price paid by domestic consumers, creating an additional distortion. Hence, notwithstanding the fact that the export tax is fully shifted back to the immovable factor of production, the tax still can have excise effects; that is, it distorts the production and the consumption decision. To this extent, the export tax in the long run is not necessarily equivalent to a tax on the income of the immovable factor of production. In the more general case, when the export sector employs factors of production that are movable across sectors, the distortionary effects of the export tax are straightforward.

It might also be argued that over the short run, unexpected increases in the international price of an export commodity can sometimes lead to temporary "windfall" gains to exporters that can be taxed through an export duty.[16,17] This tax is presumed to be nondistortionary and, some might argue, the windfall gains are "unnecessary" to induce the given level of exports. For the analysis here, the distinction should be made between systematic (expected) and unsystematic (unexpected) tax policy changes. A systematic export duty that applies when prices are above a certain "normal" level will discourage production and exports because if the market is,

[13]The section on "Estimation of Country Optimal Export Taxes," below, presents the elasticities of supply of export commodities that have been estimated in the literature for developing countries; they are all positive, though small.

[14]The land used in the production of certain cash crops is not necessarily suitable for the production of other crops.

[15]Owing to space considerations, the proof of this proposition is not included here. See Mussa (1974) who derives the above result for an import duty.

[16]See Davis (1980) who analyzes the resurgence of export taxation in developing countries after the second oil crisis and the increase in commodity prices in the late 1970s.

[17]For the sake of symmetry, this argument would require that producers are subsidized when a windfall loss occurs.

by and large, competitive, there will be no "excess" profits in the long run, as good years will balance out the bad ones.[18] In addition, any systematic, though temporary, export tax policy with respect to windfall gains will sooner or later be incorporated by producers in their expectations, distorting their economic behavior. Only the taxation of profits, resulting from unsystematic changes, will have no effect on producers' behavior concerning exports, although it might make smuggling more profitable.

Devaluation of the exchange rate can generate windfall profits for exporters, similar to the unexpected increase in the international price of a commodity described above; however, it will also raise the cost of imports and other costs to the exporter. Therefore, it should not be assumed automatically that after a devaluation exports must always be taxed additionally. In fact, the levy of an export tax after devaluation can hamper the achievement of an increase in exports needed to restore the balance of trade equilibrium, which was the primary reason for the devaluation.

Export Duties in Connection with Stabilization Schemes

Developing countries can also rationally use export taxes in connection with three kinds of stabilization schemes: (1) the stabilization of the international price of a commodity or group of commodities, especially in support of international commodity agreements; (2) the stabilization of foreign exchange export earnings derived from the exports of one commodity or group of commodities; and (3) the stabilization of the domestic consumer price of a traded or exportable commodity.[19]

The economic efficiency arguments in favor of commodity stabilization efforts are well known. It has been stated that the free market solution does not necessarily allocate resources efficiently because there are no perfect and complete futures and risk markets and there is no perfect information. Hence, market intervention is called for. The first-best solution would be to encourage the development of efficient futures and insurance

[18]The international price of a commodity is a random variable. Even though one might attempt to forecast future values, nobody can predict with certainty the price of a commodity at every moment of time. For some commodities there are futures or forward markets which allow producers to reduce the risk involved in the production process, but these markets do not work as efficiently for all types of commodities.

[19]Stabilization efforts in these areas have been attempted by a number of developing countries mostly through marketing boards, but export taxes have also been used as one of several complementary policy instruments to attain the desired goal. The effect of country-specific commodity stabilization schemes on the level and the variability of producer prices is analyzed in the section on "Impact of Stabilization Schemes," below.

markets. If this is not feasible, as a second-best solution, a commodity stabilization scheme can, under certain conditions, improve domestic economic welfare.[20] Since it is reasonable to assume that economic agents generally, and exporters in particular, are risk averse, a commodity stabilization program that reduces the variability of the permanent income of exporters without reducing the mean[21] will improve welfare.[22] Even when the administrative costs of the stabilization scheme are taken into account, exporters could be better off as long as the cost of administration does not exceed the welfare gain from reduced riskiness. Risk averse consumers can also benefit from domestic price stabilization. Finally, from a macroeconomic point of view, the stabilization of foreign exchange earnings can also lead to welfare gains for both producers and domestic consumers. Notice, however, that an efficient export tax used to attain commodity stabilization will not yield tax revenue in net present value terms.

The commodity stabilization schemes can also conceivably have an adverse effect on the economy in two main respects, namely, the size of the levy on producers and the uses to which the proceeds of the levy are put relative to what the producer would have done with it if he had not been subject to such an impost.[23] With respect to the size of the levy, the point is that a high level of export duty implicit in the stabilization levy may adversely affect the producer's incentive to produce the commodity concerned—the actual impact being dependent on the supply elasticity. Second, with respect to the use of the levy, the adverse impact may stem from the fact that the outlays undertaken by the stabilization scheme are much less productive (in terms of additional output generated) than those which the producer would most probably have undertaken in the absence of the levy.

II. Methodology for Estimating Country Optimal Export Duties and Their Effects

This section develops a methodology derived from the optimal export duty argument for estimating the country optimal level of export taxation

[20]See Newbery and Stiglitz (1981) for the economic rationale for stabilization.

[21]Helleiner (1964) and (1966a) examined the role of commodity marketing boards in Nigeria in stabilizing prices paid to producers and their incomes.

[22]See Newbery and Stiglitz (1981) for cases where the stabilization of prices is likely to lead to the stabilization of incomes. Johnson (1977) makes a case where price stabilization around the trend will decrease revenue, since the supply curve of exports is upward sloping. See Behrman (1977) for the generalization of the Johnson result.

[23]See Helleiner (1966b, Chapter 6) for this line of approach.

by commodity. Thus, optimality in this section, and throughout the remainder of the paper, is understood in this limited sense incorporating only the optimal export duty argument (see section on "Monopoly Power of the Exporter," above). It should be recalled at this stage that the optimal export duty is only optimal from the point of view of the country that imposes it; it is not optimal from the point of view of the world as a whole. By comparing the actual level with the optimal level of export taxation estimated with the help of the methodology developed below (data on the former are given in the Annex), it is possible to indicate the distortionary effect of export taxation of a given country on the level of its exports and to measure the supply effect of export duties.

Country Optimal Export Duties

As mentioned in Section I, the country optimal export duty ($\overset{*}{t}{}^i_k$) on commodity k by country i, which faces a less than perfectly elastic demand curve, is given by the inverse elasticity rule:

$$\overset{*}{t}{}^i_k = 1/\eta^i_k. \tag{1}$$

In equation (1), η^i_k is the absolute value of the country-specific long-run elasticity of demand of commodity k. Most of the demand elasticities have been estimated in the literature for commodity markets and not for individual countries. The following formula, based on partial equilibrium considerations, therefore, transforms the market elasticity of demand of a commodity into the country-specific elasticity of demand for the same commodity.[24] As can be seen, the country-specific elasticity of demand is higher in absolute terms than the market demand elasticity:

$$\eta^i_k = \eta_k/S^i_k + \epsilon^o_k\,(1 - S^i_k)/S^i_k, \tag{2}$$

where η_k is the absolute value of the long-run market elasticity of demand of commodity k, S^i_k is the share (in percent) of country i in world exports of commodity k, and ϵ^o_k is the long-run elasticity of supply of all other exporters of k (excluding country i) who are assumed to act independently of each other. The value of this elasticity of supply is given by

$$\epsilon^o_k = \sum_{j \neq i} \epsilon^j_k S^j_k/(1 - S^i_k), \tag{3}$$

where ϵ^j_k is the long-run elasticity of supply of exports of commodity k by country j. By substituting the estimated value of equations (2) and (3) into

[24]Equations (2) and (3) result from the logarithmic changes of exports of commodity k by each exporting country resulting from a given change in the export price.

equation (1), one can calculate the country optimal export tax by commodity that, as can be seen from equation (1), will be higher the larger the share of country i in world exports of commodity k, the lower the absolute value of the market demand elasticity of commodity k, and the lower the elasticity of supply of other exporters of commodity k.[25,26]

Estimate of the Effect of Export Duties on Exports

The effect of export taxes on the level of exports can be estimated by assuming a constant elasticity of supply of exports. The equation below measures the change in exports of commodity k by country i that would result if the country in question adopted country optimal export taxes,[27]

$$\frac{\Delta X_k^i}{X_k^i} = \epsilon_k^i \left[\frac{\Delta P_k}{P_k} + \frac{(t_k^i - \overset{*}{t}{}_k^i)}{1 - t_k^i}\right]. \tag{4}$$

In equation (4), P_k is the price of commodity k that would prevail if country i adopted the country optimal export duty, ΔP_k is the change in price that would result, and t_k^i is the actual export duty applied by country i.

An estimate of the effect of export taxes on the market price $(\Delta P_k/P_k)$ can be obtained, likewise, assuming a constant price elasticity of demand function for exports. Namely,

$$\left(\frac{\Delta X_k}{X_k}\right)_d = -\ \eta_k\ \frac{\Delta P_k}{P_k}, \tag{5}$$

where $(\Delta X_k/X_k)_d$ measures the change in the market demand of world exports of commodity k that would result from country i adopting country optimal export taxes. Combining equations (4) and (5), using the market-

[25] The country optimal export tax given by equations (1) to (3) assumes that exporting countries act independently of each other. Hence, for a given value of the export market demand elasticity and the elasticity of supply of other exporters, the optimal export tax of commodity i in country k will be higher the larger the export market share. An alternative estimate of the optimal export tax would result from the assumption that the exporting countries collude and agree on a common export tax, which, in order to be optimal, should be equal to $1/\eta_k$. The collusion agreement is not pursued further in this paper. See Gately (1984) and Panayotou (1979) who analyze cases of international commodity cartels.

[26] Equations (1) and (3) also assume that no new producers enter (or leave) the market when the price of the commodity increases (or falls). The inclusion of such an effect would, of course, increase the country-specific elasticity of demand for the product.

[27] Equation (4) measures the change in exports that would result if the country in question adopted country optimal export taxes. It is derived from the definition of the elasticity of supply and from the fact that exporters receive a price net of export duties equal to $P_k(1 - t_k)$.

clearing condition that the total change in supply of exports equals the sum of the changes in each exporting country:

$$\left(\frac{\Delta X_k}{X_k}\right)_s = \sum_j S_k^j \frac{\Delta X_k^j}{X_k^j} = \sum_{j \neq i} S_k^j \epsilon_k^j \frac{\Delta P_k}{P_k} + S_k^i \epsilon_k^i \left[\frac{\Delta P_k}{P_k} + \frac{t^i - \overset{*}{t}{}_k^i}{(1 - t_k^i)}\right] \tag{6}$$

and solving for $\Delta P_k / P_k$ gives the effect of the export duties on the international price of the commodity:

$$\frac{\Delta P_k}{P_k} = - \left[\frac{\epsilon_k^i S_k^i}{\eta_k + \Sigma S_k^i \epsilon_k^i}\right] \frac{(t_k^i - \overset{*}{t}{}_k^i)}{(1 - t_k^i)}. \tag{7}$$

The effect of export taxes on the level of exports of commodity k by country i can then be estimated by substituting equation (7) into equation (4). The effect on foreign exchange earnings is estimated by adding equations (7) and (4).

Equation (7) is derived under the assumption that other exporting countries do not react to the tax change introduced by country i. This assumption, which could be reasonable in the case of small countries, is not likely to hold when the country that changes its tax policy is an important exporter. That is because other affected exporters would tend to react so as to maintain their relative market shares by *simultaneously* adjusting their present levels of export taxation. One can, of course, attempt to formulate a complex behavioral model to incorporate the impact of simultaneous reactions of the numerous exporting countries. The available data, however, which permit analysis of the impact of changes in the existing tax rates but only on an illustrative basis, do not facilitate the more complex assessment involving alternative interdependent behavioral and closure rules. The scope of the analysis in this paper, therefore, has been restricted to a situation in which all other countries keep their present tax levels unchanged; it nonetheless takes into account the impact of the adoption of the optimal tax by any one country i on the market shares of all major exporters of the taxed commodity.

The methodology developed above can be generalized further by including the effect that the export duty would have on the price of substitutes and complements in both demand and production. However, this adjustment has also not been made in the empirical application of the methodology that follows, since it is assumed for the purpose of the illustration that the prices of all other commodities remain constant. Furthermore, it should be stressed that the methodology derived here assumes that there are no other relevant distortions, whether in this market or in other markets, that are introduced by the imposition of the export duty.[28]

III. Appraisal of the Impact of Existing Export Taxes

This section evaluates the impact of existing export taxes on the supply of commodity exports and foreign exchange earnings for a group of selected developing countries within the analytical framework and methodology formulated in the preceding section. In doing this, the paper uses the readily available estimates of demand and supply elasticities without making any judgment on their reliability. Were these estimates to be accepted, the main conclusion of the exercise would be that the observed level of export taxation applied by the majority of developing countries exceeds the *country optimal* level. Hence, export taxes as currently applied are in most cases distortionary and thereby discourage exports.

Estimation of Country Optimal Export Taxes

Most of the export tax revenue in developing countries is derived from a select group of commodities that have relatively inelastic demand and supply elasticities (Table 1). Furthermore, for some of these commodities, a small number of developing countries seem to have a large share of the world market. This suggests that the country optimal export taxation of these commodities could be different from zero, at least for such countries.

Table 1 shows ranges of long-run supply elasticities estimated according to the methodology developed by Nerlove (Askari and Cummings (1977)) and demand elasticities for a group of selected commodities by country given in Valles (1968), Labys and Hunkeler (1974), Adams and Behrman (1976), Askari and Cummings (1977), and Baldwin (1983) (see footnotes in Table 1 for details). The supply elasticities are, in all cases, positive and different from zero, indicating that suppliers do respond to price incentives. The demand elasticities are in all cases negative, as expected, and generally larger than minus one. The exports of the selected commodities are also concentrated in a handful of developing countries.

[28]It is easy to transform the optimal export duty formula to take into account the abovementioned distortions. It can be shown that if the factors of production released by the taxed activity have a social return which is a fraction α of the social return obtained in the taxed activity, then the optimal export duty formula becomes

$$t_k^i = \frac{1}{\alpha}\left[\alpha - 1 + \frac{1}{\eta_k^i}\right].$$

Table 1. Estimates of Country Optimal Export Duties for Selected Commodities

(In percent)

	Supply Elasticity for the Country (1)	Share in World Market 1979–81 (2)	Actual Export Duty Rate 1979–81 (3)	Estimated Country Optimal Export Duty Rate	
				High (4)	Low (5)
Coffee					
Demand elasticity[1] (−0.2, −0.6)					
Supply elasticity for others[1] (0.3)					
Brazil	0.6[2]	17.90	59.00[3]	47.57	30.85
Burundi	0.6[4]	0.70	21.00[3]	1.55	0.89
Colombia	0.6[5]	17.60	13.00[3]	37.59	20.47
Costa Rica	0.5[6]	2.50	10.00[3]	4.91	2.82
Côte d'Ivoire	0.3[4]	5.80	64.00[7]	18.14	11.14
El Salvador	0.5[6]	5.20	47.00[7]	14.61	8.71
Ethiopia	0.6[4]	2.40	37.00[3]	6.41	3.77
Guatemala	0.5[6]	3.50	24.00[3]	7.59	4.38
Haiti	0.5[6]	0.50	25.00[3]	1.10	0.63
Honduras	0.5[6]	1.50	32.00[7]	3.56	2.06
Rwanda	0.6[4]	0.60	35.00[3]	1.34	0.77
Sierra Leone	0.6[4]	0.20	34.00[3]	0.53	0.61
Tanzania	0.6[4]	1.30	41.00[7]	3.88	2.28
Uganda	0.6[4]	2.70	28.00[3]	6.31	3.67
Togo	0.3[1]	0.20	77.00[7]	4.82	3.58
Total	...	62.60	...	...	...
Cocoa					
Demand elasticity[1] (−0.3, −0.4)					
Supply elasticity for others[1] (0.3)					
Côte d'Ivoire	0.8[8]	23.40	62.00[7]	46.73	43.24
Ghana	0.9[9]	20.50	60.00[7]	43.12	39.82
Grenada	0.3[10]	1.00	18.00[3]	1.27	1.14
Sierra Leone	0.3[10]	0.70	24.00[3]	0.92	0.82
Togo	0.3[10]	1.20	77.00[7]	9.16	8.55
Total	...	46.80	...	...	...
Tea					
Demand elasticity[1] (−0.1, −0.4)					
Supply elasticity for others[1] (0.3)					
India	0.6[11]	26.70	...	54.07	28.78
Sri Lanka	0.7[11]	18.70	46.00[3]	44.73	33.12
Total	...	45.40	...	...	...

Table 1 (*continued*). Estimates of Country Optimal Export Duties for Selected Commodities

(In percent)

	Supply Elasticity for the Country (1)	Share in World Market 1979–81 (2)	Actual Export Duty Rate 1979–81 (3)	Estimated Country Optimal Export Duty Rate	
				High (4)	Low (5)
Rubber					
Demand elasticity[1] (−0.5, −0.8)					
Supply elasticity for others[1] (0.4)					
Indonesia	0.4[12]	25.00	10.00[3]	34.05	24.36
Malaysia	0.2[12]	49.10	21.00[3]	66.67	47.89
Sri Lanka	0.4[10]	3.90	53.00[3]	8.02	5.92
Thailand	0.2[12]	14.50	40.00[7]	20.60	14.97
Total	...	92.50	...	...	...
Bananas					
Demand elasticity[1] (−0.5)					
Supply elasticity for others[1] (0.1)					
Costa Rica	0.1[13]	17.30	12.00[3]	29.20	17.51
Honduras	0.1[13]	17.00	29.00[7]	29.15	17.53
Total	...	34.30	...	...	...
Cotton					
Demand elasticity[1] (−0.2, −0.4)					
Supply elasticity for others[1] (0.8)					
Chad	0.1[10]	0.50	7.00[3]	0.51	0.42
Sudan	0.5[14]	3.20	40.00[7]	4.66	2.89
Togo	0.1[10]	0.10	12.00[3]	0.10	0.09
Total	...	3.80	...	...	...
Sugar					
Demand elasticity[1] (−0.2, −1.9)					
Supply elasticity for others[1] (0.4)					
Dominican Rep.	0.8[10]	2.60	13.00[3]	4.71	1.26
Mauritius	0.8[10]	1.90	17.00[3]	3.61	0.97
Total	...	4.50	...	...	...

Table 1 (*concluded*). Estimates of Country Optimal Export Duties for Selected Commodities

(In percent)

	Supply Elasticity for the Country (1)	Share in World Market 1979–81 (2)	Actual Export Duty Rate 1979–81 (3)	Estimated Country Optimal Export Duty Rate	
				High (4)	Low (5)
Rice					
Demand elasticity[1] (−0.4, −0.8)					
Supply elasticity for others[1] (0.6)					
Brazil	0.3[10]	0.10	40.00[7]	0.13	0.09
Thailand	0.3[15]	19.60	40.00[7]	24.05	17.04
Total	...	19.70	...	...	...
Bauxite					
Demand elasticity[1] (−1.3)					
Supply elasticity for others[1] (0.4)					
Jamaica	0.4[10]	6.90	28.00[3]	4.70	4.70
Tin					
Demand elasticity[1] (−0.2, −0.5)					
Supply elasticity for others[1] (1.2)					
Malaysia	0.7[16]	33.40	20.00[3]	30.42	4.29

Note: ... = not available.

Sources: International Monetary Fund, *International Financial Statistics* (Washington), various issues, and *Government Finance Statistics Yearbook, 1984,* Vol. 8 (Washington); World Bank, *Commodity Trade and Price Trends* (Washington); and Jere R. Behrman, *International Commodity Agreements: An Evaluation of the UNCTAD Integrated Commodity Programme,* Monograph No. 9 (Washington: Overseas Development Council, 1977). Estimates are based on equation (2) of Section II.

[1]All demand elasticities and supply elasticities for other countries are from Behrman (1977). Estimates of demand elasticities generally have a low and a high figure.

[2]Simple average for the country as reported in Hossein Askari and John Thomas Cummings, "Estimating Agricultural Supply Response with the Nerlove Model: A Survey," *International Economic Review* (Osaka, Japan), Vol. 18 (June 1977), pp. 257–92.

[3]Includes explicit and implicit export taxes. The explicit export tax is calculated as the ratio of export tax revenue to the value of exports of a given commodity and the implicit export tax is derived from World Bank, *World Development Report, 1981* (New York: Oxford University Press, 1981).

[4]Estimate for Africa in World Bank (1981).

[5]Average in World Bank (1981).

[6]Estimate for Latin America (excluding Brazil and Colombia) in World Bank (1981).

[7]Incorporates only explicit export taxes calculated as the ratio of export tax revenue to the value of exports of a given commodity.

Table 1 also shows estimates of actual average export duty rates by commodity and by country. In the cases where information was available, the actual export duty rates incorporate both explicit and implicit export duties (see Table 8 for details on implicit export duties); in other cases only explicit export duties were considered. Hence, tax rates shown in column 4 are not fully comparable across commodities and countries.

The last column of Table 1 shows the authors' estimates of country optimal export taxes, by country, for commonly taxed export commodities, based on the methodology derived in Section II.[29]

The values of supply and demand elasticities and market shares are combined through equations (1), (2), and (3) to estimate the country optimal export duty for each commodity. Since the changes in tax rates simulated in this section give rise to changes in market shares, an iterative procedure is used to reflect these changes. Hence, country optimal export duties are first calculated for each country using historical data on the observed market shares. The export tax is adjusted to the level that is country optimal, giving rise to a change in price and exports that is reflected in the market shares. The new shares are then used to recalculate the country optimal export taxes again; this procedure is repeated over and over. The results are shown as high and low estimates, using the high and low values for the elasticity of demand that appear in the first column of Table 1. It goes without saying that the estimated optimal tax rates given in Table 1 should be interpreted with extreme caution, as the reliability of the elasticity estimates compiled in that table has not been checked. The estimated optimal tax rates should at best be considered *illustrative* of the way the methodology developed in this paper can be used; this point cannot be

[29]For a similar approach to estimating optimal export taxes see Tolley, Thomas, and Wong (1982) who estimate optimal export taxes for Thailand's rice and Repetto (1972) who studies the taxation of jute in Bangladesh.

---

[8]Estimate for Côte d'Ivoire reported in Askari and Cummings (1977).

[9]Average for Ghana in Askari and Cummings (1977).

[10]See Behrman (1977).

[11]Reported in W. Labys and J. Hunkeler, "Survey of Commodity Demand and Supply Elasticities," United Nations Conference on Trade and Development, Research Memorandum No. 48 (unpublished, March 19, 1974).

[12]As reported for individual countries in Askari and Cummings (1977).

[13]See Jean Paul Valles, *The World Market for Bananas, 1964–72: Outlook for Demand, Supply, and Prices* (New York: Praeger, 1968).

[14]Reported for Sudan in Askari and Cummings (1977).

[15]Average reported in Askari and Cummings (1977).

[16]Reported in William L. Baldwin, *The World Tin Market: Political Pricing and Economic Competition* (Durham, North Carolina: Duke University Press, 1983).

overemphasized. Determining the specific optimal tax rates for any export commodity, by country, requires that accurate and country specific elasticity estimates be made and more detailed study conducted, neither of which the authors have done in this paper.

Subject to this qualification, the main results derived from analyzing the estimated optimal tax rates given in Table 1 are as follows.

First, as far as the levels of export taxation in developing countries are concerned, the country optimal export tax rates for selected export commodities, which include coffee, cocoa, rubber, tea, bananas, and tin, are greater than zero for several countries. These commodities frequently have relatively inelastic demand and supply schedules. As is apparent from Table 1, the production of a few export commodities is concentrated heavily in a handful of developing countries; consequently, the estimated country optimal tax rates are high for a few countries, which are the main producers. If the *illustrative* estimates given in Table 1 are to be relied upon, Colombia and Brazil could tax coffee at a marginal rate between 20 percent and 48 percent; Ghana and Côte d'Ivoire could tax cocoa at a rate between 40 percent and 45 percent; and Malaysia could tax rubber exports and India could tax tea exports at a rate of about 50 percent. The rates for the smaller producers, however, are considerably lower than those calculated for the main producers. For instance, for 22 of the 37 cases analyzed in Table 1, the country optimal export duty rates estimated under the high assumption are below 10 percent, and for 17 of the cases, the country optimal export duty rates estimated under the high assumption are below 5 percent.

Second, the information given in the third column of Table 1 and the Annex shows that developing countries generally tax the exports of those commodities that can be taxed according to the country optimal criteria. However, the levels of taxation adopted by individual countries do not seem to correspond to the estimated country optimal tax levels. Most developing countries seem to overtax exports as a result of high "explicit" and "implicit" export taxes (see Table 1).[30] There are 31 cases, out of a total of 37 in Table 1, in which export taxes exceed the estimated country optimal level of taxation.

The empirical evidence, therefore, shows that the majority of developing countries in the sample are overtaxing exports and further that, in general, the observed level of export taxation cannot be justified on the basis of the

[30]Note that, strictly speaking, the country optimal export duty should be compared against the marginal tax rates on exports. No information is available on the latter. However, it is generally safe to assume that the marginal export tax rate is higher than the average, so that the comparison in Table 1 underestimates the extent of the overtaxation of exports.

country optimal export duty criterion. The reliability of this conclusion, of course, hinges on the reliability of the elasticity estimates used above as well as the methodology used in this study for estimating the country optimal export duty rates.

This section also estimates, with the help of the methodology developed in Section II, the effect of high export taxes (relative to country optimal levels) on the supply of exports and foreign exchange earnings of developing countries.[31] The country optimal tax rates estimated above are plugged into equation (7) to estimate the effect on the price of the commodity, and this value is used to estimate the effect of the tax change on exports through equation (4). It should be mentioned at this point that the methodology measures the net impact on the total volume of exports of the country only if the factors of production released by the taxed export activity are employed by nonexport activities. Table 2 shows the estimated effects of explicit and implicit export taxes on commodity exports by country, taking as a point of reference the levels of exports that would result if the high and low values of the country optimal export taxes, estimated in Table 1, were applied. The main conclusion that can be derived from Table 2 is that the overtaxation of exports by most of the selected developing countries has a significant depressing effect on the volume of output of the taxed commodities.

The estimated reduction in output for the generally overtaxed commodities, such as coffee, cocoa, cotton, rice, and bauxite, is quite high, especially if the low estimated values of the country optimal tax rates are used as the point of reference.[32] It would appear that for many of the individual

[31]A word of caution is needed here. The effect of the export duty on the supply of exports and on the supply of foreign exchange should not be taken as a measure of the effect of the tax on economic welfare. A more appropriate measure of the effect of the tax on economic welfare is derived from the consumer and producer surpluses and would be given by

$$-\int_{t_k^i}^{\overset{*}{t}{}_k^i} (MC_k^i - MR_k^i)dX_k^i,$$

where MC_k^i is the marginal social cost of producing commodity k, MR_k^i is the marginal social revenue derived from exporting k, and dX_k^i is the change in output induced by the export duty relative to the level that would prevail in the country optimal situation.

[32]Other circumstantial evidence supporting the above conclusion is substantial. For instance, Ghana has overtaxed exports of cocoa to such an extent that its ranking among producer countries has slipped from first to third place (after Côte d'Ivoire and Brazil). Haiti has also suffered a decline in coffee exports from three fourths to one half of total output over the last twenty-five years. Production has remained stagnant, and consumption has increased substantially. The export duty was reduced to 25 percent in 1983 from a high of 40 percent, but no effect has been felt in production yet. See Tanzi (1976), who deals with coffee in Haiti, and Okonkwo (1978), who studies cocoa in West Africa.

Table 2. Partial Effects of Adopting Country Optimal Export Duties on Exports and Foreign Exchange

(Percentage change)

	Effect on Exports		Effect on Foreign Exchange	
	High[1]	Low[2]	High[1]	Low[2]
Coffee				
Brazil	14.80	48.67	6.74	17.02
Burundi	17.38	18.06	15.73	16.34
Colombia	−14.45	−7.70	128.07	68.51
Costa Rica	2.84	4.09	0.67	0.99
Côte d'Ivoire	56.50	73.27	47.55	60.65
El Salvador	39.71	51.84	29.37	37.56
Ethiopia	38.92	44.69	32.08	36.63
Guatemala	11.61	14.45	7.10	8.77
Haiti	18.83	19.32	17.81	18.27
Honduras	25.85	27.89	22.69	24.40
Rwanda	20.11	20.83	18.62	19.29
Sierra Leone	43.53	44.03	42.80	43.29
Tanzania	58.34	63.37	53.08	57.53
Uganda	21.08	24.72	15.54	18.13
Togo	1,197.54	1,581.41	1,169.84	1,534.17
Cocoa				
Côte d'Ivoire	28.59	38.54	14.99	18.96
Ghana	35.53	46.03	18.09	22.20
Grenada	6.48	6.55	5.86	5.92
Sierra Leone	9.99	10.04	9.52	9.57
Togo	528.05	559.25	505.14	533.83
Tea				
India	−17.48	−6.44	50.24	18.69
Sri Lanka	1.27	10.87	0.44	4.84
Rubber				
Indonesia	−8.73	−5.55	78.69	50.03
Malaysia	−9.54	−5.97	63.08	39.67
Sri Lanka	57.59	62.64	29.41	31.79
Thailand	6.58	8.74	0.66	0.80

countries, the lowering of export tax rates would significantly increase the output of the taxed commodity, if the elasticity estimates are to be trusted. For instance, coffee exports from Côte d'Ivoire, El Salvador, Ethiopia, Sierra Leone, Tanzania, and Togo, cocoa exports from Togo, rubber exports from Sri Lanka, and cotton exports from Sudan could increase more than 40 percent if these countries lowered their export duties to the country optimal level. Furthermore, exports of coffee from Honduras, Rwanda,

Table 2 (*concluded*). Partial Effects of Adopting Country Optimal Export Duties on Exports and Foreign Exchange

(Percentage change)

	Effect on Exports		Effect on Foreign Exchange	
	High[1]	Low[2]	High[1]	Low[2]
Bananas				
Costa Rica	−1.87	−0.61	24.26	7.96
Honduras	−0.05	1.58	0.16	−5.52
Cotton				
Chad	0.70	0.71	0.63	0.64
Sudan	40.26	41.61	36.64	37.85
Togo	1.37	1.37	1.36	1.36
Sugar				
Dominican Rep.	7.94	11.69	3.93	5.63
Mauritius	14.33	17.75	10.36	12.71
Rice				
Brazil	24.88	24.91	24.79	24.83
Thailand	7.98	12.06	2.83	4.14
Bauxite				
Jamaica	14.43	14.43	6.69	6.69
Tin				
Malaysia	−7.00	12.48	3.77	7.47

Sources: International Monetary Fund, *International Financial Statistics* (Washington), various issues, and *Government Finance Statistics Yearbook, 1984,* Vol. 8 (Washington); and Jere R. Behrman, *International Commodity Agreements: An Evaluation of the UNCTAD Integrated Commodity Programme,* Monograph No. 9 (Washington: Overseas Development Council, 1977). See Section II for methodology employed.

[1]The high estimate corresponds to the high value of the elasticity of demand employed and measures the effect on output and foreign exchange relative to the level that would prevail if optimal export duties were adopted.

[2]The low estimate corresponds to the low value of the elasticity of demand.

and Uganda, exports of cocoa from Côte d'Ivoire and Ghana, and rice exports from Brazil could increase from 20 percent to 40 percent if these countries lowered their export duties. Other countries, such as Guatemala, Haiti, Jamaica, Mauritius, and Thailand, would have more modest, but still significant, increases in their volume of exports of the taxed commodities if they lowered their export taxes. Very few countries with large world market shares, such as Colombia for coffee and Malaysia for rubber, would *decrease* the volume of exports of the indicated commodity if country optimal export duties were adopted.

High export taxation also has a depressing effect on the average foreign exchange earnings by commodity. In most cases, the impact on foreign exchange earnings is similar to, though somewhat smaller than, the effect on output. Those countries that are overtaxing the export commodities could increase their foreign exchange earnings if they lowered the level of export tax rates (for example, on coffee, see Côte d'Ivoire, Tanzania, and Togo; on cocoa, see Togo; on rubber, see Sri Lanka; and on cotton, see Sudan).

To conclude, in the majority of cases analyzed, the observed levels of export taxation seem high and are detrimental to both the level of exports and foreign exchange earnings. Hence, the supply-side prescription of reducing export taxes, in most cases, would not only increase the volume and the value of exports but could also enhance welfare. Furthermore, a number of countries could lower export taxes to the country optimal level and increase tax revenue by transforming the nonrevenue-yielding implicit export taxes into revenue-yielding export taxes. The last result is particularly relevant for those countries that have a relatively large share in the world market and that are currently overtaxing exports by way of nonrevenue-yielding implicit taxes.[33]

Qualifying the Interpretation of Country Optimal Export Duties

The preceding generalizations need to be qualified. First, certain imperfections in the commodity markets could preclude some developing countries from benefiting, in the short run, from lowering export taxes. As was noted before, the commodity agreements and certain import restrictions imposed by industrial countries predetermine, in the short run at least, the feasible level of exports. Any small country that wants to increase output by lowering export taxes may have to sell its output in nonquota markets at a discount. This qualification applies especially to commodities such as coffee, cocoa, tin, rubber, sugar, cotton, and tobacco.

Second, the methodology developed throughout this paper assumes that there are no other relevant distortions in the economy. For the actual application of the above methodology as a tool for policymaking, this as-

[33]Multiple exchange rate practices, for instance, are an implicit form of export taxation that does not yield revenue. In many instances, it might be feasible to eliminate multiple currency practices and keep the explicit ad valorem level of taxation constant; this would certainly increase the yield of the export tax.

sumption should be checked. In most developing countries, it is likely that other agricultural producer prices are also distorted. The increase (or decrease) in production of the taxed commodity would lead to a reduction (or increase) in the production of other agricultural products and could generate positive or negative external effects that should be taken into consideration.

Third, the country optimal export duty should, in general, be estimated taking into account the effect of the export duty on the price of close substitutes and complements in demand and in production. The adjustment is particularly relevant for such commodities as coffee, tea, and cocoa that are close substitutes in demand, but it should also be made in other pertinent cases. The adjustment, however, is expected to increase the value of the optimal export duty relative to the estimates derived above.[34]

Fourth, the approach used here, static partial equilibrium, has its limitations. In a dynamic context it could be expected that a high price of export commodities would lead to technical innovation, either in the form of more efficient use of inputs or creation of substitutes; either of the two would reduce further the demand for the commodity. The dynamic demand function is thus expected to be more elastic than the static one. When general equilibrium considerations are taken into account, the increase in exports in one sector could be compensated by the decline of exports in other activities. The only way of solving this problem is by estimating optimal export duties in a general equilibrium model that takes into account all the interaction that one policy measure generates in the economy.

Fifth, the assumption of constant elasticities for demand and supply has its limitations that can lead to error, because the correct functional specification could be a variable supply function.

Sixth, it is assumed in the analysis that all countries act independently, so that there is no strategic reaction from either producers or consumers when the export duty is changed. In the real world, countries might react strategically to tax changes in forms that could invalidate the optimality of a given export duty derived under the assumption of nonstrategic behavior.

Seventh, the approach followed to estimate country optimal export duties in this paper does not incorporate any distributional considerations. Since export commodities are often produced by low-income farmers in

[34]For instance, the increase in the price of the taxed commodity induced by an increase in the export duty will tend to increase the price of the close substitutes. These higher prices of substitutes counteract the own-price effect. As can be seen, the effect on the price of complements will also tend to counteract the own-price effect.

developing countries, it is very likely that export taxes are quite regressive (Tanzi (1976) and Booth (1980)). It should be noted, however, that governments could reduce and even eliminate the regressivity of export taxes by way of income redistribution through expenditure policy. This is unlikely to happen in practice, however, because government expenditure tends to have an urban bias.

Finally, should production of the export commodity be mainly undertaken by a government enterprise, the effect of the reduction in export duty on production could be blurred:[35] For example, the taxation of oil in Mexico, where it is produced under government monopoly, and the taxation of minerals in Zaïre, where production is dominated by a public enterprise, La Générale des Carrières et des Mines (GECAMINES).[36] In Togo, a public enterprise, Office Togolais des Phosphates (OTP), is responsible for the production and marketing of phosphates, the principal export commodity. In all such cases, the tax payment is determined in accordance with the budgetary needs of the government, the financial situation of the public enterprise, and international market conditions. A reduction in the prevailing level of export taxes, however, might have an effect in terms of attracting new private investment into these sectors, provided market entry were permitted.

Impact of Stabilization Schemes

Whether or not the commodity agreements have attained the purported objectives and improved economic well-being is an empirical question that lies beyond the scope of this paper.[37] Nonetheless, one can still form some notion of their impact on the efficiency of production given the theoretical proposition that a stabilization scheme that reduces the variability of the producers' income without reducing the mean would improve welfare (see section on "Export Duties in Connection with Stabilization Schemes," above).

Table 3 shows the coefficient of variation in domestic producer and export prices. Wherever the coefficient of variation of the former is less than

[35]In the case of commodities handled by state-controlled marketing boards, the reduction in the tax burden implicit in their operations may hamper their role, albeit limited (see section on "Impact of Stabilization Schemes "), in stabilizing prices paid to producers and their incomes.

[36]GECAMINES exports 95 percent of the copper and 85 percent of the cobalt—the two most important mineral exports from Zaïre.

[37]See Behrman (1977) who estimates the benefits and the distribution of the stabilization program proposed by the Fourth United Nations Conference on Trade and Development, and Baldwin (1983) who estimates the stabilization effect of the tin agreement.

Table 3. Selected Developing Countries: Selected Indicators of the Impact of Stabilization Schemes on Producer Prices

(In percent)

	Period Covered	Coefficient of Variation		Ratio of Producer Price to Export Price
		Producer price	Export price	
Coffee				
Côte d'Ivoire	1972–81	34	51	40
Haiti	1970–84	52	49	51
Papua New Guinea	1979–83	13	21	171
Rwanda	1974–84	15	19	57
Sierra Leone	1972–83	66	59	57
Cocoa				
Côte d'Ivoire	1972–81	35	40	55
Ghana	1971–83	126	131	52
Nigeria	1972–81	51	41	68
Papua New Guinea	1979–83	16	27	128
Sierra Leone	1972–83	52	39	58
Palm kernels				
Nigeria	1972–81	28	37	92
Sierra Leone	1972–83	53	76	59
Groundnuts				
Senegal	1976–84	25	35	33
Gambia, The	1975–83	11	33	
Copra				
Papua New Guinea	1979–83	23	39	103
Rice				
Thailand	1970–82	35	42	43
Cotton				
Chad	1974–84	22	20	45

Sources: Publications of marketing organizations, central banks, statistical bureaus, and other official agencies.

that of the latter, the stabilization scheme could be judged as having achieved its objectives. Calculations given in Table 3 suggest that the marketing agencies stabilized domestic producer prices only in 12 out of 17 cases.

The extent of stabilization in producers' prices was particularly well pronounced with respect to exports of coffee, cocoa, and copra from Papua New Guinea and groundnuts from The Gambia. In contrast, the schemes proved to be destabilizing with respect to exports of coffee from Haiti and Sierra Leone, exports of cocoa from Nigeria and Sierra Leone, and exports of cotton from Chad.

The stabilization of producer prices does not, of course, reflect the efficiency gain, which depends on the reduction in the variability of producers' income and such other factors as transfers to consumers and overall macroeconomic impact of the schemes.[38] While data on producers' incomes and export earnings are available only on a fragmentary basis for some countries (only for three commodities exported from three countries), no statistics whatsoever are available on other factors. The available data have provided the basis of computing the coefficients of variations in producers' incomes and export earnings, set out in Table 4, which suggest that out of six observations, only in two cases, namely, exports of palm kernels from Nigeria and Sierra Leone, did the producers' incomes vary to a smaller extent than export earnings. In contrast, in two other cases, namely, exports of cocoa from Ghana and Sierra Leone, the activities of

Table 4. Selected Developing Countries: Coefficients of Variations in Producers' Incomes and Export Earnings

	Period Covered	Coefficient of Variation in	
		Producers' incomes	Export earnings
Cocoa			
Ghana	1971–83	102	95
Nigeria	1972–81	32	31
Sierra Leone	1972–83	62	49
Coffee			
Sierra Leone	1972–83	59	59
Palm kernels			
Nigeria	1972–81	30	53
Sierra Leone	1972–83	45	59

Sources: Publications of marketing organizations, central banks, statistical bureaus, and other official agencies.

[38]It does not take into account the impact of the STABEX, the scheme to stabilize export earnings between the EC and the ACP (African, Caribbean, and Pacific) countries because the compensation under the scheme, which is in the form of grants for most of the countries covered here, accrues directly to the budget and not to the stabilization fund or to producers.

the marketing agencies destabilized producers' incomes. In the remaining two cases, stabilization schemes seemed to have had no impact.

The stabilization of producers' prices for these commodities was financed by means of formal export duties accruing to the marketing agencies in some of these countries and, more important, by way of implicit export taxes in the form of the differential between export prices received by these agencies and the amount paid to growers. Table 3 sets out such differentials with respect to these commodities exported, in the form of the ratio of average producer prices to export prices realized over extended periods of time. Although the ratios incorporate the distribution costs incurred by these agencies, one can still infer from them that the agencies absorb an inordinately large proportion of export receipts, ranging from 8 percent on palm kernels exported from Nigeria to 67 percent on groundnuts exported from Senegal. Insofar as not all of the revenues collected by the marketing agency are distributed to producers over time, they represent the tax implicit in the administration of the scheme. The figures in Table 3 also suggest that in Papua New Guinea the producers of coffee, cocoa, and copra have been subsidized by the Government.

IV. Conclusions

Two major conclusions can be derived. First, most of the developing countries used as illustration in this chapter seem to be overtaxing exports of the selected commodities. This becomes particularly apparent when the high implicit export taxes prevalent in many of these countries are also taken into account. The overtaxation of exports is also suggested by the operation of commodity stabilization schemes that, as indicated above, markedly reduce the present value of revenue to producers without similarly reducing riskiness. Hence, the observed levels of export taxation cannot, in general, be justified on grounds of the country optimal export duty argument or based on commodity stabilization. Second, the estimates made here show that the overtaxation of exports of certain commodities may have reduced substantially the level of exports of these commodities for the majority of the countries under study. It also seems to have reduced the level of foreign exchange earnings in most of the cases analyzed.

The main policy recommendation that emerges is that lowering the explicit and implicit levels of export taxation would be advisable not only from a supply-side perspective but also from the point of view of economic efficiency. Over the short and medium runs, however, the existence of market imperfections, introduced by both commodity agreements and protectionism imposed by industrial countries, could well preclude exporting countries from benefiting from the supply-side effects of lowering export taxes and expanding their exports;[39] at the same time government revenues would be lowered.

The ensuing loss of government revenue, in most cases, may turn out to be a major obstacle in lowering export taxes. Many of the developing countries have few alternative sources of revenue, given the difficulties that could be encountered in the administration of more sophisticated, but less distortive, tax systems. It should be mentioned that many of the countries under review could reduce effective levels of taxation and promote exports without losing revenue (and in a few cases even gaining revenue), if the implicit (nonrevenue-yielding) export duties were transformed into formal (revenue-yielding) export taxes. Furthermore, in many instances the reduction of export duties could be undertaken along with the devaluation of the exchange rate, in which case the impact of lowering the tax rates on tax revenue would be reduced and could even lead to an increase in government revenue.

ANNEX

Levels and Structure of Export Duties in Developing Countries

Export taxes exist in 71 developing countries, as shown in Table 5, and are levied on a wide range of primary commodities. In 29 developing countries, export tax revenue constitutes more than 1 percent of GDP and, with some minor exceptions, over 10 percent of the total tax revenue (Table 6). This Annex will, therefore, focus on the levels and structure of export taxes in these 29 developing countries only. In most cases, the export tax revenue is derived from one or two commodities that feature prominently in the exports of these countries. Coffee is the most widely taxed commodity and is the most important source of export tax revenue in 13 of the 29 countries listed in Table 6. Furthermore, beverage crops, which comprise coffee, tea, and cocoa, are the most important source of tax revenue in 17 of the 29 countries under review. Other export commodities commonly taxed are rice, sugar, copra, bananas, groundnuts, palm kernels, cotton, rubber, wood, bauxite, tin, phosphates, copper, and petroleum.

Levels and Structure of Export Taxation

To analyze the level of export taxes and to make comparisons across countries, the section examines three different indicators.

[39]See Golub and Finger (1979) who discuss the impact of protectionism and taxation on the world commodity market.

Table 5. Developing Countries: Significance of Export Taxes

	GNP Per Capita, Around 1980	Period[1]	Ratio of: Total tax to GDP	Export duties to GDP	Export duties to total tax	Export duties to total exports
	(In U.S. dollars)			*(In percent)*		
Gabon	3,420	1974–76	20.69	0.99	5.34	1.49
Bahamas	2,770	1977–79	16.36	0.32	1.95	...
Uruguay	2,620	1980–82	20.98	—	0.01	0.02
Argentina	2,590	1979–81	14.11	0.17	1.25	2.62
Brazil	2,160	1979–81	17.10	0.32	1.84	4.35
Mexico	1,980	1979–81	14.29	2.56[2]	17.71[2]	32.01
Panama	1,730	1979–81	21.03	0.40	1.88	4.07
Fiji[3]	1,650	1979–81	18.77	0.44	2.34	2.22
Seychelles	1,580	1975–77	19.22	0.14	0.72	...
Malaysia	1,580	1979–81	22.82	4.40	19.32	8.43
Syrian Arab Rep.	1,480	1979–81	9.96	0.28	2.76	1.84
Paraguay	1,410	1979–81	10.10	0.07	0.66	0.45
Costa Rica	1,390	1979–81	16.95	2.04	12.07	...
Tunisia	1,260	1979–81	24.66	0.28	1.12	1.02
Colombia	1,260	1977–79	10.96	1.47	13.30	12.01
Côte d'Ivoire	1,110	1980	20.65	2.30	11.15	7.69
Ecuador	1,100	1979–81	10.49	0.40	3.95	1.84
Jamaica	1,090	1975–77	23.09	6.79[4]	29.27[4]	0.82
Peru	1,080	1980–82	17.19	1.66	9.44	8.65
Mauritius	1,080	1979–81	19.21	2.85	14.78	9.00
Guatemala	1,080	1979–81	9.42	1.50	15.85	...
Congo	880	1980	26.87	0.07	0.27	0.13
Nigeria	870	1976–78	19.78	0.01	0.04	...

Table 5 (*concluded*). Developing Countries: Significance of Export Taxes

	GNP Per Capita, Around 1980	Period[1]	Ratio of			
			Total tax to GDP	Export duties to GDP	Export duties to total tax	Export duties to total exports
Morocco	830	1979–81	21.57	0.28	1.31	2.00
Papua New Guinea	780	1979–81	17.78	0.45	2.62	1.30
Nicaragua	760	1978–80	14.75	0.56	3.29	. . .
Cameroon	730	1980–82	21.50	1.59	8.75	7.48
Vanuatu	715	1982–84	. . .	. . .	10.14	6.13
Philippines	710	1979–81	11.18	0.20	1.75	1.30
El Salvador	670	1980–82	11.18	2.69	24.06	. . .
Thailand	670	1980–82	12.71	0.38	3.00	1.92
Grenada	650	1975–77	19.68	3.29	17.00	. . .
Swaziland	650	1978–80	26.07	2.02	7.76	. . .
Western Samoa	574	1983–85	26.24	3.35	11.76	13.49
Bolivia	570	1980–82	6.24	0.04	0.62	0.24
Honduras	560	1979–81	13.50	2.42	17.94	0.82
Egypt	550	1977–79	27.80	0.34	1.11	. . .
Guyana	520	1985	34.37	0.34	1.00	0.74
Liberia	500	1979–81	22.70	0.14	0.63	0.23
Solomon Islands	490	1983–85	21.33	4.13	19.25	7.79
Lesotho	470	1975–77	19.92	0.16	0.82	2.12
Indonesia	450	1979–81	20.18	0.66	3.39	. . .
Yemen Arab Rep.	430	1979–81	18.02	—	0.01	0.33
Senegal	420	1978–80	20.56	0.69	3.41	1.87
Mauritania	400	1977–79	16.64	0.11	0.67	0.47
Ghana	390	1980–82	6.04	1.01	13.49	11.21
Kenya	390	1979–81	20.63	0.18	0.85	0.88

Sudan	360	1978-80	11.40	0.38	3.21	5.23
Togo	350	1978-80	26.70	1.27	4.71	4.65
Madagascar	350	1972-73	15.52	0.93	6.01	. . .
Pakistan	310	1979-81	12.96	0.19	1.49	1.13
Central African Rep.	310	1981-81	14.97	1.57	10.45	13.86
Sierra Leone	300	1979-81	15.18	1.65	10.93	10.21
Niger	300	1978-80	11.72	0.55	4.70	2.70
Benin	290	1977-79	16.33	0.29	1.77	. . .
Haiti	280	1980-82	10.16	0.95	9.53	. . .
Tanzania	270	1979-81	17.78	1.00	5.73	8.87
Sri Lanka	270	1979-81	19.27	6.25	31.99	23.05
Somalia	260	1976-78	19.65	0.38	1.96	2.62
India	230	1979-81	10.75	0.09	0.79	1.55
Rwanda	220	1978-80	11.13	2.88	25.42	33.03
Gambia, The	220	1976-78	14.64	1.50	10.36	. . .
Burundi	210	1979-81	11.94	1.41	11.19	15.94
Zaïre	200	1979-81	17.95	3.22	17.88	15.26
Burkina Faso	200	1978-80	13.29	0.43	3.26	. . .
Uganda	200	1980-82	2.09	0.67	28.24	68.53
Mali	190	1979-81	12.61	0.58	4.59	. . .
Nepal	140	1979-81	6.75	0.25	3.72	. . .
Bangladesh	130	1976-78	7.54	0.13	1.72	. . .
Ethiopia	130	1976-78	12.07	2.91	23.44	31.04
Chad	110	1974-76	9.33	0.77	8.37	0.13

Note: . . . = not available; — = negligible.

Sources: International Monetary Fund, *Government Finance Statistics Yearbook, 1984,* Vol. 8 (Washington), and *International Financial Statistics* (Washington), various issues; and Fund staff estimates.

[1]Tax data given in this table pertain to these years.

[2]Export taxes have been abolished and the corresponding revenue is raised through the transfer of profits by Petróleos Mexicanos (PEMEX).

[3]Export duty on sugar suspended since 1983.

[4]Includes production tax on bauxite.

Table 6. Selected Developing Countries: Significance of Export Taxes

	Ratio of Export Duties to GDP	Ratio of Export Duties to Total Taxes	Ratio of Export Tax Revenue to Exports	Main Taxable Commodities (Proportion of total exports)[1]
				(In percent)
Burundi	1.4	11.2	15.9	Coffee (88)
Cameroon	1.6	8.7	7.5	Coffee (16)
Central African Rep.	1.6	10.4	13.9	Coffee (31)
Colombia	1.5	13.3	12.0	Coffee (50)
Costa Rica	2.0	12.1	8.9	Coffee (27)
Côte d'Ivoire	2.3	11.1	7.7	Cocoa (29)
El Salvador	2.7	24.1	11.1	Coffee (57)
Ethiopia	2.9	23.4	31.0	Coffee (66)
Gambia, The	1.5	10.4	5.5	Groundnuts (54)
Ghana	1.0	13.5	11.2	Cocoa (71)
Grenada	3.3	17.0	7.6	Cocoa (41)
Guatemala	1.5	15.8	8.5	Coffee (30)
Haiti	1.0	9.5	9.9	Coffee (56)
Honduras	2.4	17.9	7.6	Coffee (24)
Jamaica	6.8	29.3	21.7	Bauxite-alumina (74)
Malaysia	4.4	19.3	8.4	Rubber (16)
Mauritius	2.8	14.8	9.0	Sugar (60)
Mexico	2.6	17.7	32.0	Petroleum (61)
Peru	1.7	9.4	8.6	Minerals (40)
Rwanda	2.9	25.4	33.0	Coffee (66)
Sierra Leone	1.6	10.9	10.2	Coffee (. . .)
Solomon Islands	4.1	9.8	7.8	Copra (21)
Sri Lanka	6.2	32.0	23.0	Tea (34)
Swaziland	2.0	7.8	. . .	Sugar (. . .)
Tanzania[2]	1.0	5.7	8.9	Various
Togo	1.3	4.7	4.6	Phosphates (29)
Vanuatu	. . .	10.1	6.1	Copra (47)
Western Samoa	3.4	11.8	13.5	Coconut products (66)
Zaïre	3.2	17.9	15.3	Copper (47)

Note: . . . = not available.

Sources: International Monetary Fund, *Government Finance Statistics Yearbook, 1984*, Vol. 8 (Washington), *International Financial Statistics* (Washington), various issues, and *International Financial Statistics: Supplement on Trade Statistics* (Washington, 1982); and respective countries' tax summaries.

[1]Represent an average of statistics available for three most recent years or part thereof, as shown in Table 5.

[2]Export duties on coffee, cotton, and sisal were abolished in early 1981.

First, Table 6 shows the ratio of export tax revenue to total exports for the 29 countries under analysis. The ratio varies from a high of 33 percent for Rwanda to a low of 4.6 percent for Togo and has an average level of 12.9 percent for the whole sample. Seventeen countries are below the average level and only five countries have a ratio exceeding 20 percent.

Second, export taxes are not necessarily payable on all exports, or at a uniform rate on all commodities. Even though the statutory rates can take the form of an ad valorem rate, a specific rate, or a composite rate, the composite (or sliding scale) rates are by far the most prominent form of duty, as can be seen from Table 7. Such composite tax rates take the form of a fixed amount of tax (i.e., basic tax) on up to a specified export price (i.e., floor price) and a progressively rising (sliding) rate of tax on successive increments in export price. With some minor exceptions, the sliding rate applies to the incremental value of export.[40] A specific rate is the least common form of export duties as it applies in only 6 of the 29 countries under review (Burundi, Cameroon, the Central African Republic, Honduras, Pakistan, and Western Samoa). To maintain their comparability with ad valorem and sliding scale tax rates, such specific rates are expressed in Table 7 in terms of an ad valorem equivalent derived on the basis of prevailing price levels of export commodities to which they apply. The table indicates that the statutory rates vary from a low of 1 percent on bananas in Costa Rica to a high marginal rate of 100 percent on coffee in Rwanda and Uganda.

Third, Table 8 (column 1) shows the effective rate of export tax for each commodity. This is measured as a ratio of tax revenue to total export value (f.o.b.) of that commodity. There is substantial variability by country and by type of commodity. Coffee, for instance, is taxed, on the average, at 17 percent; however, actual rates may range between a high of 25 percent in Tanzania to a low of 1 percent in Brazil. Cocoa is taxed at an average rate higher than that of coffee (20 percent); the actual rate, however, reaches 23 percent in Côte d'Ivoire. The average export tax rate for all commodities and all countries included in the first column of Table 8 is about 17 percent—somewhat higher than the ratio of export tax revenue to total exports shown in Table 6, since most countries tend to tax only the export of selected commodities.

Implicit Taxes on Exports

The second column in Table 8 shows the estimated implicit tax for some of the commodities. It is based on the estimation of the nominal protection coefficients (NPCs) of selected export commodities made by the World Bank (1981) and (1982), which takes into account "tariffs, quotas, and nontariff barriers that protect farmers as well as the impact of export taxes on restrictions that penalize

[40]A major exception is Ethiopia, where the sliding rate applies to the volume of export. Mauritius and Senegal apply a dual rate (a variant of sliding rate) under which the lower rate applies to small-scale producers in the former and to small shipments in the latter.

Table 7. Selected Developing Countries: Structure of Formal Taxes on Specific Commodities

	Type of Tax	Tax Base	Tax Rate (Ad Valorem or Equivalent)
			(In percent)
Coffee			
Burundi	Specific	Unit volume	8.0[1]
Cameroon	Specific	Unit volume	7.7
Central African Rep.	Ad valorem	Standard value (*valeur mercuriale*)	13.8[2]
	Specific	Unit volume	1.1[2]
Colombia	Ad valorem	Turnover value	9
Costa Rica	*Composite:*[3]		
	Basic: ad valorem	F.o.b. floor price	4
	Marginal: ad valorem	F.o.b. floor price	2.5–24.0
Côte d'Ivoire	Ad valorem	Standard value	23
El Salvador	Ad valorem	F.o.b. value	10–30
Ethiopia	*Composite:*		
	Basic: specific	Reference (or floor) price	2.9[4]
	Marginal: specific	Excess over it	9.2–34.9[4]
Guatemala	*Composite:*		
	Basic: ad valorem	F.o.b. floor price	0
	Marginal: ad valorem	Excess over it	20
Haiti	*Composite:*		
	Basic: specific	F.o.b. floor price	0
	Marginal: ad valorem	Excess over it	1–15
Honduras	*Composite:*		
	Basic: ad valorem	F.o.b. floor price	10
	Marginal: ad valorem	Excess over it	5–10
Kenya	*Composite:*		
	Basic	F.o.b. floor price	0
	Marginal: ad valorem	Excess over it	10–25
Papua New Guinea	Ad valorem	...	1.5–7.5
Rwanda	Customs: ad valorem	...	0–30
	Fiscal: ad valorem	...	0–100
Uganda	*Composite:*		
	Basic	F.o.b. floor price	0
	Marginal: ad valorem	Excess over it	100

Table 7 (*continued*). Selected Developing Countries: Structure of Formal Taxes on Specific Commodities

	Type of Tax	Tax Base	Tax Rate (Ad Valorem or Equiv-alent)
Cocoa			
Cameroon	Specific	Unit volume	9.9
Côte d'Ivoire	Ad valorem	Standard value *(valeur mercuriale)*	23
Ghana	*Composite:*		
	Basic: ad valorem	F.o.b. floor price	0
	Marginal	Excess over it	100
Grenada	*Composite:*		
	Basic: specific	F.o.b. floor price	7.1
	Marginal: ad valorem	Excess over it	20
Papua New Guinea	Ad valorem	. . .	1.5–7.5
Tea			
Kenya	*Composite:*		
	Basic	F.o.b. floor price	0
	Marginal: ad valorem	Excess over it	10–25
Sri Lanka	*Composite:*		
	Basic: specific	F.o.b. floor price	24.3
	Marginal: ad valorem	Excess over it	35
Sugar			
Mauritius	*Composite:*		
	Basic	Up to specified output of producer	0[5]
	Additional: ad valorem	Excess over it	12.3–23.6[5]
Swaziland	*Composite:*		
	Basic	Up to specified price paid to millers	0
	Marginal: ad valorem	Excess over it	50
Bananas			
Costa Rica	Ad valorem	F.o.b. value	1
Honduras	Specific	Unit volume	9.8

Table 7 (*continued*). Selected Developing Countries: Structure of Formal Taxes on Specific Commodities

	Type of Tax	Tax Base	Tax Rate (Ad Valorem or Equivalent)
Rice			
Pakistan	Specific (on *Basmati* rice)	F.o.b. price	8
	Ad valorem (on other)	F.o.b. price	30
Thailand	Ad valorem (tax)	Posted price of paddy	5
	Specific (premium)	F.o.b. price	5.4
Nutmeg			
Grenada	*Composite:*		
	Basic: specific	Floor price	12.3
	Marginal: ad valorem	Excess over it	20
Groundnuts			
Gambia, The	Ad valorem (on unshelled)	Sales contract price	8
	Ad valorem (on shelled)	Sales contract price	10
Groundnut oil			
Gambia, The	Ad valorem	Sales contract price	9
Senegal	. . .	. . .	0[6]
Palm oil			
Malaysia	*Composite (on unprocessed oil):*		
	Basic	Gazetted floor price	0
	Marginal	Excess over it	30–50
Solomon Islands	Ad valorem	F.o.b. value	10
Copra			
Papua New Guinea	Ad valorem	F.o.b. value	1.5–7.5
Philippines	Ad valorem	F.o.b. value	7.5
Solomon Islands	Ad valorem	F.o.b. value	15
Tanzania	Ad valorem	F.o.b. value	5

Table 7 (*continued*). Selected Developing Countries: Structure of Formal Taxes on Specific Commodities

	Type of Tax	Tax Base	Tax Rate (Ad Valorem or Equivalent)
Vanuatu	*Composite:*		
	Basic	Specified f.o.b. floor value	0
	Marginal	Excess over it	2–10
Western Samoa	Ad valorem	F.o.b. price over threshold	5
Coconut oil			
Western Samoa	Specific	Unit volume	7.3
Rubber			
Malaysia	*Composite:*		
	Basic	Gazetted price	0
	Marginal: ad valorem	Gazetted price	20–50[7]
Cotton			
Chad	Fiscal duty: ad valorem	Standard value (*valeur mercuriale)*	8
	Statistical tax: ad valorem	F.o.b. value plus fiscal duty	6
Pakistan	Ad valorem	F.o.b. value of raw cotton	10
Sudan	Ad valorem	F.o.b. value of cottonseed	15[8]
Syrian Arab Rep.	Ad valorem	F.o.b. value of cotton	15
Tanzania	*Composite:*		
	Basic	Unit price of lint	10[9]
	Marginal: ad valorem	Excess of unit price of lint	0–30[9]
Wood			
Gabon	Ad valorem	F.o.b. value	9–38[10]
Philippines	Ad valorem	F.o.b. value	20
Tanzania	Ad valorem	F.o.b. value	5
Copper			
Zaïre	Export tax: ad valorem	Sales value (net)[11]	40
	Surtax: ad valorem	Excess over floor sales value	10
	Statistical tax	F.o.b. export value[12]	1–10
	Turnover tax	Bank deposits of export proceeds	7

Table 7 (*concluded*). Selected Developing Countries: Structure of Formal Taxes on Specific Commodities

	Type of Tax	Tax Base	Tax Rate (Ad Valorem or Equivalent)
Bauxite			
Jamaica	*Composite:*		
	Basic: ad valorem	Average realized floor price	6
	Marginal: ad valorem	Excess over it	3.6
Tin (ore and concentrates)			
Malaysia	Basic	Gazetted floor price	0
	Marginal: ad valorem	Excess over it	20–50
Phosphates			
Senegal	Ad valorem	Size of shipment	2.5–5
Togo	Ad valorem	Administered price over f.o.b. price	17.1
Diamonds			
Sierra Leone	Ad valorem	F.o.b. value	3

Note: . . . = not available.

Sources: Respective countries' tax summaries, most current versions available.

[1]Comprises separate levies for ordinary budget, extraordinary budget, and for development projects.

[2]Export taxes consist of regular export duty and turnover and quality control taxes which apply at ad valorem rates and a special levy which applies at a specific rate.

[3]Comprises taxes collected on the net income of sales to the coffee processing plant and on exports but not some nominal taxes collected for the Coffee Institute.

[4]Basic tax consists of turnover tax at the rate of 2 percent, ad valorem equivalent of the specific rate of coffee cess (at reference prices prevailing in 1982/83) of 1.9 percent, and surtax at zero rate on specified reference (floor) prices. Marginal rates are ad valorem equivalents of specific rates of duty (also based on 1982/83 prices).

[5]A flat rate of 10 percent on molasses.

[6]No formal export taxes but a separate price stabilization levy applies.

[7]Additional replanting and research cess are payable.

[8]Suspended since the 1979/80 crop season.

[9]Abolished since 1981.

[10]Comprises export duty (0.5–22 percent), turnover tax (2 percent on okoumé wood), reforestation tax (1–3.5 percent), timber felling tax (0.1–5 percent), stamp tax (5 percent), and an ad valorem equivalent of several other imposts, such as the chamber of commerce and public works levies and the national unity tax, at specific rates on unit volume.

[11]Net of marketing costs, export tax, and statistical tax.

[12]Net of export duties.

Table 8. Selected Developing Countries: Estimated Implicit Export Tax Levels by Commodity

(In percent)

	Formal Export Tax[1] 1979-81	Total Implicit and Formal Export Tax[2] 1980-81
Coffee		
Brazil	1	59
Côte d'Ivoire	23	64
El Salvador	16	47
Honduras	15	32
Tanzania	25	41
Togo	20	77
Cocoa		
Côte d'Ivoire	23	62
Ghana	18	60
Togo	16	77
Rubber		
Thailand	10	40
Bananas		
Honduras	11	29
Cotton		
Sudan	15	40
Rice		
Brazil	. . .	40
Thailand	23	40

Sources: International Monetary Fund, *Government Finance Statistics Yearbook* (Washington), various issues, and *International Financial Statistics* (Washington), various issues; and World Bank, *Accelerated Development in Sub-Saharan Africa: An Agenda for Action* (New York: Oxford University Press, 1981), *World Development Report, 1981* (New York: Oxford University Press, 1981), and *World Development Report, 1982* (New York: Oxford University Press, 1982).

[1]Ratio of export tax to value of exports of the taxable commodity. This is called the formal export tax.

[2]Estimated in *World Development Report, 1981* and *World Development Report, 1982.* The sources of the estimation of rates of formal and implicit export taxes are different; therefore, the two columns may not be comparable. Estimated implicit tax is inclusive of the formal tax as indicated in the estimates of total export taxation made in *World Development Report, 1981* and *World Development Report, 1982.*

farmers."[41] To the extent that protection is also a function of the country's exchange rate, it is also included in the computation of NPCs.[42] Implicit tax data incorporate the effect of both formal export taxes and implicit export taxes. Even though information is incomplete, it is clear that implicit export taxes can substantially raise the total effective burden of export taxation, such that the average implicit rate on export is more than doubled when implicit export taxes are incorporated.

REFERENCES

Adams, F. Gerard, and Jere R. Behrman, *Econometric Models of World Agricultural Commodity Markets: Cocoa, Coffee, Tea, Wool, Cotton, Sugar, Wheat, Rice* (Cambridge, Massachusetts: Ballinger Publishing Co., 1976).

Aguirre, Carlos A., Peter S. Griffith, and M. Zühtü Yücelik, *Taxation in Sub-Saharan Africa, Part I: Tax Policy and Administration in Sub-Saharan Africa*, Occasional Paper No. 8 (Washington: International Monetary Fund, 1981).

Askari, Hossein, and John Thomas Cummings, "Estimating Agricultural Supply Response with the Nerlove Model: A Survey," *International Economic Review* (Osaka, Japan), Vol. 18 (June 1977), pp. 257–92.

Baldwin, William L., *The World Tin Market: Political Pricing and Economic Competition* (Durham, North Carolina: Duke University Press, 1983).

Behrman, Jere R., *International Commodity Agreements: An Evaluation of the UNCTAD Integrated Commodity Programme*, Monograph No. 9 (Washington: Overseas Development Council, 1977).

Booth, Anne, "The Economic Impact of Export Taxes in ASEAN," *Malayan Economic Review* (Singapore), Vol. 25 (April 1980), pp. 36–61.

Corden, W.M., *Trade Policy and Economic Welfare* (Oxford: Clarendon Press, 1974).

Davis, Jeffrey M., "The Economic Effects of Windfall Gains in Export Earnings, 1975–78" (unpublished, International Monetary Fund, February 29, 1980).

Gately, Dermot, "A Ten-Year Retrospective: OPEC and the World Oil Market," *Journal of Economic Literature* (Nashville, Tennessee), Vol. 22 (September 1984), pp. 1100–14.

Golub, Stephen S., and J.M. Finger, "The Processing of Primary Commodities: Effects of Developed-Country Tariff Escalation and Developing-Country Export Taxes," *Journal of Political Economy* (Chicago), Vol. 87 (June 1979), pp. 559–77.

[41]World Bank (1982, p. 48).

[42]NPCs do not, however, incorporate the impact of subsidies on inputs, such as fertilizers, seeds, insecticides, water, fuel, transport, storage, and farm machinery, which are extended to producers in various forms, including the exemption from relevant taxes (import and excise duties, sales tax, etc.), fixed prices which do not fully reflect the cost, and preferential interest rates on loans to producers.

Goode, Richard, *Government Finance in Developing Countries* (Washington: Brookings Institution, 1984).

———, George E. Lent, and P.D. Ojha, "Role of Export Taxes in Developing Countries," *Staff Papers*, International Monetary Fund (Washington), Vol. 13 (November 1966), pp. 453-501.

Hart, Albert G., "Taxation in the Management of Primary Commodity Markets," in *Taxation and Development*, ed. by Nian-Tzu Wang (New York: Praeger, 1976).

Helleiner, Gerald K., "The Fiscal Role of the Marketing Boards in Nigerian Economic Development, 1947-61," *Economic Journal* (London), Vol. 74 (September 1964), pp. 582-610.

——— (1966a), "Marketing Boards and Domestic Stabilization in Nigeria," *Review of Economics and Statistics* (Cambridge, Massachusetts), Vol. 48 (February 1966), pp. 69-78.

——— (1966b), *Peasant Agriculture, Government, and Economic Growth in Nigeria* (Homewood, Illinois: Richard D. Irwin, Inc., 1966).

International Monetary Fund, *Government Finance Statistics Yearbook, 1984*, Vol. 8 (Washington, 1984).

———, *International Financial Statistics Yearbook, 1984* (Washington, 1984).

———, *International Financial Statistics: Supplement on Trade Statistics* (Washington, 1982).

Johnson, Harry G., "The Gain from Exploiting Monopoly or Monopsony Power in International Trade," *Economica* (London), Vol. 35 (May 1968), pp. 151-56.

———, "Commodities: Less Developed Countries' Demands and Developed Countries' Response," in *The New International Economic Order: The North-South Debate*, ed. by Jagdish N. Bhagwati (Cambridge: Massachusetts: MIT Press, 1977).

Labys, W., and J. Hunkeler, "Survey of Commodity Demand and Supply Elasticities," United Nations Conference on Trade and Development, Research Memorandum No. 48 (unpublished, March 19, 1974).

Mussa, Michael, "Tariffs and the Distribution of Income: The Importance of Factor Specificity, Substitutability, and Intensity in the Short and Long Run," *Journal of Political Economy* (Chicago), Vol. 82 (November/December 1974), pp. 1191-1203.

Newbery, David M.G., and Joseph E. Stiglitz, *The Theory of Commodity Price Stabilization: A Study in the Economics of Risk* (Oxford: Clarendon Press, 1981).

Okonkwo, Ubadigbo, "Export Taxes on Primary Products in Developing Countries: The Taxation of Cocoa Exports in West Africa" (unpublished, International Monetary Fund, November 29, 1978).

Panayotou, Theodore, "OPEC as a Model for Copper Exporters: Potential Gains and Cartel Behavior," *Developing Economies* (Tokyo), Vol. 17 (June 1979), pp. 203-19.

Prest, Alan R., *Public Finance in Underdeveloped Countries* (London: Weidenfeld and Nicholson, 2nd ed., 1972).

Repetto, Robert, "Optimal Export Taxes in the Short and Long Run, and an Application to Pakistan's Jute Export Policy," *Quarterly Journal of Economics* (Cambridge, Massachusetts), Vol. 86 (August 1972), pp. 396–406.

Singh, Shamser, and others, *Coffee, Tea and Cocoa: Market Prospects and Development/Lending* (Baltimore: Johns Hopkins University Press, 1977).

Tanzi, Vito, "Export Taxation in Developing Countries: Taxation of Coffee in Haiti," *Social and Economic Studies* (Kingston, Jamaica), Vol. 25 (March 1976), pp. 66–76.

———, "Quantitative Characteristics of the Tax Systems of Developing Countries," in *The Theory of Taxation for Developing Countries*, ed. by David Newbery and Nicholas Stern (New York: Oxford University Press, 1987).

Tolley, George S., Vinod Thomas, and Chung Ming Wong, *Agricultural Price Policies and the Developing Countries* (Baltimore: Johns Hopkins University Press, 1982).

Valles, Jean Paul, *The World Market for Bananas, 1964–72: Outlook for Demand, Supply, and Prices* (New York: Praeger, 1968).

World Bank, *Accelerated Development in Sub-Saharan Africa: An Agenda for Action* (New York: Oxford University Press, 1981).

———, *Commodity Trade and Price Trends* (Washington, 1983).

———, *Commodity Trade and Price Trends* (Washington, 1986).

———, *World Development Report, 1981* (New York: Oxford University Press, 1981).

———, *World Development Report, 1982* (New York: Oxford University Press, 1982).

12

Limitations of the Role of Tax Policy in Economic Development

Parthasarathi Shome

The role of taxation and associated incentives in development is one piece of a large puzzle. Tax incentives may assume importance if tax policy is seen to play an instrumental role in development. Tax policy, in turn, may have perceptible ramifications on the savings rate and, therefore, on investment in the economy which, in the traditional literature, is the king-pin in an economy's development. There have, however, been other "structural positions" regarding the force behind or limiting development where natural resources are not a constraint. These are (1) the inadequacy of export markets due to protectionism abroad in the case of countries with a high degree of dependence on trade; (2) "investment" (even though this is treated as current expenditure by economists) in health, education, and other social infrastructure; (3) population control in countries such as India and China, or the lack of a large population (i.e., the smallness of market size) in others; (4) the role of appropriate technology, that is, the choice of techniques; and (5) the role of agriculture (e.g., land reform, extension services, innovation) independent of the effects of savings and investment. Therefore, in our attempt to study the effects of taxation on output—growth and development—we need to go back to the drawing board to see where taxation fits into the development picture and how important it is to the development process. Since the role of taxation is inherently linked with that of savings, this chapter begins by reviewing the treatment of savings in the development literature and then contrasts and compares it with the role of other measures of development. This is not to belittle the role of fiscal policy in economic development but to gauge it more comprehensively and to better understand its possibilities and limitations.

A perusal of the postwar literature reveals that, while the proponents of savings as a vehicle of growth were in the forefront of the discussions on growth, issues such as the role of economic infrastructure and social dynamics in the development process were being raised at the same time, even though the latter became more fashionable in the 1970s. At times the traditionalist view—savings and investment—of the development literature is perceived as an alternative to the structuralist view—financial intermediation, social infrastructure, population pressure, agricultural reform and adoption of modern technology, and factor-substitution problems. At other times, their roles are cast as complementary, for example, a better financial structure or a more educated public aiding in the savings performance of the economy. Whether treated as substitutes or complements, tax policy emerges as a modus operandi for the various tenets of development. Section I discusses the different factors that have been cast as instrumental in the development process and Section II assesses the role of tax policy in affecting these factors. Section III offers some concluding remarks.

I. The Determinants of Development

The savings literature is inherently connected with issues of external economies and of surplus labor and labor productivity, problems which are related to those of sectoral factor proportions. The issue of surplus labor—removal of a laborer from a peasant economy does not diminish productivity—is usually set against the backdrop of a lack of sufficient capital for growth. The right technique of production, that is, the right combination of labor and capital, therefore, assumes importance in the debate on the determinants of development. Among the seminal works in this area are those of Lewis (1954), Eckaus (1955), and Sen (1960) for the factor-proportions problem[1] and for the implication of a labor surplus on an economy's development, and those of Rosenstein-Rodan (1943), Scitovsky (1954), and Bator (1958) for the effects of external economies and for the need for additional investment to internalize them.

Immediately, savings—and, consequently, investment—rise in significance in that savings form the scarce factor of production. Improved savings performance thus becomes the vehicle of growth since investment follows savings. Much of the related literature derives from Harrod (1939) and Domar's (1946) early formulations of the relationship between savings and growth. The Harrod-Domar framework emphasizes the relationship

[1]These issues are inextricably linked with the "structural" feasibility or infeasibility of capital-labor substitutability—as posed by more recent literature—and are, therefore, addressed in this context, below.

between the savings rate and the growth rate of an economy by stipulating that, in an economy with v as the capital-output ratio and s as the savings rate, a unit of capital, K, produces $1/v$ units of output Y, of which s/v is saved, that is, the rate of growth of capital stock. This is also the rate of growth of output g, since the capital-output ratio is kept constant.[2]

While investment determines the rate of growth in the early literature, later literature sees the conversion of savings to investment as a possible bottleneck for development in the forms of external as well as domestic structural rigidities. For example, investment goods may have, necessarily, a foreign exchange component. In the event of foreign exchange difficulties arising from export and import inelasticities, a country may be faced with a "foreign exchange gap" even when its "savings-investment gap" is closed. External constraints in the form of foreign exchange to transform domestic savings into investment, of which imported capital goods are an integral part, are considered by Chenery and Strout (1966), Joshi (1967), Atkinson (1969), and Nelson (1970) among others. The foreign exchange constraint is also caused by the nature of the primary commodities exported—tea, coffee, cocoa, jute—usually represented by inelastic supplies so that their price responsiveness is limited and by various forms of protectionism against imports of light manufactured goods.

Domestic constraints on growth have several sources. First, as Nurkse (1953) points out, the problem in many developing countries is not a shortage of savings, but the limited size of the market leading to low investment: "Many articles that are in common use in the United States can be sold in a low-income country in quantities so limited that a machine working only a few days or weeks can produce enough for a whole year's consumption" (p. 7). This problem of limitation is linked not only with the low standard of living in many a populous developing country but also with the low absorptive capacity of those developing countries that are sparsely populated.

Second, investment in machinery that produces consumer goods is seen as a leakage from the long-run rate of growth by Mahalanobis (1953) and other "planner" economists. In other words, varying the composition of capital stock—in its respective uses as producing consumption or investment goods—provides an extra handle to attain higher growth rates. Investment in the production of consumption goods that cannot be decreased, therefore, limits growth.

Third, the difficulties in the transfer of technology from developed to developing countries are seen to reveal the insufficiencies of savings for development. Bruton (1955), in a review of the Harrod-Domar models in

[2]See Sen (1970, pp. 9–14).

the context of developing countries, writes, "In the literature on economic development . . . emphasis is always placed on the need for more and more capital. This is surely correct and was never a secret. It would appear, however, that, though more capital is a necessary condition for speeding up the rate of development, it is not a sufficient condition. . . . There is no reason at all to assume that [modern] technology . . . can be bodily transferred to other countries" (pp. 335–36).

Fourth, the conversion of domestic savings or potential savings to investment is seen to be arrested due to the lack of adequate financial institutions by Patrick (1966), Gurley and Shaw (1967), Goldsmith (1969), McKinnon (1973), and others. Gurley and Shaw (1967) emphasize four "technologies" for savings mobilization and allocation: self-finance, taxation, debt-asset ratio, and foreign aid. Each technology has a yield and a cost component, the net yield being its ability to raise savings and investment, the economy's capital stock and, thus, the flow of consumption. While they treat all of the technologies as substitutes, they assert that, in each phase of development, an economy has an optimal combination of savings-investment technologies, there being no optimal combination across space and over time. Patrick (1966) emphasizes the role of financial policy in encouraging savers to shift from tangible to financial assets and also in increasing savings, investment, and production. He calls this an approach of "supply-lending finance" where financial institutions are established and instruments created even before the emergence of a perceptible demand for them in an effort to stimulate growth. Growth is thus cast as a direct result of an efficient financial system, whose success requires government participation and innovation as well as public confidence.

The literature since the 1970s focuses more on the role of government in the development of the financial sector, for example, in Tanzi (1976), Bhatt and Meerman (1978), and Von Pischke and others (1983). Tanzi (1976), for example, states, "It would certainly be desirable for the developing countries to have financial institutions that worked smoothly and efficiently to promote economic development. Unfortunately, many developing countries . . . do not have the benefits of such institutions. . . . There is then a particular and rather obvious role that the government of these countries can perform" (p. 911). Bhatt and Meerman (1978) continue in the same vein by bringing attention to the role of the central bank in the development of the financial sector. Emphasizing that the function of a sound financial structure is to improve the mobility of financial resources and that innovations in financial structure are at least as important for development as those relating to the production structure, they identify the central bank as the agency that should carry the responsibility for promoting a sound financial structure. Von Pischke and others (1983) have brought together a number of essays testifying to the importance of the role of "financial markets in rural areas, to their performance, structure, institutions, operations, costs, and the nature of their services to rural people" (p. 5). To conclude, the ramifications of having a sound financial structure as an economy progresses along its path of development have been seen to be significant since at least the 1960s.

Other scholars such as Myint (1954), Myrdal (1968), Haq (1971), and Meier (1976) differentiate between concepts of growth and development, and expenditures in areas traditionally perceived as consumption, such as health and education, are perceived as causal factors in the development process, most notably by Streeten (1967). Thus, development is perceived by them as a conglomeration of policy objectives comprising an increase in real per capita income sustained over a long time, pari passu with a minimally acceptable structure of distribution (such that no one is below a clearly defined poverty line), attained through a process that generally increases social welfare. Associated with these concerns, infrastructure in education, social services, health, and other issues under comprehensive phrases such as "minimum needs strategy" and "human resource development" are emphasized.

In this broader context of development, additional "structural" factors in the development process may be listed. First, population has been perceived as a leading determinant of development. In the postwar literature this is addressed by Clark (1953), Ohlin (1967), Walsh (1970), and Chandrasekhar (1972) and later by Hauser (1979) and Birdsall (1980). Among demographers, the accelerating rate of world population growth —especially in developing countries—is seen as the one basic impediment to a nation's progress since population strains an economy's resources to the hilt. Countering this proposition is the argument that population growth makes market expansions possible. Thus, population growth during the modern era has both positive and negative influences on economic development: China, the country with the largest population in the world, has modified its population policy significantly over the years, stressing, relaxing, and once again stressing population control in recent years, as reported by Coale (1981) and others. In conclusion, the pressure of population on a country's economic performance cannot be denied. In countries with high population densities, the economic game may be reduced to one of perennially catching up with population growth.

Second, the impact of the agricultural sector on development is a much discussed topic. It cannot be adequately covered here except by noting certain benchmark trends.[3] While in the 1950s some, like Viner (1953) and

[3]The authors cited here certainly do not comprise an exhaustive list of those who have addressed these issues.

Lewis (1954), envisage the agricultural sector as important, most economists, including these two, also perceive it as a means for industrialization. In the 1960s, however, agriculture is assigned a direct role in development (Eicher and Witt (1964)). It begins to be realized that the squeeze on agriculture in the 1950s has had negative ramifications for domestic demand as well as for exports during the 1960s. By the late 1960s, agricultural development becomes congruous with the concept of "development from below," and the literature of the 1970s, for example, Yudelman and others (1971), Lele (1975), Benor and Harrison (1977), Singh (1979), and Berry and Cline (1979), focuses on land reform, extension work, technological change and innovation and the like. The relevance of agricultural incomes is reflected in the concern for the agricultural and nonagricultural-industrial terms of trade, predictably resulting in inconclusive debates through the 1970s and 1980s. As in the case of rural-urban terms of trade, the debate over land reform has not yielded clear conclusions either.

In spite of the above-mentioned uncertainties, today the development of agriculture per se is understood to be a vital component in the improvement of the quality of rural life and, given that significant proportions of the population of developing countries remain rural, an independent determinant of development. Raising the rate of financial savings may often have little effect on an impermeable nonmonetized agrarian sector, and the latter's welfare may need to be addressed directly if the goal is the development of the country as a whole.

Third, a considerable portion of the development literature, for example, Acharya (1975) and Rhee and Westphal (1977), considers the question of relative factor-substitutability in production functions—its responsiveness to price signals—as a structural problem, employing linear programming techniques in the analysis of the modern sector of developing economies. If labor and capital were easily substitutable, population would not be such a limiting factor, but empirical evidence on the factor-substitution question is certainly not conclusive. The econometric approach, usually measuring the factor-substitution elasticity between labor and capital, is often termed as casual empiricism (Bhalla (1975), White (1978)). Little (1982), in a survey of the evidence on various country experiences, points out that low-income countries use more labor-intensive techniques compared with middle-income countries and very often use machinery that is obsolete in the latter. Therefore, he concludes that, where production is for export markets where both compete, production factors are substitutable for the same commodity. But this argument seems to be valid only when confined to goods that fit the argument.

In conclusion, one might say that the extent of factor-substitution possibilities in a developing economy depends on the pattern of its production.

During the 1950s and 1960s, when many of these countries achieved independence, a significant number of them opted for prestigious, capital-intensive projects in both the manufacturing and agricultural sectors. As a result, and in the absence of domestic technology, the difficulty with factor substitution was seen by many of them as structural, leading, in turn, to the belief that foreign exchange was the dominant gap in development, a consideration that we have addressed above. By the 1970s, however, the often minuscule returns from these unsuccessful programs re-educated these countries regarding shifting techniques and production structures, even if through the endurement of stresses and strains.

II. Tax Policy and the Determinants of Development

If a comprehensive concept of development includes raising the rates of saving and investment in order to increase output, raising social investment in health, education and welfare, streamlining the rate of population growth with the rate of accumulation of capital stock, and safeguarding a reasonable terms of trade for the agricultural sector such that the latter's growth is assured, the role of tax policy is automatically extended from one of aiding the first criterion to all the others as well. Indeed, under appropriate assumptions, tax policy can theoretically be a powerful instrument in targeting all of the above factors of development. Whether such assumptions hold in many developing countries then becomes the question to ponder. Below we summarize the possibilities for and limitations of tax policy as a means of affecting the above-mentioned components of development.

Among the various means by which a developing economy may increase its investment rate is taxation. By taxation, the government reserves a portion of the national resources for itself, often for capital construction projects, or offers it to the private sector for similar purposes. The Union of Soviet Socialist Republics has used a sizable turnover tax to finance capital formation. Japan, in its early development, has used a land tax for the same reason. Several low-income and middle-income countries—especially in South Asia and Latin America—have attempted to raise domestic savings through payroll taxes or compulsory social security schemes. While these endeavors have mostly been mired by inflation in the case of Latin America, they have been significantly successful in Asia—Malaysia, the Philippines, Singapore, and Sri Lanka—where provident and pension funds seem not only to not have affected voluntary savings (Datta and Shome (1981)) but have also made available to their governments long-term investment funds for development purposes, as the accumulated funds of these institutions have become the primary source of financing of public debt (Shome (1986)). Theoretically, they can also be used to maximize an economy's utility from consumption at an equilibrium factor proportion, that is, take an economy to its "golden path," with appropriate financing methods (Shome and Squire (1983)).

Apart from direct quantitative controls, tax policy has been used in attempts by developing countries to close their foreign exchange gaps through import tariffs, free trade zones, income tax incentives for export diversification, such as in the case of light manufacturing goods, or contrarily, export duties in the case of traditional primary exports with low elasticities of supply. Indeed, theoretically, export subsidies and import taxes can have the same effects as those of exchange rate policies since a 10 percent ad valorem subsidy on all exports matched by a 10 percent ad valorem duty on all imports has similar economic implications as a 10 percent devaluation, with one difference: the devaluation affects all items of the balance of payments, while the tax-subsidy mix affects only the mercantile items. Arguments that have been put forward in favor of a tax-subsidy mix are its selective nature and the lower inflationary pressure it generates.

Tax policy is utilized to encourage financial intermediation through special tax treatment of both dividends, to encourage the development of the stock market, and interest, including interest from banks, governments, housing authorities, and insurance institutions, as well as from unit trusts and the like. The role of fiscal policy, in general, as a complement to the development of the financial sector has already been discussed above. Tax policy, to change factor proportions, is also used widely through incentive packages including accelerated depreciation, income tax holidays, labor-utilization relief, deductions for research and development, and so on. Almost all developing countries boast a complex system of tax incentives, the ramifications of which are often difficult to trace through the economic system. Corporate tax incentives that tend to reduce the cost of capital and subsidize capital use exist side by side with labor-utilization relief that should encourage labor intensity, the net effect of the two often being intractable. However, tax policy usually remains the main tool in a country's cache of instruments in handling the factor-proportions problem.

Tax policy can similarly be used to affect the other factors of development. China now uses a heavy tax on married couples who have more than one child. India and several other developing countries also experimented with the same type of tax in the early 1970s by offering higher personal income tax breaks for smaller families, or by reducing the number of children for which tax credits and allowances are given. Thus, tax rates can be manipulated to make the choice between having and not having children more dependent on an opportunity cost that reflects an economic rather than a social cost.

The issue of a favorable treatment for agriculture in the literature on agricultural taxation has been much debated. Indeed, in the early literature, several economists have argued that agricultural taxation is necessary in developing countries to extract the agricultural surplus or for reasons of inter-sectoral equity. Gandhi (1966), for example, quantifies the "undertaxation" of Indian agriculture relative to other sectors. According to World Bank (1982), in the last two decades not only has the proportion of gross domestic product (GDP) accruing from the agricultural sector fallen sharply in developing countries but so have the output per worker and the differentials in outputs per worker between agricultural and nonagricultural sectors. This type of reasoning has again brought about arguments for rehabilitating the agricultural sector with the aid of tax-subsidy policies, for example, export duty removal and import duty exemptions for tractors, seeds, and fertilizers. It must be noted in this context that even the United States has long utilized direct subsidies to the farm sector for leaving land fallow or reducing the production of milk in order to assure a domestically acceptable terms of trade for this sector.

Tax and expenditure policy is, of course, the primary vehicle through which human resource development—social security, social welfare, education, nutrition—has been attempted. Many developed countries, especially those in Europe, have very high social expenditures in relation to GDP and the ratio has grown rapidly in recent years (Tanzi (1986)). Indeed, it has been argued that the huge deficits of European nations are now being caused primarily by social welfare coverage and that further taxation on this account is almost impossible (Mach (1979)). For developing countries, the use of tax policy to achieve the human welfare component of development is not yet exhausted. Countries such as Sri Lanka have demonstrated what can be achieved in terms of literacy and longevity when government fiscal policy takes these up as focal points of development, while others such as India have yet a long way to go.

Taxation has its limitations and difficulties, however. In general, the success of tax policy depends on four tenets: that everyone is covered by the tax regime, that the incidence of taxation is known, that the rate of the tax is adequate, and that behavior is affected solely by price. If the first criterion is not met, for example as is the case in most developing countries where the rural sector hardly pays any income tax, experimentation with higher marginal tax rates on families with large numbers of children could be expected to have rather limited results for the country as a whole since a high proportion of the population may be rural. If the second condition is not satisfied—tax incidence is difficult to determine with certainty—then the tax policy may yield results far removed from its objective. For example, if the corporate tax is passed on to labor, then an increase in the corporate tax rate may not reduce capital-intensity (Shome (1978)). So the question of incidence is quite important in issues of factor-substitution. Third, if the rate of tax is not high enough, its potency is reduced. For example, legislating an array of taxes with low rates may have a smaller overall impact than a single tax with a high rate where the objective is the same. Fourth, if behavior is price responsive but is also affected by other less observable and noneconomic determinants, then the use of tax policy—by affecting price—to modify behavior may be vitiated. Sending children—especially female—to school to receive primary education may not depend on whether it is free but on whether it is permitted by society.

Actual experience bears witness to all these concerns with respect to the exercise of tax policy. Taxes on the poor are limited by existing poverty. Taxes on the rich may affect savings adversely and are often difficult to institute politically. In primarily agricultural countries, tax collection is a major hurdle as farmers are difficult to tax and often, marketed surpluses may be small as a proportion of production. Similarly, the incidence of direct taxation is an issue that has remained unresolved through the decades. Finally, not much space needs to be devoted here to the issue of nonprice determinants of economic behavior since these are of greater concern to sociologists and anthropologists than to economists.

The limitations of tax policy may emerge from another direction. It is argued that if marginal tax rates are prohibitive, they may have detrimental effects on the rate of growth by truncating the rates of saving, investment, and labor supply. These concerns regarding the excessive use of tax policy have recently been revived under the banner of supply-side economics, which advocates the reduction of high marginal tax rates in order to release the forces of supply of savings, investment, and labor. As the supply of factors of production is purported to increase, output increases and so does the rate of growth. However, as Tanzi (1983) points out by citing the example of the United States, even if supply did respond to tax changes in the long run, tax policy by itself may not be able to yield supply-side effects in the face of noncomplementary changes in other policies, such as those relating to the monetary and financial sector. Also, whether or not tax policy affects marginal tax rates may be crucial to the success of tax policy from the supply-side point of view. Thus, while economists have to, and indeed, do assign a major role to tax policy in tackling development and growth, and sometimes successfully, it must be done with perspicacity.

III. Concluding Remarks

The above review, albeit selective, has attempted to put into perspective the role of the orthodox savings-investment strategy in the development process as a prior step to a study of the importance of fiscal policy since, traditionally, fiscal policy has been treated as an integral part of a composite orthodox strategy for development. In that endeavor, the chapter has reviewed some of the seminal works in the growth literature based on the effects of savings on growth, and forming the major building blocks in their application to the early development literature on surplus-labor economies. It then touched on the ensuing literature on the limitations of this strategy, such as the foreign exchange gap, the lack of an optimal financial structure as well as of economic and social infrastructure, the population explosion, the role of the agricultural as opposed to the industrial sector, and the difficulties with neoclassical assumptions of factor-substitution. Indeed, it is found that the literature has often treated financial development, infrastructure, and agricultural development as alternative "technologies" to development. Some economists have also emphasized the complementary roles that these elements can and need to play during the development process.

What emerges from this review for our ultimate purpose of the study of the effectiveness of tax policy is the following. Tax policy and, generally, fiscal policy form one component of the savings-investment strategy of development. There are ample views, however, in the literature on which route to take for development, the savings-investment strategy being only one among several or, at most forming a complement with other factors. The role of tax and fiscal policy, therefore, should be seen in this perspective as an atomistic part of a much larger whole. Before placing excessive reliance on tax and fiscal policy, therefore, it is important to bear in mind the relative position of tax and fiscal policy as a determinant of development. This is not to belittle the role of fiscal policy, however. Once we have a clearer impression of its limitations, we may be better able to form objectives and pursue goals to be addressed by tax and fiscal policy.

REFERENCES

Acharya, Shankar N., "Fiscal Financial Intervention, Factor Prices and Factor Proportions: A Review of Issues," *Bangladesh Development Studies* (Dhaka), Vol. 3 (October 1975), pp. 429–64.

Atkinson, A.B., "Import Strategy and Growth Under Conditions of Stagnant Export Earnings," *Oxford Economic Papers*, Vol. 21 (November 1969), pp. 325–38.

Bator, Francis M., "The Anatomy of Market Failure," *Quarterly Journal of Economics* (Cambridge, Massachusetts), Vol. 72 (August 1958), pp. 351–79.

Benor, Daniel, and James Q. Harrison, *Agricultural Extension: The Training and Visit System* (Washington: World Bank, 1977).

Berry, R. Albert, and William R. Cline, *Agrarian Structure and Productivity in Developing Countries* (Baltimore: Johns Hopkins University Press, 1979).

Bhalla, A.S., ed., *Technology and Employment in Industry: A Case Study Approach* (Geneva: International Labor Organization, 1975).

Bhatt, V.V., and Jacob Meerman, "Resource Mobilization in Developing Countries: Financial Institutions and Policies," *World Development* (Oxford), Vol. 6 (January 1978), pp. 45-64.

Birdsall, Nancy, "Population and Poverty in the Developing World," World Bank Staff Working Paper No. 404 (Washington, 1980).

Bruton, Henry J., "Growth Models and Underdeveloped Economies," *Journal of Political Economy* (Chicago), Vol. 63 (August 1955), pp. 322-36.

Chandrasekhar, S., *Infant Mortality, Population Growth, and Family Planning in India* (Chapel Hill: University of North Carolina Press, 1972).

Chenery, Hollis B., and Alan M. Strout, "Foreign Assistance and Economic Development," *American Economic Review* (Nashville, Tennessee), Vol. 56 (September 1966), pp. 679-733.

Clark, Colin, "Population Growth and Living Standards," *International Labour Review* (Geneva), Vol. 68 (August 1953), pp. 99-117.

Clower, Robert W., George Dalton, Mitchell Harwitz, and A.A. Walters, *Growth Without Development: An Economic Survey of Liberia* (Evanston: Northwestern University Press, 1966).

Coale, Ansley J., "Population Trends, Population Policy, and Population Studies in China," *Population and Development Review* (New York), Vol. 7 (March 1981), pp. 85-97.

Datta, Gautam, and Parthasarathi Shome, "Social Security and Household Savings: Asian Experience," *Developing Economies* (Tokyo), Vol. 19 (June 1981), pp. 143-60.

Domar, Evsey D., "Capital Expansion, Rate of Growth, and Employment," *Econometrica* (Evanston, Illinois), Vol. 14 (April 1946), pp. 137-47.

Eckaus, R.S., "The Factor Proportions Problem in Underdeveloped Areas," *American Economic Review* (Nashville, Tennessee), Vol. 45 (September 1955), pp. 539-65.

Eicher, Carl, and Lawrence Witt, eds., *Agriculture in Economic Development* (New York: McGraw-Hill, 1964).

Gandhi, V.P., *Tax Burden on Indian Agriculture* (Cambridge, Massachusetts: Harvard University Law School, 1966, mimeographed).

Goldsmith, R.W., *Financial Structure and Development* (New Haven: Yale University Press, 1969).

Gurley, John G., and E.S. Shaw, "Financial Structure and Economic Development," *Economic Development and Cultural Change* (Chicago), Vol. 15 (April 1967), pp. 257-68.

Haq, Mahbub ul, "Employment and Income Distribution in the 1970's: A New Perspective," *Pakistan Economic and Social Review* (Lahore), Vol. 9 (June-December 1971), pp. 1-9.

Harrod, R.F., "An Essay in Dynamic Theory," *Economic Journal* (London), Vol. 49 (March 1939), pp. 14-33.

Hauser, Philip M., ed., *World Population and Development: Challenges and Prospects* (New York: Syracuse University Press, 1979).

International Labor Office, "Investment Practice of Social Security Institutions in Developing Countries," Working Paper of the Social Security Department (Geneva, November 1983).

Joshi, Vijay, "Foreign Exchange Bottlenecks or Unwillingness to Save?" *Economic and Political Weekly* (Bombay), Vol. 2 (March 4, 1967), pp. 485-86.

Lele, Uma J., *The Design of Rural Development: Lessons from Africa* (Baltimore: Johns Hopkins University Press, 1975).

Lewis, W. Arthur, "Economic Development with Unlimited Supplies of Labour," *Manchester School of Economic and Social Studies*, Vol. 22 (May 1954), pp. 139-91.

Little, Ian M.D., *Economic Development: Theory, Policy and International Relations* (New York: Basic Books, 1982).

Mach, E.P., "Selected Issues on Health and Employment," *International Labour Review* (Geneva), Vol. 118 (March-April 1979), pp. 133-45.

Mahalanobis, P.C., "Some Observations on the Process of Growth of National Income," *Sankhya* (Calcutta), Vol. 12 (September 1953), pp. 307-12.

McKinnon, Ronald I., *Money and Capital in Economic Development* (Washington: Brookings Institution, 1973).

Meier, Gerald M., *Leading Issues in Economic Development* (New York: Oxford University Press, 3rd ed., 1976).

Myint, H., "An Interpretation of Economic Backwardness," *Oxford Economic Papers*, Vol. 6 (June 1954), pp. 132-63.

Myrdal, Gunnar, *Asian Drama: An Inquiry into the Poverty of Nations* (New York: Twentieth Century Fund, 1968).

Nelson, Richard R., "The Effective Exchange Rate: Employment and Growth in a Foreign Exchange-Constrained Economy," *Journal of Political Economy* (Chicago), Vol. 78 (May-June 1970), pp. 546-64.

Nurkse, Ragnar, "Some International Aspects of the Problem of Economic Development," *American Economic Review, Papers and Proceedings of the Sixty-Fourth Meeting of the American Economic Association* (Nashville, Tennessee), Vol. 42 (May 1952), pp. 571-83.

———, *Problems of Capital Formation in Underdeveloped Countries* (Oxford: B. Blackwell, 1953).

Ohlin, Goran, *Population Control and Economic Development* (Paris: Organization for Economic Cooperation and Development, 1967).

Patrick, Hugh T., "Financial Development and Economic Growth in Underdeveloped Countries," *Economic Development and Cultural Change* (Chicago), Vol. 14 (January 1966), pp. 174-89.

Rhee, Yung W., and Larry E. Westphal, "A Micro, Econometric Investigation of Choice of Technology," *Journal of Development Economics* (Amsterdam), Vol. 4 (September 1977), pp. 205-37.

Rosenstein-Rodan, P.N., "Problems of Industrialization of Eastern and South-Eastern Europe," *Economic Journal* (London), Vol. 53 (June-September 1943), pp. 202-11.

Scitovsky, Tibor, "Two Concepts of External Economies," *Journal of Political Economy* (Chicago), Vol. 62 (April 1954), pp. 143-51.

Sen, Amartya, *Choice of Techniques: An Aspect of the Theory of Planned Economic Development* (Oxford: B. Blackwell, 1960).

———, ed., *Growth Economics: Selected Readings* (Harmondsworth, England: Penguin, 1970).

Shaw, Edward S., *Financial Deepening in Economic Development* (New York: Oxford University Press, 1973).

Shome, Parthasarathi, "The Incidence of the Corporation Tax in India: A General Equilibrium Analysis," *Oxford Economic Papers*, Vol. 30 (March 1978), pp. 64-73.

———, ed., *Fiscal Issues in South-East Asia: Comparative Studies of Selected Economies* (Singapore: Oxford University Press, 1986).

———, and Lyn Squire, "Alternative Mechanisms for Financing Social Security," World Bank Staff Working Paper No. 625 (Washington, 1983).

Singh, Inderjit, "Small Farmers and the Landless in South Asia," World Bank Staff Working Paper No. 320 (Washington, 1979).

Streeten, Paul, "The Use and Abuse of Models in Development Planning," in *The Teaching of Development Economics: Its Position in the Present State of Knowledge*, ed. by Kurt Martin and John Knapp (London: Frank Cass, 1967).

Tanzi, Vito, "Fiscal Policy, Keynesian Economics and the Mobilization of Savings in Developing Countries," *World Development* (Oxford), Vol. 4 (October-November 1976), pp. 907-17.

———, "The Policy Lessons of Supply-Side Economics: A Very Personal Interpretation," paper presented at the Fifty-Third Annual Conference of the Southern Economic Association (Washington, November 1983, mimeographed).

———, "The Growth of Public Expenditure in Industrial Countries: An International and Historical Perspective" (unpublished, International Monetary Fund, February 11, 1986).

Viner, Jacob, *International Trade and Economic Development*, lectures delivered at the National University of Brazil (Oxford: Clarendon Press, 1953).

Von Pischke, J.D., Dale W. Adams, and Gordon Donald, eds., *Rural Financial Markets in Developing Countries: Their Use and Abuse* (Baltimore: Johns Hopkins University Press, 1983).

Walsh, B. Thomas, *Economic Development and Population Control: A Fifty-Year Projection for Jamaica* (New York: Praeger, 1970).

White, Lawrence J., "The Evidence on Appropriate Factor Proportions for Manufacturing in Less Developed Countries: A Survey," *Economic Development and Cultural Change* (Chicago), Vol. 27 (October 1978), pp. 27-59.

World Bank, *World Development Report, 1982* (New York: Oxford University Press, 1982).

Yudelman, Montague, Gavan Butler, and Ranadev Banerji, *Technological Change in Agriculture and Employment in Developing Countries* (Paris: Organization for Economic Cooperation and Development, 1971).

APPENDICES

APPENDIX I

Statistical Tables

Jitendra R. Modi, Somchai Richupan, and Chris Wu

Many of the statistical tables included in this Appendix were prepared in 1984 as background material for the research project and, therefore, cover published data readily available at that time. As the focus of the project was on direct taxes, most tables in the Appendix cover information relating to these taxes only.

List of Tables

Table A1. Selected Industrial and Developing Countries: Total Tax Revenue as Percentage of Gross Domestic Product, 1980–82

	1980	1981	1982	Average 1980–82
Industrial countries				
United States[1]	28.793	29.228	28.906	28.975
Canada[1]	31.854	34.071	34.733	33.553
Australia[1]	29.306	30.280	31.130	30.238
Japan	25.944	26.794	27.179	26.639
New Zealand[1]	30.933	32.136	33.143	32.071
Austria[1]	40.846	42.080	40.511	41.146
Belgium[1]	43.548	43.498	44.721	43.922
Denmark[1]	45.456	45.331	44.351	45.046
Finland[1]	33.026	34.749	34.434	34.070
France[1]	40.974	41.111	41.982	41.356
Germany, Fed. Rep. of[1]	39.413	39.253	39.373	39.346
Iceland	26.112	27.525	28.578	27.405
Ireland[1]	33.405	34.561	36.442	34.803
Italy	33.344	34.180	37.277	34.933
Luxembourg[1]	36.656	34.122	31.456	34.078
Netherlands	44.367	43.857	44.370	44.198
Norway[1]	46.166	47.720	46.947	46.944
Spain[1]	24.360	25.004	27.479	25.615
Sweden[1]	48.065	49.436	48.892	48.798
Switzerland[1]	30.304	30.110	30.529	30.314
United Kingdom[1]	34.532	35.588	38.271	36.131
Maximum				*48.798*
Minimum				*25.615*
Mean				*36.171*
Variance				*48.839*
Standard deviation				*6.989*
Number of observations				*21*
Developing countries				
Oil exporting countries				
Indonesia[1]	21.206	21.813	19.535	20.851
Iran, Islamic Rep. of[1]	7.257	9.111	8.146	8.171
Kuwait	3.027	3.590	3.266	3.294
Nigeria	25.254	23.323	19.840	22.806
Oman	10.762	13.096	11.407	11.755
Venezuela	21.926	30.054	23.135	25.038
Maximum				*25.038*
Minimum				*3.294*
Mean				*15.319*
Variance				*77.902*
Standard deviation				*8.826*
Number of observations				*6*

Table A1 *(continued).* Selected Industrial and Developing Countries: Total Tax Revenue as Percentage of Gross Domestic Product, 1980–82

	1980	1981	1982	Average 1980–82
Non-oil developing countries				
Africa				
Benin	13.245	15.457	15.977	14.893
Botswana	25.093	26.494	22.615	24.734
Burkina Faso	13.298	13.668	13.538	13.501
Burundi	12.586	11.743	14.220	12.850
Cameroon	15.530	15.549	16.061	15.713
Central African Rep.	12.411	12.282	13.540	12.744
Congo	19.812	30.877	27.733	26.141
Côte d'Ivoire	21.924	23.926	23.271	23.040
Djibouti	23.677	24.361	26.070	24.702
Ethiopia	15.325	15.303	15.400	15.343
Gabon	23.632	29.646	28.553	27.277
Gambia, The	19.242	16.774	16.158	17.391
Ghana	7.942	5.048	5.145	6.045
Kenya[1]	21.972	22.334	22.122	22.143
Lesotho	28.470	25.533	26.522	26.842
Liberia	20.778	23.452	27.241	23.824
Madagascar[1]	17.187	15.612	12.467	15.089
Malawi[1]	18.144	17.376	18.523	18.014
Mali	11.956	13.551	14.563	13.357
Mauritania	13.360	15.214	16.214	14.929
Mauritius[1]	19.840	19.349	18.068	19.086
Morocco	21.499	21.678	21.803	21.660
Niger	12.337	10.723	10.145	11.068
Rwanda	10.407	9.976	9.403	9.929
Senegal	21.959	19.903	19.621	20.494
Sierra Leone	14.764	15.392	11.433	13.863
Somalia	8.798	9.757	8.151	8.902
Swaziland	26.224	21.316	25.891	24.477
Tanzania	17.685	18.917	19.455	18.686
Togo	27.041	22.858	25.667	25.188
Tunisia[1]	24.105	24.971	26.324	25.134
Uganda	2.266	0.976	4.410	2.551
Zaïre	19.458	17.447	17.897	18.267
Zambia	23.143	21.550	21.589	22.094
Zimbabwe	19.313	22.816	27.263	23.131
Maximum				*27.277*
Minimum				*2.551*
Mean				*18.089*
Variance				*39.317*
Standard deviation				*6.270*
Number of observations				*35*

Table A1 *(continued)*. Selected Industrial and Developing Countries: Total Tax Revenue as Percentage of Gross Domestic Product, 1980–82

	1980	1981	1982	Average 1980–82
Asia				
Bangladesh	7.122	7.459	7.150	7.244
Burma	9.612	9.928	9.907	9.815
Fiji[1]	18.653	20.565	19.213	19.477
India[1]	15.447	16.181	16.154	15.927
Korea	15.588	15.736	16.131	15.818
Malaysia	24.191	23.361	21.356	22.969
Maldives	4.959	6.011	9.630	6.867
Nepal	6.565	7.478	7.331	7.124
Pakistan	13.157	13.286	12.732	13.058
Papua New Guinea	17.620	20.155	17.914	18.563
Philippines[1]	12.306	10.899	10.499	11.235
Singapore	17.319	18.395	19.626	18.447
Sri Lanka[1]	19.472	17.320	16.105	17.632
Thailand[1]	13.631	13.695	13.099	13.475
Maximum				*22.969*
Minimum				*6.867*
Mean				*14.118*
Variance				*26.245*
Standard deviation				*5.123*
Number of observations				*14*
Europe				
Cyprus	17.383	18.507	18.982	18.290
Greece[1]	27.602	26.442	32.270	28.771
Malta	27.633	27.716	27.077	27.475
Portugal	27.150	28.843	28.699	28.231
Romania[1]	12.554	12.971	12.083	12.536
Turkey	16.040	17.804	14.405	16.083
Maximum				*28.771*
Minimum				*12.536*
Mean				*21.898*
Variance				*50.585*
Standard deviation				*7.112*
Number of observations				*6*
Middle East				
Bahrain	3.563	3.900	4.339	3.934
Egypt	30.756	28.864	29.191	29.603
Israel[1]	47.434	46.912	53.084	49.144
Jordan	16.828	18.377	18.908	18.038
Syrian Arab Rep.	10.431	8.782	9.415	9.542
Yemen Arab Rep.	17.908	18.834	20.778	19.174
Maximum				*49.144*
Minimum				*3.934*
Mean				*21.572*

Table A1 ***(continued).*** **Selected Industrial and Developing Countries: Total Tax Revenue as Percentage of Gross Domestic Product, 1980–82**

	1980	1981	1982	Average 1980–82
Variance				*259.750*
Standard deviation				*16.117*
Number of observations				*6*
Western Hemisphere				
Argentina[1]	22.169	19.562	17.893	19.875
Bahamas	17.500	17.068	15.130	16.566
Barbados	25.034	24.069	25.339	24.814
Belize	21.170	21.575	21.487	21.411
Bolivia	7.052	7.554	4.296	6.301
Brazil[1]	22.836	23.022	24.558	23.472
Chile[1]	26.267	25.850	23.850	25.322
Colombia[1]	12.393	12.021	11.584	12.000
Costa Rica	16.737	16.894	16.699	16.777
Dominican Rep.[1]	11.165	10.765	8.931	10.287
Ecuador	11.867	10.269	10.508	10.881
El Salvador	11.095	11.590	10.740	11.142
Grenada	22.222	20.981	22.651	21.951
Guatemala[1]	10.569	9.588	9.096	9.751
Guyana	25.497	30.063	31.355	28.972
Haiti	9.275	8.851	12.583	10.236
Honduras	14.057	13.208	12.841	13.369
Jamaica	18.767	21.448	23.026	21.080
Mexico[1]	17.805	17.426	17.735	17.655
Nicaragua	19.295	20.957	22.638	20.963
Panama[1]	21.437	21.854	20.873	21.388
Paraguay	10.080	9.304	10.014	9.799
Peru	18.853	16.288	15.797	16.979
St. Lucia	26.358	25.866	27.585	26.603
St. Vincent	23.139	21.233	23.954	22.776
Trinidad and Tobago[1]	35.360	35.867	33.889	35.039
Uruguay	21.025	22.141	19.433	20.866
Maximum				*35.039*
Minimum				*6.301*
Mean				*18.381*
Variance				*48.237*
Standard deviation				*6.945*
Number of observations				*27*
Developing countries				
Maximum				*49.144*
Minimum				*2.551*
Mean				*17.870*
Variance				*56.965*
Standard deviation				*7.548*
Number of observations				*94*

Table A1 ***(concluded).*** **Selected Industrial and Developing Countries: Total Tax Revenue as Percentage of Gross Domestic Product, 1980–82**

	1980	1981	1982	Average 1980–82
All countries				
Maximum				*49.144*
Minimum				*2.551*
Mean				*21.212*
Variance				*105.468*
Standard deviation				*10.270*
Number of observations				*115*

Sources: International Monetary Fund, *Government Finance Statistics Yearbook, 1984,* Vol. 8 (Washington, 1984), *International Financial Statistics* (Washington), various issues, and Fund staff estimates; and Organization for Economic Cooperation and Development, *Revenue Statistics of OECD Member Countries, 1965–1983* (Paris, 1984).

[1]Including revenue from state and local taxes.

Table A2. Selected Developing Countries: Total Tax Revenue by

	Year	Total Taxes	Income Taxes			
			Total	Individual	Corporate	Other
Argentina[1]	1981-83	18.12	2.47	0.04	0.01	0.76
Bangladesh	1978-80	7.43	1.14	1.08	0.06	—
Barbados	1982-83	26.00	9.17	3.10	5.57	0.51
Belize	1980-82	21.45	5.59	...	...	...
Benin	1977-79	16.33	2.82	0.53	1.72	0.57
Bolivia	1983	5.52	0.81	0.35	0.27	0.19
Botswana	1981-83	24.83	11.40	—	—	11.40
Brazil[2]	1981-83	23.83	3.39	0.17	1.37	1.85
Burkina Faso	1981-83	12.73	2.41	1.47	0.54	0.41
Burma	1980-82	9.77	0.46	...	...	...
Burundi	1979-81	12.86	2.70	1.18	1.34	0.18
Cameroon	1982-84	20.05	11.00	1.99	8.90	0.11
Central African Rep.	1981	14.96	2.65	1.27	1.38	0.01
Chad	1974-76	9.33	1.67	0.97	0.70	—
Chile[3]	1982-84	23.38	4.30	2.28	2.01	—
Colombia[2]	1979-81	12.21	2.93	1.34	1.57	0.03
Congo	1980	26.87	17.13	2.95	14.15	0.03
Costa Rica	1981-83	18.26	3.13	2.90	0.23	—
Côte d'Ivoire	1980	20.33	2.86	1.38	1.34	0.14
Cyprus	1981-83	19.32	4.67	2.92	1.00	0.75
Dominican Rep.[3]	1981-83	9.74	2.35	0.90	1.44	0.02
Ecuador	1981-83	10.79	5.66	—	4.24	1.42
Egypt	1982-84	27.69	7.00	...	...	...
El Salvador	1982-84	11.17	2.42	1.08	1.03	0.31
Ethiopia[3]	1978-80	14.89	3.37	1.28	1.60	0.49
Fiji	1980-82	19.13	10.55	7.55	2.74	0.27
Gabon	1976-78	19.75	11.60	0.62	10.81	0.17
Gambia, The[3]	1976-78	15.04	2.23	0.84	1.27	0.12
Ghana	1983-84	6.32	1.29	0.75	0.55	—
Greece[3]	1979-81	27.27	4.92	3.57	1.13	0.21
Grenada	1975-77	19.68	4.18	2.96	1.22	—
Guatemala[3]	1981-82	9.34	1.22	0.24	0.97	0.01
Guinea	1982-83	22.84	9.06	...	...	...
Guyana	1982-84	38.88	13.62	4.52	9.10	—
Haiti	1982-84	10.79	2.02	0.37	1.73	—
Honduras	1979-81	13.48	3.80	1.32	2.45	0.03
Hungary[3]	1983-84	53.06	13.76	...	...	...
India[1]	1981-83	14.53	2.40	0.94	1.33	0.14
Indonesia[1]	1981-83	19.87	16.16	0.45	14.78	0.92
Iran, Islamic Rep. of[3]	1981-83	8.42	2.15	0.19	1.96	0.01

Type of Tax as Percentage of Gross Domestic Product, Three-Year Averages

Domestic Taxes on Goods and Services				Foreign Trade						
Total	General sales, turnover, or value-added tax	Excises	Other	Total	Import duties	Export duties	Other	Social Security	Wealth and Property	Other
8.26	2.61	3.70	0.34	2.00	1.11	0.73	0.17	2.42	1.36	1.60
2.89	1.31	1.49	0.09	2.98	2.74	0.18	0.07	—	0.22	0.19
6.11	4.18	0.31	1.62	4.24	3.92	0.08	0.24	3.93	1.30	1.25
2.36	—	1.50	0.86	10.48	9.79	0.62	0.07	0.99	0.19	1.84
2.30	0.75	1.10	0.45	9.34	8.58	0.29	0.47	1.57	0.04	0.25
2.24	0.28	0.77	1.19	0.75	0.52	0.02	0.21	1.31	0.19	0.22
0.58	0.32	—	0.27	12.77	12.71	0.06	—	—	0.08	—
11.28	0.28	4.25	6.75	0.79	0.48	0.31	—	6.69	0.39	1.30
2.40	1.12	0.85	0.43	5.91	5.26	0.25	0.39	1.36	0.17	0.47
6.70	6.03	0.02	0.43	2.61	2.61	—	—	—	—	—
3.59	—	3.43	0.16	5.10	3.58	1.51	0.01	0.43	0.96	0.07
2.83	1.34	1.08	0.41	4.57	3.91	0.65	0.01	1.06	0.35	0.24
3.42	0.99	1.23	1.21	6.55	4.97	1.56	0.02	1.68	0.07	0.58
1.47	0.92	0.29	0.27	5.27	4.50	0.77	—	0.19	0.15	0.65
12.54	9.18	2.48	0.04	1.92	1.77	—	0.16	2.41	0.90	1.32
4.01	1.96	0.78	1.27	2.30	1.50	0.77	0.02	1.42	0.30	1.25
2.69	2.45	0.17	0.07	4.56	4.44	0.07	0.05	2.07	0.02	0.41
5.30	2.27	2.96	0.07	4.99	1.31	3.09	0.59	4.71	0.11	0.07
5.45	2.16	1.84	1.45	9.42	7.13	2.28	—	2.07	0.47	0.06
4.61	—	3.66	0.95	4.73	4.73	—	—	4.40	0.63	0.27
3.45	—	2.94	0.51	3.11	2.49	0.47	0.15	0.50	0.10	0.24
2.18	1.46	0.69	0.03	2.74	2.26	0.32	0.16	—	0.16	0.06
5.15	...	...	—	7.58	7.58	—	—	5.30	0.49	2.18
4.89	2.49	2.06	0.35	3.05	0.96	2.09	—	—	0.76	0.05
3.87	1.22	2.33	0.11	6.94	3.27	3.68	—	—	0.55	0.16
2.37	—	1.85	0.52	6.02	5.61	0.41	—	—	0.08	0.20
1.68	1.50	0.07	0.04	6.03	5.28	0.56	0.06	0.07	—	—
0.52	—	0.13	0.33	11.80	10.28	1.50	0.02	0.09	0.51	0.05
1.29	0.16	1.08	0.04	3.73	1.34	2.09	0.30	—	—	—
10.06	5.59	3.31	1.07	1.41	1.40	—	—	8.29	0.96	1.63
4.20	1.53	0.22	2.45	8.97	5.41	3.29	0.27	—	0.57	1.76
3.20	1.97	1.04	0.19	1.79	1.06	0.68	0.06	1.17	0.09	1.87
1.64	0.60	—	1.04	11.07	2.71	7.48	0.89	1.00	0.01	0.05
13.38	9.52	2.68	1.18	4.30	1.82	0.08	2.41	6.60	0.68	0.29
3.39	0.77	2.05	0.57	3.54	2.78	0.76	—	0.10	0.16	1.59
3.61	1.00	2.35	0.26	5.80	3.38	2.42	0.01	—	0.12	0.15
19.51	9.16	0.13	...	3.62	3.00	—	0.62	10.69	3.69	1.78
8.53	0.13	5.08	0.04	3.12	2.98	0.04	0.11	—	0.15	0.32
2.27	1.06	0.99	—	1.01	0.84	0.17	—	—	0.31	0.13
0.89	0.12	0.30	0.47	2.18	2.18	—	0.01	2.33	0.33	0.54

Table A2 *(continued).* Selected Developing Countries: Total Tax Revenue by

	Year	Total Taxes	Income Taxes			
			Total	Individual	Corporate	Other
Israel[3]	1981-83	33.87	16.13	11.49	3.35	1.29
Jamaica	1979-81	27.23	8.38	4.47	3.92	—
Jordan	1981-83	18.80	3.29	...	...	0.13
Kenya[3]	1980-82	22.18	6.61	...	...	...
Korea	1982-84	16.59	4.37	2.32	2.05	—
Lesotho	1983	34.90	3.90	2.57	1.33	—
Liberia	1982-84	26.53	10.23	7.99	2.09	0.15
Madagascar[3]	1980-82	15.09	2.58	1.39	1.19	—
Malawi	1981-83	16.60	6.20	2.71	3.49	—
Malaysia	1981-83	22.81	10.32	2.28	8.05	—
Mali	1982-83	14.07	2.34	0.59	1.53	0.22
Malta	1981-83	27.08	10.25	5.71	4.49	0.04
Mauritania	1978-79	15.12	4.89	4.01	0.77	0.12
Mauritius[3]	1982-84	19.77	3.28	2.00	1.27	—
Mexico[1]	1981-83	17.09	4.98	2.30	2.52	0.09
Morocco	1981-83	21.74	4.54	2.31	1.99	0.24
Nepal	1980-82	7.12	0.53	0.38	0.15	—
Nicaragua	1981-83	23.62	2.93	...	...	...
Niger	1978-80	11.72	3.62	0.71	2.54	0.37
Nigeria	1976-78	17.88	13.90	0.01	13.89	—
Oman	1982-84	11.48	10.28	—	10.24	0.04
Pakistan	1981-83	12.92	2.49	...	...	...
Panama[3]	1980-82	21.41	6.24	—	—	6.24
Papua New Guinea	1981-83	18.39	10.84	6.12	4.68	—
Paraguay	1980-82	9.80	1.71	—	1.63	0.08
Peru	1980-82	17.26	3.67	0.39	3.23	0.05
Philippines[3]	1981-83	10.75	2.40	1.13	1.29	—
Portugal	1981-83	30.51	7.42	2.68	1.72	3.02
Romania[3]	1981-83	12.29	0.31	...	...	...
Rwanda	1978-80	11.13	2.17	0.82	1.24	0.11
Senegal	1982-83	18.82	4.19	2.39	1.10	0.71
Seychelles	1975-77	19.34	6.21	3.82	2.40	—
Sierra Leone	1982-84	9.34	2.58	1.29	1.27	0.03
Singapore	1981-83	19.28	9.77	...	...	...
Somalia	1976-78	19.65	1.64	1.49	0.15	—
South Africa[2]	1980-82	20.35	12.18	4.65	7.10	0.42
Sri Lanka	1981-83	16.69	2.70	0.74	1.96	—
Sudan	1980-82	11.06	2.04	0.77	1.17	0.10
Suriname	1984	16.66	6.25	3.90	2.36	—
Swaziland	1981-83	23.90	6.77	3.51	2.89	0.36

Type of Tax as Percentage of Gross Domestic Product, Three-Year Averages

Domestic Taxes on Goods and Services				Foreign Trade						
Total	General sales, turnover, or value-added tax	Excises	Other	Total	Import duties	Export duties	Other	Social Security	Wealth and Property	Other
9.98	9.03	0.78	0.15	1.84	1.71	—	0.13	5.04	1.27	—
14.40	6.45	6.98	0.97	1.34	1.34	—	—	1.44	0.57	1.10
2.37	—	1.94	0.44	10.33	10.33	—	—	—	1.71	1.10
9.20	6.25	2.21	0.64	5.21	5.03	0.19	—	—	0.66	0.12
8.49	4.09	2.51	1.88	2.79	2.79	—	—	0.22	0.17	0.55
3.92	3.40	—	0.52	26.66	25.46	1.20	—	—	0.01	0.39
7.53	0.74	3.23	3.56	8.09	7.94	0.09	0.06	—	0.28	0.40
6.01	3.44	1.43	1.13	3.64	3.17	0.47	—	1.88	0.32	0.67
5.99	4.82	0.89	0.29	4.30	4.30	—	—	—	0.01	0.10
4.73	1.50	1.80	1.43	7.04	3.85	3.19	—	0.15	0.15	0.42
5.62	2.94	2.46	0.22	3.01	2.68	0.29	0.04	1.14	0.59	1.37
2.10	—	1.05	1.05	7.19	7.19	—	—	6.66	0.78	0.10
3.82	2.51	0.75	0.56	6.12	5.95	0.16	0.01	1.55	0.18	—
4.31	0.74	2.22	1.36	11.13	7.66	3.37	0.10	—	0.69	0.36
7.16	2.81	1.79	2.54	3.68	0.78	2.90	—	2.30	0.14	—
8.77	5.88	2.21	0.68	5.23	4.94	0.28	—	1.35	0.54	1.31
3.15	1.89	0.94	0.32	2.77	2.55	0.22	—	—	0.63	0.05
11.47	2.63	5.95	2.89	4.32	2.36	0.34	1.61	3.10	1.40	0.40
2.60	1.69	0.81	0.10	4.69	4.04	0.55	0.11	0.62	0.35	—
0.57	—	0.57	—	3.40	3.39	0.01	—	—	—	0.01
0.24	—	—	0.24	0.80	0.80	—	0.01	0.16	—	—
5.21	0.99	4.22	—	5.17	4.76	0.16	0.25	—	0.05	—
4.39	1.88	1.79	0.72	2.81	2.41	0.37	0.03	6.03	0.48	1.47
2.80	—	2.68	0.12	4.49	4.18	0.25	0.06	—	—	0.27
2.04	0.55	1.15	0.35	2.19	1.59	0.05	0.55	1.59	0.83	1.44
7.77	5.48	2.09	0.20	5.13	3.44	1.66	0.02	0.76	1.09	—
4.86	1.56	2.06	1.00	2.80	2.69	0.09	0.02	—	0.43	0.26
10.66	4.72	4.83	1.12	1.49	1.49	—	—	8.80	0.48	1.65
0.07	...	...	...	—	—	—	—	9.84	0.35	1.72
2.12	—	2.11	0.01	6.06	3.18	2.88	—	0.51	0.12	0.15
5.71	3.64	1.71	0.35	7.25	7.10	0.14	—	1.05	0.50	0.12
1.92	—	1.16	0.75	9.47	9.33	—	—	—	0.52	1.23
2.34	—	2.25	0.10	4.18	3.51	0.54	0.12	0.04	—	0.20
3.88	—	1.37	2.51	1.46	1.46	—	—	0.50	2.81	0.86
5.00	—	2.49	2.51	10.76	10.38	0.38	—	—	0.59	1.66
6.25	3.16	2.63	0.08	0.96	0.90	0.04	0.02	0.30	1.37	—
6.76	4.18	2.44	0.14	6.90	3.67	3.21	0.01	—	0.07	0.26
2.71	—	2.39	0.32	6.22	5.84	0.39	—	—	0.02	0.07
1.82	—	1.16	0.66	6.98	4.49	1.98	0.51	1.18	0.13	0.30
0.39	—	—	0.39	16.58	15.77	0.80	—	—	0.06	0.11

Table A2 *(concluded)*. Selected Developing Countries: Total Tax Revenue by

	Year	Total Taxes	Income Taxes			
			Total	Individual	Corporate	Other
Syrian Arab Rep.	1979–81	9.96	2.47	—	—	2.47
Tanzania	1979–81	17.07	5.40	1.65	3.39	0.37
Thailand[3]	1982–84	14.12	3.03	1.54	1.49	—
Togo	1982–84	24.46	10.09	2.03	7.38	0.68
Trinidad and Tobago[3]	1979–81	33.83	28.39	4.59	22.34	1.46
Tunisia[3]	1980–82	25.13	4.95	2.17	2.26	0.42
Turkey	1983–84	16.01	9.16	7.26	1.78	0.13
Uganda[3]	1982–84	6.93	0.71	0.04	0.39	0.02
Uruguay	1982–84	18.74	1.42	0.28	1.07	0.06
Venezuela	1984	25.58	17.69	1.09	16.60	—
Western Samoa	1984	26.82	7.17	...	...	...
Yemen Arab Rep.	1982–84	20.49	2.90	1.87	0.95	0.07
Yugoslavia[2]	1979–81	32.64	1.74	...	...	...
Zaïre	1981–83	17.51	6.56	3.18	3.37	0.01
Zambia	1980–82	22.09	8.43	3.88	4.18	0.38
Zimbabwe[3]	1981–83	27.85	13.54	7.12	5.85	0.56
Maximum		*53.06*	*28.39*	*11.49*	*22.34*	*11.40*
Minimum		*5.52*	*0.31*	—	—	—
Mean[4]		*18.71*	*5.85*	*2.13*	*3.26*	*0.49*
Variance		*61.92*	*23.33*	*4.65*	*17.16*	*2.15*
Standard deviation		*7.87*	*4.83*	*2.16*	*4.14*	*1.47*
Number of observations		*96*	*96*	*83*[5]	*83*[5]	*84*[6]

Note: Components may not add to totals because of rounding; ... = data not available; — = negligible.

Sources: International Monetary Fund, *Government Finance Statistics Yearbook, 1985,* Vol. 9 (Washington, 1985) and *International Financial Statistics* (Washington), various issues.

[1]Including revenue from state taxes.

[2]Including revenue from state and local taxes.

[3]Including revenue from local taxes.

Type of Tax as Percentage of Gross Domestic Product, Three-Year Averages

Domestic Taxes on Goods and Services				Foreign Trade						
Total	General sales, turnover, or value-added tax	Excises	Other	Total	Import duties	Export duties	Other	Social Security	Wealth and Property	Other
1.47	—	0.11	1.36	3.62	3.31	0.28	0.02	0.51	0.53	1.37
8.34	7.96	0.22	0.15	3.07	2.07	0.98	0.02	0.05	0.13	0.09
7.44	2.80	3.29	0.73	3.20	2.79	0.41	0.01	—	0.35	0.10
3.92	2.92	0.34	0.66	8.32	6.67	0.17	1.48	1.69	0.36	0.06
1.73	0.71	0.28	0.74	2.76	2.75	—	0.01	0.62	0.11	0.22
7.51	1.63	2.64	3.11	8.42	8.14	0.27	—	3.08	0.79	0.38
4.44	0.81	1.12	2.50	1.37	1.23	—	0.13	—	0.34	0.69
1.83	1.36	0.38	0.09	4.38	0.93	2.77	0.67	—	—	—
8.59	4.84	3.60	0.15	2.37	1.82	0.47	0.08	5.21	0.88	0.28
1.29	—	1.25	0.05	5.38	1.26	—	4.12	0.96	0.21	0.05
4.19	—	3.88	0.31	15.29	14.14	0.14	1.01	—	0.09	0.08
1.78	—	1.16	0.59	12.10	12.10	—	—	—	0.22	3.49
8.85	5.77	...	...	3.34	3.34	—	—	17.67	0.13	0.01
4.14	3.01	1.10	0.03	5.61	4.32	1.28	0.01	0.54	0.02	0.64
10.92	3.14	7.69	0.10	1.97	1.95	—	0.02	0.65	0.01	0.10
9.59	6.44	2.83	0.11	3.59	3.59	—	—	—	0.85	0.28
19.51	*9.52*	*7.69*	*6.75*	*26.66*	*25.46*	*7.48*	*4.12*	*17.67*	*3.69*	*3.49*
0.07	—	—	—	—	—	—	—	—	—	—
4.92	*2.18*	*1.83*	*0.76*	*5.30*	*4.34*	*0.75*	*0.20*	*1.69*	*0.45*	*0.55*
12.77	*5.97*	*2.33*	*1.00*	*15.89*	*14.74*	*1.44*	*0.30*	*8.33*	*0.32*	*0.45*
3.57	*2.44*	*1.53*	*1.00*	*3.99*	*3.84*	*1.20*	*0.55*	*2.89*	*0.56*	*0.67*
96	*94*[7]	*93*[8]	*93*[8]	*96*	*96*	*96*	*96*	*96*	*96*	*96*

[4]Unweighted arithmetic mean.

[5]Excluding Belize, Burma, Egypt, Guinea, Hungary, Jordan, Kenya, Nicaragua, Pakistan, Romania, Singapore, Western Samoa, and Yugoslavia.

[6]Excluding Belize, Burma, Egypt, Guinea, Hungary, Kenya, Nicaragua, Pakistan, Romania, Singapore, Western Samoa, and Yugoslavia.

[7]Excluding Egypt and Romania.

[8]Excluding Egypt, Romania, and Yugoslavia.

Table A3. Selected Developing Countries: Percentage Shares of

	Years	Total Taxes	Income Taxes: Total	Income Taxes: Individual	Income Taxes: Corporate	Income Taxes: Other
Argentina[1]	1981-83	100	13.58	0.21	0.03	4.17
Bangladesh	1978-80	100	15.41	14.55	0.85	—
Barbados	1982-83	100	35.32	11.96	21.42	1.94
Belize	1980-82	100	26.08	...	...	...
Benin	1977-79	100	17.19	3.24	10.47	3.48
Bolivia	1983	100	14.66	6.26	4.94	3.46
Botswana	1981-83	100	45.83	—	—	45.83
Brazil[2]	1981-83	100	14.22	0.73	5.72	7.77
Burkina Faso	1981-83	100	19.02	11.65	4.21	3.16
Burma	1980-82	100	4.74	...	...	...
Burundi	1979-81	100	21.23	9.31	10.51	1.41
Cameroon	1982-84	100	53.80	10.33	42.97	0.50
Central African Rep.	1981	100	17.73	8.47	9.21	0.05
Chad	1974-76	100	18.16	10.60	7.57	—
Chile[3]	1982-84	100	18.34	9.74	8.60	0.01
Colombia[2]	1979-81	100	23.97	10.95	12.80	0.22
Congo	1980	100	63.75	10.96	52.67	0.11
Costa Rica	1981-83	100	17.10	16.02	1.08	—
Côte d'Ivoire	1980	100	14.05	6.79	6.59	0.67
Cyprus	1981-83	100	24.14	15.06	5.18	3.89
Dominican Rep.[3]	1981-83	100	24.20	9.18	14.79	0.22
Ecuador	1981-83	100	52.40	—	39.24	13.16
Egypt	1982-84	100	25.21	...	...	...
El Salvador	1982-84	100	21.70	9.69	9.24	2.77
Ethiopia[3]	1978-80	100	22.54	8.60	10.73	3.21
Fiji	1980-82	100	55.26	39.58	14.28	1.39
Gabon	1976-78	100	58.71	3.15	54.70	0.87
Gambia, The[3]	1976-78	100	14.66	5.58	8.36	0.73
Ghana	1983-84	100	21.55	10.52	11.03	—
Greece[3]	1979-81	100	18.04	13.08	4.15	0.75
Grenada	1975-77	100	21.40	15.09	6.31	—
Guatemala[3]	1981-82	100	13.04	2.52	10.44	0.08
Guinea	1982-83	100	38.01	...	...	...
Guyana	1982-84	100	35.02	11.62	23.40	—
Haiti	1982-84	100	18.61	2.90	15.75	—
Honduras	1979-81	100	28.08	9.79	18.11	0.19
Hungary[3]	1983-84	100	25.94	...	...	...
India[1]	1981-83	100	17.01	6.62	9.47	0.92
Indonesia[1]	1981-83	100	81.22	2.30	74.28	4.64
Iran, Islamic Rep. of[3]	1981-83	100	25.27	2.23	22.95	0.10
Israel[3]	1981-83	100	47.50	33.92	9.71	3.87
Jamaica	1979-81	100	30.56	16.29	14.27	—
Jordan	1981-83	100	17.51	...	...	0.69
Kenya[3]	1980-82	100	29.80	...	...	...
Korea	1982-84	100	26.36	13.97	12.39	—

Type of Tax in Total Tax Revenue, Three-Year Averages

Domestic Taxes on Goods and Services				Foreign Trade						
Total	General sales, turnover, or value-added tax	Excises	Other	Total	Import duties	Export duties	Other	Social Security	Wealth and Property	Other
45.47	14.34	20.45	1.85	11.17	6.07	4.18	0.92	13.36	7.54	8.87
38.93	17.67	20.11	1.16	40.09	36.79	2.39	0.91	—	3.03	2.55
23.51	16.05	1.21	6.25	16.29	15.05	0.32	0.92	15.10	5.00	4.78
10.99	—	7.00	3.99	48.88	45.66	2.91	0.31	4.59	0.86	8.59
14.03	4.52	6.74	2.77	57.33	52.68	1.77	2.88	9.67	0.25	1.54
40.56	5.07	13.99	21.50	13.58	9.47	0.31	3.81	23.83	3.39	3.98
2.36	1.29	—	1.07	51.49	51.26	0.23	—	—	0.31	—
47.33	1.15	17.87	28.32	3.32	2.02	1.30	—	28.04	1.62	5.47
18.90	8.71	6.79	3.41	46.26	41.18	1.99	3.09	10.78	1.30	3.74
68.58	61.71	0.20	6.67	26.67	26.67	—	—	—	—	—
28.18	—	26.92	1.26	39.01	27.77	11.19	0.06	3.44	7.58	0.55
14.36	6.80	5.52	2.04	23.36	19.92	3.38	0.06	5.41	1.83	1.24
22.87	6.61	8.20	8.07	43.79	33.21	10.45	0.12	11.24	0.48	3.89
15.72	9.79	3.12	2.81	56.66	48.29	8.37	—	2.08	1.51	6.78
53.59	39.20	10.63	0.16	8.23	7.56	—	0.45	10.30	3.91	5.63
32.85	16.08	6.41	10.37	18.84	12.32	6.33	0.19	11.64	2.45	10.25
9.99	9.12	0.62	0.25	16.96	16.52	0.27	0.17	7.69	0.09	1.53
28.70	11.99	16.35	0.36	27.67	7.25	17.31	3.11	25.74	0.63	0.41
26.82	10.64	9.07	7.11	46.32	35.09	11.23	—	10.18	2.33	0.29
23.87	—	18.95	4.92	24.49	24.47	—	0.02	22.82	3.28	1.39
35.54	—	30.30	5.24	31.60	25.56	4.52	1.52	5.12	1.08	2.47
20.18	13.50	6.42	0.27	25.39	21.01	2.94	1.45	—	1.45	0.58
18.64	...	...	—	27.37	27.37	—	—	19.16	1.75	7.87
43.72	22.09	18.48	3.15	27.29	8.54	18.73	0.02	—	6.88	0.40
25.75	8.11	15.52	0.72	47.00	22.11	24.89	—	—	3.61	1.10
12.39	—	9.68	2.71	31.40	29.27	2.13	—	—	0.42	1.01
8.50	7.58	0.35	0.57	30.55	26.74	2.86	0.94	1.11	0.01	—
3.41	—	0.83	2.18	78.83	68.60	10.12	0.11	0.59	3.23	0.35
25.88	2.51	22.86	0.51	52.50	19.40	30.42	2.68	0.01	—	0.06
36.89	20.50	12.14	3.91	5.13	5.12	—	—	30.44	3.51	5.98
21.20	7.78	1.24	12.18	46.03	27.81	17.00	1.22	—	2.92	8.44
34.34	21.17	11.14	2.03	19.10	11.28	7.22	0.61	12.53	0.97	20.02
6.05	2.34	—	3.71	50.47	12.54	33.88	4.05	5.18	0.06	0.23
34.43	24.50	6.89	3.04	11.07	4.66	0.21	6.20	16.96	1.76	0.75
32.32	7.80	19.19	5.33	33.14	26.01	7.14	—	0.99	1.49	13.45
26.82	7.44	17.42	1.96	43.12	25.13	17.94	0.05	—	0.87	1.10
36.77	17.27	0.13	...	6.82	5.65	—	1.18	20.16	6.96	3.36
57.69	0.94	36.49	0.26	22.34	21.25	0.29	0.80	—	1.00	1.96
11.50	5.36	5.01	—	5.04	4.21	0.82	—	—	1.59	0.66
10.68	1.41	3.57	5.70	26.08	26.02	—	0.06	27.64	3.89	6.44
29.60	26.76	2.33	0.44	5.49	5.02	—	0.47	14.87	3.54	0.01
53.10	23.74	25.74	3.62	4.92	4.92	—	—	5.23	2.10	4.08
12.60	—	10.27	2.33	55.00	55.00	—	—	—	9.08	5.82
41.46	28.02	9.41	3.03	25.21	24.58	0.63	—	—	2.98	0.55
51.16	24.68	15.12	11.36	16.80	16.80	—	—	1.33	1.05	3.30

Table A3 *(continued)*. Selected Developing Countries: Percentage

	Year	Total Taxes	Income Taxes			
			Total	Individual	Corporate	Other
Lesotho	1983	100	11.19	7.38	3.81	—
Liberia	1982-84	100	38.59	30.14	7.87	0.57
Madagascar[3]	1980-82	100	17.01	9.19	7.82	—
Malawi	1981-83	100	37.32	16.31	21.01	—
Malaysia	1981-83	100	45.26	9.98	35.27	0.01
Mali	1982-83	100	16.64	4.24	10.81	1.59
Malta	1981-83	100	37.86	21.07	16.64	0.15
Mauritania	1978-79	100	32.22	26.34	5.06	0.82
Mauritius[3]	1982-84	100	16.69	10.16	6.52	—
Mexico[1]	1981-83	100	29.08	13.44	14.74	0.52
Morocco	1981-83	100	20.86	10.61	9.15	1.10
Nepal	1980-82	100	7.40	5.31	2.09	—
Nicaragua	1981-83	100	12.34	...	...	...
Niger	1978-80	100	30.97	6.09	21.72	3.16
Nigeria	1976-78	100	77.20	0.07	77.13	—
Oman	1982-84	100	89.54	—	89.18	0.36
Pakistan	1981-83	100	19.29	...	...	...
Panama[3]	1980-82	100	29.12	—	—	29.12
Papua New Guinea	1981-83	100	58.76	33.39	25.15	—
Paraguay	1980-82	100	17.44	—	16.61	0.83
Peru	1980-82	100	20.89	2.28	18.34	0.27
Philippines[3]	1981-83	100	22.35	10.52	12.01	0.02
Portugal	1981-83	100	24.28	8.77	5.67	9.85
Romania[3]	1981-83	100	2.50	...	...	...
Rwanda	1978-80	100	19.52	7.34	11.20	0.97
Senegal	1982-83	100	22.25	12.69	5.85	3.71
Seychelles	1975-77	100	32.11	19.76	12.36	—
Sierra Leone	1982-84	100	27.94	14.03	13.67	0.23
Singapore	1981-83	100	50.66	...	...	...
Somalia	1976-78	100	8.59	7.82	0.77	—
South Africa[2]	1980-82	100	59.91	22.80	35.01	2.09
Sri Lanka	1981-83	100	16.24	4.45	11.80	—
Sudan	1980-82	100	18.44	6.96	10.62	0.87
Suriname	1984	100	37.54	23.39	14.14	—
Swaziland	1981-83	100	28.64	14.87	12.22	1.55
Syrian Arab Rep.	1979-81	100	25.19	—	—	25.19
Tanzania	1979-81	100	31.63	9.62	19.83	2.18
Thailand[3]	1982-84	100	21.45	10.87	10.58	—
Togo	1982-84	100	41.34	8.34	30.19	2.80
Trinidad and Tobago[3]	1979-81	100	83.82	13.60	66.05	4.18

Shares of Type of Tax in Total Tax Revenue, Three-Year Averages

Domestic Taxes on Goods and Services				Foreign Trade						
Total	General sales, turnover, or value-added tax	Excises	Other	Total	Import duties	Export duties	Other	Social Security	Wealth and Property	Other
11.23	9.74	—	1.50	76.41	72.96	3.45	—	—	0.04	1.13
28.36	2.79	12.18	13.39	30.48	29.93	0.34	0.21	—	1.04	1.53
40.01	23.03	9.50	7.49	23.92	20.75	3.17	—	12.59	2.11	4.36
36.11	29.05	5.33	1.73	25.91	25.91	—	—	—	0.06	0.61
20.73	6.55	7.89	6.30	30.84	16.90	13.94	—	0.65	0.66	1.86
39.85	20.93	17.34	1.58	21.43	19.09	2.05	0.29	8.12	4.20	9.75
7.78	—	3.90	3.88	26.53	26.53	—	—	24.60	2.87	0.36
25.22	16.65	5.01	3.56	40.71	39.53	1.12	0.07	10.35	1.23	—
21.76	3.54	11.32	6.91	56.20	38.55	17.15	0.50	—	3.50	1.85
42.79	16.57	10.57	15.52	21.17	4.54	16.63	—	13.48	0.81	—
40.35	27.07	10.17	3.12	24.04	22.75	1.29	—	6.20	2.50	6.04
44.18	26.48	13.23	4.48	38.94	35.81	3.13	—	—	8.83	0.65
48.60	11.24	25.35	12.02	18.21	10.23	1.63	6.35	13.22	5.92	1.71
22.26	14.43	6.96	0.87	40.01	34.38	4.70	0.92	5.26	2.98	—
3.33	—	3.33	—	19.41	19.37	0.04	—	—	—	0.05
2.07	—	—	1.37	6.98	6.94	—	0.04	1.41	—	—
40.35	7.69	32.66	—	39.99	36.87	1.23	1.88	—	0.35	0.02
20.50	8.76	8.36	3.38	13.11	11.26	1.71	0.13	28.17	2.24	6.86
15.27	—	14.60	0.67	24.51	22.82	1.38	0.30	—	—	1.47
20.79	5.61	11.70	3.49	22.40	16.26	0.56	5.58	16.25	8.47	14.65
45.20	31.83	12.20	1.17	29.70	20.11	9.45	0.14	4.41	6.30	—
45.20	14.49	19.12	9.27	26.00	25.04	0.80	0.16	—	4.03	2.42
34.93	15.48	15.80	3.65	4.90	4.89	0.01	—	28.89	1.58	5.42
0.57	...	...	...	—	—	—	—	80.07	2.89	13.97
19.21	—	19.07	0.14	54.23	28.81	25.42	—	4.61	1.10	1.34
30.34	19.41	9.08	1.86	38.52	37.74	0.76	0.03	5.61	2.65	0.63
9.87	—	6.01	3.86	48.89	48.18	—	—	—	2.66	6.46
25.17	—	24.01	1.16	44.19	37.39	5.64	1.16	0.44	—	2.27
20.13	—	7.11	13.02	7.57	7.57	—	—	2.59	14.55	4.50
26.19	—	13.17	13.01	53.95	51.99	1.96	—	—	2.90	8.37
30.70	15.48	12.95	0.38	4.69	4.41	0.19	0.09	1.46	6.73	—
40.50	25.03	14.64	0.83	41.29	21.98	19.25	0.05	—	0.43	1.53
24.35	—	21.50	2.85	56.38	52.85	3.53	—	—	0.21	0.62
10.90	—	6.96	3.94	41.88	26.96	11.87	3.05	7.08	0.78	1.83
1.65	—	—	1.65	68.97	65.26	3.71	—	—	0.27	0.47
14.80	—	1.01	13.79	36.33	33.32	2.76	0.25	5.15	5.23	13.29
48.81	46.59	1.33	0.90	17.98	12.14	5.74	0.10	0.28	0.78	0.51
52.69	19.81	23.32	5.14	22.64	19.67	2.89	0.08	—	2.49	0.73
16.04	11.91	1.40	2.73	33.97	27.22	0.72	6.03	6.92	1.48	0.25
5.16	2.12	0.84	2.20	8.18	8.16	—	0.03	1.85	0.32	0.66

Table A3 *(concluded)*. Selected Developing Countries: Percentage

	Year	Total Taxes	Income Taxes			
			Total	Individual	Corporate	Other
Tunisia[3]	1980-82	100	19.69	8.64	8.97	1.67
Turkey	1983-84	100	56.85	45.19	11.27	0.39
Uganda[3]	1982-84	100	10.90	0.69	5.70	0.39
Uruguay	1982-84	100	7.54	1.54	5.67	0.32
Venezuela	1984	100	69.15	4.24	64.90	—
Western Samoa	1984	100	26.72	...	...	...
Yemen Arab Rep.	1982-84	100	14.15	9.13	4.65	0.36
Yugoslavia[2]	1979-81	100	5.33	...	...	...
Zaïre	1981-83	100	37.44	18.20	19.21	0.03
Zambia	1980-82	100	38.10	17.55	18.84	1.71
Zimbabwe[3]	1981-83	100	48.89	25.67	21.16	2.06
Maximum		*100*	*89.54*	*45.19*	*89.18*	*45.83*
Minimum		*100*	*2.50*	—	—	—
Mean[4]		*100*	*29.40*	*10.92*	*16.98*	*2.49*
Variance		—	*330.47*	*81.86*	*332.60*	*43.41*
Standard deviation		—	*18.18*	*9.05*	*18.24*	*6.59*
Number of observations		*96*	*96*	*83*[5]	*83*[5]	*84*[6]

Note: Components may not add to totals because of rounding; ... = data not available; — = negligible.

Sources: International Monetary Fund, *Government Finance Statistics Yearbook, 1985,* Vol. 9 (Washington, 1985) and *International Financial Statistics* (Washington), various issues.

[1]Including revenue from state taxes.

[2]Including revenue from state and local taxes.

[3]Including revenue from local taxes.

Shares of Type of Tax in Total Tax Revenue, Three-Year Averages

Domestic Taxes on Goods and Services				Foreign Trade						
Total	General sales, turnover, or value-added tax	Excises	Other	Total	Import duties	Export duties	Other	Social Security	Wealth and Property	Other
29.92	6.50	10.51	12.44	33.45	32.35	1.10	—	12.27	3.16	1.51
27.24	5.60	6.68	14.96	9.47	8.89	—	0.58	—	1.96	4.48
27.10	19.92	5.88	1.30	61.96	14.61	38.55	8.81	—	—	0.04
45.87	25.86	19.23	0.78	12.66	9.73	2.48	0.45	27.80	4.66	1.47
5.06	—	4.88	0.18	21.04	4.93	—	16.11	3.74	0.83	0.19
15.62	—	14.48	1.15	57.01	52.71	0.53	3.77	—	0.34	0.30
8.68	—	5.69	2.89	59.12	59.12	—	—	—	1.06	16.99
27.20	17.78	...	...	10.15	10.15	—	—	54.16	0.41	0.03
23.63	17.18	6.27	0.18	32.09	24.68	7.36	0.04	3.10	0.09	3.65
49.51	14.24	34.82	0.46	8.91	8.83	—	0.08	2.96	0.05	0.47
34.38	23.03	10.19	0.40	12.62	12.62	—	—	—	3.08	1.04
68.58	*61.71*	*36.49*	*28.32*	*78.83*	*72.96*	*38.55*	*16.11*	*80.07*	*14.55*	*20.02*
0.57	—	—	—	—	—	—	—	—	—	—
26.94	*11.45*	*10.95*	*4.26*	*30.29*	*24.25*	*5.04*	*1.00*	*8.03*	*2.40*	*3.23*
225.26	*134.51*	*72.65*	*25.36*	*325.39*	*268.24*	*63.47*	*5.23*	*153.04*	*6.53*	*17.25*
15.01	*11.60*	*8.52*	*5.04*	*18.04*	*16.38*	*7.97*	*2.29*	*12.37*	*2.56*	*4.15*
96	*94*[7]	*93*[8]	*93*[8]	*96*	*96*	*96*	*96*	*96*	*96*	*96*

[4]Unweighted arithmetic mean.
[5]Excluding Belize, Burma, Egypt, Guinea, Hungary, Jordan, Kenya, Nicaragua, Pakistan, Romania, Singapore, Western Samoa, and Yugoslavia.
[6]Excluding Belize, Burma, Egypt, Guinea, Hungary, Kenya, Nicaragua, Pakistan, Romania, Singapore, Western Samoa, and Yugoslavia.
[7]Excluding Egypt and Romania.
[8]Excluding Egypt, Romania, and Yugoslavia.

Table A4. Selected Industrial and Developing Countries: Revenue Significance of Individual Income Tax, Five-Year Averages

(In percent)

	Year	Ratio of Individual Income Tax: To GDP	Ratio of Individual Income Tax: To total tax revenue
Industrial countries			
United States	1978–82	9.55	48.51
Canada	1977–81	6.42	41.22
Australia	1978–82	13.35	55.19
Japan	1977–81	4.12	36.72
New Zealand	1977–81	19.04	64.61
Austria	1977–81	6.01	18.78
Belgium	1977–81	13.99	33.92
Denmark	1978–82	11.42	36.62
Finland	1977–81	7.60	28.47
France	1978–82	4.89	13.07
Germany, Fed. Rep. of	1977–81	4.28	16.00
Iceland	1977–81	2.41	9.21
Ireland	1977–81	10.43	32.08
Italy	1977–81	7.80	24.91
Luxembourg	1977–81	10.10	28.94
Netherlands	1978–82	11.54	26.23
Norway	1977–81	5.23	14.45
Spain	1976–80	3.32	15.43
Sweden	1978–82	5.79	17.46
Switzerland	1977–81	2.30	12.57
United Kingdom	1978–82	10.90	35.40
Maximum		*19.04*	*64.61*
Minimum		*2.30*	*9.21*
Average		*8.12*	*29.04*
Variance		*17.85*	*210.44*
Standard deviation		*4.22*	*14.51*
Number of observations		*21*	*21*
Developing countries			
Oil exporting countries			
Indonesia	1977–81	0.43	2.35
Iran, Islamic Rep. of	1977–81	0.18	1.97
Nigeria	1974–78	0.04	0.18
Venezuela	1978–82	0.99	4.40

Table A4 *(continued)*. Selected Industrial and Developing Countries: Revenue Significance of Individual Income Tax, Five-Year Averages

(In percent)

	Year	Ratio of Individual Income Tax	
		To GDP	To total tax revenue
Non-oil developing countries			
Africa			
Burundi	1977-81	0.99	8.04
Cameroon	1978-82	2.44	13.23
Central African Rep.	1981	1.27	8.47
Chad	1973-76	0.98	10.16
Congo	1976-80	2.25	8.96
Côte d'Ivoire	1980	1.39	6.74
Ethiopia	1974-78	1.16	10.29
Gabon	1973-76	0.66	3.27
Ghana	1978-82	0.86	12.65
Kenya	1973-77	1.24	7.37
Lesotho	1973-77	1.91	9.33
Liberia	1977-81	3.99	17.47
Mauritania	1975-79	3.76	22.05
Mauritius	1977-81	2.61	12.64
Morocco	1977-81	1.82	6.01
Niger	1976-80	0.67	6.70
Rwanda	1976-80	0.74	6.70
Senegal	1977-81	2.04	10.72
Sierra Leone	1977-81	1.09	7.09
Somalia	1974-78	1.29	7.73
South Africa	1976-80	4.77	25.19
Sudan	1976-80	0.47	3.97
Tanzania	1977-81	1.20	6.69
Togo	1977-80	1.37	5.17
Tunisia	1977-81	2.23	9.01
Uganda	1977-81	0.07	1.91
Zaïre	1977-81	3.22	19.48
Zambia	1977-81	4.51	19.72
Zimbabwe	1977-81	5.82	28.36

Table A4 ***(continued).*** **Selected Industrial and Developing Countries: Revenue Significance of Individual Income Tax, Five-Year Averages**

(In percent)

		Ratio of Individual Income Tax	
	Year	To GDP	To total tax revenue
Asia			
Fiji	1977–81	7.48	40.54
India	1977–81	1.16	10.92
Korea	1977–81	2.32	14.25
Malaysia	1977–81	2.10	9.48
Nepal	1977–81	0.38	5.79
Pakistan	1976–80	0.98	8.45
Papua New Guinea	1977–81	4.72	28.60
Philippines	1977–81	1.51	13.48
Sri Lanka	1977–81	0.73	3.81
Thailand	1978–82	1.17	9.19
Europe			
Cyprus	1977–81	2.32	14.21
Greece	1974–78	2.81	10.66
Malta	1976–80	4.79	18.97
Portugal	1976–80	2.08	8.08
Turkey	1977–81	7.89	45.54
Middle East			
Jordan	1975–79	0.72	3.84
Yemen Arab Rep.	1977–81	0.70	3.86
Western Hemisphere			
Argentina	1977–81	0.02	0.18
Barbados	1977–81	5.66	22.68
Bolivia	1978–82	0.76	10.88
Brazil	1977–81	0.17	0.98
Chile	1978–82	2.75	11.29
Colombia	1975–79	1.67	15.29
Dominican Rep.	1977–81	0.92	7.98
El Salvador	1978–82	1.11	9.42
Guyana	1975–79	3.69	12.20
Honduras	1977–81	1.32	9.93
Jamaica	1975–77	4.61	19.93
Mexico	1977–81	2.49	18.29
Paraguay	1975–79	0.04	0.37
Peru	1977–81	0.47	2.95
Suriname	1973–76	1.98	8.50
Trinidad and Tobago	1977–81	4.10	12.46

Table A4 *(concluded)*. **Selected Industrial and Developing Countries: Revenue Significance of Individual Income Tax, Five-Year Averages**

(In percent)

		Ratio of Individual Income Tax	
	Year	To GDP	To total tax revenue
Maximum		*7.89*	*45.54*
Minimum		*0.02*	*0.18*
Average		*2.03*	*11.19*
Variance		*3.09*	*74.11*
Standard deviation		*1.76*	*8.61*
Number of observations		*66*	*66*

Source: International Monetary Fund, *Government Finance Statistics Yearbook, 1983,* Vol. 7 (Washington, 1983).

Table A5. Selected Industrial and Developing Countries: Proportion of Individual Income Taxpayers in Total Population

(In percent)

	Year	Proportion of Taxpayers in Total Population
Industrial countries		
United States	1980	40.84
Canada	1979	57.64
Australia	1979/80	39.03
Japan	1980	28.57
New Zealand	1976	49.87
Austria	1976	50.39
Belgium	1977	34.88
Denmark	1980	77.80
Finland	1979	70.54
Germany, Fed. Rep. of	1978	34.25
Ireland	1979/80	24.91
Netherlands	1975	41.49
Norway	1979	52.60
United Kingdom	1978/79	43.53
Maximum		*77.80*
Minimum		*24.91*
Average		*46.17*
Variance		*226.02*
Standard deviation		*15.03*
Number of observations		*14*
Developing countries		
Brazil	1981	5.89
Cyprus	1980	10.00
India	1978	0.30
Indonesia	1973	0.14
Kenya	1978	0.56
Korea	1981	3.73
Malaysia	1979	6.95
Papua New Guinea	1979	3.79
Philippines	1979	6.33
Singapore	1980	2.18
Thailand	1980	4.39
Turkey	1976	11.88
Maximum		*11.88*
Minimum		*0.14*
Average		*4.68*
Variance		*14.03*
Standard deviation		*3.75*
Number of observations		*12*

Sources: Computed from annual reports of the taxation departments of various countries; International Monetary Fund, *International Financial Statistics* (Washington), various issues; and Organization for Economic Cooperation and Development, *Tax Elasticities of Central Government Personal Income Tax Systems: A Report by the Committee on Fiscal Affairs* (Paris, 1984).

Table A6. Selected Industrial and Developing Countries: Proportion of Income Assessed to Individual Income Tax in Gross Domestic Product

(In percent)

	Year	Proportion of Income Assessed to GDP
Industrial countries		
United States	1980	62.52
Canada	1979	65.38
Australia	1979/80	59.95
Japan	1980	40.42
New Zealand	1976	56.07
Austria	1976	48.45
Belgium	1977	47.66
Denmark	1980	84.32
Finland	1979	56.31
Germany, Fed. Rep. of	1978	47.39
Ireland	1979/80	54.15
Netherlands	1975	49.61
Norway	1979	52.13
Sweden	1979	65.25
United Kingdom	1978/79	63.42
Maximum		*84.32*
Minimum		*40.42*
Average		*56.87*
Variance		*112.87*
Standard deviation		*10.62*
Number of observations		*15*
Developing countries		
Brazil	1981	3.15
Cyprus	1980	23.39
India	1970	4.36
Korea	1981	23.58
Singapore	1980	27.61
Thailand	1975	8.83
Turkey	1976	6.32
Maximum		*27.61*
Minimum		*3.14*
Average		*13.89*
Variance		*110.24*
Standard deviation		*10.50*
Number of observations		*7*

Sources: Computed from annual reports of the taxation departments of various countries; International Monetary Fund, *International Financial Statistics* (Washington), various issues; and Organization for Economic Cooperation and Development, *Tax Elasticities of Central Government Personal Income Tax Systems: A Report by the Committee on Fiscal Affairs* (Paris, 1984).

Table A7. Selected Industrial and Developing Countries: Proportion of Individual Income Tax Collected from Wage and Salary Incomes

(In percent)

	Year	Proportion of Tax
Industrial countries		
Canada	1980	82.05
Japan	1981	81.54
Luxembourg	1981	68.36
Netherlands	1982	82.02
Sweden	1982	93.86
United Kingdom	1981	81.68
United States	1982	83.64
Average		81.88
Developing countries		
Benin	1979	92.96
Cameroon	1982	16.82
Chad	1976	63.44
Côte d'Ivoire	1980	44.23
Cyprus	1980	73.23
Djibouti	1980	99.02
Gabon	1976	92.84
India	1978	25.28
Indonesia	1973/74	69.46
Israel	1980	59.82
Kenya	1976	95.32
Korea	1975	57.73
Mali	1981	33.57
Mauritania	1979	58.18
Mexico	1981	74.96
Morocco	1981	76.33
Niger	1980	62.31
Romania	1976	100.00
Rwanda	1980	100.00
Singapore	1982	69.12
Thailand	1975	78.04
Togo	1980	98.16
Turkey	1976	67.40
Upper Volta	1980	84.99
Zaïre	1981	94.78
Zambia	1981	94.78
Average		72.41

Sources: Computed from annual reports of the taxation departments of various countries; and International Monetary Fund, *Government Finance Statistics Yearbook, 1983,* Vol. 7 (Washington, 1983).

Table A8. Selected Industrial and Developing Countries: Proportion of Individual Income Tax Collected Through Tax-Withholding Schemes

(In percent)

	Year	Proportion of Withholding Taxes
Industrial countries		
United States	1978	91.00
Australia	1978	89.00
Denmark	1978	87.00
Finland	1978	83.00
France	1978	63.00[1]
Ireland	1978	90.00
Netherlands	1978	80.00
Norway	1978	95.00
Sweden	1978	91.00
United Kingdom	1978	89.00
Average		85.80
Developing countries		
Brazil	1981	80.88
Greece	1978	60.00
India	1978/79	37.06
Jamaica	1981/82	93.09
Kenya	1978	75.10
Korea	1981	59.58
Philippines	1979	77.51
Portugal	1978	54.00
Thailand	1982	76.65
Turkey	1976	69.80
Average		68.37

Sources: Computed from annual reports of the taxation departments of various countries; and Organization for Economic Cooperation and Development, *Income Tax Collection Lags: A Report by the Committee on Fiscal Affairs* (Paris, 1983).

[1] Including prepayments and monthly withholding.

Table A9. Selected Developing Countries: Characteristics of the Existing Nominal Income Tax Rate Schedule, Around 1985

(Tax rates in percent; income levels in U.S. dollars and as multiples of per capita gross domestic product in parentheses)[1,2]

	Minimum Tax Rate	Income Level up to[3]	Median Tax Rate[4]	Income Level Exceeding	Maximum Tax Rate	Income Level Exceeding
Argentina	7	5,180 (2.9)	26	30,210 (13.5)	45	64,750 (29.0)
Brazil	0	1,546 (0.9)	30	6,418 (3.7)	60	48,992 (28.5)
Chile	0	3,120 (1.8)	25	21,840 (12.8)	50	46,800 (27.5)
Colombia	10	917 (1.2)	. . .	. . . (. . .)	49	37,747 (. . .)
Côte d'Ivoire	0	795 (1.1)	35	7,000 (9.9)	60	26,730 (37.9)
Cyprus	0	2,968 (0.8)	30	8,905 (2.4)	60	29,670 (8.1)
Egypt	0	2,860 (3.0)	40	85,800 (89.6)	65	286,000 (298.5)
Ghana	0	85 (0.2)	30	534 (1.5)	60	1,250 (3.6)
Guyana	5	120 (0.2)	25	2,482 (4.1)	70[5]	7,970 (13.3)
India	0	1,480 (6.3)	30	2,055 (8.7)	50	8,220 (34.9)
Indonesia	15	8,890 (18.6)	25	8,890 (18.6)	35	44,445 (93.1)
Israel	20	5,124 (0.8)	35	9,897 (1.6)	60	16,685 (4.1)
Jamaica	0	1,565 (2.1)	33.3	1,566 (2.1)	33.3	1,566 (2.1)
Kenya	10	2,210 (7.7)	35	6,635 (23.0)	65	15,480 (53.8)
Korea	6	2,022 (1.1)	27	14,040 (7.6)	55	67,400 (36.3)
Malaysia	5	1,030 (0.5)	25	14,400 (6.7)	40	41,150 (10.1)
Mexico[6]	3.3	272 (0.2)	28.6	5,690 (3.6)	60.5	86,090 (55.1)
Morocco	0	625 (1.0)	30	3,740 (6.1)	60	31,185 (50.8)
Nigeria	10	2,000 (3.2)	40	10,000 (16.2)	75	30,000 (48.7)
Pakistan	0	1,500 (4.8)	25	4,630 (14.9)	45	14,020 (45.1)
Papua New Guinea	0	945 (1.4)	28	6,060 (9.5)	50	30,300 (47.4)
Peru	0	1,335 (2.3)	24	10,670 (18.6)	48	32,000 (55.9)

Philippines[7]	0	130	(0.2)	19	3,150	(19.2)	35	26,275 (44.6)
Singapore	4	2,370	(0.3)	22	16,590	(2.3)	40	355,450 (48.8)
Sudan[8]	0	1,200	(6.4)	. . .	. . .	(. . .)	40	. . . (. . .)
Syrian Arab Rep.[7]	14	510	(0.3)	30	1,275	(0.7)	60	5,100 (2.6)
Thailand	7	1,500	(2.0)	30	11,260	(14.7)	55	75,050 (97.9)
Trinidad and Tobago	5	555	(0.1)	35	4,170	(0.9)	70	22,225 (4.7)
Tunisia[9]	0	1,710	(1.5)	42	5,265	(4.5)	80	131,580 (112.4)
Turkey	25	5,180	(8.0)	35	10,365	(15.9)	50	82,920 (127.4)
Venezuela	4.5	2,665	(0.9)	28	106,665	(37.1)	45	1,066,650 (370.6)
Zaïre	0	80	(1.3)	30	1,840	(30.6)	60[5]	5,377 (89.4)

Note: . . . = relevant information not available.

Source: Based on Jitendra R. Modi, "Levels of Personal Income Taxation in Selected Developing Countries" (unpublished, International Monetary Fund, February 1985).

[1] Income levels are rounded to the nearest figure. Tax rates and corresponding income levels reflect some major adjustments (which follow supply-side policy recommendations) to the statutory tax rate schedules that some of these countries have introduced in recent years. These include reductions in tax rates ranging from 0-66 percent to 0-50 percent by India; 0-55 percent to 0-33.3 percent by Jamaica; 6-60 percent to 6-55 percent by Korea; 6-55 percent to 5-40 percent by Malaysia; 0-66 percent to 0-45 percent by Pakistan; 0-65 percent to 0-48 percent by Peru; 0-70 percent to 0-40 percent by Sudan; and 0-65 percent to 0-55 percent by Thailand and Venezuela. In contrast, tax rates were raised from 0-55 percent to 0-66 percent by Egypt, from 0-45 percent to 0-60 percent by Morocco, and from 10-70 percent to 10-75 percent by Nigeria.

[2] Conversion of income levels in U.S. dollars is based on the market rate or par/central rate (line ae or ag) for 1985 published in International Monetary Fund, *International Financial Statistics* (Washington), September 1986. Per capita GDP data are based on GDP at current market rates and population data published in *IFS* and World Bank, *World Development Report, 1986* (Washington), respectively, for the year nearest to the one in which tax rates are in force. In some instances (e.g., Argentina and Cyprus), data represent estimates.

[3] Income levels are defined as chargeable (or taxable) incomes in the tax schedules of all countries with some very minor exceptions where the tax rate schedules are defined with reference to total or annual incomes.

[4] The median tax rate is the rate which, in each country's schedule of nominal tax rates, lies midway between the maximum and minimum tax rates.

[5] However, in practice, the maximum applicable marginal rate is restricted to 50 percent.

[6] Tax rates include earthquake relief levy equivalent to 10 percent of tax due.

[7] On employment income in the Philippines and on rental income in the Syrian Arab Republic; different schedules of tax rates apply to other income.

[8] Refers to social justice tax in lieu of individual income tax.

[9] Refers to surtax (CPE) on individuals.

Table A10. Selected Developing Countries: Tax Deductions and Exemptions Provided for Promotion of Personal Savings Under Individual Income Tax

Deductions			Exemptions				
Life insurance premiums	Contributions to pension and retire-ment funds	Other[1]	Interest on demand and time deposits	Interest from other financial institutions[2]	Interest on certain public sector bonds	Other interest earnings[3]	Dividend earnings[4]
Argentina	Argentina	—	Argentina	Argentina	Argentina	Argentina	—
Brazil	Brazil	—	—	—	—	Brazil	—
Colombia	—	—	—	—	Colombia[5]	Colombia	—
Cyprus	Cyprus	Cyprus	Cyprus	—	Cyprus	—	Cyprus[6]
Egypt	Egypt	Egypt	Egypt	Egypt	Egypt	Egypt[7]	—
Ghana	Ghana	—	Ghana	Ghana	Ghana[8]	—	—
Guyana	Guyana	—	—	—	—	—	—
India	India	India	India	India	India	India	India[9]
Indonesia	Indonesia	—	Indonesia	Indonesia		—	Indonesia[10]
Israel	Israel	. . .	. . .	. . .	. . .	. . .	. . .
. . .	Côte d'Ivoire	. . .	. . .	. . .	Côte d'Ivoire[11]	. . .	. . .
Jamaica	—	Jamaica	—	Jamaica	Jamaica	Jamaica	—
Kenya	Kenya	—	Kenya	Kenya	Kenya[12]	Kenya[12]	—
Korea	—	—	Korea[13]	Korea[13]	Korea[13]	Korea[13]	—
Malaysia	Malaysia	—	Malaysia	Malaysia	—	—	Malaysia[14]
Mexico[15]	Mexico[15]	—	—	Mexico	—	—	—
—	Morocco	—	—	—	—	—	—
Nigeria	Nigeria	—	—	Nigeria	Nigeria[16]	—	—
Pakistan	Pakistan	Pakistan	—	Pakistan	Pakistan[16]	Pakistan[17]	Pakistan[18]
—	—	—	—	—	—	—	Papua New Guinea[19]
Peru	—	Peru[20]	—	Peru	—	—	Peru[20]
—	—	—	Philippines	Philippines	—	—	—

Singapore	Singapore	—	Singapore[21]	Singapore[21]	Singapore	Singapore[21]	—
—	—	—	—	—	—	—	Sudan
—	—	—	—	Syrian Arab Rep.	—	—	—
Thailand	—	—	—	Thailand	Thailand	Thailand[22]	Thailand[23]
Trinidad and Tobago	Trinidad and Tobago[24]	Trinidad and Tobago	—	Trinidad and Tobago	—	—	—
Tunisia	—	Tunisia[25]	—	—	—	Tunisia[25]	—
Venezuela	—	Venezuela	Venezuela	Venezuela	Venezuela	Venezuela[26]	Venezuela[27]
Zaïre[28]	Zaïre[28]	—	—	—	—	—	—

Note: . . . = information not available; — = does not apply.

Source: Based on Jitendra R. Modi, "Levels of Personal Income Taxation in Selected Developing Countries" (unpublished, International Monetary Fund, February 1985).

[1] Such as subscriptions to shares of an approved company, unit-linked insurance plan, Investment Fund, special government bonds, credit union and cooperative shares, and employees' savings funds.

[2] Such as post office savings, development or housing banks, and investment trusts.

[3] Such as interest paid on foreign loans or accruing to nonresident account holders.

[4] Other than from "tax holiday" companies and stock dividends. [5] On some pre-1974 securities only.

[6] Up to specified amounts received from public companies. [7] Interest mainly on joint stock companies' bonds. [8] If held by nonresidents.

[9] Up to specified amounts received from domestic companies and an additional amount received from the Unit Trust of India.

[10] "Participation" dividends, that is, if the shareholder is entitled to participate in the enterprise's profits.

[11] On treasury bills. [12] On tax reserve certificates and on specified government securities held by nonresidents.

[13] Minor amounts earned on bank accounts, specified government bonds, and investments.

[14] Specified maximum on unit trust holdings. [15] Contributions to institutions authorized by the Treasury Department. [16] On government savings certificates.

[17] Payable by an industrial undertaking and nonresident account holdings.

[18] Up to specified amounts received by resident taxpayers from all public and "listed" private companies and by nonresidents from the State Enterprises Mutual Fund.

[19] Arising from revaluation of assets and dividends paid to nonresident shareholders in petroleum companies.

[20] Reinvestment of income free of tax, in certain enterprises.

[21] From approved banks, post office savings bank, and Asian Eurodollar bonds held by nonresidents.

[22] On long-term foreign currency borrowing registered with the central bank and up to a specified rate of interest (8.5 percent) on savings deposits with the lotteries, on savings deposits with the Government, and on time deposits with the cooperatives.

[23] Specified amount of dividends from "listed" (on local stock exchange) companies. [24] Deferred annuity premiums.

[25] Reinvested interest income. [26] On loans from foreign governments and international public financial organizations.

[27] From public companies and up to 50 percent from "listed" companies. [28] On compulsory employer schemes.

Table A11. Selected Developing Countries: Final Withholding Tax Rates Payable on Certain Investment Incomes

	Source of Income	Final Withholding Tax	Relevant Maximum Nominal Tax Rate
		(In percent)	
Argentina	Interest and dividends received by nonregistered taxpayers	5–17	45
Brazil	Dividends on nonbearer shares	15	60
Korea	Specified interest and dividends	5–25	55
Mexico	Fixed income from bank deposits, bonds, debentures, and mortgage certificates	21	55
Peru	Bearer bonds	40	48
Philippines	Dividends and interest on savings and time deposits	15–20	60
Thailand	Interest on government bonds or debentures; interest on deposits with cooperatives; and specified interest received on deposits from finance companies[1] or banks[2]	15	55
Tunisia	Interest on deposits and reinvested dividends	11.5–16.7	80
Venezuela	Dividends from mining companies	20	45
Zaïre	All interest and dividend earnings	15	60

Source: Based on Jitendra R. Modi, "Levels of Personal Income Taxation in Selected Developing Countries" (unpublished, International Monetary Fund, February 1985).

[1] Established to lend money for the promotion of agriculture, commerce, or industry.

[2] Interest exceeding the specified rate (8.5 percent) on savings deposits with the lotteries, on savings deposits with the Government, and on time deposits with the cooperatives.

Table A12. Selected Developing Countries: Minimum Income at Which Individual Income Tax Applies to a "Representative Taxpayer"[1] in 1985

(In multiples of per capita gross domestic product)[2]

	Threshold Income Level
Argentina	2.3
Brazil	1.6
Chile	2.0
Colombia	1.5
Cyprus	1.2
Egypt	4.4
Ghana	0.4
Guyana	1.6
India	6.3
Indonesia	4.5
Jamaica	2.1
Kenya	1.7
Korea	0.7
Malaysia	1.6
Mexico	1.1
Morocco	1.8
Nigeria	3.3
Pakistan	4.8
Papua New Guinea	3.3
Peru	5.8
Philippines	1.5
Singapore	0.3
Thailand	1.9
Trinidad and Tobago	0.3
Tunisia	1.8
Turkey	0.2
Venezuela	1.1
Zaïre	1.7

Source: Based on Jitendra R. Modi, "Levels of Personal Income Taxation in Selected Developing Countries" (unpublished, International Monetary Fund, February 1985).

[1] A married person with a nonworking spouse and two dependents.

[2] At current market prices.

Table A13. Selected Developing Countries: Nominal Tax Rates Applicable to Corporate Profits[1]

	Regular Tax Rate (RTR)	Special Tax Rate (STR)	Comments
Argentina	33	45	Special tax rate (STR) on branches of foreign corporations.
Brazil	35	6	STRs on agriculture and public transportation companies.
Chile	37	10	STR on undistributed income.
Colombia	40	Varies	Regular tax rate (RTR) subject to reduction in proportion to additional investment under certain conditions.
Côte d'Ivoire	40	None	RTR excludes 10 percent national contribution tax which is refundable on reinvestment.
Cyprus	42.5	25;4.25	STRs on public and offshore companies, respectively.
Egypt	40	32–42.5	STRs on industrial or export activities and on oil exploration and oil producing companies.
Ghana	55	35–45;45;50	STRs on wholly Ghanaian-owned small companies; on agriculture and mining companies; and on industrial companies.
Guyana	55	45	20 percentage points of RTR is company income tax which is creditable to shareholder; STRs apply to nontrading and life insurance profits (for the latter the entire tax is creditable to taxpayer).
India	50	55–60;20–65	Tax rates exclusive of 5 percent surcharge (refundable if deposited with Industrial Development Bank); STRs on closely held companies and on specific earnings of foreign companies.
Indonesia	15–35	35	STR on certain mining companies in first ten years of operation plus 60 percent tax on profit in excess of standard return (15 percent) on investment.
Israel	61	10–25;30;52	RTR comprises income tax of 35 percent on profits net of corporation tax (21 percent on total profits) and is creditable to shareholders. STRs apply to foreign companies, approved investment (mainly industrial) companies, and industrial ventures, respectively.
Jamaica	45	12.5;35;40; 47.5;55	RTR includes additional 10 percent company profit tax creditable to shareholders; STRs apply to international finance companies, agricultural enterprises, industrial and provident societies, and banks, respectively.

Table A13 *(continued)*. Selected Developing Countries: Nominal Tax Rates Applicable to Corporate Profits[1]

	Regular Tax Rate (RTR)	Special Tax Rate (STR)	Comments
Kenya	45	27.5-45;40; 52.5	STRs apply to mining, resident insurance, and foreign companies, respectively.
Korea	25.9-43.8	25.9-40.8	RTR includes defense tax of 20-25 percent and resident tax of 7.5 percent; STR applies to "listed" companies, that is, those with shares quoted on local stock exchange.
Malaysia	48	50;0	RTR inclusive of 5 percent development tax and 3 percent excess profit tax; STR (inclusive of 5 percent development tax) applies to petroleum companies and shipping lines, respectively.
Mexico	5-42	2.5-21;3-25.2	STRs on book publishers and agricultural companies, respectively.
Morocco	44-52.8	None	RTR includes 10 percent National Solidarity Tax.
Nigeria	45	55;65.75	STR on banks and petroleum companies (the latter prior to full cost amortization—85 percent thereafter); construction firms are subject to a 2.5 percent minimum turnover tax.
Pakistan	55	65;50;45;40	RTR comprises 30 percent income tax and 25 percent supertax. STRs apply on account of the varying rebates granted to the following: banks, specified small companies, agricultural food processing companies, foreign incomes, and specified public companies.
Papua New Guinea	35	38.5;48;50	STRs apply, respectively, to real estate companies (inclusive of 10 percent surcharge on tax due) and to petroleum companies and other mining companies (at full cost during amortization period and at 75 percent and 67.5 percent thereafter).
Peru	20-40	0;10-20	RTR scaled to profit levels; STRs apply to agricultural companies and regional activities, respectively.
Philippines	25-35	10;35-45	RTR scaled to profit levels; STRs apply to mutual life insurance companies, educational establishments, and closely held companies, respectively.
Singapore	40	10	STR applies to certain finance companies.
Sudan	20-50	60	RTR scaled to profit levels; STR includes 10 percent surtax on profits exceeding specified amount.

Table A13 ***(concluded).*** **Selected Developing Countries: Nominal Tax Rates Applicable to Corporate Profits**[1]

	Regular Tax Rate (RTR)	Special Tax Rate (STR)	Comments
Syrian Arab Rep.	14.5-92.4	None	RTR includes a war surtax of 30 percent and a municipal surcharge of 2 percent to 10 percent of the tax due.
Thailand	35	30;43-46	STRs on "listed" companies and on company profits remitted abroad (additional remittance tax is 20 percent of posttax profit on both listed and unlisted companies), respectively.
Trinidad and Tobago	50	20;58.3;80.3	RTR includes 5 percent unemployment levy; STRs apply to life insurance companies, petroleum companies, and marine enterprises, respectively.
Tunisia	38;44	6-15;20	All companies subject to a standard advance minimum tax (deductible from final assessment) payable at 1 percent of turnover. RTR applies to commercial and industrial companies, respectively, and STR to agricultural and artisan companies, respectively.
Turkey	47.38	0-42.38	RTR includes 3 percent defense fund payable on regular corporate tax due. STR effectively applicable on account of varying levels of rebates available on different sources of export earnings.
Venezuela	18-50	67.7;60	STR on oil and other mining companies, respectively.
Zaïre	50	0;24-60	STRs apply to "free zone" profits during first five years and to real estate companies, respectively, the latter being subject to a special schedular tax on profits. STRs also apply to petroleum and other mining companies as stipulated in the agreement between the Government and the companies concerned.

Source: Based on Jitendra R. Modi, "Major Features of Corporate Profit Taxes in Selected Developing Countries," International Bureau of Fiscal Documentation, *Bulletin* (Amsterdam), Vol. 41 (February 1987), pp. 65-74.

[1]The table reflects recent revisions that have taken place in the tax codes of individual countries.

Table A14. Selected Industrial and Developing Countries: Effective Corporate Tax Rates

(In percent)

	Year	Effective Tax Rate[1]	Nominal Tax Rates
Industrial countries			
United States	1980	35.4[3]	17-46
Canada	1980	35.6	50
United Kingdom	1979	35.9	40; 52[2]
Developing countries			
Brazil	1981	17.6	35-40
Cyprus	1980	14.6	42.5
India	1978/79	49.8	46.1-56.4
Kenya	1977	40.9	45
Korea	1978	34.7	28.1-50.4
Malaysia	1976	39.6	50
Papua New Guinea	1977	28.0	36.5
Syrian Arab Rep.	1976	27.1	14.5-92.4
Thailand	1978	32.4	40

Source: Based on Jitendra R. Modi, "Major Features of Corporate Profit Taxes in Selected Developing Countries," International Bureau of Fiscal Documentation, *Bulletin* (Amsterdam), Vol. 41 (February 1987), pp. 65-74.

[1]The ratio of corporation tax assessed to total assessed income of the corporation.

[2]The lower rate applies to small companies.

[3]Relates to returns of active corporations.

Table A15. Selected Developing Countries: Incentives Available to Corporate Entities Subject to Profits Tax

	Depreciation				Availability of Investment Allowance, Tax Credit, or Development Rebate	Maximum Shifts and Percentage Increases in Normal Depreciation	Basis of Inventory Valuation[1]	Carry-Over of Losses	Period of Tax Holiday
	Formula	Asset price	Initial	Annual					
			P&M;B;V	P&M;B;V	P&M				
			(In percent)					(Number of years)	
Argentina	St.line	Curr.	—;—;—	10;2;20	10-35(ITC)	. . .	Cost/Market[1]	5	10
Brazil	St.line	Curr.	—;—;—	10;4;20	—	DS-TS (50-100)	Cost/Market[1]	4	10-15
Chile	St.line	Curr.	6.6;3.3-5.3; 18.6	5;2.5-4;14	—	Unspec.	Replacement cost	Unltd.	None
Colombia	St.line	Hist.	40;40;40	10;5;20	—	TS(25-50)	LIFO	5	None
Côte d'Ivoire	St.line	Hist.	20;5;33.3	10;5;33.3	—	—	Cost/Market/LIFO	3[2]	7-11[2]
Cyprus	St.line	Hist.	100;100;—	10;3-4;20	10-55(IA)[3]	—	Cost/Net sale price[1]	Unltd.	10
Egypt	Opt.	Hist.	35-45;2-5; 20-25	10-15;2-5; 20-25	—	—	Opt. LIFO/FIFO	5	5
Ghana	Dec.bal.	Hist.	20;10;20	5-20;3;5-10	5(IA)	—	. . .	Varies[4]	3[4]
Guyana	Dec.bal.	Hist.	7-33.3; 2-5;10	7-33.3; 2-5;10	—	—	Cost/Market[1]	Unltd.	. . .
India	Dec.bal.	Hist.	—;25-40;—	15-100;5-10; 5-20	25(IA)[5]	DS-TS (50-100)	Cost/Market[1]	Varies[6]	8[7]
Indonesia	Dec.bal.[8]	Hist.[8]	10;5;20-50	10;5;20-50[8]	—	—	Av. cost/FIFO	5-8	None
Israel	St.line	Curr.[9]	10-15;2-8; 15-20	10-15;2-8; 15-20	—	—	FIFO/Av. cost	Unltd.	5[10]
Jamaica	Dec.bal.	Hist.	20;20;12.5	7.5-10;2.5-5; 12.5	20;40; 70(IA)[11]	Unspec.	Cost/Market[1]	5	5-10

Kenya	Dec.bal.[12]	Hist.	12.5–37.5; 2.5–4;25	12.5–37.5; 2.5–4;25	50(IA)[13]	. . .	Av. cost/Market	Unltd.[14]	None
Korea	Opt.	Hist.[15]	100;1.7–4;20	6.6–20;1.7–4; 16.6–33.3	3–5(ITC)[16]	DS-TS(20–50)	Cost/Market/LIFO	3	5
Malaysia	St.line	Hist.	100;12;. . .	6–20;2;. . .	25(ITC)[17]	Unspec.	Cost/Market[1]	Unltd.	2–8
Mexico	St.line	Curr.[9]	25–50;25–50; 20	10;5;20	30(ITC)[17]	—	Market/LIFO	4	None
Morocco	St.line	Curr.[9]	—;—;—	15–20;—;—	12(IA)	—	FIFO/Av. cost	5	10
Nigeria	St.line	Hist.	20;5–15;25	9;9–10;25	—	—	FIFO	4	3–5
Pakistan	Dec.bal.	Hist.	40;10;—	10;5;20	15–30(ITC)	DS-TS (50–100)	Cost/Market/LIFO	6	5
Papua New Guinea	Opt.	Hist.	40–50;23;. . .	20;3;20	20(IA)	Unspec.	Av. cost/Market[1]	7	3–7[18]
Peru	St.line	Curr.[9]	5–30;3;5–15	5–30;3;5–15	Varies(ITC)[19]	—	Av. cost/FIFO[1]	4	Unltd.[18]
Philippines	Opt.	Hist.	Unspec.	Reasonable	25–100(IA)	DS	Cost/Market[1]	6	None
Singapore	St.line	Hist.	20–100;25;10	16–0;3;10	Up to 50(IA)	—	Av. cost/FIFO[1]	Unltd.	5
Sudan	St.line	Hist.	5–15;2.5–10; 20–25	5–15;2.5–10; 20–25	—	—	FIFO	5	5
Syrian Arab Rep.	St.line	Hist.	. . .;5–20;. . .	5–10;—;20[20]	—	—	. . .	5	None
Thailand	St.line	Hist.	Unspec.	20;5;20	—	—	Cost/Market[1]	5	3–8[21]
Trinidad and Tobago	Dec.bal.	Hist.	20–50;10;25	10–25;2;25	30(IA)[22]	—	Cost/Market[1]	Unltd.	10
Tunisia	St.line	Curr.[9]	12.5;20;20	12.5;20;20	—	—	. . .	3	3–5
Turkey	Opt.	Curr.[9]	—;—;—	6–20;2–4;. . .	30–60(IA)	—	Av. cost	5	None
Venezuela	St.line	Hist.	—;—;—	Unspec.	10–30(ITC)	—	Cost/Market	3	10
Zaïre	St.line	Hist.	20–25;3–5; 20–25	20–25;3–5; 20–25	—	—	Cost/Market	2	5

Note: . . . = relevant information not available; — = the countries concerned do not extend the incentive.
The following abbreviations have been used in the table:
P&M = Plant and machinery
B = Industrial buildings
Hist. = Historical
TS = Triple shift

Table A15 *(concluded)*. Selected Developing Countries: Incentives Available to Corporate Entities Subject to Profits Tax

V = Vehicles
St. line = Straight line
Curr. = Current
ITC = Income tax credit on cost of investment
DS-TS = Double or triple shift
Unspec. = Unspecified
Unltd. = Unlimited

LIFO = Last in, first out
IA = Investment allowance, usually on plant and machinery
Opt. = Optional
FIFO = First in, first out
Dec. bal. = Declining balance
Av. cost = Average cost
DS = Double shift

Source: Based on Jitendra R. Modi, "Major Features of Corporate Profit Taxes in Developing Countries," International Bureau of Fiscal Documentation, *Bulletin* (Amsterdam), Vol. 41 (February 1987), pp. 65–74.

[1] Whichever is lower, but not LIFO.
[2] Deferred depreciation indefinitely; tax holiday period extendable to 15 years by special convention with host country.
[3] To manufacturing and certain agricultural companies only; allowance to public companies 5 to 15 percentage points higher than to others.
[4] Unlimited carryover for agricultural companies; nil for others. Tax holiday phased out on a diminishing basis.
[5] On new ships, aircraft, and machinery.
[6] Duration for carryover of losses is four years for long-term capital losses and eight years for short-term capital losses, except unabsorbed depreciation for which it is unlimited.
[7] Only on 75 percent of manufacturing profits.
[8] Except buildings for which straight line method is applied; depreciation rates depend on life of assets (e.g., 50 percent for assets having a life of up to four years and 10 percent for those over eight years).
[9] After revaluation of the balance sheet.
[10] Exempt from income tax at 35 percent but not from corporation tax of 40 percent.
[11] Higher rates apply to agriculture and sugar industry and to motion picture companies.
[12] Except on industrial buildings and hotels.
[13] On new industrial buildings and hotels and on machinery installed therein, located outside main cities.
[14] Losses can be offset only against profits from the same source.
[15] Except when assets are revalued.
[16] To machinery and electronics industry only.
[17] As an alternative to accelerated depreciation.
[18] On export income in full (Papua New Guinea) or partially (Peru).
[19] On reinvested profits.
[20] For industrial buildings the annual rental value of property is deductible in lieu of depreciation.
[21] For additional five years, exemption of 50 percent.
[22] As an alternative to tax holiday.

Table A16. Selected Industrial and Developing Countries: Export Duties as Percentage of F.o.b. Value of Exports, 1980–82

	1980	1981	1982	Average 1980–82
Industrial countries				
Canada	1.063	1.106	0.450	0.873
Australia	0.455	0.301	0.282	0.346
New Zealand	0.144	0.122	0.139	0.135
Austria	0.217	0.214	0.082	0.171
Iceland	0.045	0.043	0.039	0.042
Norway	0.048	0.057	0.060	0.055
United Kingdom	0.023	0.020	0.018	0.020
Maximum				*0.873*
Minimum				*0.020*
Mean				*0.235*
Variance				*0.092*
Standard deviation				*0.303*
Number of observations				*7*
Developing countries				
Oil exporting countries				
Indonesia	2.220	0.914	0.560	1.231
Nigeria	0.007	—	—	0.002
Maximum				*1.231*
Minimum				*0.002*
Mean				*0.617*
Variance				*0.755*
Standard deviation				*0.870*
Number of observations				*2*
Non-oil developing countries				
Africa				
Benin	5.711	4.118	2.932	4.254
Botswana	0.125	0.146	0.131	0.134
Burkina Faso	6.362	5.121	4.633	5.372
Burundi	22.638	2.654	13.927	13.073
Cameroon	7.759	10.016	4.799	7.525
Central African Rep.	4.101	13.600	9.870	9.190
Congo	0.156	0.091	0.061	0.103
Côte d'Ivoire	8.027	8.504	7.348	7.960
Ethiopia	33.832	23.377	22.108	26.439
Gabon	1.677	0.920	0.986	1.194
Gambia, The	13.708	0.933	3.827	6.156
Ghana	26.781	6.860	14.359	16.000
Kenya	1.357	0.592	0.932	0.960
Lesotho	6.184	5.107	3.584	4.958
Liberia	0.250	0.208	0.230	0.229
Madagascar	3.298	4.495	4.710	4.168
Mali	6.225	7.549	4.010	5.928

Table A16 *(continued)*. Selected Industrial and Developing Countries: Export Duties as Percentage of F.o.b. Value of Exports, 1980–82

	1980	1981	1982	Average 1980–82
Mauritania	0.707	3.616	4.515	2.946
Mauritius	8.598	8.942	9.472	9.004
Morocco	2.229	2.080	1.974	2.095
Niger	2.594	3.156	3.467	3.072
Rwanda	37.868	16.413	13.747	22.676
Senegal	2.749	1.126	0.722	1.532
Sierra Leone	11.089	9.385	10.150	10.208
Swaziland	4.672	3.615	0.380	2.889
Tanzania	11.094	4.472	1.017	5.528
Togo	4.659	1.309	0.736	2.234
Tunisia	1.072	1.038	0.987	1.033
Uganda	51.372	3.624	22.385	25.794
Zaïre	14.950	10.587	10.296	11.944
Maximum				*26.439*
Minimum				*0.103*
Mean				*7.153*
Variance				*52.998*
Standard deviation				*7.280*
Number of observations				*30*
Asia				
Bangladesh	24.292	25.746	20.459	23.499
Fiji	1.378	2.253	0.957	1.529
India	1.748	0.850	0.769	1.122
Malaysia	9.076	8.208	6.119	7.801
Maldives	1.533	0.153	0.854	0.846
Nepal	6.492	4.015	3.636	4.714
Pakistan	1.721	2.474	1.393	1.863
Papua New Guinea	1.262	0.792	0.792	0.949
Philippines	0.985	0.713	0.679	0.792
Sri Lanka	21.927	18.662	12.832	17.807
Thailand	2.600	2.044	1.108	1.917
Maximum				*23.499*
Minimum				*0.792*
Mean				*5.713*
Variance				*60.638*
Standard deviation				*7.787*
Number of observations				*11*
Europe				
Greece	0.032	0.004	0.035	0.024
Portugal	0.018	0.013	0.011	0.014
Maximum				*0.024*
Minimum				*0.014*
Mean				*0.019*
Variance				—
Standard deviation				*0.007*
Number of observations				*2*

Table A16 *(continued).* **Selected Industrial and Developing Countries: Export Duties as Percentage of F.o.b. Value of Exports, 1980–82**

	1980	1981	1982	Average 1980–82
Middle East				
Syrian Arab Rep.	1.704	1.454	0.641	1.267
Yemen Arab Rep.	0.097	0.092	0.056	0.082
Maximum				*1.267*
Minimum				*0.082*
Mean				*0.675*
Variance				*0.702*
Standard deviation				*0.838*
Number of observations				*2*
Western Hemisphere				
Argentina	2.442	2.693	7.076	4.070
Bahamas	0.059	0.108	0.131	0.099
Barbados	—	—	0.483	0.161
Belize	1.066	0.889	1.114	1.023
Bolivia	0.550	0.045	0.123	0.239
Brazil	6.049	1.697	2.347	3.364
Colombia	7.257	6.332	3.630	5.740
Costa Rica	6.579	8.566	9.971	8.372
Dominican Rep.	6.165	7.399	1.342	4.969
Ecuador	1.501	0.899	0.372	0.924
El Salvador	10.298	11.828	11.409	11.178
Grenada	10.225	10.125	7.986	9.445
Guatemala	9.617	5.447	4.188	6.418
Guyana	0.131	0.164	0.124	0.140
Haiti	11.321	5.905	5.572	7.599
Honduras	7.735	7.486	7.074	7.431
Mexico	38.180	41.188	34.325	37.897
Nicaragua	5.642	4.846	0.442	3.643
Panama	3.495	4.724	3.975	4.065
Paraguay	1.026	0.838	0.753	0.872
Peru	10.956	8.456	6.551	8.654
St. Lucia	0.121	0.205	0.944	0.423
St. Vincent	1.399	1.063	1.258	1.240
Trinidad and Tobago	—	—	0.001	—
Uruguay	—	0.023	0.049	0.024
Maximum				*37.897*
Minimum				*0.024*
Mean				*5.333*
Variance				*60.292*
Standard deviation				*7.765*
Number of observations				*24*
Developing countries				
Maximum				*37.897*
Minimum				*0.002*

Table A16 *(concluded)*. Selected Industrial and Developing Countries: Export Duties as Percentage of F.o.b. Value of Exports, 1980–82

	1980	1981	1982	Average 1980–82
Mean				*5.747*
Variance				*53.781*
Standard deviation				*7.336*
Number of observations				*71*
All countries				
Maximum				*37.897*
Minimum				*0.002*
Mean				*5.252*
Variance				*51.414*
Standard deviation				*7.170*
Number of observations				*78*

Note: — = negligible.

Sources: International Monetary Fund, *Government Finance Statistics Yearbook, 1984*, Vol. 8 (Washington, 1984), *International Financial Statistics* (Washington), various issues, and Fund staff estimates; and Organization for Economic Cooperation and Development, *Revenue Statistics of OECD Member Countries, 1965–1983* (Paris, 1984).

Table A17. Selected Industrial and Developing Countries: Import Duties as Percentage of C.i.f. Value of Imports, 1980–82

	1980	1981	1982	Average 1980–82
Industrial countries				
United States	2.891	2.985	3.496	3.124
Canada	4.353	4.090	3.953	4.132
Australia	7.834	7.882	7.860	7.859
Japan	2.457	2.578	2.502	2.512
New Zealand	4.115	5.089	4.621	4.609
Austria	1.542	1.462	1.537	1.513
Belgium[1]	0.005	0.004	0.004	0.004
Denmark	0.943	0.875	0.876	0.898
Finland	1.785	1.541	1.586	1.637
France	0.070	0.076	0.066	0.071
Germany, Fed. Rep. of	0.023	0.022	0.027	0.024
Iceland	14.414	15.733	15.064	15.070
Ireland	8.357	10.048	10.754	9.720
Italy	0.255	0.224	0.290	0.256
Luxembourg[1]	—	0.065	0.063	0.042
Netherlands	0.006	—	—	0.002
Norway	0.854	0.982	0.840	0.892
Spain	9.140	8.558	9.685	9.128
Sweden	1.514	1.684	0.782	1.327
Switzerland	5.208	5.398	5.620	5.409
Maximum				*15.070*
Minimum				*0.002*
Mean				*3.411*
Variance				*17.156*
Standard deviation				*4.142*
Number of observations				*20*
Developing countries				
Oil exporting countries				
Indonesia	6.595	6.395	4.680	5.890
Iran, Islamic Rep. of	18.580	17.233	22.453	19.422
Kuwait	3.060	3.547	3.648	3.418
Nigeria	15.286	13.672	13.203	14.054
Oman	1.454	1.430	1.587	1.490
Venezuela	8.858	9.851	12.604	10.438
Maximum				*19.422*
Minimum				*1.490*
Mean				*9.119*
Variance				*46.675*
Standard deviation				*6.832*
Number of observations				*6*

Table A17 *(continued).* Selected Industrial and Developing Countries: Import Duties as Percentage of C.i.f. Value of Imports, 1980–82

	1980	1981	1982	Average 1980–82
Non-oil developing countries				
Africa				
Benin	30.409	26.943	24.597	27.317
Botswana	19.001	15.674	16.267	16.981
Burkina Faso	21.351	19.453	18.052	19.618
Burundi	21.159	18.147	16.598	18.635
Cameroon	19.321	20.006	21.364	20.230
Central African Rep.	57.029	30.414	23.483	36.975
Congo	12.810	17.435	12.545	14.263
Côte d'Ivoire	25.828	28.692	25.972	26.831
Ethiopia	16.017	18.660	16.882	17.186
Gabon	39.070	27.997	25.193	30.753
Gambia, The	19.275	19.554	25.219	21.349
Ghana	12.429	15.518	29.376	19.108
Kenya	10.688	15.653	21.768	16.036
Lesotho	19.789	15.765	13.430	16.328
Liberia	12.345	17.232	17.697	15.758
Madagascar	22.399	15.556	16.231	18.062
Malawi	11.770	16.007	16.349	14.709
Mali	11.270	14.051	16.087	13.803
Mauritania	16.617	16.689	21.083	18.130
Mauritius	13.564	14.234	13.656	13.818
Morocco	19.740	17.411	18.077	18.410
Niger	19.454	17.977	16.722	18.051
Rwanda	14.250	14.270	15.046	14.522
Senegal	22.388	16.019	17.111	18.506
Sierra Leone	15.531	23.052	18.780	19.121
Swaziland	18.537	12.077	20.894	17.169
Tanzania	7.945	6.529	6.255	6.910
Togo	14.300	15.914	16.254	15.489
Tunisia	18.461	17.439	21.843	19.247
Uganda	8.321	3.480	10.652	7.484
Zaïre	33.362	40.865	49.038	41.088
Zambia	6.153	5.642	7.807	6.534
Zimbabwe	3.921	8.792	13.528	8.747
Maximum				*41.088*
Minimum				*6.534*
Mean				*18.399*
Variance				*55.688*
Standard deviation				*7.462*
Number of observations				*33*

Table A17 *(continued)*. Selected Industrial and Developing Countries: Import Duties as Percentage of C.i.f. Value of Imports, 1980–82

	1980	1981	1982	Average 1980–82
Asia				
Bangladesh	15.588	15.492	14.578	15.219
Burma	39.276	45.069	44.870	43.072
Fiji	11.529	12.415	11.945	11.963
India	28.192	31.782	35.235	31.736
Korea	7.485	6.686	7.425	7.199
Malaysia	8.831	8.442	7.976	8.417
Maldives	5.228	6.960	7.614	6.600
Nepal	13.279	16.408	14.949	14.879
Pakistan	22.893	24.341	22.685	23.306
Papua New Guinea	6.930	7.499	9.001	7.810
Philippines	12.509	11.265	12.262	12.012
Singapore	0.851	0.737	0.810	0.799
Sri Lanka	8.618	8.818	9.403	8.946
Thailand	10.055	10.093	10.084	10.077
Maximum				*43.072*
Minimum				*0.799*
Mean				*14.431*
Variance				*126.138*
Standard deviation				*11.231*
Number of observations				*14*
Europe				
Cyprus	7.764	7.715	8.190	7.890
Greece	5.737	3.961	4.055	4.584
Malta	11.052	10.597	10.235	10.628
Portugal	4.058	3.932	3.673	3.888
Turkey	8.495	7.095	10.157	8.582
Maximum				*10.628*
Minimum				*3.888*
Mean				*7.114*
Variance				*7.978*
Standard deviation				*2.825*
Number of observations				*5*
Middle East				
Bahrain	1.919	1.715	2.406	2.014
Egypt	36.929	23.342	26.857	29.042
Israel	4.153	4.542	7.456	5.384
Jordan	14.130	11.782	12.312	12.741
Syrian Arab Rep.	11.247	10.111	14.142	11.833
Yemen Arab Rep.	19.154	20.356	26.514	22.008
Maximum				*29.042*
Minimum				*2.014*
Mean				*13.837*
Variance				*102.882*
Standard deviation				*10.143*
Number of observations				*6*

Table A17 *(continued)*. Selected Industrial and Developing Countries: Import Duties as Percentage of C.i.f. Value of Imports, 1980–82

	1980	1981	1982	Average 1980–82
Western Hemisphere				
Argentina	20.148	19.146	13.833	17.709
Bahamas	2.542	3.481	5.034	3.686
Barbados	8.560	7.784	6.745	7.696
Belize	11.377	11.514	12.007	11.632
Bolivia	16.527	14.878	11.810	14.405
Brazil	6.711	6.346	6.330	6.462
Chile	7.466	8.609	7.304	7.793
Colombia	11.350	10.568	10.426	10.781
Costa Rica	6.190	3.419	2.954	4.188
Dominican Rep.	13.857	10.997	12.069	12.308
Ecuador	16.266	16.852	14.709	15.942
El Salvador	4.097	3.530	3.707	3.778
Grenada	16.154	15.609	20.944	17.569
Guatemala	7.003	6.287	5.611	6.301
Guyana	3.704	3.881	3.166	3.584
Haiti	10.417	10.723	11.994	11.045
Honduras	7.420	10.547	12.719	10.229
Jamaica	2.214	3.503	4.921	3.546
Mexico	10.815	10.508	10.261	10.528
Nicaragua	10.794	6.751	9.108	8.884
Panama	5.875	6.130	6.563	6.189
Paraguay	14.444	14.756	9.695	12.965
Peru	21.945	22.012	18.975	20.977
St. Lucia	9.122	9.372	9.936	9.476
St. Vincent	12.451	11.394	14.347	12.731
Trinidad and Tobago	5.537	6.257	6.081	5.958
Uruguay	19.092	19.153	18.123	18.789
Maximum				*20.977*
Minimum				*3.546*
Mean				*10.191*
Variance				*25.323*
Standard deviation				*5.032*
Number of observations				*27*
Developing countries				
Maximum				*43.072*
Minimum				*0.799*
Mean				*13.820*
Variance				*69.668*
Standard deviation				*8.347*
Number of observations				*91*

Table A17 *(concluded)*. Selected Industrial and Developing Countries: Import Duties as Percentage of C.i.f. Value of Imports, 1980–82

	1980	1981	1982	Average 1980–82
All countries				
Maximum				*43.072*
Minimum				*0.002*
Mean				*11.945*
Variance				*76.115*
Standard deviation				*8.724*
Number of observations				*111*

Note: — = negligible.

Sources: International Monetary Fund, *Government Finance Statistics Yearbook, 1984,* Vol. 8 (Washington, 1984), *International Financial Statistics* (Washington), various issues, and Fund staff estimates; and Organization for Economic Cooperation and Development, *Revenue Statistics of OECD Member Countries, 1965–1983* (Paris, 1984).

[1]Import data refer to Belgium-Luxembourg and exclude transactions between the two countries.

APPENDIX II

Selected Bibliography

This bibliography covers major publications containing the views of popular supply-side economists in the United States on taxation and the Laffer curve. It also covers a few publications on related subjects such as tax incentives, tax evasion, and progressivity of tax rates.

Agell, Jonas, "Subsidy to Capital Through Tax Incentives in the ASEAN Countries: An Application of the Cost of Capital Approach Under Inflationary Situations," *Singapore Economic Review* (Singapore), Vol. 28 (October 1983), pp. 98–128.

Bartlett, Bruce R., *Reagonomics: Supply Side Economics in Action* (New York: Quill, updated ed., 1982).

———, "Supply-Side Economics: Theory and Evidence," *Quarterly Review,* National Westminster Bank (London), February 1985, pp. 18–29.

Bird, R., *Tax Incentives for Investment: The State of the Art,* Canadian Tax Paper No. 64 (Toronto: Canadian Tax Foundation, 1980).

Bosworth, Barry P., *Tax Incentives and Economic Growth* (Washington: Brookings Institution, 1984).

Canto, Victor A., Douglas H. Joines, and Arthur B. Laffer, *Foundations of Supply-Side Economics: Theory and Evidence* (New York: Academic Press, 1983).

Chatterji, M., "A Note on Progressive Taxes and the Supply of Labor," *Journal of Public Economics* (Amsterdam), Vol. 12 (October 1979), pp. 215–20.

Cozzi, Terenzio, "Supply-Side Economics," *Rivista di Politica Economica: Selected Papers* (Rome), LXXII, 3rd Series (December 1982), pp. 59–86.

Evans, Michael K., *The Truth About Supply-Side Economics* (New York: Basic Books, 1983).

Federal Reserve Bank of Atlanta and Emory University Law and Economics Center, *Supply-Side Economics in the 1980s: Conference Proceedings* (Westport, Connecticut: Quorum Books, 1982).

Fink, Richard H., ed., *Supply-Side Economics: A Critical Appraisal* (Frederick, Maryland: University Publications of America, 1982).

Fullerton, Don, "On the Possibility of an Inverse Relationship Between Tax Rates and Government Revenues," *Journal of Public Economics* (Amsterdam), Vol. 19 (October 1982), pp. 3-22.

Gardner, Martin, "Mathematical Games: The Laffer Curve and Other Laughs in Current Economics," *Scientific American* (New York), December 1981, pp. 18-31c.

Hailstones, Thomas J., *A Guide to Supply-Side Economics* (Richmond, Virginia: Robert F. Dame, Inc., 1982).

———, ed., *Viewpoints on Supply-Side Economics* (Richmond, Virginia: Robert F. Dame, Inc., 1982).

Hall, Robert E., and Alvin Rabushka, *Low Tax, Simple Tax, Flat Tax* (New York: McGraw-Hill, 1983).

Hemming, R., and J.A. Kay, "The Laffer Curve," *Fiscal Studies* (London), Vol. 1 (March 1980), pp. 83-90.

Jameson, Kenneth P., and Joseph Philips, "Supply-Side Economics: A Skeptical View," *Economic Forum* (Salt Lake City, Utah), Vol. 12, No. 1 (Summer 1981), pp. 81-88.

Kwon, Ohchul, "Taxes, Tax Revenues, and the Laffer Curve for a Developing Country Like Korea," *International Tax Journal* (New York), Vol. 10, No. 4 (May 1984), pp. 269-72.

Meyer, Laurence H., ed., *The Supply-Side Effects of Economic Policy* (Boston, Massachusetts: Kluwer-Nijhoff, 1981).

McMullen, B. Starr, "The Laffer-Curve: Fact or Convenient Fantasy," *Economic Forum* (Salt Lake City, Utah), Vol. 12, No. 2 (Winter 1981-82), pp. 113-15.

Mirowski, Philip, "What's Wrong With the Laffer Curve?" *Journal of Economic Issues* (Sacramento, California), Vol. 16 (September 1982), pp. 815-28.

Modi, Jitendra R., "Major Features of Corporate Profit Taxes in Selected Developing Countries," *Bulletin*, International Bureau of Fiscal Documentation (Amsterdam), Vol. 41 (February 1987), pp. 65-74.

Raboy, David G., ed., *Essays in Supply Side Economics* (Washington: Institute for Research on the Economics of Taxation, 1982).

Rabushka, Alvin, *From Adam Smith to the Wealth of America* (New Brunswick, New Jersey: Transaction Books, 1985).

———, and Bruce Bartlett, *Tax Policy and Economic Growth in Developing Nations* (Washington: PPC/EA, U.S. Agency for International Development, 1985, mimeographed).

Reynolds, Alan, "The World: On the Wrong Side of the Laffer Curve," paper presented to a Conference on "The Flat Rate Tax," Policy Sciences Program, Florida State University (Tallahassee, Florida, March 1985, mimeographed).

———, "Some International Comparisons of Supply-Side Tax Policy," *Cato Journal* (Washington), Vol. 5 (Fall 1985), pp. 543-69.

Richupan, Somchai, "Income Tax Evasion: A Review of the Measurement Techniques and Some Estimates for the Developing Countries" (unpublished, International Monetary Fund, July 23, 1984).

———, "Revenue Significance of the Individual Income Tax in Developing Countries" (unpublished, International Monetary Fund, April 22, 1985).

Roberts, Paul C., *The Supply-Side Revolution: An Insider's Account of Policymaking in Washington* (Cambridge, Massachusetts: Harvard University Press, 1984).

Rousseas, Stephen, "The Poverty of Wealth," *Journal of Post Keynesian Economics* (Armonk, New York), Vol. 4, No. 2 (Winter 1981-82), pp. 192-213.

Sautter, Hermann, "Socio-Cultural Aspects of Supply-Side Economics for Developing Countries," *Intereconomics: Review of International Trade and Development* (Hamburg), No. 6 (November–December 1983), pp. 278–85.

Tanzi, Vito, "The Policy Lessons of Supply-Side Economics: A Very Personal Interpretation," paper presented at the Fifty-Third Annual Conference of the Southern Economic Association (Washington, November 1983, mimeographed).

———, "The Underground Economy: The Causes and Consequences of this Worldwide Phenomenon," *Finance & Development* (Washington), Vol. 20 (December 1983), pp. 10–13.

———, "Quantitative Characteristics of the Tax Systems of Developing Countries," in *The Theory of Taxation for Developing Countries*, ed. by David Newbery and Nicholas Stern (New York: Oxford University Press, 1987).

United States, Department of the Treasury, *Tax Reform for Fairness, Simplicity and Economic Growth: The Treasury Department Report to the President,* Vols. I–III (Washington: Office of the Secretary, Department of the Treasury, November 1984).

U.S. Congress, House Committee on the Budget, *Supply-Side Economics, Hearing Before the Task Force on Tax Policy of the Committee on the Budget, House of Representatives,* 97th Congress, 1st Session, March 10, 1981 (Washington: Government Printing Office, 1981).

Wanniski, Jude, "Taxes, Revenues, and the 'Laffer Curve,'" *The Public Interest,* National Affairs, Inc. (New York), Winter 1978, pp. 3–16.

———, *The Way the World Works* (New York: Simon and Schuster, rev. and updated ed., 1983).

Weintraub, Sidney, "Keynesian Demand Serendipity in Supply-Side Economics," *Journal of Post Keynesian Economics* (Armonk, New York), Vol. 4, No. 2 (Winter 1981-82), pp. 181-91.